Religion, Leadership and Development

A Sustainable Transformational Approach

Obaji Agbiji

Langham
MONOGRAPHS

© 2023 Obaji Agbiji

Published 2023 by Langham Monographs
An imprint of Langham Publishing
www.langhampublishing.org

Langham Publishing and its imprints are a ministry of Langham Partnership

Langham Partnership
PO Box 296, Carlisle, Cumbria, CA3 9WZ, UK
www.langham.org

ISBNs:
978-1-83973-792-3 Print
978-1-83973-922-4 ePub
978-1-83973-923-1 PDF

Obaji Agbiji has asserted his right under the Copyright, Designs and Patents Act, 1988 to be identified as the Author of this work.

All rights reserved. No part of this publication may be reproduced, stored in a retrieval system or transmitted, in any form or by any means, electronic, mechanical, photocopying, recording or otherwise, without the prior written permission of the publisher or the Copyright Licensing Agency.

Requests to reuse content from Langham Publishing are processed through PLSclear. Please visit www.plsclear.com to complete your request.

Scripture texts in this work are taken from the *New American Bible, revised edition*© 2010, 1991, 1986, 1970 Confraternity of Christian Doctrine, Washington, D.C. and are used by permission of the copyright owner. All Rights Reserved. No part of the New American Bible may be reproduced in any form without permission in writing from the copyright owner.

British Library Cataloguing-in-Publication Data
A catalogue record for this book is available from the British Library

ISBN: 978-1-83973-792-3

Cover & Book Design: projectluz.com

Langham Partnership actively supports theological dialogue and an author's right to publish but does not necessarily endorse the views and opinions set forth here or in works referenced within this publication, nor can we guarantee technical and grammatical correctness. Langham Partnership does not accept any responsibility or liability to persons or property as a consequence of the reading, use or interpretation of its published content.

This work is dedicated to

My parents,
HRH Elder (Okim) Lawrence Mbeh and Grace Achi Agbiji

My brothers and sisters,
Onor, Agbiji, Mercy, Mbeh, Ikuma, Ndifon, Nchajenor,
Oyongha, Koli, Alobi and Margaret

My family,
Emem, Anointing-Mbeh, Shalom-Achi, Majesty-
Obaji, Redarokim-Bliss and Stella

With all my love and gratitute for your immeasurable
contributions and sacrifices

Obaji Agbiji's book fills a yawning gap in the practice and literature on Christianity in Nigeria. It addresses how the Nigerian church can contribute more meaningfully to the sociopolitical and economic transformation of its society. Following an analysis that is set within an empirical-theological methodology, this book displays brilliance not only in social ethics but also in development studies. Agbiji performs the analytical, descriptive and historical tasks of this book with panache, perspicacity and profundity of knowledge.

Nimi Wariboko, PhD
Walter G. Muelder Professor of Social Ethics
Boston University, Massachusetts, USA

This book places the importance of a conscious, development-oriented ecclesiastical leadership at the centre of its consideration of the institutional church's authentic role in development in contemporary Nigeria. As such its significance lies in the way in which it draws on a considerable interdisciplinary conceptual apparatus to make a much-needed contribution to a crucially important but under-researched topical focus in the theology and development debate. It is a timely contribution that further reflects in the innovative and theologically sound conceptualization of a sustainable transformational development approach as normative framework for an engaged ecclesiastic leadership. Although this contribution steers towards the contemporary Nigerian context, the book offers theoretical insight and perspective that are undoubtedly relevant to a wider theology and development scholarship concerned with other African contexts and beyond.

Ignatius Swart, PhD
Professor and Head of Department, Religion and Theology,
University of the Western Cape, South Africa

Obaji Agbiji's thorough and concise research in *Religion, Leadership and Development* represents a critical front in scholarship aimed at constructing robust theological reflection for the express purpose of a flourishing creation. Sadly, some theological reflection is too myopic to tackle the stuff of real existence. But that is not the case here. The author has set the table for a reimagined vision for the flourishing of all of creation with God at its centre and it is a project I can get behind.

A. J. Swoboda, PhD
Associate Professor of Bible, Theology and World Christianity,
Bushnell University, Oregon, USA

Contents

Acknowledgements xv
Acronyms/Abbreviations xvii

Chapter 1 1
Research Focus and Outline
   1.1 Introduction 1
   1.2 Background to the Study 3
   1.3 Motivation for the Study 5
   1.4 Problem Statement 7
   1.5 Research Questions 7
   1.6 Goals of the Study 8
   1.7 Research Paradigm 9
   1.8 Research Design 9
      1.8.1 Practical Theological Methodology 9
   1.9 Research Methodology 12
      1.9.1 Unit of Analysis 13
      1.9.2 Population 13
      1.9.3 Sampling 14
      1.9.4 Data Collection Method 14
      1.9.5 Research Ethics 15
      1.9.6 Pilot Study 15
   1.10 Significance of the Study 16
   1.11 Delimitation of the Study 20
   1.12 Definition of Key Terms 22
      1.12.1 Forms of the Church 22
      1.12.2 Church Leadership 24
      1.12.3 Development-Oriented 24
      1.12.4 Development 25
      1.12.5 Sustainability 25
      1.12.6 Transformation 26
      1.12.7 Postmilitary Nigeria 27
      1.12.8 Poverty 27
      1.12.9 Underdevelopment 28
      1.12.10 Corruption 28
   1.13 Chapter Outline 29
      Chapter 1 – Introduction 29

Chapter 2 – Meanings and Implications of Development in Postmilitary Nigeria 29
Chapter 3 – Meanings and Implications of Leadership in Postmilitary Nigeria 29
Chapter 4 – Social and Theological Analysis of Church Leadership Discourse in Postmilitary Nigeria 30
Chapter 5 – Dissemination and Reflections on the Empirical Study 30
Chapter 6 – A Sustainable Transformational Approach to Development in Postmilitary Nigeria 31
Chapter 7 – Development-Oriented Church Leadership in Postmilitary Nigeria: Perspectives, Conclusion and Recommendations 31

Chapter 2 33
Meanings and Implications of Development in Postmilitary Nigeria
2.1 Introduction 33
2.2 The Meanings of Development 34
    2.2.1 Development as Economic and Technological Growth 34
    2.2.2 Development as Liberation 34
    2.2.3 People-Centred Development 35
    2.2.4 Development as Expanding Access to Social Power 35
    2.2.5 Development as Responsible Well-Being 36
    2.2.6 Development as a Kingdom Response to Powerlessness ... 36
    2.2.7 Development as Freedom 36
    2.2.8 Development as Transformation 37
2.3 Development Trends in Nigeria and Sub-Saharan Africa 38
    2.3.1 Capital Formation Centred Approach 39
    2.3.2 Economic Nationalism Centred Approach 39
    2.3.3 The Basic Human Needs Approach 40
    2.3.4 The Structural Adjustment Approach 41
2.4 The Quest for an African and Nigerian Model of Development 42
    2.4.1 African Development Philosophy and Philosophers 43
    2.4.2 Some African and Nigerian Voices in Development Discourse 47
2.5 The Challenges of Nigerian and African Development 53
    2.5.1 Natural Endowments 53
    2.5.2 Historical Antecedents 54
    2.5.3 Poor Internal Policies 58
    2.5.4 Institutions and Governance 59
    2.5.5 Imperialism 60

  2.5.6 Lack of Regional Integration...61
  2.5.7 International Economic Order 64
  2.5.8 Environmental Challenges..65
  2.5.9 Poor Leadership...67
 2.6 Assessing Developmental Trends in Postmilitary Nigeria...........69
  2.6.1 Economic Development 70
  2.6.2 Political Governance 72
  2.6.3 Civil Society 82
 2.7 Conclusion 87

Chapter 3 89
Meanings and Implications of Leadership in Postmilitary Nigeria
 3.1 Introduction...89
 3.2 The Meaning of Leadership..90
 3.3 Conceptualising Leadership...92
  3.3.1 Transformational Leadership...92
  3.3.2 Authentic Leadership...93
  3.3.3 Servant Leadership...94
  3.3.4 Adaptive Leadership 96
 3.4 Leadership in the African Context..98
  3.4.1 Traditional African Heritage...99
  3.4.2 The Christian Influence 100
  3.4.3 The Influence of Islam..101
 3.5 Leadership in Precolonial Nigerian Societies 103
  3.5.1 Leadership among the Hausa-Fulani and Kanem-Bornu...104
  3.5.2 Leadership among the Yoruba..105
  3.5.3 Leadership among the Igbo..106
 3.6 Leadership in the Colonial Era..108
 3.7 Leadership in Postcolonial (Independent) Nigeria......................110
 3.8 Leadership during the Military Era 112
 3.9 Leadership in Postmilitary (Democratic) Nigeria 114
  3.9.1 The Influence of Globalization 117
 3.10 The Importance of Leadership in Development and
   Social Transformation 119
 3.11 Conclusion 121

Chapter 4 125
Social and Theological Analysis of Church Leadership Discourse in Postmilitary Nigeria
 4.1 Introduction..125
 4.2 The Public Role of the Church..126

4.3 Social Analysis of Church Leadership Discourse..........................129
    4.3.1 Setting the Stage..129
    4.3.2 Charity and Social Services.......................................133
    4.3.3 The Use of Dialogue as a Tool for National Cohesion......136
    4.3.4 Church Leaders' Advocacy and Social Transformation...144
    4.3.5 Collaboration of Church Leaders and Churches
        with Other Institutions...150
4.4 Theological Analysis of the Church Leadership Discourse..........155
    4.4.1 The Quest for a Nigerian Christian Theology...................155
    4.4.2 Church Leaders and Ecumenism................................159
    4.4.3 A Theology for Church and State Relations..................161
    4.4.4 Nigerian Christianity and Moral Questions..................167
    4.4.5 Inculturation and Nigerian Christianity........................172
    4.4.6 The Concept of Good News...175
    4.4.7 The Church in Mission as an Agent of Transformation...176
    4.4.8 Church Leaders and Gender Issues..............................179
    4.4.9 The Church and the Environment...............................180
4.5 Conclusion...182

Chapter 5 185
Dissemination and Reflection on Empirical Study
5.1 Introduction..185
5.2 Empirical Study...186
    5.2.1 Research Method...187
    5.2.2 Profile of Respondents..189
    5.2.3 The Social Engagement Rating of the Church..................196
    5.2.4 More Meaningful Social Engagement on the part of
        Nigerian Church Leaders..200
    5.2.5 More Meaningful Social Engagement of Nigerian
        Church Members..219
    5.2.6 More Meaningful Social Engagement of the
        Ecumenical Church..222
    5.2.7 More Meaningful Social Engagement on the
        Denomination/Congregational Levels.........................228
    5.2.8 Leadership Style and Social Transformation in Nigeria...233
    5.2.9 More Meaningful Social Engagement on the
        Part of Church Leaders and the Constituents
        of a Sustainable Transformational Approach to
        Development in Nigeria..237
5.3 Conclusion...263

Chapter 6 265
A Sustainable Transformational Approach to Development in Postmilitary Nigeria
   6.1 Introduction 265
   6.2 Sustainable Transformational Development 268
      6.2.1 Definition of the Concept 268
      6.2.2 The Goals of Sustainable Transformational Development 270
      6.2.3 Sustainable Transformational Development Domains 281
      6.2.4 The Processes of Change through Sustainable Transformational Development 295
   6.3 Development-Oriented Church Leadership as a Vital Component of Sustainable Transformational Development in Nigeria 301
      6.3.1 The Development-oriented Church Leader as the Facilitator of Sustainable Transformational Development 302
      6.3.2 The Development-Oriented Church Leader as the Conscientiser of the Faithful 305
      6.3.3 The Development-Oriented Church Leader as the Mentor of Transformational Leaders 307
      6.3.4 The Development-Oriented Church Leader as the Shepherd of the Faithful into the Public Domain as Agents of Change 312
      6.3.5 Harnessing the Resources of the Church, Nigeria and the Global Community for Sustainable Transformational Development through Church Leaders 314
   6.4 Conclusion 319

Chapter 7 321
Development-Oriented Church Leadership in Postmilitary Nigeria: Perspectives, Conclusion and Recommendations
   7.1 Introduction 321
   7.2 Development-Oriented Church Leadership in Postmilitary Nigeria: Perspectives 323
      7.2.1 Development-Oriented Church Leadership, Nigerian Development and Sustainable Transformational Development 324

  7.2.2 Development-Oriented Church Leadership,
    Nigerian Leadership/Followership and Sustainable
    Transformational Development 327
  7.2.3 Development-Oriented Church Leadership, the
    Various Expressions of the Church and Sustainable
    Transformational Development 329
  7.2.4 Development-Oriented Church Leadership,
    Sociopolitical and Economic Systems and
    Sustainable Transformational Development......................330
  7.2.5 Development-Oriented Church Leadership,
    Globalization and Sustainable Transformational
    Development..331
  7.2.6 Development-Oriented Church Leadership, Civil
    Society and Sustainable Transformational
    Development..333
  7.2.7 Development-Oriented Church Leadership,
    the Dignity of Creation and Sustainable
    Transformational Development 334
 7.3 Conclusion and Recommendations..335
  The Church..336
  The Nigerian Sociopolitical and Economic Institutions............337
Appendix 339
 Questionnaire to Leaders of National CAN/ CAN Bloc/LPC
Bibliography..341

List of Tables

Table 5.1: The position, duration of term, ecumenical bloc of origin and development engagement indicator of the nine national CAN respondents..191

Table 5.2: Bloc, position, duration of term and development engagement of CAN bloc respondents..193

Table 5.3: LPC leaders' position, years of service and development engagement..194

Table 5.4: Total number of research participants and the groups they represent 195

Acknowledgements

The journey which has culminated in this work was made possible by the immense and diverse contributions of many persons too numerous to be mentioned in two pages. However, in as much as it is not possible for me to mention all their names and their valued contributions, it is also impossible to completely avoid mentioning some names.

Emmanuel Nwabuikwu and Florence Iheoma Nnorom, you provided almost everything that my family and I needed in my academic endeavours in South Africa and during our visits to Nigeria, and we are still unable to comprehend your love, care and magnanimity. Prof. Karel Thomas August, thank you for your supervision and your many contributions to both my personal life and my academic journey. Without you my path would have been more difficult to navigate.

Ekeoma and Ngozi Ekeoma, Nkechi Ene-Obong, Akim and Obaje Mbeh, Ude and Ngozi Nkama, Nnachi and Ogbonne Ibiam, Vincent and Nkechi Ukoh, Nsan Ojong Tiku, James Okwara, Sally Agbor, Kingsley Oti, Henry Onugha, Richard Ezeoke, Margaret Obono, Olivier Eya, Mabel Offiong, Nkereuwem and Peace Akpan, Tony and Natalie de Ruiter, John and Heather Harrison, Tim Hawkridge, Duncan and Ann Mackenzie, Relin du Toit, Paul Okey, Joseph Eton and Obong Ndueso, thank you for your friendship and the varied ways it was expressed. You have all proved your abilities in your respective competencies in turning around situations financially, psycho-sociologically and in many other ways. You are the best group of friends anyone could ever dream of having.

Prof. Hans Jurgens Hendriks and Prof. Ignatius Swart, your contributions to my family, my studies, my general well-being and my future will always be cherished. Your mentoring, counselling, prayers and guidance made a great difference; far more than anyone could ever imagine. Thanks to my spiritual sons and daughters for your untiring support.

Prof. N. Wariboko, Prof. AJ. Swoboda, Prof. N. Koopman, Prof. E. Mouton, Prof. J. Cilliers, Dr. D. X. Simon, Dr. C. Thesnar, Dr. I. Nell, Dr. A. Cloete, Prof. D. J. Louw, Prof. D. Smith, Prof. H. Bosman, Prof. J. Punt, Prof. R. Voslo and Prof. J. Claassens, thank you. My personal experiences with each of you in both formal and informal settings have impacted me in unforgettable ways. You have taught me a beautiful combination of humour, humility, godliness, civility and academic excellence. Thanks to Mark Arnold and the staff of Langham Publishing for their enormous contributions leading to the publication of this work. Thanks also to the leadership and the staff of CAN and LPC for your kind assistance.

Both my nuclear family and my extended family have made immense sacrifices and contributions that are too numerous to be mentioned. Thank you especially to my treasure, Emem. What would I have done without you and our children?

Above all, to the Father of all creation, *oko me ra mete reda* (my owner and loving Father), promisekeeper and only wise God who alone is able best to transform the deplorable conditions of the poor and suffering, be all the glory, honour, power and majesty forever!

Acronyms/Abbreviations

AD	*Anno Domino*
AFREG	African Forum on Religion and Governance
AIDS	Acquired Immune Deficiency Syndrome
ATR	African Traditional Religion
AU	African Union
CAN	Christian Association of Nigeria
CAQDAS	Computer Aided Qualitative Data Analysis
CCN	Christian Council of Nigeria
COCEN	Congress on Christian Ethics in Nigeria
CPC	Congress for Progressive Change
CPFN/PFN	Christian Pentecostal Fellowship of Nigeria/Pentecostal Fellowship of Nigeria
CSN	Catholic Secretariat of Nigeria
EAC	The East African Community
ECOWAS	Economic Community of West African States
ECWA/TEKAN	Evangelical Church of West Africa/Tarrarya Ekkelisiyar Kristi a Nigeria
EFCC	Economic and Financial Crimes Commission
FBO	Faith-Based Organization
FRL	Full Range of Leadership
FRIG	Forum for Righteousness in Governance
GDP	Gross Domestic Product
GSM	Global System for Mobile Communication
HIV	Human Immunodeficiency Virus

ICPC	Independent Corrupt Practices and Other Related Offences Commission
IFIs	International Financial Institutions
IMC	International Mission Conference
IMF	International Monetary Fund
ING	Interim National Government
LPC	Lagos Presbyterian Church
NADECO	National Democratic Coalition
NAPEP	National Poverty Empowerment Programme
NASR	Nigerian Association for the Study of Religions
NEPAD	New Partnership for Africa's Development
NEEDS	National Economic Empowerment and Development Strategy
NGOs	Non-governmental Organizations
NIREC	National Inter-Religious Council
OAIC	Organization of African Instituted Churches
OAU	Organization of African Unity
OIC	Organization of Islamic Countries
PDP	Peoples' Democratic Party
PKP	Promise Keeper's Partners
SADC	Southern African Development Community
SAPs	Structural Adjustment Programmes
SCIA	Supreme Council for Islamic Affairs
SNG	Save Nigeria Group
TD	Transformational Development
TI	Transparency International
TNCs	Transnational Corporations
UNICEF	United Nations Children's Fund
WCC	World Council of Churches

CHAPTER 1

Research Focus and Outline

1.1 Introduction

Humans have long dreamed of a thriving world filled with communities that offer ecologically balanced, sociopolitical, economic and spiritually fulfilling lives. Africans move within a spiritual heritage of *ubuntu* (I am because you are)[1] which is a unique sense of value for community.[2] The role and importance of good leadership that often translates into socioreligious, political economic and ecological well-being in the various strata of human society is hardly in doubt. However, the issue is whether or not this type of leadership is available within both the Nigerian ecclesial community and in society as a whole. The plethora of literature on development, leadership and social transformation attests to the importance of these concepts and the issues related to them. Indeed, the need for visionary and result-oriented leadership is common in political, economic, social, cultural and religious circles, while the need for greater engagement directed towards the transformation of both Nigeria and other African nations from their plight of poverty, underdevelopment, corruption and poor leadership is, in fact, crucial.

Development-oriented church leadership through a sustainable transformational approach to social change seeks to be based on the biblical tenets regarding the kingdom of God and the mission of God to the world. In this type of engagement, both leadership and socioeconomic and political

---

1. Korten, "Telling a New Story," 259.
2. Agbiji, "Religious Practitioners and Ecological."

change are conducted with a deep sense of moral value, compassion and human/extrahuman dignity. Such a social vision encourages the clergy and lay Christians alike to accept the responsibility, while depending on God's promise of guidance, to function as agents of change in the societies in which they live. This, in turn, requires of them to become more accessible and to build relationships that enable them to serve as stewards, mentors, coaches and role models. These are the kind of leaders that can help others navigate their transformation as they live through change.[3] It is a vision of leadership that the clergy and the laity of the church are being called upon by God to provide to humanity.

The struggle of the Age of Enlightenment to separate religion and secular society has not only failed, but it has left the post-modern age facing huge challenges, especially within the sociopolitical and economic realms as well as the realm of leadership. As a fallout of modernism, ecological challenges are staring humanity in the face while our value systems and human dignity are under threat.[4] To a certain extent, these issues are related to the kind of leadership that humankind is offering to the created order and the irresponsible manner in which some human beings are using the gifts received from God for their own selfish ends without due consideration for the wellbeing of all creation. In terms of the Nigerian and the African worldview, the religious and the secular are inseparable and it is for this reason that whatever the positive or negative developments that we encounter in the church/mosque/shrine, these will be reflected in wider society and vice versa. It is common knowledge that the Nigerian nation and, indeed, the whole of Africa are confronting huge challenges of leadership and poverty issues while the leadership crisis in these areas is, in fact, reinforcing poverty, underdevelopment, corruption and other vices.

In focusing on the underdevelopment and poverty in Nigeria, leadership seems to constitute the natural starting point. The absence of basic infrastructure in a country is a strong indicator of the presence of poverty and poor leadership as it is the duty of political leaders to provide basic infrastructure for their citizens. Nigerians are, indisputably, a religious people and a large proportion of the leadership cartel (political, social and economic) is

---

3. Rolls, "Transformational Leadership," 65–84.
4. Nurnberger, *Prosperity, Poverty and Pollution*, 177–88.

Christian. It is, thus, essential to ascertain the kind of leadership which the Christian community is providing to both its constituency and the Nigerian public, especially in terms of the reversal of poverty, underdevelopment, corruption and bad leadership.

It is vital that an effective church leadership that is able to offer the much-needed help in bringing a nation out of poverty and underdevelopment be passionate about the plight of the people both within and outside the church context with this kind of leadership representing the biblical symbolism of the church (Christians), namely, "The salt of the earth and the light of the world."[5] This kind of leadership strives to see the church, through its clergy and the laity, working vigorously in collaboration with both sociopolitical and economic structures towards the liberation of the Nigerian society and the environment. A development-oriented church leadership will function in such a manner. In addition, besides influencing the Nigerian society, such a church leadership could make a significant contribution beyond the country's borders to African development as a whole and, in collaboration with the World Council of Churches (WCC), to the quest for global justice and transformation. The contributions of the WCC towards global social justice and transformation represent a good example of the possible contributions that the church is able to make in human society.[6] However, such contributions are not possible without a development-oriented leadership.

1.2 Background to the Study

There is little doubt that many Nigerians do not have access to food, clean water, healthcare and adequate shelter,[7] while much of the infrastructure in the country, including hospitals, roads, railway lines, electricity supply, communication, oil refineries and education institutions, are in a state of disrepair. The high rate of unemployment, underemployment and job insecurity has

---

5. Matthew 5:13–16.

6. The interests of the World Council of Churches are indicated by the widespread reporting of its pronouncements, studies, meetings and other actions in the world's newspapers. Its strength lies in speaking for the poor, the sufferers from discrimination, and those experiencing other forms of injustice, whether they are Christian or not. One of such actions of the Council was the consultation on "Equity and Emission Trading – Ethical and Theological Dimensions" held at Sascatoon, Canada, May 9–14, 2000.

7. Aluko, "Poverty and Illness in Nigeria," 231–34.

made it easy for the youth to be recruited by militia groups, political thugs and cults. These are all indications of a country that has suffered from poor leadership over long periods of time, particularly in terms of sociopolitical and economic structures.

Political turmoil in Nigeria is evidenced by the coup d'états and appalling election malpractices that have characterized successive military, as well as civilian, regimes. Despite the fact that it is possible to attribute the socioeconomic and political challenges facing Nigerians to the political leadership that has kept watch over the nation since the country's independence, the greater part of the blame should, nevertheless, be attributed to the military regimes. Commenting on the leadership record in Nigeria, Chinua Achebe, the renowned Nigerian poet and novelist and one of the most prominent contemporary African writers, laments the fact that Nigeria has been less than fortunate in its leadership. A basic element of this misfortune, he argues, is the seminal absence of intellectual rigor in the political thought of our founding fathers. Achebe further argues that these leaders have a tendency to pious materialistic woolliness and self-centered pedestrianism.[8]

This issue of poor leadership, which has endured since independence and to which Achebe alludes in his reference to the founding leaders, is still a feature of the Nigerian state today. The situation was exacerbated by the military regimes that institutionalized corruption and which mismanaged Nigeria throughout the many years of their rule. The political class followed suit and the hopes of Nigerians have been consistently dashed by the successive administrations that have come into power.[9] In the same vein, Onyeani, a Nigerian-American social critic, asserts: "We [Africa/Nigeria], have leaders who are not ruthless with themselves in pursuit of excellence but who are quick being ruthless to their citizens."[10] However, this situation will probably not change in the near future unless concerted efforts are made in this regard. It is this challenge that the Christian community is being encouraged to address in a more sustainable way through its leadership and membership in order to transform the sociopolitical and economic horizons of Nigeria.

---

8. Achebe, *Trouble with Nigeria*, 11.
9. Chinne, "Building a Future," 2.
10. Onyeani, *Capitalist Nigger*, 38.

The Nigerian Christian community possesses resources that may, if used in collaboration with certain strands of Nigerian sociopolitical and economic structures, and with the resources of emerging global institutions such as peoples' movements, contribute more meaningfully to the transformation of Nigerian society. It may be best for those Nigerian church leaders, who are concerned about the enduring challenges facing the majority of Nigerians and that seem to defy the numerous attempts to transform them, to coordinate the engagement of such Christian resources with those of the Nigerian and global societies. In addition, it is essential that such leadership be consistent with the tenets of the concept of sustainable transformational development which promise to be innovative and courageous, if the anticipated change is to go beyond the traditional boundaries that the church has always maintained in order to transform the sociopolitical and economic life of Nigerians in a more meaningful way.

The 1995 UNICEF report on the importance of faith-based organizations in community development states that faith-based organizations are able to play an important role in development practice in the sense that religion plays a central, integrative role in the social and cultural life of most developing countries, including Nigeria. Religious leaders are in closer and more regular contact with all age groups in many of the societies in the developing countries and their voices are often highly respected. In traditional communities, religious leaders are often more influential than either the local government officials or the secular community leaders. Okaalet further notes that "[r]eligious leaders can influence communities, societies, nations, and the course of human events."[11] Accordingly, this study intends to explore the way in which Nigerian church leaders may, in the light of the current challenges facing Nigerian society, namely, poverty, underdevelopment, corruption and poor leadership, contribute more meaningfully to the sociopolitical and economic transformation of the Nigerian society.

1.3 Motivation for the Study

There are a number of reasons motivating this study. First, it was motivated by a passion for a holistic ministry that reaches out to the various strata of human

---

11. Okaalet, "Role of Faith-based Organizations," 275, 277.

and extrahuman life. This passion has always informed both my practice and my quest for the fulfillment of my ministry as a church leader and it led to my involvement in both the establishment of the Elim Micro-Finance Bank (which provides training and loans for small- and medium-scale enterprises), and in NGOs such as the Covenant Partners' Fellowship and WELFOUND, schools, youth empowerment programmes and political/socioeconomic participation organizations such as PAYIES and FRIG. Second, my postgraduate studies in practical theology (theology and development studies at the postgraduate diploma and master's levels) have further deepened my convictions and concerns regarding the unfortunate sociopolitical and economic challenges facing my country, Nigeria.

Third, whereas concerted efforts are being made in various fields of study, including economics, political science and philosophy, to address the challenges of poverty, underdevelopment, corruption and poor leadership in Nigeria, the voice of the church – especially that of the church leadership – needs to be heard more clearly in a manner that moves beyond mere church statements to the taking of concrete action that engages both the individuals and the systems that perpetuate the current sociopolitical and economic challenges in Nigeria. In addition, it is essential that such a bold approach should include innovative and collaborative efforts on the part of both the church and sociopolitical and economic institutions that may be instrumental in the transformation of society. However, unlike the transformational development approach which has been useful to Christian NGOs such as World Vision in several community development projects elsewhere, the aim of this study is to formulate a development framework that is church-based and that may complement other frameworks for social transformation through the action of church leaders, church institutions and other institutions, including faith-based organizations (FBOs) and non-governmental organizations (NGOs), in Nigeria and sub-Sahara Africa. As Chris Sugden, a development scholar and practitioner, suggested almost a decade ago, "to be sustainable, transformational development needs to be linked with the church."[12] In other words, an approach to social change that emanates from the church should necessarily be linked to the church but should also go beyond the scope of the church in connecting with other institutions if far-reaching and lasting

---

12. Sugden, "Transformational Development," 72.

results are to be attained. Accordingly, this study aims both to reflect upon existing Nigerian and global church-based approaches to social change and to investigate the potential of engaging other change institutions and measures within the Nigerian context in order to realize social transformation in the light of current challenges emanating from poverty, underdevelopment, corruption and poor leadership.

Komakoma, Muyebe and Muyebe, Van Bergen, and Mitchell have all reflected upon the activities of church leaders on social issues within Africa, with their roots in Zambia, Tanzania and Malawi.[13] Fortunately, many of these advocates for a socially transformational conscious church leadership are church leaders. But there is still a lack of substantial reflection upon this issue within the Nigerian context, although Nigeria accounts for a substantial proportion of the total population of the African continent. In addition, whereas these African scholars have voiced their concerns regarding the deplorable conditions of Africans, they have hardly proposed a development framework that can be engaged by Christian religious leaders and the faithful in their bid to address the huge challenges they face daily. This study makes a bold step in this direction.

1.4 Problem Statement

In adopting a sustainable transformational development approach, this study explores the possibility of, and the potential ways in which, a development-oriented Nigerian church leadership would be able to contribute more meaningfully to the transformation of the sociopolitical and economic realms of Nigerian society.

1.5 Research Questions

How may church leaders in Nigeria, in light of the country's poverty, underdevelopment, corruption and poor leadership, contribute more meaningfully to the sociopolitical and economic transformation of Nigerian society? In what

---

13. Komakoma, *Social Teaching of Catholic*, 3–9; Muyebe and Muyebe, *African Bishops on Human*, 96–294; Van Bergen, *Development and Religion*, 208–10; Mitchell, "Living Our Faith," 5–18.

ways would Nigerian church leadership be able to achieve this? When translated into a sustainable transformational development approach (with a view to more meaningful engagement on the part of church leaders in the sociopolitical and economic change within Nigerian society), what would the possible constituent elements of such an approach be? Underlying the research questions is the assumption that Nigerian church leaders have the potential to contribute more meaningfully to the social transformation of Nigeria.

1.6 Goals of the Study

The major purpose of this study is to explore the way in which a development-oriented church leadership in Nigeria may make more meaningful contributions towards the sociopolitical, economic and religious transformation of Nigerian society. This study has the following objectives: First, to evaluate the Nigerian historical context so as to uncover the root cause(s) of the perennial challenge of poor leadership and underdevelopment that have, in turn, given rise to poverty, corruption and other forms of injustice. Second, to ascertain the type of leadership to which Nigerians have been exposed in the sociopolitical and economic spheres of Nigerian society. Third, to appraise the involvement of the Nigerian church – both the leaders and their adherents – in the development of Nigeria from 1999 to 2010 (the reasons for focusing on this era will be explained in section 1.11 – Delimitation of the Study). Fourth, to undertake a qualitative empirical study in terms of which open-ended questionnaires will be issued to church leaders in the Christian Association of Nigeria (CAN) and the Lagos Presbyterian Church (LPC). The author will subsequently reflect on and disseminate the results of the study. Moreover, the intention is to ascertain from both the literature review and the empirical study whether the sustainable transformational development approach will result in making Nigerian church leaders engage more meaningfully in the country's sociopolitical and economic transformation. Finally, perspectives and recommendations regarding the engagement of church leaders in social change in Nigeria will be presented.

1.7 Research Paradigm

The research in this study is guided by the qualitative research paradigm. This paradigm will be discussed in the following sections. The presentation and interpretation of the data will be viewed mainly from a postmodern perspective and will focus on the contextual, local value of the research. The study exhibits transformatory characteristics as it seeks to address the challenge of inefficient leadership with the attendant consequences of poverty, underdevelopment and corruption in Nigeria. The study will assess the possibility of a development-oriented church leadership channelling the efforts of the church through a sustainable transformational approach that may, in turn, have a more positive impact on the sociopolitical and economic transformation of Nigeria as against the predominantly social service and advocative posture of church leadership to sociopolitical and economic challenges.

1.8 Research Design

Based on the research questions cited in 1.5 above, this research study comprises qualitative field research. The study focuses on impact assessment, although not in the technical meaning of the term, but in the sense that the study assesses how the church leadership in Nigeria from 1999 to 2010 contributed to the transformation of Nigerian society. The essence of this exercize is to explore ways and means through which a development-oriented church leadership may engage more meaningfully in the social transformational process of Nigerian society. The empirical study is conducted in compliance with the requirements of social research in conjunction with a practical theological approach.

1.8.1 Practical Theological Methodology

This research follows the steps identified by Richard Osmer in his extensive methodology for practical theology, which he describes with reference to the following four tasks:

- The first task is descriptive-empirical and it addresses the question: What is going on in this particular social context or field of experience? This task accords special attention to the religious praxis with a particular approach being selected because

it represents the approach that is best suited to the purpose of a specific project.
- The second task is interpretive. Research findings are not self-interpretive and, thus, the interpretive task of practical theology seeks to position such findings within an interpretive framework and providing an answer to the question: Why are these phenomena happening? The important point is that contemporary, practical theologians move beyond the findings of their own empirical research and place them within an interpretive framework.
- The third task is normative. Practical theology does more than merely investigate and interpret contemporary forms of religious praxis and, indeed, it seeks to assess such praxis normatively from the perspective of Christian theology and ethics, with an eye to reform should this be needed. Thus, the normative task addresses the question: What form ought the current religious praxis take within this specific social context?
- The fourth task of practical theology is pragmatic. This task focuses on the development of rules of art – a concept first introduced by Friedrich Schleiermacher in his seminal description of practical theology. Rules of art are open-ended guidelines that may assist those who are either leading or participating in a particular form of religious praxis. This task, thus, asks the question: How might this area of praxis be shaped to embody more fully the normative commitments of a religious tradition within a particular context of experience?[14]

In light of the above, the *descriptive-empirical* task will be engaged in this study in order to assist in the understanding of what is taking place in the Nigerian social context by paying particular attention to the religious and social praxis of church leaders and the happenings within the developmental and leadership context within the sociopolitical and economic realms in Nigeria. The *interpretive* task will be utilized in order to make meaning of the occurrences within the Nigerian context both in literature and in the

---

14. Osmer, *Practical Theology*, 4–12.

empirical study as "research findings are not self-interpretive. Accordingly, the interpretive task of practical theology seeks to place such findings within an interpretive framework and to provide an answer to the question: Why are these things going on?"[15] However, the practical theological focus of this study does more than merely investigate and interpret contemporary forms of religious, sociopolitical and economic praxis. "It seeks to assess such praxis normatively from the perspective of Christian theology and ethics, with an eye to reform when this is needed."[16] As such, the normative task will be employed in this study in order to understand what constitutes a more meaningful social engagement that may inform the involvement on the part of church leaders as agents of change in Nigeria. Through the pragmatic task, the development approach that may assist church leaders' religious, sociopolitical and economic transformation of Nigerian society will be proposed.

G. D. J. Dingemans points out that, in recent times, practical theologians in many parts of the world have come to agree on the principle of starting their investigations with practice itself.[17] Accordingly, this approach moves from practice to theory and then back to practice. Dingemans is, furthermore, of the opinion that the practical theologian is able to interpret his/her context correctly only if he/she uses the tools of the social sciences. In line with this view, he argues that practical theologians are currently collaborating with social scientists in an interdisciplinary approach which integrates theology and the social sciences.[18] This study will, therefore, evaluate the impact of development-oriented church leaders on Nigerian society by using the theories and methods of both the social sciences and those of theology.[19] Accordingly, the study will engage first in theory through the study of relevant literature before moving onto an empirical study which, it is hoped, will complement the relevant theory in aiding social change.

---

15. Osmer, 4–12.
16. Osmer, 4–12.
17. Dingemans, "Practical Theology in Academy," 83–91.
18. Dingemans, 83–84.
19. For example, social research guidelines in empirical research data collection, management and analysis as espoused by Graham Gibbs (2007) in his work *Analysing Qualitative Data* and Richard Osmer's work *Practical Theology* may be useful to this study.

1.9 Research Methodology

All research methodology rests upon a bedrock axiom: "The nature of the data and the problem for research dictate the research methodology."[20] The aim of this study is to discover more meaningful contributions that a development-oriented church leadership may make to the sociopolitical and economic transformation of Nigerian society with regard to ameliorating poverty, underdevelopment, corruption and poor leadership. In view of the nature of the study, the study is empirical and will employ the qualitative method. Earl Babbie uses the term qualitative field research "to distinguish this type of observation method from methods designed to produce data appropriate for quantitative (statistical) analysis."[21] Qualitative data is derived from field research with this type of data being based on observations that may not easily be reduced to numbers. C. B. Fouche has pointed out that the focus of qualitative data is "to gain insight into a situation, phenomenon, community or individual."[22] In qualitative research, the researcher pays close attention to words, reports detailed views of the informants and endeavours to conduct the study in a natural environment.[23]

This research study focuses on the qualitative data collected pertaining to the involvement of development-oriented church leaders in postmilitary Nigeria from 1999 to 2010, especially their impact on both the church and the wider Nigerian society as regards the political and socioeconomic transformation of Nigeria. For the purposes of assessment and analysis, open-ended questionnaires were distributed to former and serving church leaders of the Christian Association of Nigeria (CAN) and its constituencies in Nigeria, who have served in leadership positions between 1999 and 2010, as well as to the minister and elders of the Lagos Presbyterian Church, Yaba in Nigeria. Whereas the leaders of CAN represent the denominational and interdenominational expressions of the church leaders in Nigeria, the minister and elders of the Lagos Presbyterian Church will represent the congregational expression of the church. For the purpose of the study, coding was applied in a broader sense, with all the questions in the questionnaires, as informed

---

20. De Vos and Strydom, *Research at Grassroots*, 15.
21. Babbie, *Practice of Social Research*, 282.
22. Fouche, "Qualitative Research Designs," 109.
23. Sandelowski, *Handbook for Synthesizing Qualitative*, 67.

by the literature study, being coded and then formulated into themes for discussion. Codes were also derived from the empirical data and thematized for discussion.

The analysis of the broader context was based mainly on secondary literature – scholarly journals, newspapers, internet sources and books – and primary documents available, including documents and communiqués from both CAN and the Lagos Presbyterian Church. This aspect of the research provided the grounds for the theoretical analysis and linked the outcomes from the empirical research to broader discussions on socioreligious, economic, political, development-oriented church leadership and social transformation issues.

1.9.1 Unit of Analysis

Units of analysis "are those things we examine in order to create summary descriptions of all such units and to explain differences among them."[24] Units of analysis are, thus, units of observation and may include individuals, groups, organizations or social artifacts. For the purposes of this study, the units of analysis comprise Nigerian church leaders from both CAN and the Lagos Presbyterian Church during 1999–2010.

1.9.2 Population

According to Babbie, a population refers to a group of people or items possessing the attribute one wishes to understand and about which one wishes to draw conclusions.[25] Strydom and De Vos define a population as "the total set from which the individuals or units of the study are chosen. A population is the totality of persons, events, organization units, case records or other sampling units with which our research problem is concerned."[26]

The population in this research study refers to development-oriented church leaders, cutting across ecumenical and local expressions of the church in Nigeria, specifically from 1999 to 2010.

---

24. Babbie, *Practice of Social Research* (10th ed.), 94, 97.
25. Babbie, *Practice of Social Research* (11th ed.), 111.
26. Strydom and De Vos, "Sampling and Sampling Methods," 90.

1.9.3 Sampling

A sample is "[t]he element of the population considered for actual inclusion in the study. Or it can be viewed as a subset of measurements drawn from a population in which we are interested."[27] The purpose of studying a sample is to understand the population from which the sample is drawn since it is impossible to study the entire population. Sampling is, therefore, the act of taking any portion of a population as representative of that population. In this study the non-probability, purposive sampling method was adopted.[28] According to Jeffrey C. Johnson, qualitative research uses non-probability sampling as this type of research does not aim at drawing statistical inferences. The purposive sampling technique is also often employed in qualitative research. The strength of this technique does not lie in the number of individuals who participate, but is in the criteria used to select the participants, with the characteristics of the participants being considered as the basis for selection. The participants are often selected to reflect the diversity and scope of the sample population.[29] The sampling frame of this research study comprises thirty-one Nigerian church leaders drawn from the Christian Association of Nigeria (CAN) and its constituencies and leaders of the Lagos Presbyterian Church (LPC), Yaba. The selection criterion was, thus, the fact that these individuals had served or were serving in leadership positions in both CAN and LPC and, specifically, between 1999 and 2010.

1.9.4 Data Collection Method

Questionnaires were used to collect the data for the purposes of this study.[30] Smith defines a questionnaire as a series of written questions a researcher supplies to subjects, requesting their response. However, Smith cautions that "different kinds of questions solicit different types of data (e.g. open or closed questions, quantitative or qualitative questions)."[31] In this study, open-ended questions were used to solicit the required qualitative data.

---

27. Strydom and De Vos, 191.
28. Babbie, *Practice of Social Research* (10th ed.), 182–83.
29. Johnson, *Selecting Ethnographic Informants*, 34.
30. See Appendix A.
31. Smith, *Academic Writing and Theological*, 161.

Depending on the preference of the respondent, soft (electronic) or hard copies of the questionnaire were issued to the respondent and the data was collated over a period of eleven months, namely, April 2010 to March 2011.

1.9.5 Research Ethics

All the questionnaires used adhered to the ethical requirements of social research. The prospective participants were invited to participate in the study and, in conformity with the ethical requirements and standards of Stellenbosch University, were informed of the scope and purpose of the research. The consent of the various institutions to which the participants were affiliated was also obtained. The respondents were, thus, voluntarily engaged in the study and no harm whatsoever was either foreseen nor did it result from their participation. Both anonymity and confidentiality were also ensured. The issue of confidentiality was explained to the participants in the requisite consent forms which each participant was obliged to complete. Ethical clearance was also obtained from the Research Ethics Committee of Stellenbosch University prior to the commencement of the empirical study.

1.9.6 Pilot Study

According to N. K. Denzin and Y. S. Lincoln, the aim of a pilot study in qualitative research is to enable the researcher either to focus on specific areas that may have been unclear or to test certain questions. The researcher is, thus, able to make adjustments with a view to asking the right questions during the main enquiry. A pilot study may, furthermore, assist the researcher to obtain an idea of the probable costs and time the study will require as well as other challenges that may arise during the main research.[32] The participants in the pilot study in this research project included three church leaders from the ecumenical and local expressions of the Christian community in the Western Cape, South Africa, and all of whom had served as leaders for a period of no less than ten years.

---

32. Denzin and Lincoln, *Handbook of Qualitative Research*, 213.

1.10 Significance of the Study

Scholars such as C. A. Ndoh and A. Njoku, and Myles Munroe are of the opinion that, even before independence, Nigerians were filled with an overwhelming desire for development. However, after independence it became clear that they lacked the skills necessary for development.[33] In addition, long years of military rule with brief interludes of democratic rule did little to improve the situation and, instead, the corruption and poor governance on the part of its leaders plunged the nation more deeply into underdevelopment and poverty. Before the independence, military and postmilitary eras, Munroe suggests that Nigerians, in common with the other inhabitants of the so-called "Third World countries," were products of their colonial past with their colonial heritage leaving them with certain dehumanizing characteristics such as timidity, dependency and lack of self-confidence. These elements of slavery and (the) colonial hangover"[34] are still the weapons of neo-colonialism[35] which remains prevalent in various spheres in national life, including in a number of churches and in the Muslim community. Although the masses are colluding with the political elite in the perpetuation of underdevelopment, corruption and poverty, some scholars, such as Toyin Falola, are of the opinion that the leadership of the Nigerian state should be held largely responsible for the sufferings of Nigerians.[36] Thus, all attempts to deal with poverty, underdevelopment and corruption will prove abortive, unless the primary challenge of poor leadership is addressed.

If there is indeed corrupt and irresponsible leadership in Nigeria, as some scholars argue, and which this study will investigate in chapter 3, there is no doubt that a morally bankrupt, timid and dependent leadership will also lack self-confidence. The critical role of leadership, which may either have a positive or a negative influence, implies that many Nigerians are replicas of their

---

33. Ndoh and Njoku, "Nigerian Nationalism in Nigeria," 51, 56; Munroe, *Becoming a Leader*, 16, 18.

34. Munroe, 17.

35. Munroe and Onyeani argue that the impact of slavery and colonialism on the psyche of Africans and Nigerians still endures and that it may be responsible for their inability to meet the challenges facing them because of a lack of confidence to undertake initiatives that may translate into substantial sociopolitical and economic development. As such, transnational corporations, international financial institutions such as the IMF and the countries of the Northern hemisphere still control the political and economic trends in underdeveloped countries such as Nigeria. Munroe, 17; Onyeani, *Capitalist Nigger*, 38.

36. Falola, *History of Nigeria*, 153.

leaders. This view is in alignment with that of O. I. Mbachu who argues that leaders allocate moral values to their followers and also serve as models for sociopolitical socialization.[37] If this is indeed true, then it is in this context that the church must rise to fulfil its role, which is deeply rooted in the following biblical mandates, namely, "Go, therefore, and make disciples of all nations, baptizing them in the name of the Father, and of the Son, and of the holy Spirit, teaching them to observe all that I have commanded you"[38] and "You are the salt of the earth . . . You are the light of the world . . . Just so, your light must shine before others, that they may see your good deeds and glorify your heavenly Father."[39] Munroe, commenting on Matthew 28:19–20, states that "This is a direct mandate to the church [through her leadership and faithful] to provide leadership for nations, instructing them to live according to the principles of the kingdom of God."[40] Ngara is convinced that Matthew 5:13–16 is Jesus's declaration regarding the leadership role he expects his followers (the church) to fulfil in the world. He (Jesus) expected Christians to work for a more humane and caring society so that the world can be a better place for all to live in. Should the church abdicate its leadership responsibility, Ngara is of the opinion that Christians negate their role as "the light of the world" and "the salt of the earth," "if we see that our continent is crying out for leaders who are dedicated to the development of the people, and do nothing about the aspirations of the people in this regard."[41] According to Munroe, the church has the responsibility and possesses the capability to produce quality leadership that may lead to the sociopolitical and economic transformation of both the church itself and Nigerian society as a whole.

The significance of this study is, therefore, in accordance with the fundamental concerns of practical theology as pointed out by Jurgens Hendriks, namely, that practical theology includes personal, ecclesiastical, secular, public, scientific and ecological levels of actions. He elaborates on these levels of action as follows: At a "personal level," we have been called to be followers or disciples of Jesus Christ. At an "ecclesiastical level," within the faith

---

37. Mbachu, "Leadership and Accountability," 59.
38. Matthew 28:19–20 (NABRE).
39. Matthew 5:13–16 (NABRE).
40. Munroe, *Becoming a Leader*, 17.
41. Ngara, *Christian Leadership*, 35.

community, we are the body of Christ, a missional church that acts in worship, witness, help, service, fellowship and planning. At the level of secular society, the church has an important role to play. In addition, it faces the public and should influence it in a positive way. At a "scientific level," the church should participate in the academic and intellectual aspects of theology. It is therefore important that theology should not happen alone and in splendid isolation. In addition, theology should be multidisciplinary in so far as it should relate to other disciplines when addressing issues that confront us. This does not mean that theology has to compromise its normative element. At the ecological level, as the body of Christ, we must be humble custodians of God's creation.[42]

First, in arguing for a development-oriented church leadership in postmilitary Nigeria with a sustainable transformational approach, this study seeks to call especially on all Nigerian church leaders and Christians to rise to the challenge of responsible Christian living. Through its leadership, the church should imbue its members with a leadership mentality that is geared towards social change which will address poverty, underdevelopment, corruption and poor leadership. Accordingly, individual Christians may naturally become agents of social change as they go about their daily lives and it is in this way that the Nigerian Christian may set a good example even among persons who are not of the Christian persuasion.

Second, the essence of the existence of the church is to serve the purposes of God in the spreading of the kingdom of God. The leadership of the ecclesial community (within the local and ecumenical expression of that community) may, in fellowship, be afforded the opportunity to equip and nurture that community so as to enable its members to be sent out to serve in the world. Accordingly, this study intends to evaluate the degree of success with which both the church leadership and the faithful are fulfilling the divine mandate within the ecclesial community and beyond for the purpose of exploring a more meaningful way of engagement, should there be a need to engage in that regard.

Third, this study seeks to respond to the key practical theological question, where are we now?, and to provide some critical theory about the ideal situation, and some understanding of the processes, spiritual forces, and

---

42. Hendriks, "Change of Heart," 33.

technologies required to get from where we are to the ideal future. Nigerian society is plagued with poor leadership with the resultant effect of poverty, underdevelopment, corruption and other forms of injustice. The Christian community accounts for about 40 percent[43] of the Nigerian population of about 150 million, as in 1998 or thereabout. The country's population at the time of conducting this study is well over 230 million. This study is, thus, a call to the church to fulfil its public role by influencing Nigerian society in a positive way through a sustainable transformational approach to development, an approach flowing from the church into the public arena. As such, this study may contribute to the promotion of a development paradigm which may, in turn, result in collaborative, innovative stewardship and value laden endeavours between leaders of the church in Nigeria and other social institutions within Nigeria and the global community.

Fourth, this study is concerned about burning issues that are relevant to Nigeria. However, the issues of poor leadership, social transformation, poverty, underdevelopment, corruption, ecology and other forms of injustice are not only African issues but also global issues as well as being interdisciplinary issues. Although this study uses theology as its point of departure, the study aims at presenting the church (leadership and faithful) as comprising stewards imbued with both a divine calling and the capabilities to serve the kingdom of God and the mission of God in the world. As such, this study may be applicable as a learning opportunity for African or any other countries facing similar issues and it may contribute, on a theological and socioreligious level, to the global discourse on leadership and development.

Fifth, in view of the fact that the leadership challenge and its consequences within Nigeria are common to several countries in Africa and the global south, there is no doubt that some aspects of this study will be relevant to those churches and countries that are faced with similar challenges. It is, therefore, hoped that the findings and perspectives that will emerge from this study will influence the church's leadership and followership regarding a new vision of the economic and sociopolitical emancipation of Nigerians and, to some extent, all Africans and persons living in developing countries. In addition, this study may also prove to be useful in other parts of the African

---

43. Falola, 4. This figure may be contested as some writers believe that Christians comprise not less than 46% of the Nigerian population.

continent and the global south as a result of the astronomical growth of the church in some African and southern hemisphere countries and the ongoing influence of church leaders in such countries.

1.11 Delimitation of the Study

This research study does not reflect upon leadership in the general sense but is rather concerned with ecclesiastical leadership that is geared towards the religiosocial, political and economic transformation of Nigerian and sub-Saharan African societies. Furthermore, it is not a prescriptive work on either political and economic management or leadership, nor does it investigate or report on all the developmental activities of churches in Nigeria. On the contrary, its focus is on development-oriented church leadership as a means through which the church in Nigeria may contribute to the socioeconomic and political realms within Nigerian society. The level of corruption, poverty and underdevelopment in Nigeria has been attributed to the poor leadership that has controlled the country since independence.[44] Accordingly, this study seeks to explore ways and means by which the church in Nigeria, through its leaders, may make more meaningful contributions to overcoming the challenge of misrule and the attendant consequences from the perspective of church leadership and social transformation.

This study, furthermore, aims at addressing the challenge of leadership and underdevelopment in Nigeria, specifically within the context of the post-military or democratic era of Nigerian history (1999–2010). However, this is not the only era of democratic rule in independent Nigeria. The first years of independence from British colonial rule, popularly termed the First Republic, was also characterized by democratic rule. However, this period lasted for five years only (1960–65) and, from 1965, the Nigerian military held the reins of power with short interludes of democratic rule.[45] In 1998, when Nigeria had been an independent state for approximately thirty-eight years, thirteen years only had been marked by civilian/democratic rule with the rest witnessing the military at the helm of government. Nigerian political history may, therefore, be demarcated roughly as civilian (democratic) rule (1960–65),

---

44. Achebe, *Trouble with Nigeria*, 11; Falola, *History of Nigeria*, 224, 230.
45. Falola, 179.

military rule (1966–98) and civilian/democratic rule (1999 to the present). The period from 1999 to the present may, thus, be termed a postmilitary era. This research study focuses on this period for the following reasons: First, this period of approximately ten years is a reasonable period for investigating the challenges of the leadership in Nigeria – leadership which is assumed to have given rise to poverty, underdevelopment and corruption. For the purpose of this study, this is also a manageable period in which to collect the necessary data to enable the researcher to make well-informed conclusions.

Second, should the challenges of leadership to be addressed in this study have, indeed, arisen from the misrule of Nigeria by Nigerians themselves (military or civilian), as many commentators suggest, if these Nigerian leaders are to be held liable for their failures, then it is essential that sufficient time be allowed for the learning period involved in self-rule. Despite the fact that there are still powerful controlling tendencies on the part of countries in the Northern Hemisphere,[46] and these should by no means be underrated, it is time that Nigerians/Africans took responsibility for the mistakes and failures of their own making instead of laying the entire blame on their colonial masters who have long since disengaged from effective occupation of countries on the African continent. With regard to leadership of the churches which remained under the control of foreigners long after independence, it has now, for some time, been in the hands of Nigerians. The period under study has witnessed not only a tremendous growth of the church in Nigeria, but it has also afforded Nigerian church leaders the opportunity to demonstrate their development consciousness, with the degree to which the latter has occurred comprising an important element of this study.

Third, military regimes across the world are usually despotic and/or repressive and, therefore, unacceptable. Accordingly, evaluating the governance and leadership performance of churches during the years of military rule would be ineffective and even, perhaps, unreasonable as such an era would not have provided an enabling environment for the optimum performance of both nonmilitary and church leaders. In addition, if, as some commentators suggest, the challenge of leadership within both the church and the Nigerian

---

46. What is referred to here are countries in Europe and North America and their powerful influence on the economic and political scenarios of Nigeria and other underdeveloped countries on other continents. Cf. Nurnberger, *Prosperity, Poverty and Pollution*; Chambers, *Whose Reality Counts?*

context is worse now than ever before, then this would be an appropriate time to rise to meet this huge challenge in a sustainable transformational manner through a development-oriented church leadership.

1.12 Definition of Key Terms

1.12.1 Forms of the Church

D. Hughes and M. Bennett have pointed out that the Greek word "*ekklesia*" which was translated by the translators of the Authorized Version of the Bible to mean "church," is an inappropriate translation and the word "congregation," as used by Tyndale is more appropriate.[47] According to Hughes and Bennett, "church has a strong inclination to place, whereas ekklesia means a particular group of people gathered together – a congregation." In line with this understanding, in the Septuagint, *ekklesia* is often used to translate *qahal*, the "congregation" of Israel, "the nation in its theocratic aspect, organized as a religious community." "Church" in the New Testament, therefore, does not refer to buildings or hierarchical structures but simply the people whose life is focused on Jesus Christ. The whole body of those who believe in and worship Jesus, wherever they may be are the "church."[48]

The implication of Hughes and Bennett's argument is that the term church refers to the whole body of those who are followers of Jesus Christ in a particular locality. However, it may also refer to the congregants who gather together to worship Jesus Christ in people's houses or when Christians congregate anywhere to worship Jesus and to honour God. John W. De Gruchy has argued that there is a slight variation between the constitution of the Hebrew *qahal* and the Christian *ekklesia* (used to translate *qahal* in the Septuagint). Whereas the former is constituted ethnically, the latter refers to a people bound by Jesus Christ, and not by nationality.[49]

Mercy Oduyoye and D. S. Long agree that the church is the one body of Christ that is mystically constituted with the unification of this body being made possible by the sacraments (Baptism and Eucharist).[50] Long terms this

---

47. Hughes and Bennett, *God of the Poor*, 72.
48. Hughes and Bennett, 72.
49. De Gruchy, *Christian Community*, 126.
50. Oduyoye, *Hearing and Knowing*, 145; Long, *Goodness of God*, 156.

body (*ekklesia* or church) "a different city" – "alterna civitas" and points out further that it does not have a fixed, geographical boundary.[51] Interestingly, T. M. Monsma has observed that social scientists refer to the church as an organization or an institution as compared to other institutions. This term is most appropriate when applied to either congregations or denominations.[52] Monsma stands with Abraham Kuyper (Dutch pastor, theologian and politician), who refers to an aspect of the church using a biological term, namely, "organism." According to Monsma, Kuyper used this term to describe church members when they are not in worship but when they are doing work that honours Christ their King out in the world, in terms of their respective engagement. In the light of this view, the church as an organism (individual Christians in their respective daily preoccupations), exists and works alongside the church as an organization or institution.[53] It may further be stressed that the church is an organic community, comprising citizens of a kingdom whose entire lives are guided by their membership of that community.

Based on the above, the church may be conceived as comprising the followers of Jesus in a particular place (venue, city or country) or the congregants who gather to worship Jesus and to honour God through Christian witness anywhere. In other words, the church is the one body of Christ that is mystically constituted. It is an organization or institution among other institutions such as a nation or political entity. The church may also be seen as an organized community with its component membership drawn from congregations and denominations within a nation for the purpose of fostering unity among the followers of Jesus and acting as a collective witness to the broader society. In this study, I will use the term church and Christians interchangeably and in a generic sense. The term church will also be used in reference to the various expressions of the communities of the followers of Jesus as regards congregations, denominations and interdenominational collaborations (ecumenical formations) for the purpose of worship and witness.

---

51. Long, 156.
52. Monsma, *Hope for the Southern World*, 122, 128.
53. Monsma, 128.

1.12.2 Church Leadership

Whereas there are different understandings of the concept of church leadership, and the kinds of leadership categories and roles both play in various ecclesial traditions such as Episcopalians, Congregationalists, Reformed and Presbyterian, this study uses the term in the simplified sense to denote all ordained and nonordained persons in leadership positions in churches (congregations, denominations and ecumenical bodies) with individuals in the categories of clergy, elders, women and youth leaders all being included. Accordingly, the term includes designations such as, inter alia, cardinal, archbishop, bishop, reverend, pastor, deacon, (deaconess) and elder.

Thus, the range of church leadership covered in this study, especially in the empirical study, includes categories such as youth and women leaders, elders, pastors, reverends, bishops, archbishops, prelates, moderators, presidents, cardinals, general secretaries, centre managers, treasurers, and leaders of denominations, congregations and ecumenical bodies.

1.12.3 Development-Oriented

This expression has been coined expressly for the purpose of this study and refers to a consciousness/inclination (mental and concrete engagement) on the part of clergy and other persons who hold leadership positions in the Christian fold towards human, political, economic, and social transformation, tailored to the reversal of poverty and underdevelopment. In the development discourse, this expression has a connection with "the pragmatic ecumenical development discourse including its moderate and radical perspectives.[54]

The expression refers to the ordained and nonordained persons who are entrusted with leadership responsibilities at different levels of the Christian

---

54. Swart, *Churches and Development Debate*, 62. Richard Dickinson is the most prominent exponent of the "moderate" pragmatic debate. Articulating a central aspect of the "moderate" pragmatic debate, it is proclaimed that there is a meaningful place for the project system besides a more overt structural approach to development. It suggests that there is the remaining factor of people and local societies' fundamental needs, which cannot be neglected amidst the concentrated participation in programmes for structural change. In this light, the development projects of the churches are to be positively viewed as "serving meaningful and qualitative efforts to meet these needs." The major exponent of the "radical" pragmatic debate is Charles Elliot. According to Swart, Elliot affirms that "however well-intentioned and carefully circumscribed with non-discriminatory provisions, aid is aid and an agent of the maintenance of a dependent relationship. Therefore, the best aid that can be given to the poor countries is the means of breaking that relationship. In addition, that means starting with the marginados."

community and with a concern for and engagement in social transformation. The scope of such leadsership includes denominational and ecumenical expressions of the Christian community.

1.12.4 Development

Development scholars and practitioners such as Burkey, Ndem Ndiyo and others have suggested different definitions for the concept of development. Burkey, for example, argues that development refers to the process of gradual change or transformation of human beings and/or economic, political and social structures.[55] Ndiyo agrees with this view and takes into account the concept of development within the Nigerian context as basically refering to socioeconomic and political wellbeing.[56] There is a detailed discussion on the concept of development in chapter 2. For the purpose of this study, development is understood as referring to the general wellbeing of humankind, animals and plants, as well as the environment and sociopolitical and economic systems. Such wellbeing includes the spiritual, psychological and physical/material realms.

1.12.5 Sustainability

This term is used in the sense of the consciousness that, for social change to be successful, it is essential that the various stakeholders be acknowledged. These stakeholders include God, humankind, plants/animals and the environment. The indispensability of these players must inform every endeavour that is directed towards the eradication of poverty and underdevelopment. The term is also used in reference to the church's assets as regards its engagement in development. These assets include the church's spiritual and moral foundations (a ground which may be explored in interfaith dialogue), access to the poor at grassroots level, a high premium on the family as the smallest unit of the human society, membership with diverse influence at all levels of society, international influence/communication networks,[57] numerical strength, financial capability and environmental consciousness. The church's development-oriented leadership must ensure that its developmental vision

---

55. Burkey, *People First*, 39.
56. Ndiyo, *Poverty to Sustainable Development*, 8, 11.
57. Nurnberger, *Prosperity, Poverty and Pollution*, 371–72.

and endeavour is channelled through these assets for the benefit of all. In addition, the term is used in reference to the church's innovativeness as it engages in development and exploring new opportunities and making the necessary adjustments, but bearing in mind the vision of its calling, as it navigates change in Nigeria. The sustainability of development as reflected upon in this study also refers to development in the sense of it being in the hands of Nigerians who understand the challenges of poverty, underdevelopment, corruption and bad leadership through firsthand experience. The role of non-Nigerian development agents or agencies in the developmental exercise in Nigeria should be that of catalysts for a season only,[58] while it is recommended that the developmental "stick"[59] be in the hands of Nigerians, and not foreign agents. Finally, development should be sustainable in the sense of being holistic in terms of the development being advocated, and covers the physical, mental, social, ecological and spiritual realms coupled with a concern that the gains of social transformation be transmitted to future generations.

1.12.6 Transformation

In this study, the word transformation is used in preference to the term development and is used synonymously or interchangeably with the term development. The latter term is imbued with meaning, with even negative and suspect connotations. Wayne Bragg argues that development refers to human endeavours while transformation refers to God's direct endeavours in which humankind is engaged as his agents or instruments for the realization of his purposes. In addition, development is often used to differentiate between the conditions of the poor and the rich with no reference to the spiritual while transformation transcends physical and spiritual issues. Based on this view, transformation means "to take what is and turn it into what it could and should be."[60] In the case of Nigeria, this would mean that Nigerians should

---

58. Expatriate or foreign development consultants and agencies will need to see themselves as facilitators or enablers of Nigerians who should in turn equip and motivate the locals to take responsibility for the development and sociopolitical and economic transformation of their nation.

59. Chambers, *Whose Reality Counts?*

60. Bragg, "From Development to Transformation," 38–39.

have the opportunity to take what is at their disposal and turn it to what could and should be.

1.12.7 Postmilitary Nigeria

Postmilitary Nigeria refers to the era in Nigerian history that began in May 1999, after twenty-eight years of military rule. Military rule had been characterized by corruption, political instability and civil unrest. In addition, it had suspended the democratic structures of governance and had ruled through intimidation and fear. Nigerians anticipate that, in the so-called postmilitary or democratic era, a new sociopolitical and economic course will be charted, a course that will herald the advances of democracy. These advances include the eradication of poverty, job creation and employment opportunities, provision of infrastructure, freedom of speech and all the other benefits that characterize societies that have embraced the democratic ethos in their policies.

1.12.8 Poverty

Development scholars and practitioners have proffered a number of definitions for the word poverty, including Stand Burkey who argues that poverty may be defined in terms of basic needs. Absolute poverty refers to the inability of an individual, a community or a nation to meet its basic needs in a satisfactory way while relative poverty refers to the condition in which basic needs are met, but where, in addition to these basic needs, there is an inability to meet perceived needs and desires. Whereas people living in absolute poverty need relief in order to survive, those existing in relative poverty need development assistance to help them to become independent of such assistance over time.[61] The classification of the various degrees of poverty has also been viewed from the financial perspective. In terms of this view, individuals, households or communities are considered relatively poor if their equivalized income is less than 60 percent of the median income in that year, taking into account the context in which they live. This is termed relative poverty because the poverty line varies from year to year as median income changes – if median income goes up, then so does the poverty line. Essentially, changes in the relative poverty rate are informative about whether poorer households are keeping

---

61. Burkey, *People First*, 3–4.

up with those on middle incomes. An individual is defined as being in absolute poverty if their household income is less than 60 percent of real median income[62] in a given year and given context. Besides these views on what it means to be poor, like other Africans, Nigerians also view poverty as a lack of meaningful relationships among kinsmen/women and the community.[63] In a sense, when the physical and spiritual needs are considered, poverty refers to the lack of basic needs such as food, shelter, clean water and healthcare as well as a lack of finances to meet one's needs, skill and knowledge; and, as regards the non-Christian poor, a lack of knowledge of God and the good news of Jesus Christ. The term is used in this study as detailed above.

1.12.9 Underdevelopment

According to Amartya Sen, "underdevelopment has to do with the presence of major sources of unfreedom: poverty as well as tyranny, poor economic opportunities as well as systemic social deprivation, and neglect of public facilities."[64] S. A. Ekanem suggests that underdevelopment depicts "conditions that inhibit real development in any country, usually signified by stagnation, retardation, and lack of economic prosperity or progress, and moral decadence, among other social ills."[65] The use of the term underdevelopment in this study will be in line with the definitions of both Sen and Ekanem and will, thus, refer to poverty as inadequate economic opportunities, neglect of public infrastructure and systemic social deprivation.

1.12.10 Corruption

Ndiyo argues that corruption "is the offering, giving, receiving or soliciting, directly or indirectly, of anything of value to influence improperly the actions of another party."[66] He goes on to suggest that corrupt practices vary enormously in kind from place to place but usually include fraudulent, collusive, coercive and obstructive practices. In this study, the use of the term corruption is in accordance with Ndiyo's definition of the term.

---

62. Hood and Waters, "Living Standards, Poverty," 27.
63. Agbiji, "Religion and Ecological Justice," 10.
64. Sen, *Development as Freedom*, 3.
65. Ekanem, *How the Military Underdeveloped*, 124.
66. Ndiyo, *Poverty to Sustainable Development*, 175.

1.13 Chapter Outline

Chapter 1 – Introduction

This chapter serves as an introduction to the study and, as such, it presents the background, motivation, problem statement, research question, goals of the study and the theoretical frameworks that inform the study. It also elucidates the research paradigm, research methodology and research design guiding the study. In addition, chapter 1 discusses the significance, delimitations and definitions of key terms used in the study.

Chapter 2 – Meanings and Implications of Development in Postmilitary Nigeria

Chapter 2 focuses on the meanings and implications of development. In line with Osmer's practical theological methodology,[67] this chapter seeks to carry out the descriptive-empirical and interpretive tasks. The chapter addresses the following questions: What is going on in the Nigerian social context with regard to development and why are these things going on? The aim of this chapter is to uncover the root causes of the perennial challenges of underdevelopment and the resultant consequences in Nigeria, in particular, and to suggest concerns that may be built into a development agenda that may be of benefit to Nigerian society. To this end, issues pertaining to development, including the various approaches to and views on the concept of development, development trends in Nigeria and sub-Saharan Africa, the quest for an African model of development and the challenges confronting development in Nigeria are discussed. Development trends in Nigeria are also assessed.

Chapter 3 – Meanings and Implications of Leadership in Postmilitary Nigeria

The main focus of this chapter is an exploration of relevant literature on the Nigerian historical context from precolonial times to the present era, especially as it relates to leadership in the country. The chapter engages both the descriptive-empirical and interpretive lenses as proposed by Osmer.[68] The aim of the chapter is to understand the root cause(s) of the persistent challenge of poor leadership and the consequences arising from this poor

---

67. Osmer, *Practical Theology*, 4–12.
68. Osmer, 4–12.

leadership, with particular reference to underdevelopment and poverty. In accordance with the aim of the chapter, the chapter offers both a definition and a conceptualization of the concept of leadership. Reflections on leadership in precolonial, colonial, postcolonial, military and postmilitary (democratic) Nigerian society are preceded by a presentation of the African understanding of leadership and the sources that influence that understanding. In addition, the importance of leadership as the pivot of development and social transformation in Nigerian society are also discussed.

Chapter 4 – Social and Theological Analysis of Church Leadership Discourse in Postmilitary Nigeria

The goal of this chapter is to appraise the involvement of the Nigerian church leaders in the social and theological development discourses within the Nigerian context, using the descriptive-empirical and interpretive practical theological approaches,[69] as discussed in 1.8.1. This chapter seeks to answer the question, whether and how, based on the extensive population of the church and the rich resources the church possesses, church leaders have utilized these resources to address the material/physical, psychological and spiritual challenges facing Nigerians? The chapter is divided into three parts: The first part deals with the public role of the church, the second with the social discourse of church leaders and the third with matters arising from the theological discussions of church leaders pertaining to development in Nigeria.

Chapter 5 – Dissemination and Reflections on the Empirical Study

The aim in this chapter is to present and reflect on the results of the empirical study that was carried out among church leaders of CAN and the LPC in Nigeria. The focus of the empirical study was on finding out whether church leaders have made any contribution to social transformation in Nigeria and, if so, the extent of such contribution and whether it may, perhaps, be made more meaningful in the light of the poverty, underdevelopment, corruption and poor leadership in Nigeria. Accordingly, the focus of the study will be on the responses to the open-ended questionnaires as these responses relate to the research questions. These questions are intended to uncover important

---

69. Osmer, 4–12.

themes that may aid the proposal and assessment of a social transformational approach to the social engagement of church leaders in Nigeria in the interest of a more meaningful social agenda. The enunciated task of chapter 5 is guided by the descriptive-empirical, interpretive, normative and pragmatic tasks of practical theological methodology, as enunciated by Osmer.[70]

Chapter 6 – A Sustainable Transformational Approach to Development in Postmilitary Nigeria

In line with the pragmatic task of practical theology,[71] this chapter proposes a developmental framework which may be used by church leaders and the Christian community in Nigeria, as agents of change, in order to engage their resources adequately in collaboration with other institutions in Nigeria and beyond. The contents of the proposed framework are drawn from themes derived from both the literature study and empirical research – See chapters 2, 3, 4, and chapter 5 respectively.

Chapter 7 – Development-Oriented Church Leadership in Postmilitary Nigeria: Perspectives, Conclusion and Recommendations

Also, in line with the normative and pragmatic tasks of practical theological methodology,[72] the final chapter of this study concludes by highlighting some important perspectives in the study and by making recommendations that may aid the sociopolitical and economic transformation of Nigerian society. The perspectives presented include the proposed goals regarding development in Nigeria, Nigerian leadership/followership, the various expressions of the church in Nigeria, sociopolitical and economic systems, globalization, civil society and the dignity of creation; as well as the way in which the development-oriented church leader and those concerns that may be vital to social change in Nigeria relate to the sustainable, transformational, development paradigm.

---

70. Osmer, 4–12.
71. Osmer, 4–12.
72. Osmer, 4–12.

CHAPTER 2

Meanings and Implications of Development in Postmilitary Nigeria

2.1 Introduction

Central to the discussion on the meanings and implications of development in Nigeria is the evaluation of the historical context of Nigeria through the study of relevant literature from precolonial to present times. In line with Osmer's practical theological methodology, as discussed in chapter 1, this chapter attempts to carry out the descriptive-empirical and interpretive tasks.[1] The chapter also seeks to provide answers to the following questions: What is going on in the social environment in Nigeria as it pertains to development? And why are these things going on? The aim of this chapter is to uncover the root causes of the perennial challenge of underdevelopment and the resultant consequences in Nigeria. This study assumes that the poverty, underdevelopment and corruption, as are currently being experienced in Nigeria, may be a result of the failure of the political leadership in Nigeria in terms of both the development of a relevant development agenda and the proper management of the resources in the country over time. This chapter will, therefore, explore the meanings and implications of development. In addition, issues peripheral to development, including the various approaches to and views on the concept of development, development trends in Nigeria and sub-Saharan Africa, the quest for an African model of development and the challenges

---

1. Osmer, *Practical Theology*, 4–12.

confronting development in Nigeria will be discussed. Development trends in Nigeria will also be assessed. The meanings of the term development will be discussed first.

2.2 The Meanings of Development

The concept of development has more than one meaning, with meanings ranging from development from an economic angle to development as an overall social process. The latter includes the various facets of the social process, including economic, social, political, religious and cultural aspects.

2.2.1 Development as Economic and Technological Growth

From an economic perspective, P. Land suggests that, initially, the primary focus of development was economic.[2] Regarding the origin of this view of development, T. Sine argues that Western development was a product of the European and American Enlightenment era and it was based primarily on unlimited technological and economic growth. This vision first emerged in Francis Bacon's book, *The New Atlantis*. And this view is believed to be the first indication in Western history of a technological paradise which was possible through human agency. This view of development gave impetus to the colonial era with all its ramifications. Sine further maintains that the seventies sounded the death knell for the Enlightenment belief that humanity could achieve a utopia here on earth. Yet, the essential image of the better future as synonymous with economic growth, which is implicit in contemporary development theory, has not significantly changed since the beginning of Western expansion. Nations that have experienced major economic and technological growth are described as "developed"; those that have not are characterized as "underdeveloped," in spite of the growing awareness of the negative human and environmental consequences of unrestrained growth.[3]

2.2.2 Development as Liberation

In terms of development, Latin American theologian Gustavo Gutierrez Merino argues from a perspective which he maintains is both biblically oriented

---

2. Land, "What Is Development?," 181.
3. Sine, "Development: Its Secular Past," 3, 5.

and economically, socially, politically and culturally relevant. According to him, an approach to development as an overall social process necessarily implies ethical values, which presupposes, in the last analysis, a concept of man. It is this all-embracing approach to development that Merino deems to be the most appropriate and which he prefers to call liberation. Accordingly, he argues that liberation expresses more clearly both the aspirations of oppressed peoples and the completeness of a perspective in which man is seen, not as a passive factor, but as the agent of history.[4] Merino's view on development chiefly calls to question the mechanistic and industrial understanding of the word "development" which privileges the rich and the fact that this approach does not pay adequate attention to the sufferings and aspirations of the poor for more humane living conditions.

2.2.3 People-Centred Development

According to David Korten, it is essential that development be people-centred, and not production-centred. Korten therefore defines development as a process by which the members of a society increase their personal and institutional capacities to mobilize and manage resources to produce sustainable and justly distributed improvements in their quality of life consistent with their own aspirations.[5] Korten's view is animated by a spirituality and a value-based approach to human and environmental existence. In terms of this approach, the decision-making process is significantly decentralized and returned to the people. Stan Burkey's approach to development is in accordance with this position and manifests a strong emphasis on self-reliance.[6]

2.2.4 Development as Expanding Access to Social Power

In making his case for development as expanding access to social power, John Friedman defines development as "a process that seeks the empowerment of households and their individual members through their involvement in socially and politically relevant actions."[7] Central to this definition is the premise that empowerment involves local decision-making, self-reliance,

---

4. Merino, "Meaning of Development," 121–125.
5. Korten, *Post Corporate World*, 16, 301.
6. Burkey, *People First*, 41–55.
7. Myers, *Walking with the Poor*, 99.

participatory democracy and social learning while both gender equality and sustainability are closely allied to these notions. In creating life space for the poor through the household, the two areas of concern are civil society and political community.

2.2.5 Development as Responsible Well-Being

Robert Chambers views development as responsible well-being for all. He goes on to describe well-being as quality of life with ill-being as its opposite. Well-being is open to the whole range of human experience: social, mental, spiritual as well as material.[8]

2.2.6 Development as a Kingdom Response to Powerlessness

For Jayakumar Christian, the response to the "web of lies" that entraps the poor is to declare truth and righteousness while doing good works. It is, thus, essential that the most appropriate transformational development approach should seek to reverse the process of disempowerment. Accordingly, what is required is a kingdom of God response that includes three commitments: Dealing with the relational dimensions of poverty by building covenant quality communities that are inclusive; dealing with forces that create or sustain powerlessness (at all levels); and challenging the time element by rereading the history of the poor from God's perspective.[9] In Christian's opinion, such an approach would constitute development.

2.2.7 Development as Freedom

Amartya Sen postulates that development requires the removal of major sources of unfreedom: poverty as well as tyranny, poor economic opportunities as well as systemic social deprivation and neglect of public facilities. Thus, in terms of this approach, what constitutes underdevelopment is not lack of technological and economic growth; but it is the presence of poverty, tyranny, poor economic opportunities, systemic social deprivation and the neglect of public or social facilities in any given society.[10]

---

8. Chambers, *Whose Reality Counts?*, 9–10.
9. Myers, *Walking with the Poor*, 106–7.
10. Sen, *Development as Freedom*, 3.

2.2.8 Development as Transformation

Wayne Bragg is the main exponent of transformation as a developmental framework. At the Wheaton '83 consultation entitled "A Christian Response to Human Need," Bragg argues that transformation is the concept that permeates the biblical record, from the Old Testament images of shalom and the reign of God in Israel to the New Testament church and the kingdom of God. Throughout the Bible, we see how the existing reality is transformed into a higher dimension and purpose: a rag tag slave group in Egypt is changed into the Hebrew nation; a small band of powerless Jews are transformed into the church that altered the course of history. Transformation is to take what is and turn it into what it could and should be.[11]

The characteristics of Bragg's development framework, which he terms transformation, include "life sustenance; equity; justice; dignity and selfworth; freedom; hope and spiritual transformation." Bryant Myers has further given impetus to the development of the concept of transformational development wherein he proposes the twin goals of transformational development as changed people and just and peaceful relationships. In terms of changed people, these are persons that have discovered their true identity as children of God and who have recovered their true vocation as faithful and productive stewards of gifts from God for the well-being of all.[12]

In light of the various definitions of development, this study agrees with Burkey's suggestion that "[t]here can be no fixed and final definition of development; merely suggestions of what development should imply in particular contexts."[13] It is certainly hardly in doubt that Nigeria and many other African countries comprise the main underdeveloped and poorest countries in the world. However, the question arises as to what concerted efforts Nigeria and other African countries have made to deal with the challenges of poverty and underdevelopment.

---

11. Bragg, "From Development to Transformation," 38–39.
12. Myers, *Walking with the Poor*, 14.
13. Burkey, *People First*, 33.

2.3 Development Trends in Nigeria and Sub-Saharan Africa

From 1960 to 1994, when Nigeria and most of the other countries in sub-Saharan Africa, gained independence, there have been a number of economic and political policies pursued with the desire to bring about rapid development being the main motivation in the pursuit of those policies. However, M. Kankwenda has described the forty years of the development endeavour in Nigeria and in other sub-Saharan African countries as illusory. He argues that, in these forty years, there have been numerous development policies, all of which have been prolific and incoherent and which have ended up confusing and limiting African leaders in their quest for development. Most of these economic policies were informed by the pioneering work of John Maynard Keynes and others who were concerned with the problems of economic growth in the developed countries in the 1930s, soon after the recession.[14] In line with this thinking and, until recently, a lack of development was perceived as an economic issue – "lack of access to economic resources, poor growth rates, lack of industrialization, inflation, high interest rates, lack of savings, low levels of investments and so on."[15] B. S. Mongula has identified a number of these policies, namely, "[t]he capital formation centred approach, the economic nationalism centred approach, the basic human needs centred approach and the economic stabilization approach."[16]

This list may not be exhaustive but it does constitute the major developmental trends that have been witnessed in both Nigeria and in most of the African nations. However, whereas other African nations may have subscribed to different policies, Nigeria is considered to be in the "Afro-Capitalist" category.[17] Each of these policies will be discussed briefly for the purpose of assessing how well, or otherwise, each of these policies informed development in Nigeria, in particular, and in sub-Saharan Africa, in general.

---

14. Kankwenda, "Forty Years of Development illusions," 3, 5.
15. Onubogu, "Modernisation, Globalisation and Africa's," 72–73.
16. Mongula, "Development Theory and Changing," 88.
17. Deng, *Rethinking African Development*, 14.

2.3.1 Capital Formation Centred Approach

The capital formation centred approach policy came into play soon after Nigeria gained its independence from Britain in 1960. The political leadership in Nigeria was preoccupied with promoting rapid economic growth with the aim of matching up to the more advanced countries in the Northern Hemisphere. During this era, "growth was perceived to be a function of increased capital formation."[18] This policy of development closely resembles the modernization theory. However, the major disadvantages of this policy were that it did not take into account the local context, and besides the acute lack of an industrial sector, infrastructure and skilled labour were not also taken into consideration.[19]

2.3.2 Economic Nationalism Centred Approach

In terms of the economic nationalism centred developmental approach, most sub-Saharan African countries, including Nigeria, embarked on a number of strategies such as indigenous control of the public service and participation in the management and ownership of economic enterprises. In some instances, this approach encouraged collaboration between the governments of African countries and foreign investors. The main aim of the nationalization policy was to ensure the full pursuit of independence and, thus, the total liberation of these countries from colonial control. This approach was further justified by a nationalistic inclination geared towards economic development for the benefit of the citizens.[20]

Speaking on the Africanization of the civil service in Nigeria and other countries in Africa, H. Stein observes that with the exception of Hastings Banda in Malawi and Felix Houghouet-Boigny in Ivory Coast, newly formed African governments succumbed to pressures to rapidly Africanize civil services after independence. Stein estimates that between 100,000 and 200,000 expatriate-held posts were Africanized between 1958 and 1968. The "positions sought were extremely lucrative, since the salary structures inherited from the colonial period, which were aimed at maintaining a Western lifestyle, were largely kept in place." Nigeria, for example, had a top civil service salary scale

---

18. Mongula, "Development Theory and Changing," 88.
19. Mongula, 89.
20. Mongula, 89.

estimate of per capita GDP of 118 to 1. However, the poor state of human capital development, the weak economic base, poor infrastructure and ethnic imbalances, which were all colonial legacies, did not help this nationalization policy of development.[21]

Arguably, the expectation of the indigenous people that their nationalist leaders would transform their economic, political and social challenges soon after the colonial period was unrealistic. However, the major challenge was the politicized, tribalized, overbloated and incompetent personnel manning the civil service and other institutions. It is in this connection that Mongula observed that as the public sector expanded over time, this brought about a number of unprecedented problems whose size and complexity could not be handled with the existing managerial resource base, political and public administration structures and, above all, the asymmetrical economies and low domestic technological capacity.[22] The fact that African countries, especially Nigeria, had been inadequately prepared for independence by the colonial masters as well as the lifestyles, self-interests and clannish inclinations of the nationalist leaders contributed significantly to the failure of the economic nationalism approach to development in Nigeria.

2.3.3 The Basic Human Needs Approach

Unlike the socialist centred approach which, according to Mongula, represents the third developmental effort and which enjoyed the support of certain African leaders including Nkrumah (Ghana), Sekou Toure (Guinea), Nyerere (Tanzania) and others in the African socialism mould, the basic human needs approach gained a substantial following across political ideologies and also in Nigeria. The significant aspect of the basic human needs' development paradigm is its focus on human beings instead of on infrastructure. In addition, apart from being considered "neutral," this development concern was tilted to moral justice as compared with the economic bent of previous approaches. However, despite the fact that this approach did succeed in raising standards in both education and healthcare in some African countries, the

---

21. Stein, *Economic Development*, 15.
22. Mongula, "Development Theory and Changing," 90.

apparent gains did not match the population growth in these countries and this contributed substantially to the failure of the approach.[23]

2.3.4 The Structural Adjustment Approach

Following closely on the basic human needs' development approach was the structural adjustment or "economic stabilization approach," an approach which featured strongly in sub-Saharan Africa in the 1980s. As a result of the increasing difficulty experienced by the governments of Nigeria and other African countries in raising financial loans to uphold their economies in the face of the debt burden, the International Financial Institutions (IFIs) (World Bank and International Monetary Fund) introduced Structural Adjustment Programmes (SAPs).[24] It should be noted at this point that these financial institutions were the only institutions able to grant loans to these governments. A. Thomson has observed that SAPs are programmes of conditional lending. Accordingly, Nigeria and other African countries were able to access more loans only if they changed their economic policies to synchronize with the requirements of these lending institutions. "IFIs require African countries to liberalise their economies, opening them to international and domestic private capital, while at the same time reducing the role of the state in economic governance."[25] Although the policy was first instituted in Kenya, Malawi and Mauritius in the 1980s, the 1990s witnessed a proliferation of this policy in sub-Saharan Africa, including Nigeria, despite the fact that the economies of these countries were now at the mercy of Western financial institutions.

Shortly after independence, the economies of most African countries were driven by the state. However, with the introduction of SAPs, the major driving structure of these countries, namely, the state, was dismantled with the aim of shifting the focus of development from the urban areas to the rural

---

23. Mongula, 90. "African socialism" is a label that is often used to distinguish the type of socialism that was practiced in Africa from the orthodox Marxist-Leninist type of socialism.

The "basic human needs" economic approach is considered the fourth developmental approach to which most countries in sub-Saharan Africa subscribed in the post-independence era. It was a generally accepted approach in both the African continent and in the international community as the approach to development that would be most appropriate in tackling the challenge of poverty and underdevelopment in Africa. According to Mongula, the basic human needs approach appeared ideologically neutral and was a compromise between the forces that called for socialist and capitalist-oriented development.

24. Mongula, 92.
25. Thomson, *Introduction to African Politics*, 183.

communities and also of relieving the governments of their control over economic activities in order to eradicate both corruption and administrative bottlenecks. Deng, Stein and Thomson, all agree that, in view of the fact that the concern for stabilization was given precedence over development, the already poor state of the physical infrastructure and social amenities was made worse as a result of the adjustment programmes. The concrete implications of this economic policy inevitably included, inter alia, poor roads, declining health and educational systems, an increase in unemployment and moribund factories. In addition, SAPs also negatively impacted the political life of several African countries with a decline in government legitimacy. This "decline in government legitimacy led to political instability, which also impacted on the development endeavour."[26] It should be noted that the development policies that were pursued were "cut and dry" and imported to the shores of Africa. In other words, the peculiarities of African societies were not taken into consideration in both the formulation and the implementation of these developmental approaches. As a result, Nigeria in particular, and sub-Saharan Africa in general, still yearn for a developmental paradigm that would address their human, political, social, economic and environmental developmental challenges.[27]

2.4 The Quest for an African and Nigerian Model of Development

Regrettably, despite the myriad of developmental approaches that have been proposed and introduced in Nigeria and the countries of sub-Saharan Africa to help them overcome both underdevelopment and poverty, not much has changed.[28] The question, thus, arises as to whether the respective development programmes, from the colonial period until now, have been ill-intended or whether the challenge of poverty and underdevelopment within these contexts is unique and merits a special approach that will take into account the peculiarities of Nigeria in particular, and Sub-Saharan Africa in general. One way in which to address this issue may be to engage African philosophers

---

26. Thomson, 189.
27. Deng, *Rethinking African Development*.
28. Deng.

and development thinkers in a development discourse in order to find out what steps are being taken by Nigerians/Africans themselves to meet the challenge of underdevelopment.

2.4.1 African Development Philosophy and Philosophers

As a way of addressing underdevelopment, the quest for an African model of development may be considered to have been pioneered by philosophers of both European and African origin. It is feasible that the African philosophical quest for development may not have attracted much attention as a result of the domination of foreign economic, technological and structural concerns in development discourses. African development philosophical tendencies include the following: ethnophilosophy (Bantu philosophy), Africanism, theory for African revolution, professional philosophers and critics of the professional philosophers.[29]

Chachage claims that ethnophilosophy or Bantu philosophy, as enunciated by Placide Temples in his work, *Bantu Philosophy*, is considered to be a major step in the articulation of what is deemed to be African philosophy.[30] This work appeared at a time when African thinkers were searching for an African identity. From the perspective of the missionaries and colonial agents, who penetrated African societies during the colonial and missionary era with enormous challenges, Western anthropologists had been driven to the quest of understanding African societies following the impact of the World War II on the African masses, an impact which had triggered rebellion. This war had demystified the peddled superiority of the moral values of Europeans over the assumed savages (Africans). Both the imperialistic and the missionary visions for Africa came under public scrutiny and were found to be wanting. The resistance of Africans to the notion of Western superiority over Africans made it clear to the missionaries that the colonial authorities could no longer continue to treat Africans in a shabby way with the missionaries realizing that Western civilization was destructive in the African context. Despite the fact that the superiority of the West's science and technology could be of benefit

---

29. Chachage, "Discussion on Development."
30. Chachage, 51. According to Chachage, ethnophilosophy or Bantu philosophy was systematized by the agents of colonisation and was aimed at the re-appropriation of African cultures for colonial use.

to the Africans it was, nevertheless, also necessary to consider the effects of Western civilization which "gave birth to boundless egoism and threatened to annihilate society itself." The conclusion of the anthropologists is remarkable with "condemnation of 'savage' religions having to be abandoned with the realization that primitive religion and magic also fulfil specific functions, as do other aspects of culture. Primitive religion and magic may also have economic advantages, and could be used for the control and organization of societies."[31]

Tempels's African philosophy emerged at a time when the Marshall Plan and modernization theories were coming to the forefront. According to Tempels, these schemes were directed towards the mastery of nature by a vital force with Africans also wanting to share in the benefits of development. It is worth noting that this era also witnessed the building up of nationalist movements at a time when the colonial rulers were devising strategies to keep the colonized countries dependent on them, even after the attainment of self-rule. There is no doubt that African nationalists, who also constituted the bulk of African intellectuals, absorbed much both of Tempels's philosophies and of the prevailing ideologies of their time.

Broadly speaking, there were three categories of African philosophers, namely, ethnophilosophers, professional philosophers and the critics of the ethnoprofessional philosophies. African philosophers and intellectuals such as Leopold Senghor, Alexis Kagame and John Mbiti were greatly influenced by the ethno (Bantu) philosophy of Placide Tempels. Drawing from Frobenius, Griaule and Tempels, Senghor devized his famous philosophy of Negritude. In arguing for a distinctive African spirituality and worldview, which he deemed a vital component of his apprehension, he laid stress on the point that "Emotion is African as reason is Hellenic." Despite the fact that Kagame upheld the Bantu ontological philosophy through a linguistic analysis of the Rwandan people's historical narrative, he made a shift by universalising the Bantu ontological philosophy as compared to Tempels's particularising it to Africa.[32] From a political perspective, Aime Cesaire viewed Tempels's philosophy as a decoy with which to safeguard the colonial exploitation of Africa while, at the same time, breaking the resistance of the African people. Sheikh Anta Diop considered Tempels's Bantu philosophy to be both false and useless.

---

31. Chachage, 51–52.
32. Chachage, 53, 60.

He argued that it was the duty of African philosophers to understand their origin and to develop the necessary infrastructure, and reconnect with Egypt (home of African philosophy) for the purpose of integrating such a rich heritage with modern thoughts. Diop, another African philosopher, maintained that Judaism, Christianity and Islam as well as arithmetic, science and other fields of study are not strange to Africa but that they have, in fact, emerged from Africa. As a result, no thought, no ideology is foreign to Africa which was the land of their birth. Africans must draw from the common intellectual heritage of humanity, guided by notions of what is useful and effective. Affirming Jeffreis Jr.'s position on African development, Chachage echoes Diop's view when he argues that development is a process of transformation from the clan to monolinguistic ethnic groups to nation or nationality. Important factors in this process are socialization (clan), production (division of labor), accumulation (surplus), and militarization (classes). The liberation of Africa can only be conducted along three lines: (1) Linguistic: Selection of one language to a continental language. (2) Political: The unity of Africa as in the past. Colonial and neocolonial states are false as they do not have the material capacity for the transformation of Africa, hence the need for a federated Africa. (3) Industrialization: The need for an industrialization plan in which all the resources of the continent (Thermo-nuclear, oil, etc.) can be fully utilized, and, thereby, combat the problems of investment and research which must accompany the plan.[33]

With regard to the challenge of underdevelopment, African professional philosophers such as Frantz Fanon foresaw the possibility of African development through the total liberation of African nations, which he perceived as the ultimate goal of independence. For Fanon, dwelling on the unity of African culture and a return to Egypt are not important and the major issue is the total transformation of African society.[34] Nationalist leaders such as Nkrumah (Ghana) and Azikiwe (Nigeria) and others advocated the strengthening of the state as a vehicle for development. However, while they worked for the concentration of power, especially within the presidency, they also ensured the weakening of civil society as a response to the civil upheavals which they considered to be inimical to development. The nationalist leaders

---

33. Chachage, 53, 56.
34. Fanon, *Wretched of the Earth*, 70–71.

were committed to modernization, and the general tendency was to view the mass of the people as ignorant, primitive, lazy, superstitious, resistant to change and backward. It was, therefore, necessary to defeat the working masses by concentrating the powers in the state and eroding the independence of the civil society, to pave the way for development.[35] This was the thinking of most African leaders shortly after independence. As early as 1961, the tendency of African leaders and African states was to disarm everybody politically, bully them and institute the single-party system which was the modern form of dictatorship of the bourgeoisie.[36] Chachage shares Fanon's view with regard to the attitude of African political elite towards the struggles of ordinary Africans.[37]

Fanon's view is both informative and visionary as, over time, a number of African leaders have been dictatorial and corrupt and insensitive to the voices of the masses. It would appear that the nationalist and ethno-philosophical ideologies have provided a foundation for the poor leadership and the looting of public treasuries by political and military leaders in Nigeria and across the continent. The annihilation of civil society by the powerful state through the instrumentality of a political leadership which holds the masses in low esteem has no place in the development and the transformation of African societies. In this understanding, the major hindrance to development in Africa was both the state and those in control of political power. Reversing the status quo would require instruction in the philosophical disciplines that are able to foster the development of scientific thought in Africa. Such disciplines include, for example, logic, the history of sciences, epistemology, the history of technology, the history of philosophy, and theology and religion with a view to channel the resources of these disciplines towards development.

It would appear from the various philosophical perspectives that the way out of underdevelopment in Africa is through rigorous intellectual and social engagement which aims to broaden the democratic space in African nations. The way out of underdevelopment also includes scientific creativity and the sociopolitical self-organization of the masses. Accordingly, the key issue that will foster African development is not predominantly economic policies and

---

35. Chachage, "Discussion on Development," 55.
36. Fanon, *Wretched of the Earth*, 71.
37. Chachage, "Discussion on Development," 51–60.

the transfer of technology; but it is a matter of improving the conditions in African nations in such a way that will allow for the self-mobilization and organization of the masses for the transformation of their societies. In this respect, leadership that believes in the potential of the people, respects their opinions and is willing to assist the people navigate their change is crucial. However, in addition to the contributions of certain African philosophers, there are also some African intellectuals and leaders who have also made valid inputs into the development discourse.

2.4.2 Some African and Nigerian Voices in Development Discourse

The attainment of political independence for African countries has been credited to African intellectuals in their respective countries, including, inter alia, Nnamdi Azikiwe (Nigeria), Kwame Nkrumah (Ghana), Julius Nyerere (Tanzania), Leophold Senghor (Senegal) and Nelson Mandela (South Africa). The efforts of these intellectuals have had a major positive impact within their own countries but, to a large extent, their contributions have gone beyond their countries to the entire African continent. Although the hope of the masses of having political independence translate into economic independence is still far from being realized, this was not the fault of the generation of intellectuals who have fought for independence but rather that of the following generation of intellectuals. It is essential that the attainment of African development (second independence) be the prerogative of contemporary African intellectuals – researchers and policy analysts.[38] Goran Hyden had earlier observed that "development is the product of human efforts and it is for this reason that development has both its architects and its auditors."[39] The architects of development are those persons of vision who embrace certain ideologies such as concern for the development of infrastructure and better standards of living for the masses and who often occupy positions of power. Meanwhile, the auditors of development are academics. Although these academics are often not at the forefront of events, they do hasten to express their concerns when things are going wrong. In addition, besides acting as the auditors, the academics often play vital roles in shaping the developmental

---

38. Deng, *Rethinking African Development*, 146.
39. Hyden, "Changing Ideological and Theoretical Perspectives," 308.

ideologies, policy formulation and policy implementation in their countries. It is common knowledge that a number of African leaders rely greatly on the academics to formulate policies for them as they themselves, as in Nigeria, lack the capacity to do this as a result of inadequate formal education. In the spirit of Deng's argument, it remains within the ambit of African intellectuals, as in other parts of the world, to rise to the challenge of underdevelopment in Africa. Accordingly, this study will, at this point, briefly discuss some current intellectual concerns in African development discourse.

Hyden argues that, in the past, the voices of African scholars have not been given a chance to be heard on the continent itself, let alone outside of it. However, with the shift from the neoliberal theorising on development to "institutionalism"[40] (the layer between individual actors and societal structures), African intellectuals now have an opportunity to be heard within and beyond the continent. It is hoped that the emphasis on social and cultural variables will, naturally, provide an authentic impetus to African intellectuals as they express what is peculiar to Africans as compared with other voices of the broader perspectives beyond the African continent. Deng contends that the advice of policy analysts to the effect that the "Asian miracle" development model should be put into practice in Africa, no matter how well intended, will not yield the desired impact and he calls on African intellectuals to look at African history for a possible guide to an appropriate development framework. He then proposes six leading issues that are guaranteed to dominate Africa's research and policy agenda in the twenty-first century. These issues include "economic reform; democratization; protecting the environment; controlling indebtedness; poverty reduction; and conflict resolution."[41] It is suggested that addressing these issues should be done through frameworks that integrate African social values and institutions with the economic fundamentals contained in contemporary development theories.[42] In Deng's model for development in Africa, the state is "the hub of sustainable development around which the other key elements such as agriculturally led

---

40. Hyden, 318. According to James March and Johan P. Olsen, the "new institutionalism" refers to what, in the 1990s, appeared to be the new emphasis in development theory. Although it is still to be translated into a development theory, it argues that social action is primarily integrative and is aimed at going beyond self-interest.

41. Deng, *Rethinking African Development*, 146.

42. Deng.

economic growth, social stability and ecological harmony all depend."[43] In view of the key role which the state in Africa plays in most African countries, including Nigeria, it would not be possible to sideline political leadership at all levels of the political space if any meaningful development progress is ever to be imagined. Unfortunately, poor leadership in Africa has repeatedly dashed the hopes of the masses. Most of the leaders in Nigeria identify with both the church and with other religious entities. Nigeria boasts of a large Christian population which is engaged on a daily basis at different levels in Nigerian society. Any developmental model that may be grasped by the leadership of the church with the intention of educating and urging the faithful to implement the development paradigm as a religious responsibility within the Nigerian environment may bring effective results that will be capable of transforming the political, economic, social and environmental state of the nation. Arguing for a robust and inclusive political authority capable of guaranteeing the involvement of all interest groups in the direct management of their development,[44] Deng draws inspiration from the advances brought about by the South African experience and as elucidated by Mamadou Dia. According to this view, "decentralization involving genuine empowerment of local or regional entities in an ethnically, culturally" and multireligious society without rubbishing national cohesion is worth emulating by both Nigeria and by other volatile African nations.[45]

Oladele Omosegbon, focusing on the importance of economic intelligence, has also remarked on the need for objectivity on the part of African intellectuals and advisers in their choice of economic paths for their countries. He points out the inherent difficulty in developing democratic institutions simultaneously with economic advancement and the success of both as a twin task. The ideal situation is one in which democratic norms and values benefit

---

43. Deng, 238.

44. Deng argues that South Africa and Uganda are good examples of emerging African states with an effective model of broad-based participation in development. The mass participation of both community and civil society in governance at various levels has enhanced the political authority of the state and given impetus to development. In recent times, Uganda's ruling party led by Museveni has not fared well in allowing for a robust political participation by opposing political views. This trend will have negative repercussions on the development agenda of that nation.

45. Deng, *Rethinking African Development*, 250.

from advances in material living.[46] Although Omosegbon supports the acceleration of Africa's development through diversification, he maintains that challenging issues such as corruption, civil strife and bad governance – recurrent factors in African nations like Nigeria, Kenya, Zimbabwe, Zambia, and many others – should also be taken into consideration. In addition, ecological issues should also be considered in the African model of development. In his opinion, African nations would do better by forming strong collaborations among themselves rather than following the current trend of collaboration with the powerful nations of the Northern Hemisphere. In suggesting culture and historical antecedents as guiding lights for African development, Omosegbon urges the engagement of resources including knowledge, skills, culture and values that Africans have accumulated over the years while at the same time discarding the negative Western and Ottoman influences that are hampering African development. To be sure, African institutions have adapted, and they continue to do so, but no culture is known in history to flourish without throwing away and disengaging from such negative challenges, and then resuming its normal march of history and mission. The American state did so politically and militarily, and so can Africa and must do so through functional institutions and an enduring legacy.

K. T. August, arguing from the perspective of the engagement of the church in African development discourse, has lent his voice to the important role of culture in authentic development in Africa. In his critique of Walt W. Rostow who aligns with the modernization theory of development, August argues that the agents of modernization development have neglected the cultures of the indigenous people in the developing countries, with dire consequences as a result. As a way out of the developmental logjam in the African milieu, any development approach must take into account the transformational development model which takes interculturality into consideration in its development fit. Interculturality as a development construct is theology-friendly as it makes room for theology "to influence development with its kingdom values and its biblical anthropological principles of acknowledgement of the other and dignity of all human beings."[47] Also, in view of its emphasis on hospitality and interdependency, theology is coercive of culture and this has a transformational

---

46. Omosegbon, "Role of Institutional Factors," 55.
47. August, *Equipping the Saints*, 60–61.

value in terms of benefit to humankind. It may be pertinent to note at this point that the long years of colonialism, neocolonialism and the ongoing negative impact of globalization have severely battered African cultures. However, with the current call to deconstruct African history in the interests of a possible discovery of both the strong and the weak aspects of its history in order to make way for progress, the process of interculturality should proceed with caution. It is also important that Nigerians and Africans, in general, first acknowledge what is good in their cultures before borrowing from other cultures so as to address their own deficiencies. In addition, Nigerian and African scholars should be wary of the level of Western influence on many cherished areas of African culture including language, marriage, extended family system and lifestyle. A. M. Kanduza has warned that "any diminution of language undermines a sense of identity, self-confidence and also shatters community. It is this sense of identity, this self-esteem that is fundamental to the development process."[48] In line with this sentiment, it is important to note that, in Japan, China and South-East Asia, the use of local languages coupled with a strong commitment to use local culture to domesticate all external knowledge was fundamental to economic development.

Swart's focus in his cultural input into the church's engagement as espoused in his work, *The Churches and the Development Debate: Perspectives on a Fourth-Generation Approach*, is in line with Robert Korten's fourth generation approach and Charles Elliot's radical pragmatic development debate. Encouraging the church's innovativeness in the development discussion and engagement, the fourth-generation approach is steeped in the process of change which may be brought about by social movements. As a value and idea driven institution, Swart argues that the church falls naturally within the context of people's movements which hold the greatest promise for social transformation vis-a-vis the unjust economic and political control of the masses. As a result of its moral and spiritual content, the church has sufficient space and resources to engage positively as compared to its charity posture which has merely reinforced the structures of injustice. Furthermore, building on Manuel Castell's notion of "project identities," Swart advocates the notion of "soft culture."[49] In accordance with this line of thought and as

---

48. Kanduza, "Socio-cultural Change in Africa," 95.
49. Swart, *Churches and Development Debate*, 230–31.

a way of transforming society, the church should liaise with either people's movements or civil society to transform current society which is both aggressive and egoistic. Swart argues that these "male" values are deeply embedded in institutions and structures and also in general human behavior in society. Taking a stand against the suppression of local cultural traditions, he also challenges the oppressive elements of traditional culture such as hierarchy, patriarchy, autarchy, sexism and fundamentalism.[50]

There is no doubt that God's creation has been blessed with diverse blessings which God, in his wisdom, has bestowed on different continents, languages and races. Respect for and the celebration of God's endowment and a loving adjustment aimed at the humanization of society and responsible use of the created order is inevitable as the journey towards the general good progresses. This human and environmental consciousness is crucial as the quest for a development model for Nigeria and, indeed, for Africa, continues. In addition, it is essential that such a model should be all embracing and that it encompasses the African environment, African history, values, systems, and generations as well as the global society. The transformational development paradigm with its key elements of life sustenance, equity, justice, dignity, self-worth, freedom, participation, reciprocity, cultural fit, ecological soundness, hope, and spiritual transformation is crucial to the challenge of underdevelopment and poverty in both Nigeria and the rest of sub-Saharan Africa. However, it may require a development-oriented church leadership to imbue the faithful and other Nigerians with these ideals in ideology and lifestyle, from the ecclesial community to the Nigerian public arena. Religion pervades the sociopolitical and economic landscape of Nigeria although, unfortunately, the high level of corruption and poor leadership in the country do not show the huge Christian population in a good light. It is my contention that, if the church leaders in Nigeria cultivate the right development consciousness and ensure that their church members are imbued with this consciousness in the context of their daily lives and engagements, underdevelopment and all that it involves will become a thing of the past. However, for any model of development to be effective in any African society, it is essential that the development agent or catalyst be aware of the challenges involved.

---

50. Swart, 230–31.

2.5 The Challenges of Nigerian and African Development

The challenges facing development in Nigeria and sub-Saharan Africa are not only numerous, but they are also "mostly driven by pressures in the domestic and international environment."[51] It is possible to trace these challenges by investigating some of the natural resources to be found in the sub-Saharan African countries, including Nigeria, and the antecedents that have dogged African nations from their early contacts with the Western world to present times. The challenges of Nigerian and African development will be discussed under the following themes: Natural endowments, historical antecedents, internal policies, institutions and governance, imperialism, lack of regional integration, international economic order, environmental challenges and bad leadership.

2.5.1 Natural Endowments

Nature has endowed Nigeria and other African nations with significant resources that could play a vital role in their development. However, there are other factors that may constitute possible hindrances to development. Unlike in the developed nations, natural resources such as geography, climate, demography[52] and ethnicity are not playing a favourable role in the developmental efforts of Nigeria and its sister nations.[53] From a geographical perspective, African coastlines are straight with few bays, inlets and natural ports. In addition, a number of African countries are landlocked and accessing the hinterlands for economic purposes by means of mainly "unnavigable" small rivers, poses huge challenges. The climate in Nigeria, as in many parts of sub-Saharan Africa, including Cameroon, Ghana, and Togo etc. is notorious for facilitating the spread of diseases such as malaria with all the attendant economic burdens.[54] In addition, the climate also poses huge agricultural challenges that make the cultivation of certain important economic crops difficult and, in some instances, impossible. These climatic challenges include common rainfall patterns such as heavy rains and long, dry seasons.

---

51. Ake, "Socio-political Approaches," 17.
52. Sachs, *End of Poverty*, 56, 66.
53. Osaghae, "Ethnicity in Africa," 147.
54. Sachs, *End of Poverty*, 196–97.

The huge desert area in northern Nigeria, semi-arid land and drought also poses further challenges.

African countries are facing a population crisis as a number of them are experiencing low population density as a result of low life expectancy indices. Poverty, the HIV and AIDS pandemic, poor medical facilities and war are decimating the work forces and this is impacting negatively on the economy of the continent.[55] Nigeria has as many as 250 ethnic groups and languages. However, despite the fact that this diversity could promote economic activities, in most instances in Nigeria, as in many African countries, this is not the case. As noted by Todd J. Moss, "multiple linguistic and cultural groups can make organization more difficult and can fragment markets, preventing economies of scale."[56]

2.5.2 Historical Antecedents

In tracing the antecedents operating in the history of African nations, including Nigeria, one uncovers depressing trends that are still playing a role in undermining development in Nigeria and, indeed, in Africa as a whole. Such historical signposts include trade, slavery and colonialism. Each of these historical developments played unique roles, the negative repercussions of which are still palpable in modern society and may be impossible to obliterate in the near future.

Okonta and Dauglas remind us that, long before the advent of colonial rule in Nigeria, the people in the Niger Delta had trading relations with European traders. The stock in trade was palm oil and palm kernel. In exchange for this palm oil and kernel, the Nigerian traders were offered spirits, clothing materials and gunpowder. However, not only were the tokens of exchange they were offered of inferior value, as compared to the items of trade offered by the African traders, the Europeans largely exploited the indigenous people and, in fact, there were times when the stock in trade was collected forcefully.[57] The current exploitation of crude oil in the Niger Delta by Royal Shell may be seen as a continuation of the exploitation which was carried out by the Royal Niger Company. Whereas the Royal Niger Company exploited the

---

55. Sachs, 200.
56. Moss, *African Development*, 93, 96.
57. Okonta and Douglas, *Where Vultures Feast*, 1, 50.

people in terms of the trade in palm oil, Royal Shell is exploiting the people in terms of crude oil, with all the attendant environmental challenges. There is no doubt that the economic losses suffered by successive generations of Nigerians contributed to economic gains on the part of successive generations of the Western world. Despite the fact that the European traders may have been more astute than their African counterparts, the fact remains that many of their transactions were unethical and dubious. This moral burden on the offending party is exacerbated when it is remembered that the "black man" was largely helpless, especially whenever the "white man" engaged his firepower and it was often a matter of the strong and powerful grabbing all, while the weak and powerless went empty-handed.

It may be argued that, before the Arab and trans-Atlantic slave trade, there did exist a form of slavery among indigenous African communities carried out by fellow Africans and this had impacted negatively on African societies. However, such a statement ignores the scale of the Arab and trans-Atlantic slave trade and the monumental damage they caused in African societies. The Arab slave trade was more enduring than the trans-Atlantic slave trade but on a smaller scale in terms of the human trafficking although its impact was, nevertheless, brutalising. Besides its demoralising effect on human relations, the Arab slave trade led to the disintegration of the social structures in African societies, including those in Nigeria. On the other hand, the trans-Atlantic slave trade endured for approximately four centuries and led to a monumental drain of the vital human resource in African societies. Himmelstrand has painted a vivid but disturbing picture of the monumental devastation wrought by the slave trade: The main long-term effects on African societies of the nearly four centuries of trans-Atlantic slave trade, and the less voluminous but more enduring Arab slave trade across the Indian Ocean were a brutalization and demoralization of human relations, and the implicit breakdown of fair transaction rules, and ensuing social disintegration.[58] The coastal communities including Nigeria were the most affected.

The African rulers and kings may have collaborated with the European and Arab slave traders but this does not rule out the terrible effects of the many years of trading in human cargo. It is worth noting that, while the slave merchants took Africans to work on their farms and in their industries in

---

58. Himmelstrand, "Perspectives, Controversies & Dilemmas," 22.

the interest of developing their economies, the African slave traders were rewarded with guns, gunpowder and rum. This, in turn, created a vicious cycle with the slave traders tending to go out with their guns to hunt for more slaves while under the influence of alcohol. In other words, Africans were armed with drinks and firepower by Europeans to encourage them to sell their brothers and sisters and, thus, to foster the development of the European economy with the concomitant better standards of living, while the Africans were impoverished on a daily basis and left worse off than they ever had been before. The obvious questions that come to mind at this point in our discussion are: Are the descendants of the "merchants" of the Northern Hemisphere not continuing the legacy of their forebears? Are Nigerian/African leaders not presently collaborating with the "merchants" of the developed world to sell the treasures of Nigeria/Africa to them for a pittance and arms? The reasons for the seeming incurable underdevelopment and poverty ravaging Nigerian society in particular, and Africa in general, may not be far removed from the enduring legacies of the Western merchants and their African collaborators. One wonders for how long Nigerian and other African leaders will continue to trade their oil, diamonds, gold, agricultural produce and their best brains in return for some ridiculous rewards, political power and arms.

The legacies of colonialism, including the alleged civilization of Nigeria and the lack of significant improvement in the socioeconomic and political structures have been widely seen as unfortunate colonial hangovers hampering development in Nigeria. Other negative consequences of colonialism include unequal and often exploitative international trade exchanges and the arbitrary dividing and merging of multiethnic groups.[59] Ohwofasa has remarked that the British rule of Nigeria (1900–1960) was purely for the self-interest of Britain. It was a rule that was marked by the exploitation of the country's natural resources with this exploitation laying the terrible foundation for the continued contention for state authority between northern and southern Nigeria.[60] Based on the British policy of divide and rule, these two halves of the country continue to perceive themselves as different entities. Many federal policies are often reached by compromise. However, the ongoing federal character policy which ensures the distribution of employment

---

59. Himmelstrand, 23–24.
60. Ohwofasa, *Democracy and Issues*, 25, 66.

opportunities by quota to the various ethnic groups and regions and the unwritten power sharing policy of the former ruling Peoples' Democratic Party (PDP) and current ruling party, All Progressives Congress (APC), have arisen from the British colonial system. This policy has, in turn, played a significant role in hindering the sociopolitical and economic development of Nigerian society. It has also not only institutionalized mediocrity in place of excellence, but it has provided the foundation for the perpetuation of corruption and bad leadership. Accordingly, an understanding of this legacy is pivotal to the worrisome developments that have come to the fore in Nigerian national life. Not only are Nigerians suspicious of leaders who come from the opposite divide of where they themselves come from, but they are quick either to condemn or to support policies, even when such policies are unhelpful. Nigerians evaluate a leader on the basis of where that leader comes from, instead of on the merit or demerit of the leader's policies. It is not possible for any nation to progress from underdevelopment to development under such circumstances. Leadership thrives on trust and trust is built over time. From colonial times during which leadership was imposed by the "white man" to the democratic era during which there has been massive electoral fraud, the Nigerian masses have not exercized their rights to choose creditable leaders for themselves.

The political culture that had underpinned colonial leadership came to the fore in Nigeria soon after independence in the form of the political turmoil and the authoritarian governments which are still enduring to the present day. Imposed leaders, who have been selected by some powerful individuals instead of credible electoral processes on their part, have also not proved themselves to be worthy of trust because of their corrupt and bad leadership practices. As a result, poverty and underdevelopment are commonplace in Nigeria. For the masses to trust leadership, it is essential that Nigerian leaders change the way in which they are leading the people. Leaders should seek to satisfy the needs of the ordinary people by providing job opportunities, basic social amenities and a robust social interaction platform by which the people's voices may be heard and respected.

Also, as a result of the colonial "bootprints" that are dogging African development in general, and development in Nigeria in particular, is the huge challenge of the nondevelopment of an "entrepreneurial or merchant national bourgeoisie"[61] at the time of independence. As a result of the fact that the political, economic and administrative leaders had not been developed during the colonial era, this has automatically led to the poor performance of the political and administrative structures that were inherited from the colonial masters. Leadership skills take time to be nurtured and developed and, because this had not happened prior to independence, inevitably, it could not be done after independence. Nevertheless, despite the negative impact of colonialism on Nigerian development, after fifty years of independence, Nigerian leaders and citizens ought to have developed the necessary statecraft needed to develop their country. In addition, although Nigerian development has been impeded by factors such as unfavourable natural endowments and certain historical antecedents, certain internal policies have also contributed to the challenge of underdevelopment.

2.5.3 Poor Internal Policies

There are certain bad internal policies that were initiated by the state and which have fostered underdevelopment in both Nigeria and a number of other sub-Saharan African countries. These policies have resulted in state-created problems which have arisen from the state becoming "overly involved in the economy, including failed central planning and public ownership of industry."[62] In Nigeria, the Udoji Salary Award of the mid-seventies is one example of these bad internal policies. The nation had a financial windfall as a result of the sudden high rise in the world oil prices. However, instead of the Gowon administration ploughing this windfall income into the development of infrastructure, much of the accrued income was used to increase workers' wages. "This brought about much inflation and economic instability that made Nigerians uneasy."[63] Another example of these policies is the "villagization" scheme of Nyerere's Tanzania which led to the forced relocation of citizens, sometimes at gunpoint, from their preferred places of abode to the villages, which had been developed by the government for the purpose of ensuring development. The government may, ultimately, have had the best intentions for the masses, but, in its abuse of power and violation of the rights of

---

61. Himmelstrand, "Perspectives, Controversies & Dilemmas," 23.
62. Moss, *African Development*, 94.
63. Ohwofasa, *Democracy and Issues*, 74.

the citizens, the scheme ran counter to the vision of development.[64] Nigerian leaders are also in the habit of using their offices to reward their political allies and loyalists with jobs and contracts which are then inefficiently executed. This, in turn, leads to a bloated civil service and recalcitrant attitudes on the part of government officials with the concomitant economic consequences. Nevertheless, internal policies are a reflection of governments and are realized through the institutions of government. How have the Nigerian institutions of government and the art of governance fared? Have they been helpful in the developmental process or not?

2.5.4 Institutions and Governance

Some measure of blame for the poor performance of Nigerian and African development efforts has been attributed to the institutions of state and the way in which they operate. Onyekpe has observed that "since the era of decolonization and nationalist polities (i.e. the 1950s) the main issue has been how to share political power to accommodate the elites of the different regions in central power structure where the bulk of national resources have been concentrated and consolidated especially from 1969–70 onward."[65] Although Nigeria is regarded, in practice, as a federation this concept does not appear to be working. For example, the states and local governments have, through military decrees, lost their rights to control their natural and fiscal resources to the federal government. Instead of encouraging each state and local government to develop their resources, create employment opportunities and develop their jurisdictions, there is extremely minimal income generation within the state and local tiers of government. Every month, the local and state governments look up to Abuja for revenue allocation, without which these tiers of government could be incapacitated. There is, thus, an overconcentration of power and control at the centre and this, in turn, is bringing about the weakening and dysfunctionality of those tiers of government that are closer to the people. Commenting on the practice of federalism in Nigeria, Mbachu has argued that "Nigeria's experience of federalism is problematic if not enigmatic. The reason is that Nigeria is a federal republic run like a

---

64. Moss, *African Development*, 94.
65. Onyekpe, "Globalization and Less Developed," 138.

unitary system."⁶⁶ In a proper democratic system, institutions such as the executive, legislature and judiciary ought to be independent so as to enable them to carry out the roles of checks and balances required of them for optimum performance and the well-being of the nation. Unfortunately, in Nigeria, the executive arm of government tends to maintain a tight grip over both the judiciary and the legislature. The near total collapse of the Nigerian state in early 2010, which may be attributed to the ailing president, Umaru Musa Yaradua, aptly demonstrated the weakness and poor performance of the various arms of government. A closer look at the state of Nigerian public schools, hospitals and other infrastructure testifies to the acute dysfunctionality of Nigerian institutions. Ultimately, the political systems appear obviously to favour and focus on personal gain or short-term concerns at the expense of longer term, public concerns.⁶⁷ The political systems have, therefore, not contributed sufficiently to propel the much-needed development. In addition, imperialistic influences that are often driven through the government and its institutions have also tended to negatively impact development in Nigeria.

2.5.5 Imperialism

In their work, "The Relevance of the Theories of Imperialism to the Nigerian Development," Obiezu and Ugenyi observe that Europe's move into Africa in approximately 1870 in search of cheap labour, raw materials and markets for their surplus manufactured goods marked the beginning of imperialism in Africa. Although apologists of this move have purported that the move was well intended it did, in the main, hinder the development of African countries, including Nigeria, by destroying any precolonial, sociopolitical and economic development which would have helped the African nations to develop a solid political and economic foundation. The apologists have also claimed that "imperialism is a very old concept which has been going from stage to stage with a continuous manifestation of new tactics and dimensions in the international system."⁶⁸ The quest for the control of the political, economic, sociocultural, military and religious life of the underdeveloped nations such as Nigeria by the powerful Western countries for their own

---

66. Mbachu, "Anguish of Federalism," 159.
67. Moss, *African Development*.
68. Obiezu and Ugenyi, "Relevance of Theories," 220.

benefit represents what is meant in this context as imperialism. At the moment, a clear manifestation of imperialism on Nigerian soil is being perpetrated by the multinational or transnational corporations who have enormous control over the Nigerian oil industry. Through their sharp practices and powerful connections, these corporations ensure capital flight, environmental pollution and intercommunity conflicts. In this regard, Egeonu asserts that "transnational corporations have evidently proved to be agents of imperialism by their sociopolitical and economic domination, exploitation, extortion, repatriation and unmitigated profit maximization."[69] The world's financial institutions such as the World Bank and the International Monetary Fund may also be perceived as imperialist institutions that represent the interests of the developed countries through their policies.[70] Based on the comments of Sam Aluko, a renowned professor, economist and one time chair of the National Economic Intelligence Committee (NEIC), in respect of the IMF's unfair economic policies, Obiezu and Ugenyi state that "it was wrong to go to IMF, if I were the Minister of Finance, I wouldn't."[71] Unarguably, a number of the policies that have been introduced by these institutions have done more harm than good to the development efforts in Nigeria and it was the pursuit of these unhelpful policies on the part of Nigerian financial personnel that led to the comment from the veteran economist Aluko. However, if there is justifiable criticism of Nigeria's collaboration with international institutions, to what extent has its collaboration with other African countries helped the country's developmental efforts?

2.5.6 Lack of Regional Integration

The challenge inherent in both regional and subregional integration in Africa is enormous. However, although this is not peculiar to Africa, as compared to both Europe and other continents, the challenge in Africa is exacerbated by the indiscriminate fragmentation, the lumping together of peoples from different backgrounds and the numerous language groups. African challenge in this regard is a product of the scramble and partitioning of Africa by Europe

---

69. Egeonu, "Transnational Corporations," 156–57.
70. Sachs, *End of Poverty*, 74.
71. Obiezu and Ugenyi, "Relevance of Theories," 232.

at the Berlin Conference of 1884. "Many states . . . mean many governments"[72] and, of course, segregated interests which make working together difficult. Thomas Lines has argued that African regional collaboration is a key factor that holds the key to the socioeconomic transformation of African countries. However, the economic and agricultural disparities between the developed and underdeveloped regions of the world mean that African entrepreneurial and agricultural sectors will find it increasingly difficult to compete with their Western counterparts.[73] Lines's view is premised on the fact that in the Western world, farmers, for example, are granted considerable government subsidies which, in the case of African farmers, are almost nonexistent with the result that Western farmers are able to afford to lower their prices and still enjoy comfortable profit margins, while African farmers have to go for higher prices but with lower profit margins. This situation is exacerbated when African farmers experience poor crop yield or worse still, crop disease, which renders them financially unable to continue farming. Regional collaboration would afford African governments, entrepreneurs and farmers a level playing field in terms of which, through exchanges and fair competition, Africans would be able to develop their skills and financial capabilities. In addition, aside from the benefits of technological development and capital accumulation, African countries such as Nigeria would be delivered from the huge challenges of capital flight, exploitation, food shortages and unfair competition which are all challenges arising from the current global economic arrangement.

However, despite the rebranding of the Organization of African Unity (OAU)[74] as the African Union (AU),[75] African countries have not "walked

---

72. Moss, *African Development*, 190.

73. Lines, *Making Poverty a History*, 124.

74. The Organization of African Unity (OAU) (now African Union – AU) was founded in 1963, with its headquarters in Addis Ababa, Ethiopia. The OAU arose from the political ideologies of African leaders such as Kwame Nkruma and Julius Nyerere in the wake of the independence of many African nations. Although the OAU was not exactly in line with Nkruma's dream of a "United States of Africa," he and Nyerere proposed a regional institution for the promotion of a continent-wide political union. There is no doubt that these leaders envisioned an African continent that would be unified for the purpose of collaboration, development and other benefits.

75. The ineffectiveness of the OAU led to the African Union (AU) being launched in 2002 to replace the OAU. The AU continues to maintain the same headquarters, aims and main structures of the OAU.

the talk" of African collaboration.⁷⁶ Nevertheless, the AU is known for its lofty vision for the African continent – a vision which includes a central bank, single currency, common defense and communication policy, and a continental court. In addition, with the main purpose of creating a platform for regular meetings of the leaders of all African countries in order to discuss both their common challenges and strategies on how to solve these problems, the AU envisions a regional collaboration that would be meaningful to the development of Nigeria and other African countries. The New Partnership for Africa's Development (NEPAD), launched in 2001 by the AU secretariat in Johannesburg, South Africa, represents the main economic strategy structure of the AU. "NEPAD has been hailed as, perhaps, the boldest new initiative in recent times on the appropriate path which the African continent should be taking towards its long-term development."⁷⁷ NEPAD's major concerns include regional infrastructure, agriculture, market access, education, health and the environment.⁷⁸ Other subregional bodies that are also expected to foster African collaboration are the Economic Community of West African States (ECOWAS), the Southern African Development Community (SADC), the East African Community (EAC) and the African Franc Zones.

Despite the lofty ideals of the African regional bodies about the economic, political, technological and sociocultural development of African states, the realization of the vision of collaboration in terms of development has been slow and has not had the much-desired impact. According to Schoeman, there are a number of reasons for this dismal state of affairs including overreach, duplication and overlap, a lack of political will on the part of the African leaders to implement policies, relationships between subregional economic communities, lack of resources and a nonuniform political culture.⁷⁹ It should

---

76. Moss, *African Development*, 191.
77. Olukoshi, *Governing African Developmental Process*, 5.
78. Moss, *African Development*, 193.
79. Schoeman, *African Union after Durban*, 1, 18. Schoeman argues that if, for example, one takes into account the fact that the AU will consist of eighteen organs, the immense task involved in fleshing out each of these becomes apparent especially when we bear in mind the fact that building structures and institutions requires human and material resources as well as political will.

A number of the responsibilities and institutions of the AU are replicated in the subregional bodies and even in certain organs of the AU such as NEPAD. If, for example, one looks at the issues of peace and security, the AU has a Peace and Security Council while NEPAD also has a peace and security program. The time, energy and other resources usually spent on packaging

also be noted that, in addition to the issues raised by Schoeman, there is the underlying challenge of the selfish and inordinate ambitions of some African leaders. African collaboration at the subregional levels, for example, ECOWAS and SADC, may be yielding some results, but much is still desired of the AU and its institutions such as NEPAD. In my opinion, the coordination of the African continent – but not as a United States of Africa – under existing bodies such as the AU and its institutions and organs could be of immense benefit to the development of the continent. However, despite the poor performance of African regional bodies, what promise does the international economic order hold for the development of Nigeria and other African countries?

2.5.7 International Economic Order

In terms of the current international economic order which is strongly driven by both globalization and liberalization, Nigeria and other sub-Saharan African countries have, from the beginning of the 1990s, remained largely marginalized, especially in the context of financial globalization. The current disadvantaged position of African countries in modern international economy is traceable to their imperial inheritance.[80] The Nigerian economy which was both agricultural and mining based was also an export specialized economy – a "minute manufacturing base, a lack of access to technology," but with few trained personnel in modern business and social services. In the words of Walter Rodney, "the vast majority of Africans went into colonialism with a hoe and came out with a hoe."[81] Unfortunately, an economy that is based on the production of crude oil and other raw materials which are exported cheaply and imported as refined and processed products with high costs will, probably, always be in the red. As has been clearly pointed out by Onyekpe: To be sure, the liberalization of world trade and economic relations "has been the exclusive advantage of the industrialized states." The configuration of the world economy itself is such that "the world has been polarized into two groups, namely, the industrialized and developed countries of the Northern Hemisphere (Europe, North America and Japan)

---

each of these structures are such that they definitely take a toll on the general performance of these bodies. It even becomes confusing as to the extent to which these issues are to be pursued and by which institution or organ.

80. Ndikumana and Verick, "Two-Way Linkages," 305, 329.
81. Thomson, *Introduction to African Politics*, 179.

and the primary producing and less developed countries of the Southern Hemisphere"[82] (Africa, Caribbean and Pacific countries). Liberalized trade between the powerful and weak partners has only widened and perpetuated, and cannot but continue to widen and perpetuate the gap between the two groups of states.

There is little doubt that, despite the supposed good intentions in the current global economic collaboration between the developed and underdeveloped countries such as Nigeria and the US for example, such collaboration is not in the best interests of Nigeria. In addition, besides the repeated failures of the economic policies (e.g. SAPs) of these bodies which constitute the international economic order such as IMF and World Bank, and the dire consequences of these failures, there still remains the huge challenge of issues such as, "who sets the agenda"? Are Nigeria and the other less developed countries able to overcome the technical and legal constraints of collaborating with these bodies? Regulated markets that may bring about economic justice to all of humankind and sincere collaboration without segregation could make the world a better place for the benefit of all human beings and the created order.

2.5.8 Environmental Challenges

Extensive economic and technological activities have greatly enhanced global standards of living, especially in the developed world. Environmental challenges have also arisen in such a magnitude that the very existence of planet earth is threatened. "Global climate change, acid rain, depletion of the ozone layer, rapid rates of deforestation, and significant increases in the rate of species loss suggests that the costs of global development are rising rapidly."[83]

---

82. Onyekpe, "Globalization and Less Developed," 337. Globalization may be defined as the process of making any thing, issue, idea, practice, development, etc. global, worldwide or universal. But from the international political economy point of view, it is the tendency or process towards achieving rapid integration of the world economies through the deliberate formulation and execution of policies and programs focused on the defined goals of integration and through the corresponding construction of the relevant theories and ideologies to defend, uphold and promote the integration process.

Liberalization refers to the processes of achieving unobstructed economic activities. It seeks to remove all obstacles to trade, investment and production. It emphasizes freedom of economic activities and the dominance of private enterprise and initiative. It further aims to divorce the state from interference in and control of the economy.

83. Weaver, Rock, and Kusterer, *Achieving Broad-based Sustainable Development*, 237.

Nigeria and other parts of sub-Saharan Africa are currently experiencing the severe repercussions of environmental degradation arising from the extensive oil exploitation carried out by multinational companies. The Niger Delta is not only restive, vast farm lands can no longer be cultivated and aquatic life is wasting away because of oil spillages. The American economist Jeffrey Sachs has warned that "the continuing environmental degradation at local, regional and planetary scales threatens the long-term sustainability of all our social gains."[84] There is a danger that generations of Nigerians living in the Niger Delta area will be denied their sources of livelihood if the situation is not checked. There are also the deplorable health issues arising from the gas flaring, water pollution and food poisoning caused by the ongoing environmental pollution. The poor living condition of many Nigerians is also inevitably impacting on the environment negatively. For example, if one takes the issue of deforestation and species loss. The supply of electricity in Nigeria is extremely poor and, in fact, most rural communities are not supplied with electric power and neither are they able to afford cooking gas. Accordingly, they have no other option but to cut down trees for fuel. In addition, the prevailing poverty means that communities allow the cutting down of timber for exportation at ridiculous sums of money. Hunters are forced to hunt for game in order to be able to feed and care for their families. Unfortunately, this game often includes species of animals that are facing extinction. However, in a typical rural environment in Nigeria, issues about animal rights, game reserves, forest reserves and endangered species not only sound ridiculous, they are almost nonexistent. Desert encroachment, floods, poor crop yield and food shortages which were not issues in the past have suddenly become burning issues in the local communities in Nigeria. Klaus Nurnberger has well observed that "scarcity of food is a case of over-exploitation of renewable resources."[85] While the population continues to grow, the capacity to produce food declines. This is partly due to pollution and erosion and partly to the law of declining marginal productivity.

Environmental issues are, thus, posing a monumental challenge to the developmental efforts in Nigeria, especially in the field of agriculture which accounts for the highest employment of rural dwellers. In order to guarantee

---

84. Sachs, *End of Poverty*, 367.
85. Nurnberger, *Prosperity, Poverty and Pollution*, 73.

the just and equitable co-existence of all life species on earth, both now and in the future, it is inevitable that relevant ethical considerations will include issues regarding ecological justice, economic justice and sustainable development. In all, human beings should take responsible leadership as stewards of God's creation.

2.5.9 Poor Leadership

So far, we have discussed some of the challenges that are inhibiting the development of Nigeria and, to some extent, sub-Saharan Africa. As has been previously mentioned, the challenges may vary in degree from one African country to another but they are common in all. The issues already discussed include natural endowments, historical antecedents, internal policies, institutions and governance, imperialism, a lack of regional integration, the international economic order and environmental challenges. It is essential that the important role played by each of these contributory factors to the problematic poverty and underdevelopment in Nigeria should not be underestimated, but might it be that what lies at the heart of all these issues is the failure to provide responsible leadership when such leadership is required?

Chinua Achebe summarized his "clinical diagnostic report" on the seeming incurable ailments (poverty, underdevelopment, corruption, etc.) plaguing Nigeria in his work, *The Trouble with Nigeria*, in which he asserts that "the trouble with Nigeria is simply and squarely a failure of leadership."[86] In line with Achebe's view on the problem of leadership in Nigeria, Seteolu has also argued that "the Nigerian state is governed by a predatory political class, hence personal rulership, political corruption and underdevelopment."[87] In the same vein, Mbachu asserts that the malaise of poor leadership is not a new development in Nigeria but a challenge that has continued to live on, unconquered and disheartening. "Since independence in 1960, Nigeria has ceaselessly struggled to have an authentic leadership but to no avail". Instead, "she has always had the misfortune of falling into the hands of rapacious power megalomaniacs who, owing to sheer incompetence and selfishness, are incapable of satisfying the yearnings and aspirations of her people."[88]

---

86. Achebe, *Trouble with Nigeria*, 1.
87. Seteolu, "Challenge of Leadership," 74.
88. Mbachu, "Leadership and Accountability," 57.

Unfortunately, because leadership has much to do with influence, the prevailing type of leadership tends to be replicated in its followers. In support of this statement, Achebe has also noted that "Nigerians are what they are only because their leaders are not what they should be."[89] Mbachu agrees when he states that "whatever forms of behavior the leaders engage in, tend to reflect on the behavior of the followers." This may seem like an overexaggerated comment on leadership but it is difficult to contest. Again, Mbachu further substantiates his position by echoing Vilfredo Pareto and Gaetano Mosca who claim that every society, whether authoritarian, dictatorial or democratic, certainly needs a crop of committed leaders. The centrality of leadership in any society is long established by political theory. "Society is divided into a few who have power (leaders) and the many who do not (followers)."[90] Only a "small number of persons allocate values for society," and that small number is the leaders.

It is, thus, not an overstatement to argue that leadership is a core issue in Nigerian development. Indeed, it may even be said to be the rallying point at which all the resources within Nigerian society may be harnessed for the realization of the envisioned reduction of poverty and underdevelopment which are so deeply entrenched in Nigerian society. The failure of Nigerian leadership over time has manifested in many areas such as corruption, unaccountability, dishonesty, immorality, injustices and other forms of unethical and irresponsible conduct. According to Mbachu, "Nigerian leaders ignore and undermine the principles of accountability with reckless abandon." In government, "accountability touches on the morality, integrity, honesty, ethics, and behavior of all officers in the areas of finance, money, material and management of men."[91] A survey of the Nigerian political, social, economic and religious landscape may show that the virtue of accountability is no longer upheld in many areas of Nigerian society and this may, in turn, be detracting from the efforts of some Nigerians who may be trying to bring the nation back on track. In addition, the paucity of good leadership may be assumed to be giving rise to a paucity of good followership as, where there is bad leadership, it is unlikely that there will be good followership. Followers

---

89. Achebe, *Trouble with Nigeria*, 10.
90. Mbachu, "Leadership and Accountability," 58–59.
91. Mbachu, 64.

mirror the leaders, just as leaders mirror the followers with both belonging to the same mould.

As a solution to the sorry state of Nigerian leadership, Seteolu has conducted an extremely crucial analysis and issued an invitation which are both crucial to this study. He argues that "there is a leadership crisis which constitutes a core problem. However, the analysis should include the followership link."[92] The genuine leadership will need an honest, courageous and credible followership, which is less vulnerable to the manipulative politics of the ruling elite. It should possess knowledge, sound judgment and be committed to specific causes and ideas. The civil society groups, community-based organizations may likely constitute blocs to evolve leadership that approximates the features of the charismatic, visionary, transformational types.

In his fourth-generation development debate in which he emphasizes the importance of peoples' movements as a crucial instrument for social change, David Korten suggests that the church belongs to this group (civil society).[93] It is the core argument of this study that church leaders have a responsibility to rise to the challenge of the scarcity of credible leadership in Nigeria. The challenges of development in Nigeria persist and require solutions so as to pave the way for such development and, thus, an understanding of the developmental trends in the postmilitary Nigerian context is essential.

2.6 Assessing Developmental Trends in Postmilitary Nigeria

In an effort to understand the present Nigerian context, it is vital to gain some insight into the developmental trends which have characterized the Nigerian landscape from 1999 to the present time. As has been noted in this study, this is the period that has witnessed consistent civil rule without the incursion of the military. The obvious question is whether the high expectations of the Nigerian people regarding the delivery of the benefits of democracy, including job creation, education, healthcare, the provision of basic infrastructure and improved standards of living from their democratically elected leaders

---

92. Seteolu, "Challenge of Leadership," 75.
93. Swart, *Churches and Development Debate*, 132.

have been met? Development trends will, therefore, be discussed from the economic, political governance and civil society perspectives.

2.6.1 Economic Development

The Nigerian economy is basically neocolonial capitalist, dependent and largely dominated by primary or extractive production. It may be regarded as neocolonial capitalist because the major investors in the Nigerian economy include transnational corporations (TNCs) such as Shell, Chevron, Coca Cola, May and Baker, Unilever etc. The challenge inherent in an economy that is neocolonial capitalist is that such an economy is in the hands of powerful foreign companies and their agents and the usual practice is that those resources that are generated in the process of production are usually taken away by these foreign owners to their home countries for the benefit of reinvestment and development. The Nigerian economy is dependent in the sense that "the level of production is dictated and conditioned by the dynamics and behavior of the metropolitan economies structured and organized: to feed with its primary products and, to serve as a market for industrial manufactures."[94] The above implies that the Nigerian economy is automatically at the mercy of the economies of those metropolitan centres on which it is dependent.

Within the time period which is the focus of this study, the Nigerian government, under the leadership of President Olusegun Obasanjo (1999–2007), made certain developmental efforts to revamp the Nigerian economy. Among the major programmes worth mentioning is the National Economic Empowerment and Development Strategy (NEEDS). According to Nwokoma and Nwokoma, "NEEDS is a 'home-grown' poverty reduction medium term strategy (2003–2007) which derives from the country's long-term goals of poverty reduction, wealth creation, employment generation and value reorientation."[95] It rests on four key strategies: reforming the way government works and its institutions; growing the private sector; implementing a social charter for the people; and reorientation of the people with an enduring African value system.

Despite the fact that the strategy is "lacking a proper articulation of sectoral linkages as well as not regarding the resource envelope required to

---

94. Onyekpe, "Issues in Development: Nigeria," 135.
95. Nwokoma and Nwokoma, "Appraising Employment," 102.

determine the capability of the country"[96] and which necessitated the reinvention of NEEDS II, NEEDS was, in fact, a bold step in the right direction. However, the acknowledgement of the presence of weak institutions, poor infrastructure and capacity constraints in the management of the economy of Nigeria, as enunciated in the policy documents of NEEDS from its inception, was an indication of the fact that the programme would, in all probability not achieve much. Based on the policy of NEEDS, the telecommunication system in Nigeria was given a boost through the Global System of Mobile (GSM) communication. Nevertheless, although this created some employment opportunities, it has also led to the exploitation of the masses with huge profits being made by the mobile telecommunication companies in exchange for poor services.

Onyekpe has noted that the agricultural, physical infrastructural and petroleum sectors of the Nigerian economy have suffered significant neglect. Agriculture was the major foreign earner and mainstay of the Nigerian economy before the discovery of oil in Oloibiri in the Delta region. "Today, not a little proportion of foreign exchange earnings from crude oil exports is spent on the settlement of food import bills. The nation is unable to feed itself and all sorts of food items are imported."[97] A further negative outcome of the neglect of agriculture is the high rate of unemployment and rural-urban migration. In addition, as a result of poor planning and implementation, the nation's physical infrastructure such as roads, airports, railway system, electricity and seaports etc. are in a deplorable state. Also, apart from the problem of safety, the poor condition of this vital infrastructure impedes economic activities by increasing both the cost of production and the level of the losses sustained. The situation is further exacerbated by the fact that the poor state of infrastructure has impacted negatively on the manufacturing sector and this sector is now almost nonexistent. In recent years, some companies have been forced to relocate to Ghana where the cost of production is lower as a result of a stable supply of electricity. However, the petroleum sector, which is now the mainstay of the country's export earnings and government income, is not faring any better. Crude oil is exported and refined products are imported at a higher price than the price of exportation. Local refineries are either in

---

96. Nwokoma and Nwokoma, 102.
97. Onyekpe, "Issues in Development: Nigeria," 137.

a total state of collapse or are producing below the required capacity. For a country that is the sixth largest world exporter of crude oil to still be importing refined oil is not economically logical.

The score card, when assessing NEEDS, which represents the most strategic economic development programme in Nigeria from 1999 to date is not encouraging. Commenting on NEEDS and the policies that came into existence in the wake of its implementation, Nwokoma and Nwokoma conclude that "most of the set-out objectives of these reforms, such as enhanced efficiency, service delivery and professionalism, are hardly achieved."[98] The immediate outcome of the reforms in most of the sectors is retrenchments or right-sizing of the workforce. As such for the past few years of the implementation of NEEDS, it has succeeded in creating more unemployment than the number it set out to reduce. The total dilapidation of basic infrastructure and policy inconsistencies has worsened the employment situation in the labour-abundant Nigerian economy.

2.6.2 Political Governance

Governance occupies a central position in the Nigerian development discourse, both in the national and the international arenas. "The concept of governance refers to the use of political power to manage a nation's public affairs and to shape its economic and social environment in line with perceived notions of public interest and societal progress."[99] Based on Nkom's definition of governance, good governance could, therefore, imply the use of political power by political governors or leaders to manage the affairs of a nation and to shape the economic and social environment in the interests and for the progress of the entire nation. Otobo has remarked on the important role of governance in the development agendas of both Nigeria and Africa as a whole. According to Otobo, three facts underscore the importance of political governance. First, poor governance of states has been identified as a key hindrance to economic reform and growth. Second, with the persistent failure of development policies in Nigeria and sub-Saharan Africa, economists and development practitioners are viewing ineffective governance as contributing to such failures. Third, "political governance defines the context

---

98. Nwokoma and Nwokoma, "Appraising Employment," 111.
99. Nkom, "Culture, Empowerment," 75.

in which economic governance and corporate governance – the other two main dimension[s] of governance – are practised."[100] Without diminishing the importance of economic and corporate governance, the concern of this study at this point is political governance, which is the source of the rules and organizational structures for economic and corporate governance. Having noted the extent to which political governance is pivotal to development, the study will now proceed to discuss briefly the evolution of political governance in Nigeria from 1999 to 2010. The study will also explore the contributions of this sector to both the development and underdevelopment of Nigeria within the parameters of the study.

The political governance of Nigeria that commenced on 29 May 1999 under the leadership of President Matthew Aremu Olusegun Obasanjo marked the beginning of a new era in the political history of Nigeria. This new era is termed the postmilitary or democratic era. Apart from the democratic process that resulted in the election of Obasanjo,[101] this period was preceded by certain dramatic events that signalled the ending of one era and the beginning of another era. It is the view of the researcher that this drama had begun to unfold when a military dictator in the person of General Ibrahim Badamosi Babangida[102] metamorphosed into a military president. As a result of his inability to stay in power because of pressure from both the press and some Nigerian political activists, he presided over the election of 12 June 1993 which witnessed the emergence of M. K. O. Abiola as the president-elect in "an election that has been acclaimed as the freest and fairest election in Nigerian history."[103] However, this election was annulled by Babangida on 23 June 1993. Nevertheless, succumbing to mass civil protests, Babangida set up an Interim National Government (ING) under the leadership of Earnest Shonekan, a fellow tribesman of Egba origin like Abiola and Obasanjo, on 27

---

100. Otobo, "Contemporary External Influences," 101.

101. Obasanjo was a former military ruler who was incarcerated by the military junta of Sani Abacha. He came out of prison and was elected as president of the Federal Republic of Nigeria in 1999.

102. Babangida was a self-styled "evil genius." The people named him "Maradona", after the Argentian footballing genius Diego Armando Maradona – as Maradona could outwit any defence, so Babangida could get past any political opponents. In Babangida's case this was done through consultations whose outcome was determined by Babangida's skill in bribery and corruption.

103. Ohwofasa, *Democracy and Issues*, 19.

August 1993 and stepped aside. Within a short period of Shonekan's interim government, which was initially planned to last till February 1994, "General Sani Abacha, another military junta who was the then defence minister, forced Shonekan to resign"[104] and he became the head of state on 17 November 1993. The situation was not ever going to be the same again. The people's mandate had been stolen by the Babangida government and an interim government, which was considered illegal, had been set up, although with an extremely short lifespan. Another military dictator had come into power with the usual accompaniment of martial music and promises which successive military dictators had never fulfilled. At this time, a number of political activists had gone on exile but they were not silent while the press was, despite repression, also vocal. However, more drama was unfolding. On coming to power, Abacha disbanded all the democratic institutions and replaced elected governors with military administrators. Despite the fact that he had promised to restore the civilian governors – a promise which he failed to fulfil – he refused to announce the transition timetable and held on to power until 1995.

Abacha's rule was accompanied by sanctions from the US because of the annulled election and because of its failure to secure certification for its counter-narcotics efforts. The initial euphoria that had greeted his ascendance to power was quickly replaced with public disenchantment as a result of the ever-increasing abuse of power and repression. The activities of the National Democratic Coalition (NADECO) for the restoration of democratic institutions led by Pa Abraham Adesanya were notable. In addition, Abacha's junta was further imperilled by strikes by labour unions, civil disturbances, the issuing of death sentences to top Nigerian leaders by military tribunals and human rights abuses. Abacha, who had endeavoured to remain in power, died suddenly while still scheming to metamorphose into a civilian president. His death, although mysterious, was greeted with massive public jubilation across the nation. At this point, General Abdulsalam Abubakar became the head of state. He released all military and political detainees, including those who had been handed the death penalty. Included in those released was Chief Olusegun Obasanjo who eventually became president in 1999. It was during Abubakar's rule that the timetable for a new election and the transition from military to civil rule had been drawn up, and the era which

---

104. Ohwofasa, 19.

is now called the postmilitary period was birthed. It should be noted that at this point in Nigerian history, the nation had become a pariah state because of the successive military regimes. Poverty, corruption, underdevelopment, bad leadership and infrastructural decay had become entrenched in all the political, economic and social structures of the life of the nation and this was coupled with huge national debt and a battered public image of Nigeria in the comity of nations. The situation was exacerbated by the fact that the Nigerian people had lost confidence in the leadership of the country, whether civil or military. With this background in mind, the study will discuss the era of civil rule or the postmilitary era.

The handing over of political rule from Abubakar, a military ruler, on 29 May 1999 to Obasanjo, a democratically elected president, marked the termination of both an uninterrupted fourteen years of military rule and a long history of military rule with "interregnums" of civil rule since independence from colonial rule. For the first time in Nigerian history, the country had a leader, Chief Olusegun Obasanjo, who ruled as a member of a political party, the Peoples' Democratic Party (PDP) after many years of military rule. He ruled for a period of eight years and then handed over the reins of power to another democratically elected president. However, the questions that arise are: what is special about this era in Nigerian history, and in what respect has this era made an impact, either positively or negatively, on the developmental trends in the country? There are divergent views in the assessment of the performance of the political governance under Chief Olusegun Obasanjo, both positive and negative. One of the most positive voices is that of Jonathan Power in his article entitled "Forward Nigeria." Power, a non-Nigerian syndicated columnist, the contributing editor of a London magazine and self-professed friend of Chief Obasanjo, has argued that "in the eight years of the administration of Olusegun Obasanjo, Nigeria paid off the country's huge debt, stabilised the currency, cut inflation down to single digits, expanded foreign reserves tenfold (they are now the seventh largest in the world), cracked down on money laundering, consolidated the now highly profitable banking sector, won its first sovereign credit rating, and established macroeconomic and fiscal policies that are both effective and enshrined in law by the landmark Fiscal Responsibility Act."[105] Economic growth and a

---

105. Power, "Forward Nigeria," 69.

huge investment in power stations, gas pipelines and electrical transmission are attributed to the success story of Obasanjo's presidency.

However, despite Power's positive rating of the political governance of Obasanjo's administration, the harsh realities on the ground in Nigeria are not as exciting as Power would have us believe. Arguably, the expansion of foreign reserves, the debt cancellation and the strides in telecommunications (GSM) represent some of the most positive initiatives of that administration. However, the way in which these successes have translated into the tangible public interest of ordinary Nigerians and their contribution to the progress of the Nigerian society is still in question and there are major deficiencies in some key areas which would have transformed the lives of many Nigerians for the better. These issues include electrical power generation/supply, the Niger Delta oil exploitation crisis, crackdowns on corruption, election rigging and the crisis in the banking industry. Above all, "the dismal state of the manufacturing sector, to which Power himself has admitted, the deplorable state of public schools, hospitals and roads and the huge unemployment indices are the most worrisome aspects that do not reflect well on those eight years of rule."[106] In the same vein, the perennial Niger Delta oil exploitation and pipeline crisis all of which occurred during Obasanjo's presidency cannot be ignored. In addition, "another frightening lingering problem is that of the sabotage of oil pipelines by vandals to eke out a living with high human, financial and material losses."[107] In Ohwofasa's view, these actions of Nigerians beyond the confines of the Niger Delta area are underpinned by poverty. He further warns that the lingering dilemma of unrest in the Niger Delta area over the environmental degradation prompted by oil prospecting and the unpardonable poverty of inhabitants of the oil-rich region, that is developing into a disturbing security challenge of the Gulf of Guinea demands a down-to-earth resolution. Unfortunately, this advice was not heeded by the Obasanjo administration and, instead, troops were drafted to the Niger Delta and entire communities, including Odi and Umuechem, were wiped out by military action.

Onyekpe has also observed flaws in the development endeavours of Obasanjo's government when he points out that one of the major hurdles in

---

106. Ohwofasa, *Democracy and Issues*, 23–24.
107. Ohwofasa, 23–24.

Nigeria's development is the prioritization of politics, in the sense of retaining power. Those in power deploy all available resources for the retention of power. "In the last two years of Chief Obasanjo's first term as president (1999–2003), the responsibility of administration and governance was sacrificed on the altar of the struggle and scheming to have a second term."[108] While the struggle and scheming lasted, the issue of development was relegated outright. Unfortunately, Obasanjo also indulged in the same scheming during the last few years of his second term in his bid for yet a third term of office – something which was generally opposed by Nigerians. Accordingly, Obasanjo handed over power to his alleged handpicked successor, Umaru Musa Yar'adua, who had come on board through an electoral process that was noted for its massive electoral flaws.

Umaru Musa Yar'adua assumed office as the president of the Federal Republic of Nigeria in May 2007. On the positive side, Yar'Adua instituted the Poverty Eradication Council (PEC) which comprised top functionaries of his cabinet such as the vice president, secretary of the federation, and some ministers, with Yar'Adua himself chairing the council. The main aim of this council was to eradicate poverty in Nigeria. It was taken a step further by the National Poverty Eradication Program (NAPEP) which was initiated by Obasanjo. By this act, the president demonstrated his commitment to deal with the greatest challenge facing Nigerians. He was also a fervent believer in due process and wide consultations. However, while this endeared him to many Nigerians and gained him wide acclaim, it was this style of leadership that earned him the name "Mr. Go Slow." Although he was perceived as allowing the other arms of government, such as the legislature and judiciary, to be independent – a move which is healthy for political leadership – analysts felt that this approach slowed down the decision-making process badly. This was unlike the style of his predecessor, Obasanjo, who was seen as a "corner cutter and the constitution"[109] as a result of his quick, authoritarian and sometimes unconstitutional style of leadership. Critics have attributed the poor performance of Yar'Adua's leadership to his slow pace which eventually impeded his attempts to better the lot of Nigerians. Critics also cite the nullification of some developmental efforts which had been initiated by his predecessor

---

108. Onyekpe, "Issues in Development: Nigeria," 139.
109. Power, "Forward Nigeria," 70.

and which Yar'Adua was expected to see to their fruition. Examples of the developmental efforts which he nullified include "the invitation of Mittal, the Indian-British conglomerate, to take over Nigeria's moribund steel mill, the railway which was to traverse from the south to the north of the country, the final auction of oil blocks concessions and the removal of Nuhu Ribadu, the chairperson of the Economic and Financial Crimes Commission (EFCC)."[110] In judging Yar'Adua's laudable notion of eradicating poverty and ensuring development, it is worth noting that the Poverty Eradication Council (PEC), headed by President Umaru Yar'Adua and Vice President Goodluck Jonathan as vice chairman and the Secretary of the Federation (SGF) as secretary and ministers of Agriculture, Water Resources, Works and Housing, Education, Industry, Power and Steel, Environment and Science and Technology as members did not do anything tangible as far as poverty eradication was concerned.

Meanwhile, Power has also claimed that Yar'Adua "unwittingly sabotaged his own political leadership, which he had envisioned as eradicating poverty in Nigeria, when he succumbed to the political pressure exerted by some corrupt Nigerians to remove the chairman of EFCC. EFCC had been tackling corruption in the country head-on."[111] Onyedika Agbedo has remarked that the failure of NAPEP and other poverty eradication programmes may be attributed to the fraudulent and corrupt practices of some of the leaders of the agencies and certain financial institutions.[112] However, President Yar'Adua's greatest challenge regarding his political governance of Nigeria was the health crisis which created a leadership vacuum and almost brought Nigeria to a standstill. The health crisis sparked protests and exposed the ineffectiveness of the political governance as regards the arms of the Nigerian government. Unfortunately, Yar'Adua then died and Vice President Goodluck Jonathan took over leadership amidst political tension and uncertainty.

The political leadership of President Goodluck Ebele Jonathan commenced in April 2010 and has barely lasted six months at the time that this study was conducted. Arguably, this period of time may be deemed too short for an objective assessment of performance. However, this period has been haracterized by unique challenges to the political governance of Nigeria.

---

110. Power, 69.
111. Power, 69.
112. Agbedo, "Senate Committee Indicts."

These challenges include the lack of political will on the part of Nigerian leaders to confront the challenges that arise in their governance with the aim of strengthening the arms of government so as to enable them to perform their constitutional duties for the development of the nation. A case in point was the failure of Yar'Adua's cabinet to declare the ailing president incompetent to handle the affairs of the state and also the failure of the National Assembly to initiate actions for the impeachment of the president who had failed to notify the National Assembly that he was departing on a trip for medical treatment. The issue of the president's health, which was shrouded in unnecessary mystery and his eventual secret return to Aso Rock (the presidential residence in Abuja) under the cover of darkness and a heavy military presence, was unfortunate and also disappointing as regards those that collaborated in the exercize without the knowledge of the acting president and commander-in-chief of the armed forces.

Jonathan's leadership will be discussed with reference to the Yar'Adua dispensation for two reasons. First, the two leaders came to power on the same ticket. Second, the policies which were enunciated at the beginning of Yar'Adua's administration in 2007 have, essentially, been continued under Jonathan's leadership. Suleiman Abubakar[113] has accorded an extremely poor rating to Jonathan's six months in office. In Abubakar's assessment, Jonathan's administration is void of policy direction and lacks the expected courage and experience to produce the results that will address the challenges facing the country. Abubakar bases his claims on issues such as the poor state of the social infrastructure, the unemployment rate, debt burden, and depletion of the excess crude oil account from 20 billion dollars to 500 million dollars, the 1 October 2010 bomb blast and the spate of criminal activities such as kidnapping. Such a claim may contain some kernel of truth but it remains undeniable that Jonathan has, in the main, continued with Yar'Adua's programmes. This course of action is understandable as it would have been unwise to do otherwise at the time he assumed office. Again, six months is too short a period to make an informed assessment of a leader in a complex society such as Nigeria, with the situation having been exacerbated by the way in which Yar'Adua's health saga had been handled. A realist will also understand that the political jostling for the 2011 general election in which

---

113. Abubakar, "Jonathan's 6-month Scorecard."

the serving president was an interested candidate would naturally engage his energy alongside the task of governance. However, the challenges of political governance which have undermined Nigerian development over the years continue, even in the postmilitary or democratic era which is now under the guidance of Jonathan.

Thus, from the 1999 political leadership of Chief Olusegun Obasanjo through Alhaji Umaru Yar'Adua to 2010 with Dr. Goodluck Jonathan in power in Nigeria, three leadership challenges have emerged which are not just peculiar to Jonathan's administration but common to the Nigerian sociopolitical environment. These challenges, which are inimical to political governance and, ultimately, to development include leadership fatalism, leadership instability and the absence of a leadership of virtue ethics. The latter was rated by Lanre-Abass as abysmal. According to Ukaegbu, leadership fatalism has to do with a situation in which leaders experience hopelessness and act in a helpless way when faced with challenges of critical national importance. He argues that, in the face of such challenges, Nigerian leaders have often displayed their fatalistic dispositions by their tendency to tow "the line of least difficulty and least challenge, seek and implement short-term and palliative solutions, and depend on, and outsource complex national problems to international outsiders without first exploring all domestic possibilities."[114] This attitude, which is engrained in the mindset, expression and behaviour of Nigerian leaders and, to some extent, Nigerian citizens is strongly reinforced by uninformed religiosity. For example, when Yar'Adua was presented for election in 2007 by the People's Democratic Party (PDP), the condition of his health was highly questionable. It was common knowledge that, in his eight years as the governor of Katsina state, he had made frequent visits to hospitals. Ignoring the reactions of some Nigerians, Obasanjo, the then incumbent, had inflicted Yar'Adua on Nigeria instead of recognising the reality of his ill health. Yar'Adua himself was said to have challenged whoever questioned the state of his health to a squash competition. It was not long after he became president that the dire condition of his health became obvious with death as the inevitable outcome. In the same instance, during his health crisis which led to his stay in Saudi Arabia for months, Nigerians were asked to pray for his recovery despite the leadership vacuum and the concomitant crisis that

---

114. Ukaegbu, "Leadership Fatalism," 161, 182.

ensued. The Federal Executive Council and the National Assembly experienced difficulties in addressing the obvious challenges which had placed the nation in such a precarious situation and exposed Nigeria to the ridicule of the international community. The intention here is not to make light of the challenge of ill health to which all humans are prone and the fact that health may be unpredictable. However, it is obvious that, in both instances of Yar'adua's election despite his poor state of health and his illness as president, those leaders who were in a position to take action failed in their duties and, instead, demonstrated their fatalistic tendencies. By so doing, they evaded their responsibilities and exposed the nation to unnecessary and avoidable setbacks.

On the issue of leadership instability, Odunsi suggests that factors such as "ideological incongruencies, unhealthy political competition, ethnic consciousness, corruption and mismanagement, intolerance and inflexibility on policy issues and the exclusion of the minority groups from national politics all contribute to political instability."[115] Several political analysts concur with Udensi when they point to economic imbalances and ineffective leadership as the major contributory factors to the political leadership crisis in Nigeria with the selection of an unhealthy presidential aspirant and the entire Yar'Adua ill health and eventual death crisis as an extremely good example of irresponsible leadership. In the same case (Yar'adua), the undercurrents of ethnicity, corruption, mismanagement, ideological incongruencies and the undermining of the minority groups in national politics are also present. It is these same factors that are responsible for two presidents within four years and the removal of state governors by election tribunals and the courts of law. How else is it possible to account for the absence of at least one strong opposition party in Nigeria? The issues listed above not only reflect underdeveloped political governance structures, but they also constitute barriers to the meaningful sociopolitical and economic transformation of Nigerian society.

Lanre-Abbas has pointed out how indispensable the moral and ethical rectitude of Nigerian and, indeed, sub-Saharan African leaders is to the development of their countries. Based on Aristotle, Slote and the Nigerian (Yoruba, Hausa and Igbo) cultural heritage, Lanre-Abbas emphasizes virtue ethics as "the role that diverse habits and dispositions play in moral decisions and

---

115. Odunsi, "Impact of Leadership Instability," 67, 81.

recognizes the value of both self-regarding and other-regarding virtues."[116] After repeating Aristotles's list of the good virtues that should be found in a leader, namely, courage, moderation, justice, generosity, greatness of soul, mildness of temper, truthfulness, social grace (sensitivity), proper judgment and practical wisdom, he argues that it is the absence of the requisite virtues in Nigerian leaders that has resulted in the monumental spate of corruption among both them and the Nigerian citizens. Lanre-Abbas's rebuke to religious and traditional leaders, who sometimes fail to set the example of moral and ethical rectitude, is understandable. He argues that his rebuke is based on their poor performance in terms of their obligation to set the moral standards of society and that this has also led to their failure to rectify the actions of the political leaders. This study agrees with Lanre-Abbas that both church leaders and church members have a responsibility to inculcate the right values and mindset among the faithful and society at large so as to foster the transformation of Nigerian society in the face of the challenges of poverty, underdevelopment, irresponsible leadership and corruption. Civil society is a third category that reveals the true state of a nation's success or failure. Within the period of this study, how has the Nigerian civil society fared?

2.6.3 Civil Society

F. A. Aremu and J. S. Omotola suggest that civil society refers to "that realm of organized social life that is voluntary, self-generating (largely), self-supporting, autonomous from the state, and bound by a legal or set of shared values."[117] In an ideal setting, the role of civil society includes limiting state power, promoting openness in government activities, supplementing the role of political parties in stimulating political participation, and the structuring of multiple channels beyond the political party for the purpose of articulating and representing the interests of the masses. Through election monitoring groups, democratic institutions and think tanks, civil society strengthens democracy by enhancing the accountability and responsiveness of the political system to the citizens through positive engagement. Non-governmental

---

116. Lanre-Abass, "Crisis of Leadership," 120.
117. Aremu and Omotola, "Violence as Threats," 65.

organization (NGO) is the most common term which is used to describe those groups that make up the social network that constitutes civil society.[118]

Organizations such as church groups, charities, youth groups, service clubs, trade unions, amateur soccer leagues, hobby groups, advocacy groups, community organizations, grassroots community groups, community improvement and betterment groups, self-help groups and all the respective kindred organizations fall under the gamut of civil society. These organizations perform sociocultural, economic and political functions. As regards their sociocultural function, these organizations "promote social cohesion; combat isolation, alienation, and anomie; train future leaders; develop organizational skills; and raise the self-confidence and self-esteem of members."[119] NGOs fulfil their economic roles through the provision of services, the mobilization of local resources to satisfy local needs, and by increasing self-sufficiency through decreasing dependence. On the political front, "NGOs can act as interest groups: to lobby, to mobilize people who otherwise don't have access to state power, and to gather them together in groups so that they can have some influence and participate in the governmental decision-making process."[120] Organizations such as the Human Rights Watch and Amnesty International are known for providing education to their members and, most especially, for the influence they have had on political systems in order to bring legislations and policies in line with their interests. In a broader sense, political governance belongs to civil society. However, we may recall that, in the previous section, political governance was discussed purely as it relates to political leadership. Accordingly, our particular focus on civil society in this section will be elaborated upon in the social sector, as it concerns the contributions of civil society to the political, economic and sociocultural transformation of a democratic Nigerian society vis-à-vis the current challenges of poverty, underdevelopment, ineffective leadership and corruption. In line with Osmer's practical theological methodology, my intention in the ongoing discussion is to carry out the descriptive-empirical and interpretive tasks.[121] As previously stated, this task seeks to provide answers to the

---

118. Aremu and Omotola.
119. Weaver, Rock, and Kusterer, *Achieving Broad-based Sustainable Development*, 211.
120. Weaver, Rock, and Kusterer, 214.
121. Osmer, *Practical Theology*, 4–12.

following questions: What is going on in the social environment in Nigeria as it pertains to development in its various ramifications? Why are these things going on? The point here is to uncover the root causes of the perennial challenge of underdevelopment and the resultant consequences in Nigeria, and where necessary, to suggest concepts that may be built into a possible development agenda that may be of benefit to Nigerian society.

With regard to the activities of civil society in the present democratic Nigeria, the high points include the activities of two organizations, namely, Transparency International (TI) and the Save Nigeria Group (SNG). Transparency International has consistently ranked Nigeria as one of the most corrupt countries in the world since 1999 and, by this action, it pressured Chief Obasanjo's administration to address corruption in a vigorous way. Two anti-corruption institutions were established to that effect – the Independent Corrupt Practices and Other Related Offences Commission (ICPC), founded in 2002, and the Economic and Financial Crimes Commission (EFCC), founded in 2002. Drawing on the Human Rights Watch 2007 report, Idemudia observes that, "as at 2007, the EFCC had claimed to have successfully recovered more than $5 billion of stolen money. In addition, more than eighty-two individuals have been prosecuted for corrupt and fraudulent charges."[122] Commenting further, Idemudia notes that "despite these efforts and their dividends, Human Rights Watch noted that success has so far been limited, and corruption continues to remain rampant at all levels of government: Today Nigeria ranks 121st out of 180 countries in the corruption-perception index of the Transparency International Survey."[123] The fight of Obasanjo's administration against corruption has served at least three purposes. The deplorable international reputation of Nigeria improved; the confidence of Nigerian citizens in his administration was boosted and the $18 billion debt cancellation was granted to Nigeria by the Paris Club creditors. These results, that were offshoots of an institution that belongs to civil society, have made a significant contribution to the development of Nigeria. Unfortunately, during the latter part of Obasanjo's administration, the EFCC's focus was assumed by Nigerians to have been directed at Obasanjo's enemies while his cronies were

---

122. Idemudia, "Quest for Effective Use," 9–10.
123. Idemudia, 10.

deeply enmeshed in corrupt and fraudulent practices without any apparent action being taken by the anticorruption institutions.

The Save Nigeria Group came to prominence as a result of its activities relating to the disputations that ensued following President Umaru Yar'Adua's illness in 2010. In a rare occurrence in Nigerian history, we find a church leader at the forefront of civil protest. The SNG has, therefore, brought about an interesting and vital turn to the social transformation of Nigerian society, not only through the results they have achieved in recent history concerning Yar'Adua's ill health crisis and electoral reforms, but by demonstrating the impact church leaders may have when they become development oriented. On 10 March 2010, the SNG, under the leadership of Pastor Tunde Bakare and other civil activists such as Femi Falana (Chair of the West African Bar Association) and Lt. Gen. Alani Akirinade (rtd.), together with hundreds of protesters took to the streets of Abuja after sending a letter to the then acting president, Goodluck Jonathan via the Secretary of the Government of the Federation (SGF), Yayale Ahmed. According to the editorial in the Thisday Newspaper, the letter from SNG to Jonathan read as follows:

> For more than 100 days, Nigerians have not seen or heard from President Yar'Adua since he was evacuated to Saudi Arabia for treatment. For the three months he reportedly stayed in an intensive care unit of a Saudi hospital, several of his aides continued to claim that the President was getting better. Some claimed he had started intense physical exercises. It is now more than two weeks since he was brought back to Nigeria in the dead of the night. We have not still heard from or seen President Yar'Adua. The refusal of President Yar'Adua to resign from office on account of his deteriorating ill health and failure to transmit a letter of vacation on time as required by the constitution has resulted in a severe, but avoidable, constitutional crisis. This crisis has compounded other political challenges caused by an electoral system that is designed to aid electoral malpractices. This dysfunctional electoral system threatens democracy and good governance in Nigeria.[124]

---

124. "Protesters Demand."

The SNG, in the letter to the acting president went on to demand the following: An end to the invisible presidency of Yar'Adua by activating Section 144 of the constitution so that presidential powers will be fully accountable; The dissolution of the present Executive Council of the Federation which has largely collaborated with presidential aides to foist this crisis on the nation; and quick and thorough implementation of the Uwais Report on Electoral Reform starting with the immediate removal of Professor Maurice Iwu as Chairman and the reconstitution of INEC with persons of impeccable integrity and competence.[125]

In an extremely dramatic way, the protests and activities of SNG achieved much. The full powers of the president were conferred on the then acting president by an act of the National Assembly (Senate and Federal House of Representatives) while the Executive Council of the Federation was dissolved and reconstituted. The true state of the ailing president was disclosed and the chairman of the INEC was removed from office as part of electoral reforms, while other reforms were put in progress. The power of the people's movement had been tested and had proved to be extremely effective in acting as a counterbalance in the democratic process. Civil society emerged as a crucial factor in the expression of the wishes and power of the citizens in the face of political and economic power.

There has been some degree of progress in the political and economic structures in Nigeria although it may be argued that this progress has not been translated into concrete benefits beyond the ambit of the politicians, big businessmen and their benefactors. Despite the fact that Nigerian civil society still requires a stronger resource base and more definite focus if it is to address the considerable challenges that Nigerians are facing in the socio-cultural, economic and political milieus, it remains the last hope of rescuing Nigeria from total collapse. It may, therefore, be of interest to this study to explore the way in which the church, through its leadership, could meaningfully contribute to the process of change in Nigeria by equipping the faithful with kingdom values and resources that will aid them to live as the "salt and light" in the broader Nigerian society. In addition, it may be incumbent on the Nigerian church leadership at all levels to consider collaboration with the mechanisms of civil society so as to be able to address the major structures

---

125. "Protesters Demand."

that are responsible for the poverty, underdevelopment, poor leadership and corruption in the country.

2.7 Conclusion

Aided by the practical theological methodology in terms of the descriptive-empirical and interpretive tasks,[126] I set forth to investigate and perhaps provide answers to the following questions: What is going on in the social environment in Nigeria and its broader context (sub-Sahara Africa) as it pertains to development in its various ramifications? Why are these things going on? The aim is to uncover the root causes of the perennial challenge of underdevelopment and the resultant consequences in Nigeria, and where necessary, to suggest concepts that may be built into a possible development agenda that will benefit Nigerian society.

This chapter discussed the meaning of development; trends that have characterized Nigerian developmental efforts both before and during the democratic period; the quest for an authentic development paradigm and the unique challenges that are inhibiting development in Nigeria. There are no fixed definitions for the term development. Nevertheless, it is possible for the concept to find its meaning and implications based on the challenges that relate to the concept within a particular context. By following the historical antecedents of Nigerian society, it is possible to trace the sources of poverty, underdevelopment, corruption and poor leadership to the exploitation of Nigerians, first by the European traders and colonialists. Thereafter, from postcolonial to present day Nigeria, the exploitation of Nigerians and the perpetuation of poverty, underdevelopment, corruption and poor leadership may be attributed to poor leadership on the part of both the military and the political elite, with these Nigerian elite having collaborated in their acts of injustice with neocolonialists and imperialists. Ethnicity, certain traditional/religious mores, and the negative imprints of globalization continue to serve the selfish interests of these individuals and institutions. Within the Nigerian context, development implies a process in terms of which Nigerians increase their personal and institutional capacities in order both to mobilize and to manage their resources so as to bring about sustainable and justly distributed

---

126. Osmer, *Practical Theology*, 4–12.

improvements in their quality of life and which are consistent with their own aspirations. It is anticipated that a development focused leadership could contribute significantly to the much desired sociopolitical and economic transformation of Nigerian society. The church in Nigeria, as both a component of civil society and as a community-based organization, could be harnessed through its leaders to help bring about sociopolitical and economic change. The third chapter will focus on the meanings and implications of leadership.

CHAPTER 3

Meanings and Implications of Leadership in Postmilitary Nigeria

3.1 Introduction

The main thrust of this chapter is the exploration of literature relevant to the Nigerian historical context from the precolonial to the present era, as it relates to leadership. The chapter engages both the descriptive-empirical and interpretive theological approach as proposed by Osmer.[1] The intention is to understand the root cause(s) of the ongoing phenomenon of poor leadership in the country and the consequences of this poor leadership. This study suggests that it is the failure of successive generations of Nigerian leaders that is responsible for the poverty, underdevelopment and corruption which has been a feature of life in Nigeria for some time and which is still continuing. In view of the fact that this study argues that it is leadership that should drive development in Nigeria and in order to understand the Nigerian leadership scenario, a definition of leadership and the concepts of leadership will be examined. Discussions on the leadership in the precolonial, colonial, postcolonial, military and postmilitary (democratic) Nigerian society will be preceded by a presentation of the Nigerian and African understanding of leadership and the sources that influence that understanding. Finally, the importance of leadership as the motivating force behind development and social transformation in Nigerian society will be explored.

---

1. Osmer, *Practical Theology*, 4–12.

3.2 The Meaning of Leadership

Leadership is a highly valued phenomenon, yet very complex and continues to present challenges to practitioners and researchers in its definition and conceptualization. Over the years leadership has been defined and conceptualized in varied ways. There is, therefore, no universally accepted definition of leadership. However, some researchers and practitioners have tendered definitions that are worthy of our consideration. Although this list will by, no means, constitute an exhaustive rollcall of the works on leadership, as that body of literature is enormous, I hope to engage with the most substantive literature on leadership.

Myles Munroe, John Maxwell and L. Collinson have made some interesting differentiations between what a leader is and leadership, and leadership and management. These demarcations are worth considering. According to Munroe, "leader is both a designated position and the individual who assumes that position, accepting the responsibility and accountability it entails."[2] On the other hand, he maintains that "leadership is the function of the designated position and the exercize of the responsibilities involved in that position."[3] The crucial point here is the fact that, although one may have a position of leadership, the exercising of leadership is not automatically guaranteed and there are basic qualities, competencies and skills that are essential. It is also implied that it is possible to become a leader by understanding and developing these qualities, competencies and skills. We now turn our attention to the difference between leadership and management. The difference between managers and leaders can be expressed in the saying, "there are four types of people in the world: those who watch things happen, those who let things happen, those who ask what just happened, and those who make things happen. Leaders are those who make things happen while managers are in the other groups."[4] According to Maxwell, "Managers are maintainers, tending to rely on systems and controls. Leaders are innovators and creators who rely

---

2. Munroe, *Becoming a Leader*, 34.
3. Munroe, 35.
4. Munroe, 35.

on people."[5] For John Adair, "management is prose; leadership is poetry."[6] What then is leadership?

Munroe maintains that "Leadership is the capacity to influence others through inspiration, generated by a passion, motivated by a vision, birthed from a conviction, produced by a purpose."[7] It follows then that influence, inspiration, passion, vision and purpose are key components of leadership. According to Warren Bennis and Burt Nanus, "Leadership is doing the right things."[8] For James McGregor Burns, "leadership is when persons with certain motives and purposes mobilise, in competition or conflict with others, institutional, political, psychological and other resources so as to arouse, engage and satisfy the motives of followers."[9] Burns's viewpoint presupposes that the followership should occupy the centre stage of leadership endeavour. On their part, Henry and Richard Blackaby suggest that religious or "spiritual leadership is moving people on to God's agenda."[10] They also agree that the impact of what is termed spiritual or religious leadership in terms of moving people to God's agenda is not confined to spiritual or religious issues but must show results on sociopolitical and economic matters in relation to the needs of the broader society.

Peter G. Northouse argues that "the component common to nearly all classifications of [leadership] is that leadership is an influence process that assists groups of individuals towards goal attainment."[11] He therefore defines leadership as a "process whereby an individual influences a group of individuals to achieve a common goal."[12] Ronald Heifetz on his part argues that leadership is more than influencing people and giving them what they want or occupying a position of authority. Leadership is an activity and a value-laden word. "Leadership means influencing the community to face its problems."[13]

---

5. Maxwell, *Developing Leaders*, 27.
6. Collinson, "Management Isn't Mysterious," 22.
7. Munroe, *Becoming a Leader*, 36.
8. Barna, *Leaders on Leadership*, 20, 23.
9. Barna, 20, 23.
10. Blackaby and Blackaby, *Spiritual Leadership*, 36.
11. Northouse, *Leadership: Theory and Practice*, 15.
12. Northouse, 15.
13. Heifetz, *Leadership without Easy Answers*, 14.

It also means "mobilizing people to tackle tough problems."[14] Based on this understanding, leadership is therefore defined as "the practice of mobilizing people to tackle tough challenges and thrive."[15]

Ngara suggests that leadership refers to those qualities and capabilities which some individuals possess and which enable them to influence or lead others.[16] Speaking from an African perspective, Masango declares that "Leadership has to do with someone who has commanding authority or influence within a group. In Africa a leader is viewed as someone who is a servant to the clan, tribe, community or group."[17] However, this understanding of leadership is not common to all African societies as some African societies perceive their leaders as "gods," having the power of life and death.[18] It may be deduced from the above that a significant number of scholars and leadership analysts tend to agree that leadership entails influence which is rooted in character and charisma, tailored together with a vision for the common good and encompassing a significant measure of work, passion and compassion. Having defined leadership, our task at this point is to conceptualize it.

3.3 Conceptualising Leadership

In leadership literature, there are four major leadership concepts, styles or theories that are currently driving research and practice in leadership. These are transformational, authentic, servant and adaptive leadership. A discussion of each of these leadership styles and a further attempt to adopt an appropriate concept of leadership for the purpose of this study may be helpful at this point.

3.3.1 Transformational Leadership

According to G. A. Stone, R. F. Russel, and K. Patterson, transformational leadership theory was initiated by James MacGregor Burns in 1978. This leadership theory has become an extremely popular concept in recent years. The transformational leader's main concern is with progress and development.

---

14. Heifetz, 15.
15. Northouse, *Leadership: Theory and Practice*, 258.
16. Ngara, *Christian Leadership*.
17. Masango, "Leadership in African Context," 313.
18. Mbiti, *African Religion and Philosophy*, 177, 181.

He or she "transforms the personal values of followers into support for the vision and goals of the organization by cultivating an environment in which relationships may be built and by establishing an atmosphere of trust and vision sharing."[19] The following four behaviours are encompassed in transformational leadership, namely, "idealised influence, inspirational motivation, intellectual stimulation and individualised consideration."[20] Based on his/her idealized or charismatic influence, the transformational leader becomes a role model who is respected, admired and emulated by followers. This attribute also provides impetus to vision sharing. This is what is vital for others to look at the futuristic state, which is inevitable in the tailoring of personal values and concerns to the collective aspirations of the group's purposes. With regard to inspirational motivation, the transformational leader motivates others by providing meaning and challenge to the followers' work. The combination of idealized influence and inspirational motivation gives rise to charismatic-inspirational leadership.[21] Whereas intellectual stimulation is helpful to the followers' efforts to be innovative and creative, individualized consideration helps the transformational leader to give personal attention to the followers' needs for achievement and growth. I will now discuss the concept of authentic leadership.

3.3.2 Authentic Leadership

This concept of leadership is about the authenticity of leaders and their leadership. Whereas the concept appears to be simple in definition, in fact leadership scholars find it difficult to define it. Perhaps the fact that this concept is new and as such still undergoing its formative stage of development is contributing to this challenge. One productive way to grapple with the concept is by viewing it from various angles such as intrapersonal, interpersonal and developmental perspectives. In reference to the intrapersonal perspective, authentic leadership means to lead genuinely, from conviction and being original. "This perspective emphasizes the life experiences of a leader and the meaning he or she attaches to those experiences as being critical to the

---

19. Stone, Russell, and Patterson, "Transformational versus Servant Leadership," 349, 361.
20. Northouse, *Leadership: Theory and Practice*, 65.
21. Stone, Russell, and Patterson, "Transformational versus Servant Leadership."

development of the authentic leader."[22] As an interpersonal process, authentic leadership is viewed as relational created by both leaders and followers together. "Authenticity emerges from the interactions between leaders and followers."[23] This is based on the understanding that in authentic leadership, leaders influence followers and followers influence leaders. It is the developmental perspective of authentic leadership that brings to the fore the fact that this leadership theory upholds the understanding that leadership is not a fixed trait, but a skill that can be nurtured over a period of time and that which can be "triggered by major life events, such as severe illness or a new career."[24] A leadership paradigm that has gained a lot of traction in organizations and amongst faith communities is the concept of servant leadership.

3.3.3 Servant Leadership

Robert K. Greenleaf coined the term servant leadership and is the author of seminal works on the subject matter, after working for AT&T for forty years and after his retirement. He argues that "servant leadership begins with the natural feeling that one wants to serve, to serve first. Then conscious choice brings one to aspire to lead."[25] Based on this understanding, "the difference manifests itself in the care taken by the servant – first to make sure that other people's highest priority needs are being served."[26] The test as to whether or not servant leadership is at play in a context is: "do those served grow as persons; do they, while being served, become healthier, wiser, freer, more autonomous, more likely themselves to become servants? And, what is the effect on the least privileged in society; will they benefit, or, at least, will they not be further deprived?"[27] In engaging the concept within the context of the church, Osmer argues that "It is best to think of servant leadership in the following way: Servant leadership is leadership that influences the congregation to change in ways that more fully embody the servanthood of Christ."[28] Servant leadership is not a matter of personality traits, like being self-effacing,

---

22. Northouse, *Leadership: Theory and Practice*, 198.
23. Northouse, 198.
24. Northouse, 198.
25. Greenleaf, *Servant as Leader*, 15.
26. Greenleaf, 15.
27. Greenleaf, 15.
28. Osmer, *Practical Theology*, 183, 193.

mild mannered or overly responsible. On the contrary, it requires courage, a firm resolve and the ability to empower others. Servant leaders are also known to influence others, gain the credibility and trust of their followers, as well as provide them with vision.

E. Gibbs has argued that, whereas the servant leadership style, which is generally held to have been portrayed by Jesus, is helpful in rectifying the prestige-seeking and domineering leadership that has prevailed in some ecclesial traditions, the use of the servant concept has sometimes been misunderstood and misapplied.[29] This misunderstanding and misapplication have arisen from the assumption that the servant's primary role is to meet the demands of those which he/she has been called to serve while, in some instances, this servant concept has resulted in an abdication of leadership. Gibbs notes that "Jesus unswervingly sought his Father's guidance for the direction of his ministry. Rather than simply responding to popular demand, he took the initiative in terms of his overriding purpose."[30] There is no doubt that Jesus was not a servant of people. Jesus's example of servanthood was defined very differently because of his unique connection with the will of God. Jesus came to fulfil the role of the "servant of the Lord." The idea of the servant of the Lord, as understood in the Old Testament, was by no means a demeaning one. On the contrary, it was a title of honour, applied to Israel's national leader and, even more significantly, to the servant king spoken of by Isaiah. It referred to the special messenger sent by God with whom Jesus identified – an identification that was also assumed by the early church.

Gibbs's argument implies that care should be exercized when applying the notion of servant leadership within the church and communities of today. We are not Jesus. Consequently, we are prone to be selective in our obedience and to display sinful tendencies, and are limited in our understanding of God's will for our lives; thus, we struggle to interpret and follow his day-to-day guidance. In as much as the biblical notion of servant leadership inspired Greenleaf's conceptualization of the concept of servant leadership with its possible application within the ecclesial community and beyond, Gibbs's observation on the misconception of servant leadership is significant as we seek an appropriate concept of leadership, capable of addressing the challenge

---

29. Gibbs, *Leadership Next*.
30. Gibbs, 23.

of poverty and poor leadership in Nigeria. Such a concept of leadership, as envisioned within the context of Nigerian society, should also have relevance within the Nigerian church. We turn now to the adaptive leadership approach.

3.3.4 Adaptive Leadership

Ronald Heifetz and Marty Linsky are the originators of the concept of adaptive leadership. Adaptive leadership now occupies a unique place of importance in leadership theory and practice. This development has been largely informed by the effectiveness of the concept in the explanation of how leaders can encourage effective change across multiple levels, including self, organizational, community and societal. Heifetz posits that "adaptive leadership is the process of mobilizing people to tackle tough challenges and thrive."[31] In this understanding of leadership, the leader is not seen as a saviour who solves problems for people, but as one who plays the role of assisting people who need to confront tough problems. At the core of Heifetz's view of leadership is the understanding that there are two distinctions: between technical and adaptive problems, and between leadership and authority. "The first points to the different modes of action required to deal with routine problems in contrast with those that demand innovation and learning; the second provides a framework for assessing resources and developing a leadership strategy depending upon whether one has or does not have authority."[32] Adaptive leadership incorporates ideas from a systems' perspective, a biological perspective, a service orientation perspective and a psychotheraphy perspective.[33] From the systems perspective, this approach argues that many problems people experience are embedded in complicated interactive systems. In solving problems, these systems must be taken into account. The biological perspective acknowledges that people evolve and develop as they adapt to both their internal cues and external environment and their ability to adapt also helps them to thrive in their new circumstance. Just like the physician, the adaptive leader in the service perspective uses his authority and expertise to help the people in the diagnosis of their problems while also working with them to find the solutions of new ways of coping

---

31. Heifetz, *Leadership without Easy Answers*, 15.
32. Heifetz, 8.
33. Northouse, *Leadership: Theory and Practice*.

with the problems. In the psychotherapy perspective, the adaptive leader appreciates the fact that people who are having problems need a supportive environment and that where such an environment exists, people adapt more successfully and are able to learn, resolve internal conflicts and learn new attitudes and behaviour.

Although every leader usually manifests varying degrees of the four leadership styles, as discussed above, a leader is deemed as belonging to that category that is most pronounced in his or her exercise of leadership. There is hardly any doubt that all leadership theories carry within them the possibility of manipulation and corruption, however, there are some that are more prone than others to extreme manipulation and corruption, and all persons exercising leadership are advised to be conscious of this fact. Accessibility to the people and tolerance of opposition could act as helpful checks in this regard. The adaptive leadership concept which views leadership as an activity aimed at influencing the community to face its problems and to take up its tough challenges for the purpose of thriving promises to be helpful to the Nigerian context. The concept with its orienting concepts and the tools of diagnosis of any context are extremely relevant when one considers the enormity of challenges within the Nigerian context. This leadership concept speaks to the heart of the sustainable transformational development which this study espouses when it argues that resolving societies' problems is based on the engagements of the leadership, followership and the context in the process of learning, improvisation and drawing from the repertoire of knowledge of the past and being open to new ways of problem solving. The understanding that the people and their leaders constitute both the problem and the solution as against the leader or one in a position of authority being viewed as the saviour is very informing.

Both the servant and the transformational leadership theories are considered to be extremely similar, although there are slight differences. Both theories encompass people-oriented leadership styles while their leadership frameworks include influence; vision; trust; respect or credibility; risk sharing or delegation; integrity and modelling. It has also been observed that transformational leadership and servant leadership are not antithetical, nor is either paradigm inherently superior to the other. The difference in practice may be a function of both the organizational context in which the leaders operate and the personal values of the leaders. I believe that either the transformational leadership theory or the servant leadership theory or the adaptive leadership style would satisfy the sustainable transformational approach to development that may provide a panacea for the challenge of poverty, underdevelopment, corruption and poor leadership within both the church and the Nigerian context. However, in the interests of adhering to a leadership model, this study prefers to use the transformational leadership paradigm while also engaging the resources of the adaptive leadership concept as leadership models that are suited to both the ecclesial and the wider Nigerian community.

Gibbs maintains that leadership is profoundly influenced by the context and the personality of the individual. We cannot simply transpose one style of leadership from one particular time, location and cultural setting and apply it to another. Herein lies one of the problems in trying to impose biblical or other models of leadership without distinguishing universally valid elements from those that are context-specific.[34] In Gibbs's view, it is not always possible to reproduce the models of leadership, as displayed in Scripture or elsewhere, although they do provide useful lessons to be learned. These lessons may be adapted to situations in both our own lives and in communities in which similar circumstances are to be found. The transformational and adaptive leadership concepts are, thus, capable of addressing both the individual and the institutional challenges in Nigeria for the common good. In addition, these leadership concepts or at least some of their dimensions may or may not find some commonalities with African views on leadership. A survey of the influences that have shaped the African and Nigerian view of leadership may further strengthen this view.

3.4 Leadership in the African Context

Both the concept of leadership and leadership ideology in contemporary Africa have been informed by at least four sources of influences, namely, traditional African heritage, the Christian religion[35] and Western ideas of

---

34. Gibbs, *Leadership Next*.

35. Our discussion on the influence of Christianity on the concept of leadership in Africa does not suggest the influence of colonization on the African concept of leadership, as the advent of Christianity in Africa predates the establishment of the colonial regimes in Africa. However, the influence of colonialism on African/Nigerian leadership ideology will be discussed in other sections in this study.

leadership, and the Islamic religion. We will briefly discuss each of these influences for the purpose of tracking the sources of the leadership ideologies that inform leadership practices in Nigeria and in several African countries. In so doing, a foundation will be laid for the discussion on leadership trends within Nigerian society from the precolonial to the postmilitary times.

3.4.1 Traditional African Heritage

In traditional African societies, leadership practices and styles vary from people to people and from place to place.[36] In most instances, the most prominent sources of leadership in the community are the kings, queens and rulers. However, in view of the fact that not all African societies have had rulers or leaders in the form of kings, queens and chiefs, there are other sources through which leadership has flowed to the people, for example, family, compounds and age grade structures. Most leaders in African traditional societies occupy a special place in the lives and experiences of their people by virtue of their office. Mbiti has observed that where these rulers are found, they are not simply political heads: they are the mystical and religious heads, the divine symbol of their people's health and welfare. "The individuals, as such, may not have outstanding talents or abilities, but their office is the link between human rule and spiritual government."[37] Elaborating further on the special importance of these leaders, Mbiti notes that "they are therefore, divine or sacral rulers, the shadow or reflection of God's rule in the universe. People regard them as God's earthly viceroys."[38] It is on this premise that these rulers are accorded extremely high positions and titles such as "saviour," "protector," "child of God," "chief of the divinities" and "lord of earth and life."[39] Such leaders are not only allowed to do what they wish but they are assumed to be incarnations of God who have proceeded from heaven and, therefore, possess power over natural phenomena such as rain. The sacred position of African rulers is demonstrated in a number of ways, for example, they are not seen in ordinary life; no reference must be made to either their eating or their sleeping; they must be spoken well of; their followers must bow or

---

36. Masango, "Leadership in African Context."
37. Mbiti, *African Religion and Philosophy*, 177.
38. Mbiti, 177–78.
39. Mbiti, 178.

kneel before them; they have sexual rights over the wives of their subjects, and their illnesses and death are not usually mentioned. The family members and close associates of the rulers also enjoy high esteem. While, in some societies, traditional rulers are succeeded by their son, daughter, brother or some other member of the royal family, in other societies, the ruler's successor could be chosen by a council of chiefs. Priests, prophets and the religious founders of African traditional religion constitute another source of leadership in many African societies. The duties of the priest are chiefly religious, but, since Africans do not dissociate religion from other departments of life, he has or may have other functions.[40] Where lengthy training is part of the preparation for priesthood, the priests are the depositories of national customs, knowledge, taboos, theology and even oral history.

3.4.2 The Christian Influence

Although it may be argued that Christianity may be deemed to be African indigenous religion in view of the fact that it has had a lengthy history on the continent, it may also be argued that it falls in the category of a later arrival on the shores of Africa, long after the evolution of the African traditional religion, albeit before Islam. Mbiti informs us that "long before the start of Islam in the seventh century, Christianity was long established all over North Africa, Egypt, parts of the Sudan and Ethiopia."[41] It was a dynamic form of Christianity, producing great scholars and theologians like Tertullian, Origen, Clement of Alexandria and Augustine. There is, therefore, no doubt that it was the impact of Christianity that led to the emergence of these outstanding scholars whose influence extended to a broad range of men and women. It is, thus, assumed that these men and women were able to bring their Christian-imbued leadership virtues and skills to both the church and to African society, as did Augustine and others.

Subsequent contact with Christianity on the African continent came about as a result of the activities of the missionaries who had come to Africa during the colonization of the continent. During this period, "African religion and its leaders were challenged by the missionaries, especially in the way that they brought change and used Western concepts. The leaders and

---

40. Mbiti, 183.
41. Mbiti, 223.

the people adapted to Western concepts, and some abandoned their own African religious values, customs and culture."[42] Commenting on the impact of Christianity on the concept and practice of leadership in Africa, Masango opines that from this time onward, the concept of African leadership developed steadily towards professionalism. Western organizational concepts guided new leaders to operate in a colonialist style. Change came as a result of leadership being shaped by missionary education. Africans were then evaluated according to Western concepts or standards.[43] In other words, to be civil one had to use Western concepts of leadership styles. African leaders who used traditional methods of leadership were viewed by some Westerners as barbaric. With the advent of the Christian missionaries and the colonial masters, much of the leadership role shifted from the traditional leaders, such as kings, queens, priests and chiefs, to the colonial master, missionaries and teachers. There is no doubt that the traditional styles of leadership were severely affected and that this paved the way for an upset of the traditional systems of leadership. Despite the fact that the traditional systems were not completely eradicated, they were seriously weakened.

Despite the negative aspects of the impact of both the missionaries and the colonial masters on African styles and concepts of leadership, some African leaders did derive something positive from the biblical teachings on leadership. Christian concepts such as "people being created in the image and likeness of God"; "love for one's neighbor" and "the body of Christ" enriched the value which African leaders accorded to human life and the positive assertion of leadership on their subjects. In addition, these concepts contributed to the unity of communities as the Christian converts who had attained leadership positions sought to live out the Christian ideals in their villages or communities.

3.4.3 The Influence of Islam

Within a century after the death of the prophet Mohammad in AD 632, Islam had swept through the entire North Africa as well as the Horn of Africa, reaching southwards to the east coast of Africa.[44] As is the case with

---

42. Masango, "Leadership in African Context," 316.
43. Masango.
44. Mbiti, *African Religion and Philosophy*, 236.

Christianity, Islam may, arguably, be termed an indigenous African traditional religion as a result of the length of time it has welded influence on the African continent and its interaction with a number of African communities and cultures. The trade routes as well as the commercial activities between the Arab world and north Africa and the colonization era contributed significantly to the spread of Islam on the continent.

Recounting the impact of Islam on the Nupe, a tribe in northern Nigeria (or the middle belt), Mbiti notes that "since Islam came to Nupe as a religion of conquerors and the ruling class, what counts is, first and foremost, the assimilation to upper-class culture and, only secondarily, the deliverance from unbelief."[45] This assertion implies that the social impact of Islam on the Nupe may be regarded as an example of what happened in other parts of Africa into which Islam made incursions. However, more negatively, Islam provides "a point of reference for a sense of pride and superiority"[46] in the Muslim convert instead of touching the deep levels within the soul of the convert, although these deep levels in the convert may have been informed by the mystical and ecstatic observances of Islam. In as much as Islam may have contributed positively to African communities, the inculcation of a sense of pride and superiority embodied in the ultimate culture of a class-cult has been detrimental to the development of positive leadership qualities in members of African villages and communities. It is also unlikely that Islamic converts who assume leadership positions in their communities would regard themselves as being accountable to their fellow villagers. Most importantly, because such a conversion is more social than spiritual, it may lead to the fragmentation of the community by creating class distinctions and the use of force in leadership. It may be possible to come to a greater appreciation of the challenges of social dislocation and violence as tools of Islamic evangelization if one remembers that much of the spread of Islam in Africa was as a result of the jihads led by Uthman dan Fodio. Islamic fundamentalism and terrorism continue to hold sway in the Nigerian and African context.

Throughout the chequered history of the Nigerian nation, the leadership practices of its leaders have been influenced by leadership notions that may be traced to one or more of the leadership influences derived from the

---

45. Mbiti, 240.
46. Mbiti, 240.

African traditional heritage, the Christian religious and colonial influence or the Islamic religion. A brief survey of the leadership practices within the Yoruba, Hausa and Ibo ethnic groups in precolonial times will be helpful in particularizing the leadership trends that are ingrained in most Nigerian leaders, depending on their ethnic origin. It will be discovered that, apart from other influences, Nigerians and their leaders still draw a great deal from their traditional leadership patterns which may have been influenced by religion in the distant past. An understanding of these ethnic/religious divides is vital in understanding the complexities inherent in leadership in Nigeria. It will also be useful in charting a new direction for the practice of effective leadership that will address the challenges of poverty, underdevelopment, corruption and poor leadership.

3.5 Leadership in Precolonial Nigerian Societies

Before the arrival of the colonial masters to the area which now constitutes Nigeria, there were organized entities in the form of empires, city states, clans, chiefdoms, compounds, families, houses or villages. The "basic political units in precolonial Nigeria were the village, village-group, clan, state, chiefdom, kingdom, empire and caliphate. Except those that were conquered and incorporated into the core, each of the geopolity existed as a separate and independent entity."[47] Accordingly, scholars argue that the emergence of such names as Igbo, Hausa, Yoruba, Fulani, Efik, and Ibibio etc. for the Nigerian peoples as they are known today may be traced to the emergence of the colonial state of Nigeria. It was European visitors, traders and writers who started referring to the entire group based on the language spoken by the group and not necessarily because the group was a reflection of a single, coherent and politically organized group. Ohwofasa explains that "long before 1500 A.D., much of modern-Nigeria was divided into nation-states identified with contemporary ethnic groups. These early states included the Yoruba kingdoms, the Igbo kingdom of Nri, the Edo kingdom of Benin, the Hausa cities state, Nupe, etc."[48] Using the three major tribes in Nigeria, namely, Hausa, Yoruba and Igbo, as our point of reference, we will briefly explore

---

47. Chuku-Okereke, "Evolution of Nigeria," 5.
48. Ohwofasa, *Democracy and Issues*, 9.

how these varied societies were ruled and the concepts of leadership that held sway among the people.

3.5.1 Leadership among the Hausa-Fulani and Kanem-Bornu

Trans-Saharan trade played a key role in the formation of organized communities in the savannah areas which now comprise northern Nigeria. In this area, the Kanem-Bornu Empire and the Hausa states constituted the main political structures within their respective jurisdictions. Ohwofasa argues that "Borno's history is closely associated with Kanem, which had achieved imperial status in the Lake Chad basin by the 13th century. Kanem expanded westward to include the area that became Borno."[49] The emergence of farming and other professional associations led to the founding of villages which later developed into walled cities. It is assumed that, by the eleventh century, certain Hausa states such as Kano, Katsina, Gobir and others had developed into walled cities and that trade and manufacturing were thriving in these cities. The Fulani are believed to have come from the Senegal River valley via the Mali and Songhai Empires to settle eventually in Hausaland and Borno where they became racially integrated. As a result of their religious devotion and education, the Fulani soon developed into influential leaders and were indispensable political advisers to the Hausa kings.[50]

The Hausa-Fulani and Kanem-Borno system of administration was centralized. After the ninth century AD, Islam made incursions into this region via the trans-Saharan trade routes. The arrival of Islam in this area soon altered the rhythm of the economic, political and social life. C. A. Ndoh has observed that "what appears today to be the administrative set-up in the north came about as a result of the overthrow of the traditional administrative machinery of the native Hausa system of administration and its replacement with the Fulani system. This was done through the Jihad of Uthman dan Fodio."[51] It was indeed this development that gave rise to the establishment of the emirate system with the Sokoto and Gwandu emirates as the most prominent. The emirs of Sokoto and Gwandu were assumed to have the power

---

49. Ohwofasa, 11.
50. Ohwofasa.
51. Ndoh, "Pre-Colonial Political Institutions," 27.

of life and death over the other emirates within their subdivisions. Of these two most prominent emirates, the Sokoto emirate, headed by the Sultan of Sokoto, exercized the highest level of religious and political power over the other emirates. Ohwofasa reminds us that "Islam was used to reinforce the political and social structures of the state although many established customs were preserved – women, for example, continued to exercize considerable political influence,"[52] especially within the Kanem-Borno. It should be noted that the emirs exercised both a high level of authority and enormous power over their subjects. "In most cases, they were very dictatorial or autocratic. An emir could be removed if he became a dictator"[53] by a general consensus of the senior officers of the ruling houses. However, this rule was rarely put into practice as a result of the powers which the emirs wielded. It is significant to note at this point that the prevailing leadership style was often authoritarian and also a combination of religious and political leadership was imbued in the same individual (the emir).

3.5.2 Leadership among the Yoruba

The Yoruba is the dominant group on the west bank of the Niger to the south. They are assumed to be products of mixed origin – Egyptian, Etruscan or Jewish – from the Nile valley. "The Yoruba kingdom of Ife and Oyo were founded about 700–900 AD and 1400 AD respectively."[54] Oduduwa is regarded as the creator of the earth, progenitor of the Yoruba race and the ancestor of the Yoruba kings. Traditionally, the Yoruba were an agricultural people. They were organized patrilineally in groups that formed village communities. Around the eleventh century, adjoining compounds known as "ile" transformed into a number of city-states under dynasties. It is held by the Yoruba that "Oduduwa founded Ife and dispatched his sons to establish other cities, where they reigned as priest-kings. Ife was the nucleus of as many as 400 religious cults whose traditions were contrived to political advantage by the Ooni."[55] The Benin kingdom is linked historically with the Yoruba kingdom.

---

52. Ohwofasa, *Democracy and Issues*, 11–12.
53. Ndoh, "Pre-Colonial Political Institutions," 28.
54. Ohwofasa, *Democracy and Issues*, 9.
55. Ohwofasa, 9.

Political and religious authority resided in the Oba (king) who was assumed to be a descendant of the Ife dynasty.

Commenting on the process through which the ruler (Oba) emerged, Ndoh notes that "the choice of an Oba was based on the royal family that had a royal blood of Oduduwa. However, his candidature must have the blessing of the senior chiefs."[56] Despite the fact that each Oba exercized his independence within his jurisdiction, he was traditionally expected to look to the Oni of Ife for leadership. This, naturally, gave the Oni (who was traditionally a spiritual leader) an edge in political power over the Alafin who was the original political leader. Each Oba had under him a number of towns and villages. The Oba ruled his kingdom from his headquarters and had a council of chiefs and elders to assist him in governance. Administratively, the Oba was expected to follow the advice of this council of chiefs and elders. "Any Oba who ruled autocratically would be compelled to commit suicide through the presentation of an empty calabash."[57] It is, therefore, the opinion of certain scholars that the Yoruba system of leadership was more democratic than that of either the Hausa-Fulani or the Kanem-Borno.

3.5.3 Leadership among the Igbo

The area which comprised the diverse Igbo kingdoms was to the southeast of the Niger. The Onitsha kingdom had already come into existence during the sixteenth century AD while other kingdoms included the Nri and Arochukwu. In the southeast and south of modern Nigeria, other kingdoms such as Efik, Quas, Ejagham, Olulumo, Nkome, Opobo, Bonny, Brass, Eleme, Kalabari and others flourished. Such kingdoms were under the control of groups such as the Ijaw, Urhobo, Efik and Ibibio,[58] Ejagham, Olulumo and others. It may be observed that the Efik and Opobo, for example, were ruled by kings and that there was a leadership structure in place that was different from that in other neighbouring communities. However, many other communities such as the Olulumo (Okuni), Ikom (Nkome) and Ejagham/Etung had leadership structures that were similar to that of the Igbo. It may be argued that the presence of dense tropical forests in these areas safeguarded

---

56. Ndoh, "Pre-Colonial Political Institutions," 29.
57. Ndoh, 27.
58. Ohwofasa, *Democracy and Issues*.

the area from invasion by external conquerors which may, in turn, have not given rise to the establishment of an empire as had happened in the case of the Yoruba and the Hausa-Fulani. The kind of terrain that characterized the Igbo area had also made movement and interaction between the communities extremely difficult. The reason for the lack of centrality in the administrative structure of these communities is said to have been as a result of the tropical nature of the area which was inhabited by sedimentary farmers.

All political observers agree that the village was the centre of political, economic and social life. The principal institutions were the council of elders and the village assembly of which every grown-up male was a member. The council of elders was responsible for issues affecting tradition, custom and ritual, while essential matters of policy affecting the life of the villagers were decided by the village assembly.[59] Besides the council of elders and the village assembly, the age-grade system and the village cults such as ekpe (mgbe) represented another vital structure that assisted in the enforcement of law and the provision of social services in the community. The Igbo and the other groups which were neighbours of the Igbo held personal freedom in high esteem and resented any form of autocratic government. It would, thus, not be incorrect to say that leadership in Igboland was predominantly democratic. However, the weakness of the Igbo leadership style lay in the fact that it made decision-making difficult and it was not possible to command wide followership as each community or village was a republic on its own and there was hardly any one figure to whom one could point as the leader of the community.

It is evident that, before colonization, the major tribes that constitute modern Nigeria and the other smaller groups that lived around them were diverse in history, culture, political development and religion. Anthropologists have placed these societies in two main categories, namely, centralized (state) and noncentralized (stateless). While the Igbo kingdoms in particular, and other kingdoms around them were noncentralized, the Sokoto Caliphate, the emirates of the north and the Kanem-Bornu Empire were characterized by advanced Islamic theocracies and advanced forms of state organization and were highly centralized. Also included in this category, but without the high degree of centralization, were the Benin, Oyo and other Yoruba traditional

---

59. Ndoh, "Pre-Colonial Political Institutions."

institutions. With the exception of the Benin and Yoruba areas where the taxation system was non-existent, the highly centralized institutions had in place an effective taxation system and there were clear demarcations between the rulers and the ruled. These demarcations were usually based on wealth and ascribed status. In addition, whereas the northern areas were undergoing Islamization, the southern societies comprised predominantly traditional worshippers who later came into contact with Christianity. We will now discuss the British colonial administration of these diverse groups.

3.6 Leadership in the Colonial Era

In 1885, at the Berlin Conference, Great Britain was given jurisdiction over much of west Africa, which included the area now known as Nigeria. Prior to this, British traders had expanded trade in the interior areas of Nigeria. In approximately 1886, the Royal Niger Company was chartered under the leadership of Sir George Taubman Goldie for the purpose of administering the Niger region. "In 1900, the company's territory came under the control of the British Government, which moved to consolidate its hold over the area of modern Nigeria."[60] Thus, on 1 January 1900, Nigeria became a British protectorate. Subsequently, in 1914, under the leadership of Lord Lugard, the northern and southern protectorates were amalgamated and it was this amalgamation of the two protectorates that gave birth to modern Nigeria. Nevertheless, in the administrative sense, Nigeria remained divided into the northern and southern provinces and the colony of Lagos. These areas were administered separately until 1946 when, in terms of Richard's constitution, the two protectorates were brought under the same legislative authority.[61]

As a result of the inefficiency of the British administrative staff, inadequate funding, fear of local resistance, and a lack of knowledge of, and familiarity with the local conditions, customs and traditions of the local peoples, Lugard introduced a system of "indirect rule." Lugard's motivation in instituting this system of indirect rule also stemmed from the successful implementation of the system in both Burma and Northern Protectorate of Nigeria which already had an effective administrative network in place. Indirect rule is a system of

---

60. Ohwofasa, *Democracy and Issues*, 14.
61. Ohwofasa.

British colonial "rule through the native Chiefs or traditional authorities who are regarded as an integral part of the machinery of government, with well-defined powers and functions recognized by the Government and by law, and not dependent on the caprice of an executive officer."[62] The main implication of this policy was that the administration or leadership of the indigenous people was, at the outset, the exclusive preserve of the traditional rulers. However, this policy meant that the Western, educated elements of southern origin were alienated from the political processes. "This alienation aroused the hostility of the nationalists, again, particularly in the South, not only towards the traditional rulers but also towards the native administration."[63] The policy of indirect rule succeeded in the north as a result of the existence of a highly centralized administrative structure and tax system, the inclusion of the emirs and the retention of their powers in the political system, the presence of few educated persons and the use of religious justification for authority and obedience, but the system failed in Yoruba and Igboland. In the west or Yorubaland, a number of factors contributed to this failure, namely, a noncentralized system of administration, limited power and restricted public appearances on the part of the Oba and the rise in the number of the Western, educated elite who queried the system and clamoured for independence. In Igboland, the failure was attributed to the absence of a centralized political structure, a negative perception of the system of indirect rule, the absence of a tax system, alienation of the elite from the leadership, the extremely limited power and jurisdiction of the traditional rulers and the corruption of the warrant chiefs.

The introduction of the policy of indirect rule was not well intended by the colonial government and, thus, it did not help in the development of competent leadership in Nigeria. Fanon's evaluation of colonialism is extremely informative: "By its very nature, colonialism is separatist. It does not simply state the existence of tribes, it also reinforces it and separates them."[64]. Ndoh has discussed the consequences of the policy of indirect rule: in some instances, "it led to excessive concentration of powers on the traditional rulers which made most of them dictatorial. The Chiefs and the Native Authorities

---

62. Ndoh, "Pre-Colonial Political Institutions," 42.
63. Ndoh, 45.
64. Fanon, *Wretched of the Earth*, 233.

were supported by the British and the masses were relatively neglected. The system alienated the educated elites in the society."[65] This system of rule created disunity and discord between the local chiefs and the new breed of educated elites in the society. The educated elites had embraced democratic ideas from the West and were anxious to put them into practice but were not given opportunity to do so. There was corruption among some of the chiefs and the system was inconsistent. In some cases, direct form of administration was applied and in others, it was indirect rule. The system made the traditional rulers stooges of the colonial masters.

It may therefore be deduced that the colonial era did little to develop the leadership potential of Nigerians as regards the realization of the leadership concepts and styles that would have laid a strong foundation for the leadership of the nation. Consequently, there was no platform on which the sociopolitical, economic and cultural spheres of the Nigerian nation could be supported. The question, thus, arises as to how did this leadership setback and the dislocation of the sociopolitical and cultural structures affect the postcolonial and military eras.

3.7 Leadership in Postcolonial (Independent) Nigeria

Anticolonialism may be said to have arisen as soon as the indigenous people realized that the European presence posed a threat to their social, political and economic security. Initially, the anticolonial move was economically motivated. The Brass Palm Oil Middlemen opposition against Western traders' attempts to sideline them and the Abeokuta and Aba riots of 1895, 1918 and 1929 which were as a result of taxes were the first of the nationalist moves that were geared towards ending European domination.[66] The discontent nursed by the Yoruba and Igbo elite as a result of the policy of indirect rule which had, initially, sidelined the elite from the political processes soon gave rise to a more vigorous and politically motivated nationalism. It should be noted that the 1922 Clifford constitution's elective principle paved the way for the formation of the Nigerian National Democratic Party (NNDP) in 1923 with

---

65. Ndoh, "Colonial System of Administration," 49–50.
66. Ndoh and Njoku, "Nigerian Nationalism in Nigeria," 51–52.

this party providing an opportunity for Nigerians to participate actively in the political process. It was this participation in administrative responsibilities that boosted the nationalistic consciousness of Nigerians. The NNDP was Lagos-based and had a support base which comprised scholars, chiefs, traders and other professionals. In 1934, the Lagos Youth Movement, which later became the Nigerian Youth Movement (NYM), was formed. It counted among its members some of the renowned nationalists, including Ernest Ikoli, H. O. Davies and Nnamdi Azikiwe (he joined the Movement in 1937). Within this period there were quite a number of associations with political, economic and ethnic undertones that flourished across the country. However, despite the fact that these associations were helpful during the struggle for independence, soon after independence they were used to intensify the tribal and ethnic divisions that had been set in motion by the colonial policy of divide and rule. Soon after independence from British colonial rule, these ethnic interests would engender animosity among the major tribal groups that comprised Nigeria.

Nigeria was granted independence on 1 October 1960. The country was to operate under a constitution that provided for a parliamentary system of government with a significant measure of self-government for the three regions of the country. "However, the political parties had a propensity to reflect the outlook and temperament of the three major ethnic groups, namely, the Hausa/Fulani, Yoruba and Igbo. In 1963, Nigeria became a Federal Republic with Dr. Nnamdi Azikiwe as the President."[67] Unfortunately, "Nigeria inherited a weak sociopolitical structure, a defective and unbalanced federation, an intensification of ethnic consciousness and rivalries, a subverted indigenous ethos of government and culture and, above all, an inexperienced leadership."[68] Thus, the politicization of ethnicity in Nigerian politics which had been engineered by the colonial leadership was given impetus by the nascent and inexperienced leadership of Nigeria by Nigerians. Inevitably, this led to an extremely vicious and combative struggle for the control of the federal government. "Elections were rigged in the most blatant fashion; census figures were manipulated to give political advantage to the competing regions; violence, corruption, arson and brigandage were employed in the mad desire

---

67. Ndoh and Njoku, 51–52.
68. Emezi, "Ethnic Foundations," 21.

to win or retain power both in the regions and at the centre."[69] Naturally, the backward, underdeveloped, parasitic and corruption-ridden economy inherited from the British fared very badly and dashed all hopes of meaningful development. These developments were all a reflection of the weak foundation on which the nation's leadership and national existence rested and it was these unhealthy developments that gave rise to the 15 January 1966 coup as well as the chain of upheavals that eventually led to the Nigerian civil war of 1967–70. It is estimated that one hundred thousand soldiers and one million civilians lost their lives in the civil war.

It may be said that the failure of the colonial leaders to respect the peculiarities of the peoples and their traditional divisions and cultures led these divergent groups being both forced together and, at the same time, divided in order to satisfy the selfish desires of the colonialists. Thus, to an extent, the failure of leadership in the colonial period laid the foundation for the failure of leadership in the postcolonial era while, inadvertently, the unbroken chain of leadership failure has taken an immense toll on the socioeconomic, political and cultural life of both the Nigerian people and also future generations of Nigerians.

3.8 Leadership during the Military Era

The emergence of the military on the Nigerian political stage on 15 January 1966 and their remaining there until 1999, despite some interludes of civil rule, introduced some positive, but numerous negative factors into political life in Nigeria. It is not the intention of this study to furnish a detailed account of the proceedings of the military rulers in Nigerian politics as the main concern of the study is to provide a concise account of the kind of leadership offered by these military rulers and the way in which their leadership impacted on issues such as poverty, underdevelopment and corruption. The discussion will naturally lead to a conclusion as to whether that leadership was either good or bad. Ohwofasa has summarized the reasons for the incursion of the Nigerian military into Nigerian political governance as follows: "Struggle for political power by the politicians, economic problems due to widening class distinction, modernized Army – vibrant, ambitious military

---

69. Emezi, 22–23.

officers not satisfied with the traditional constitutional roles of the military, political instability arising from disputed elections and disagreements over census figures."[70]

Political commentators agree that all the successive military governments that came to power through coups provided a litany of reasons to justify their reasons for taking over the government in Nigeria and the issues and the sentiments that they kept raising became familiar verses and refrains. For example, five years into independence, the first coup was staged with the following words that were intended to rally the support of all Nigerians: "Our enemies are the political profiteers, the swindlers, the men in high and low places that seek bribes and demand 10 percent; those that seek to keep the country divided permanently so that they can remain in office as ministers or VIPs at least."[71] The military toppled the civilian administration and tagged them tribalists, nepotists, and those that make the country look big for nothing before international circles.

Admittedly, these words of Major Kaduna Nzeogu and the passion behind them did make reference to the issues at stake but it is doubtful if this same passion characterized the intentions of the successive military coups that followed that first coup. Unfortunately, the first attempt of the military to rectify the sociopolitical and economic ills of Nigerian society were not realized as that group of officers was ousted shortly after they had taken over. The coup failed. However, other military leaders such as J. T. U. Aguiyi-Ironsi, Yakubu Gowon, Murtala Mohammed, Olusegun Obasanjo, Mohammadu Buhari, Ibrahim Babangida, Sani Abacha and Abdulsalami Abubakar then entered the Nigerian political arena and the achievements of the military included the unifying of the country after the civil war; the creation of states; the establishment of National Youth Service Corps; local government reforms and the Nigerian Enterprises Indigenization Policy Promotion.

It is worth noting that both civilian and military rule all represent institutions manned by human beings and, thus, they are all prone to mistakes and bad policies. Nwalimu Julius Nyerere had well observed when he said there is nothing "inherently sacred about civilian governments and there is nothing inherently evil about military governments. Some of the most corrupt

---

70. Ohwofasa, *Democracy and Issues*, 61.
71. Ohwofasa, 61.

regimes in Africa are, or have been headed by civilians. We must not take an over-simplified or automatic view about the merits or demerits of civilian and military governments in Africa."[72] Nevertheless, it is not easy, particularly in the Nigerian context, to dismiss the popular saying, namely that "the best military government is worse than the worst civilian rule or that the worst civilian government is better than the best military government."[73]

Thus, the Nigerian military in terms of the issue of leadership, scores low. Included in the issues held against the military are the impoverishment of the citizenry; the display of dictatorship and despotism, fraudulent practices and the embezzlement of public funds. There is no doubt that there was an escalation in the level of poverty, corruption, oppression and bad leadership at all levels of Nigerian society during the years of military rule in the country. The obvious question then arises as to whether the eleven years of civil rule have offered any solutions to the plight of Nigerians.

3.9 Leadership in Postmilitary (Democratic) Nigeria

Nigerian politicians have controlled the instruments of governance for eleven, uninterrupted years – 1999 to 2010. This is the first time in the history of Nigeria that political power has been transmitted from one democratically elected political administration to another via the electoral process. It is mainly for this reason that political analysts are referring to the current chapter of Nigerian history as "postmilitary" or "democratic" Nigeria. This period has witnessed political governance under the leadership of three presidents who emerged via the political processes. These presidents include Chief Olusegun Obasanjo (1999–2007); Alhaji Umaru Musa Yar'Adua (2007–10) and Dr. Goodluck Ebele Jonathan (2010–11). Of these three leaders, Obasanjo ruled for eight years while Yar'Adua's presidency lasted two years only as a result of ill health and his eventual death. Jonathan, who was vice-president under Yar'Adua, took over from Yar'Adua on 6 May 2010 and has been in power for some months, at the time of conducting this study. It is, thus, worth noting that much of the assessment of the current democratic Nigeria will be based

---

72. Ndoh, 28.
73. Ohwofasa, *Democracy and Issues*, 97.

on Obasanjo's tenure in office while there will also be reference made to the short term of Yar'Adua.

Chief Obasanjo's rise to democratic political power was at the behest of the military hegemony as Obasanjo was a retired military general. He won the 1999 and 2003 presidential elections under the flag of the Peoples' Democratic Party (PDP) amidst stiff opposition to his pseudo-military rule. In the course of his eight years of leadership, he was severely criticized by civil society groups, trade unions and other political parties. Seteolu's assessment of Obasanjo's political leadership is worth noting: "He was perceived as intolerant, arrogant, combative, bellicose, cantankerous and pedantic. This leadership style is linked to his military background and orientation, personal attributes and demeanour."[74] This description of Obasanjo's leadership style, which is informed by his character traits and professional influence, provides an insight into the influence which has now taken hold of the Nigerian political class, with this influence pervading the political landscape from local to federal government. It is common knowledge among the politicians that, when appointed as political officers, appointees are made to sign their letters of resignation, which are then kept in the custody of the chief executive (governor or president). This exercize is aimed at extracting absolute loyalty from the appointees and also at facilitating their easy removal from office at any time the political leader so wishes.

However, aside from the character traits of democratic Nigeria's political class, as exemplified in the chief leader, a further score card has also been presented. Obasanjo's "rulership is critically perceived for national insecurity, rising inflation, collapse of local businesses, growing human poverty, homelessness and despondency, epileptic, unreliable and inefficient social facilities, over bloated bureaucracy, and half heart struggle against corruption."[75] Nevertheless, Obasanjo did register some positive achievements while in power, including the professionalization of the military, an anti-graft crusade and the establishment of a functional Mobile Telecommunication Sector. As regards the leadership of Yar'Adua, he is best remembered for the slow pace of policy formulation and it is this slow pace of governance that earned him the name "Mr. Go Slow." He was rated as humble but lacking the will and drive

---

74. Seteolu, "Challenge of Leadership," 73.
75. Seteolu, 73.

to direct the affairs of governance although the poor state of his health may have exacted a heavy toll on his ability to take responsibility as the president of the nation. However, the bank reforms and his ability to negotiate the amnesty deal with the restive militants of the Niger Delta were all lauded by both Nigerians and the international community.

A key function of political leadership is the formulation of policy for the purpose of delivering the benefits of governance to the citizenry. It is gravely in doubt whether the political class in the postmilitary period has shown a responsible commitment to dealing with the challenges of poverty, underdevelopment, corruption and irresponsible leadership. Many Nigerians are also of the opinion that the political hegemony is still trailing in the steps of the politicians who came to power soon after independence in 1960. There is a widespread belief that the politicians are in politics for their own personal gain. It may, therefore, be argued that their fatalistic tendencies and lack of imagination in their policymaking provide clear proof of their political incompetence in running the intricate affairs of goverment. According to Ukaegbu, the political leaders in Nigeria are plagued with leadership fatalism and a lack of imagination in policymaking with these tendencies playing out in a number of areas.[76]

Such policies including the federal character are the result of a lack of imagination in policymaking as well as helplessness (fatalism) on the part of political leaders when they are under pressure and it would appear that they lack the courage to deal with ethnic pressures. The federal character policy is perpetuating mediocrity in place of excellence. In addition, the choice to import petroleum products instead of ensuring that the refineries work to capacity is highly questionable as regards the intentions of political leaders while the issue of poor infrastructure – hospitals, electricity and schools – relates to leadership incompetence. Many Nigerian leaders and their family members obtain medical services and education in foreign medical and educational institutions at an exorbitant cost. Why do the medical and educational institutions in Nigeria not function properly? Why are privately owned establishments such as schools doing extremely well but not those of the governments? Why are the roads in the country not constructed by

---

76. Ukaegbu, "Leadership Fatalism."

Nigerian engineers? Why do Nigerians have to import toothpicks? Why does almost every Nigerian home run a power generator for electricity?

There is no such thing as political ideology in Nigerian partisan politics. Nigerian politicians are not elected to positions by the power of the ballot but by the power of violence and election rigging. Political patronage and money politics (money in exchange for votes) still reign supreme in Nigerian politics. The political arena is still extremely limited as a result of the absence of formidable opposition which would act as a counterbalance to the ruling party. Until recently, in instances in which bold steps were taken to overturn illegitimate election results in courts of law, the legal system proved to be nothing more than an appendage of the executive arm of government. The legislature is also at the mercy of the executive arm of government. It is still hoped that, in the postmilitary or democratic era, the vestiges of those authoritarian and despotic regimes that were commonplace in the precolonial, colonial and military eras will be replaced by a robust and vibrant democratic political process. However, in addition to the contributions of the various historical eras to the culture of leadership in Nigeria, it is essential not to overlook both the positive and negative effects of globalization.

3.9.1 The Influence of Globalization

There is no single definition of the term globalization. However, globalization has to do with the "increasingly interconnected character of political, economic and social life of the peoples on this planet."[77] Shedding more light on the concept, Herbert Anderson notes that "globalization is a worldwide social phenomena in which things are fragmenting or splintering and reluctantly coming together simultaneously. On the one hand, there are new borders emerging daily in nations and multinational corporations because of parochial concerns within, while on the other hand universalizing forces from without make borders more porous and particularly more difficult to maintain."[78] Information technology is also playing a vital role in continuously expanding the influence of globalization.

The influence of globalization on all societies is inescapable and globalization has impacted Nigerian and other African communities, both positively

---

77. Schreiter, *New Catholicity*, 5.
78. Anderson, "Seeing the Other Whole," 7.

and negatively. An important example of the negative impact of globalization has been the extinction of the cherished traditional practice of moulding leaders around the fire. Masango has pointed out that "Africans had a very helpful model of moulding leaders around the fire. Young boys would listen in the evening to powerful stories of brave men at war and, as they listened, they developed leadership skills."[79] The main point of Masango's observation is that the practice of leadership development around the fire, which used to be part of the traditional Nigerian societies, has now been replaced by the television. Unfortunately, however, television does not mould people in the same way as a result of the content, values and culture that television programmes tend to propagate. In addition, besides the content of the television programmes, the dialogue and exchange of ideas that were crucial in the discussions around the fire are completely absent. Also, in today's world of the "haves" and the "have-nots," globalization is being used by the leaders of the powerful nations to co-opt and control the leaders of the weak nations of which many nations of Africa, including Nigeria, constitute the bulk. Chipenda argues that African countries are already threatened with cleavages: "The haves" on the one side, and "the have-nots,"[80] on the other; those who control political and economic machinery as opposed to those who are marginalized; those who can speak and others who are silent; those who work for transformation of their societies and others who keep the status quo, and; those who are well-informed and others who are ill-informed.

However, Nigeria and other African countries have also benefited from the positive aspects of globalization. Nigerian and African leaders are being afforded opportunities to relate to and connect with good leaders from other parts of the world who have also supported them in their times of crisis, for example in times of epidemics, war and natural disasters. Despotic leaders in Nigeria and other Africa countries have been pressurized by other world leaders to respect the voices of their own people while the creation of the global village through advanced technology has contributed immensely to the timely circulation of information. This, in turn, has enabled rapid and helpful interventions in African challenges by fellow African and other world leaders. It has also become easier to expose the activities of poor leaders whereas,

---

79. Masango, "Leadership in African Context," 316.
80. Chipenda, "Culture and Gospel," 23.

in the past, corrupt African leaders were able to continue with their unjust regimes without undue international pressure. However, there are also the increasing negative effects of economic globalization with TNCs and other global institutions maintaining their control over the Nigerian economy to their advantage and, thus, contributing to the economic woes of Nigeria. In addition, globalization has accelerated the spread of Islamic fundamentalism through the global communication system, such as the internet and mobile telephones. The activities of these fundamentalists have introduced into Nigerian society a dimension of violence – bomb blasts – which are alien to the society. Besides causing large scale destruction of human life and property, these happenings perpetuate a sense of insecurity that is both inimical to social-economic and political developments. It is in this study's view that effective leadership could make the desire for sociopolitical and economic development a reality within the Nigerian context.

3.10 The Importance of Leadership in Development and Social Transformation

Achebe has asserted that "the trouble with Nigeria is simply and squarely a failure of leadership."[81] Unlike Achebe, Odunsi attributes only a part of the blame for the troubles Nigerians are facing to its leaders when he opines that "the pervasive political wrangling, civil strife, economic disorder and social malaise endemic in Nigeria today flow, in part, from ineffective leadership."[82] However, all of these writers do agree that the ineffective leadership in Nigeria is problematic to its citizens. By pinpointing the appalling challenges facing Nigerians as a result of poverty, underdevelopment, corruption and bad leadership to the absence of responsible leadership, it may be possible to locate the source of the crisis and the means by which the crisis may be overcome. However, would pinpointing the challenges facing Nigerians as predominantly proceeding from poor leadership not amount to an oversimplification of the problems? Would it not demand too much from mere mortals? This study suggests that there are at least two ways in which both questions may be answered. One way would be to trace the historical antecedents of Nigeria,

---

81. Achebe, *Trouble with Nigeria*, 1.
82. Odunsi, "Impact of Leadership Instability," 66.

from precolonial times to present day Nigerian society while another way would be to explore the way in which political leadership influences development and social transformation. This study has addressed the former and will now focus on the latter.

Lanre-Abass has argued that leadership has to do with "the guidance of a group, party, or political entity undertaken by an individual."[83] In explaining his two views of leadership he argues, first, that leaders, by virtue of their inspiration or charisma, offer their followers a vision that functions as a map to new and uncharted regions. The second view of a leader is that the leader discerns, through a peculiar talent for development and sensitive listening, from the followers' discordant debating, or even from their pregnant silences, the vision implicit in what they are or even desire. Accordingly, a leader should have the capacity to navigate between the good and the just, and between wisdom and consent. At the same time, he should also be able to be flexible and principled. Ukaegbu posits that leaders innovate, focus on people, develop and inspire trust, have a long-term perspective, show originality and challenge the status quo. Leaders guide, direct, motivate, influence and make choices that enable their followers to contribute to the success or positive transformation of the entity they lead, namely, the Nigerian political economy. It would be expedient in our discussion to align these qualities of leadership with the concepts of transformational and adaptive leadership which, in this study's view, holds promise for both the church in Nigeria and Nigerian society as we seek to highlight the importance of leadership in development and social transformation. The transformational leader is imbued with charisma, inspiration, intellectual stimulation, vision and sense of mission; instils pride, and; attracts respect and trust. As I have argued in section 3.3.1 and 3.3.4, the transformational leader is concerned about progress and development. He/she transforms the personal values of his/her followers to support the vision and goals of the organization by cultivating an environment in which relationships may be built and by establishing an atmosphere of trust and vision sharing. Also, the adaptive leader mobilizes people to tackle tough challenges and thrive. This kind of leader does not give false hope to the people as a saviour who solves problems for people, but as one who plays the role of assisting people who need to confront tough

---

83. Lanre-Abass, "Crisis of Leadership," 117.

problems. It is this type of leadership that would enable the church and leaders in Nigeria to mobilize their respective constituencies and beyond in order to realize the goals of Nigerian development. Thus, the role of leadership in social transformation is indispensable and merits further explanation.

It is political leadership that has the responsibility to make decisions on public policy and resource allocation through partisan representatives, and it is at this level that the challenges of poverty, underdevelopment, corruption and other forms of injustice may be adequately addressed through imaginative policymaking. In Nigeria, the state occupies the centre stage at all levels of political, social and economic life and it is for this reason that traditional leaders, traders, teachers, contractors and farmers etc. patronize the state. In addition, leadership shapes the beliefs, behaviour and conduct of the followers through the conscious and unconscious allocation of values. Nigerian society today has lost the confidence in most of its leaders because of their moral ineptitude, incivility and ethnocentricity. However, it will still require leadership to restore character, civility and the integration of the diverse ethnic groups and interests into a single community which would command the respect and loyalty of all. Furthermore, the role of the leader in Nigeria goes beyond the allocation of values and includes serving as a political socialization model for the followers or citizens. The leader exerts influence on his/her followers and is often imitated, consciously and unconsciously, by them. It is for these reasons that many scholars agree that the long-awaited development and social transformation of Nigerian society is attainable only through responsible leadership and, in my opinion, transformational and adaptive leadership.

3.11 Conclusion

Thus far, the definition of leadership in this study has revealed that leadership has much to do with influence and that this influence may be either positive or negative. Also, leadership has to do with mobilising people and resources to solve tough problems. In our brief study of the concepts of leadership, we have noted that a leader may be termed either a servant leader or a transformational or adaptive leader depending on the degree to which the ideals of a particular concept of leadership are present in his/her style of leadership. The transformational and adaptive leadership concepts have been found to be in line with the approach this study intends to adopt. The discussions on leadership in precolonial, colonial, post-colonial, military and postmilitary (democratic) Nigeria revealed that each of these stages in Nigerian history have contributed negatively in a way which has perpetuated the challenge of poor leadership in the country. The importance of leadership as a facilitator of development and social transformation in Nigeria was also examined. The descriptive-empirical and interpretive theological approach as proposed by Osmer[84] provided the lens through which the Nigerian sociopolitical and economic context was viewed. The intention as enunciated at the beginning of the chapter was to understand the root cause(s) of the ongoing phenomenon of poor leadership in the country and the consequences of this poor leadership.

It is my opinion that it is possible to develop the capacity of Nigerians to mobilize and manage their own resources. However, such an endeavour should be informed by both a development orientation and a leadership style which has a transformative vision so as to bring about transformation that will be life sustaining, equitable and such that it will enhance the self-worth of Nigerians. Nevertheless, the leaders' efforts will be shortlived unless they intentionally pay close attention to the development of more of such leaders who will be able to take responsibility in the political, economic and sociocultural governance of Nigeria. The transformational and adaptive leader is a leader who is imbued with charisma, inspiration, intellectual stimulation, vision and a sense of mission and who is able to instil pride in his followers as well as gain their respect and trust. The transformational and adaptive leader's concern is progress and development. He/she transforms the personal values of his/her followers to support the vision and goals of the organization by cultivating an environment in which relationships may be built and by establishing an atmosphere of trust and vision sharing, and such that it can engender growth. He or she asks tough questions and supports the people to take on tough challenges. It is essential that the church leadership, which has the rare privilege of being both transformative and adaptable, be in the vanguard of such leadership mobilization, starting from its own leadership and membership.

Meanwhile, what contributions have church leaders made to transforming Nigerian society in the light of its many challenges? Or, in other words, how

---

84. Osmer, *Practical Theology*, 4–12.

are church leaders engaging in the social and theological issues in Nigeria? What could inform the church's leadership and membership as the bastion of character, civility, community and, ultimately, social transformation for the purpose of serving as a catalyst for the anticipated transformation of Nigerian society? The next chapter will focus on Nigerian church leaders' social and theological discourse.

CHAPTER 4

Social and Theological Analysis of Church Leadership Discourse in Postmilitary Nigeria

4.1 Introduction

In chapters 2 and 3, the focus was on those factors that had played a role in bringing about the enduring challenges of poverty, underdevelopment, corruption and poor leadership in Nigeria, and the consequences of these challenges for Nigeria from independence until now. It was argued that, although there is a possibility that Nigerian society may be transformed, the status quo has, in the main, not changed. The goal of this chapter is to appraize the involvement of the church (leaders/faithful) in Nigeria in the social and theological discourses within the Nigerian context using the descriptive-empirical and interpretive practical theological methodology, as discussed in section 1.8.1. The *descriptive-empirical* and *interpretive* tasks are engaged in this study in order to assist in the understanding of what is taking place in the Nigerian social context by focusing in this chapter on available literature, the religious and social praxis of church leaders and the happenings within the sociopolitical and economic realms in Nigeria.

Accordingly, and for the purpose of reiteration, the descriptive-empirical concern is to paint a picture of what is going on whilst the interpretive task of practical theology seeks to place such findings or picture "within an interpretive framework . . . and to provide an answer to the question: Why are these things going on?"[1] This chapter therefore hopes to answer the following question: Given the extensive population of the church and the church's rich resources, have church leaders utilized these resources to address the material/physical, psychological and spiritual challenges facing Nigerians and, if so, in what way? In order to answer this question, this chapter will be divided into three parts. The first part will discuss the public role of the church while the second part will deal with the social discourse of church leaders. The third part of the chapter will discuss some of the matters arising from the theological discussions of Nigerian church leaders. This study intends to explore the contributions Nigerian church leaders could make to the political, economic and social transformation of Nigerian society in the light of the current challenges of poverty, underdevelopment, corruption and poor leadership. However, in order to realize the aim of the study, it has now become necessary to understand what outcomes are arising through the engagement of the church so as to come to some understanding of what remains to be done if the church is to be a relevant and efficient agent of change, alongside other change agents within the Nigerian context. The discussion on the social analysis of the discourse of church leaders will commence by indicating the public role of the church and its leaders.

4.2 The Public Role of the Church

There are divergent views, both for and against, the engagement of the church or/and its leaders in sociopolitical and economic issues in theological discourses. S. L. S. Salifu, a former secretary of the Christian Association of Nigeria (CAN), has summarized these views into two major groups, namely, the "participatory and the non-participatory schools."[2] He maintains that the nonparticipatory school argues against the participation of the church and its leaders in sociopolitical and economic issues. This argument is based on four premises. First, there is the premise of two kingdoms – church and state – and it is not possible to be loyal to one without being disloyal to the other. Second, there is the great commission (evangelization) which should engage the energies of all believers, and engaging with the state may constitute

---

1. Osmer, *Practical Theology*, 4–12.
2. Salifu, "Christian and Nation Building," 189.

a distraction from this primary commission. Third, there is the notion of politics as a "dirty game" and, thus, participation in this "dirty game" could soil the believer through compromise, corruption and unprincipled behaviour. Fourth, there is the belief in the imminent return of Christ who will then rectify all social problems. The church should, thus, wait until Christ returns.

In contrast to the nonparticipatory stance, the participatory school focuses on the call to believers to be salt and light in the world, the spiritual and material or social ministry of Jesus while on earth, the comprehensive nature of Christian ethics, and God's care and ongoing involvement in his creation.[3] Very importantly, C. T. Kurien, a renowned evangelical and ecumenical development scholar and practitioner, has noted in another context the invaluable contributions churches through the leadership are making in identifying with the challenges of the people in their contexts. According to Kurien, "it must be noted that the church's involvement in the discussion on the practical problems of our times, whether it is development or the environmental crisis, has an indirect but significant impact on itself"[4] but also on the society. This study affirms the participatory view and will, therefore, elaborate on its position below.

In his book, *Christian Leadership: A Challenge to the African Church*, Ngara urges Christian leaders to move beyond the confines of the church into the wider public domain in order to bring about the desired impact that may transform society. He argues that the church may promote good leadership in society effectively only if it is able to exemplify a vibrant culture of leadership within its ranks in accordance with a pattern that mirrors the leadership style and qualities as epitomized by the Lord Jesus.[5] Ngara's work may be seen as a bold step in the direction of addressing the perennial challenge of poor leadership on the African continent. He makes an extremely strong case for attributing the major problems of African countries to bad leadership and to the failure of the church to exert a stronger influence in the public arena.

Dennis Jacobson clearly depicts a crucial reason why it is essential that church leaders should fulfil a public role when he poses his vital question,

---

3. Salifu.
4. Kurien, *Poverty and Development*, 14.
5. Ngara, *Christian Leadership*.

"Who takes the local church into the public arena if not the pastor?"[6] Jacobson is of the conviction that if the pastoral church leadership of the local church is resistant to a public arena ministry, even the best-intentioned laity will be blocked or deflated in their efforts to engage their congregation in public arena issues. The ambivalence, reluctance or disdain of most clergy towards the public arena keeps most churches in the sanctuary.[7]

It may be deduced from Jacobson's argument that the engagement of the church – in its various forms – in the public arena is possible only through a development-oriented church leadership with the church being sent into the public arena on the ethical imperatives of its Lord Jesus Christ, because the public arena is God's arena. Indeed, it is in the public arena where the victims of poverty and other forms of injustice are to be found. The faithful come from the public arena to the sanctuary of the church and it is from this sanctuary that they return to the public arena. Thus, should the church fail in the public arena by remaining passive in the face of the challenges of the faithful in that arena, it will, without any doubt, also fail within the confines of the sanctuary. Accordingly, the pastor and other church leaders who lead in the sanctuary must also lead the flock wherever they go. However, in addition to leading the flock, the church leaders would do well to develop the leadership capacity of their followers for the purpose of effective service within both the church and in society at large.

Ruwa, writing from a Kenyan Roman Catholic background, also joins the discourse on the church's involvement in the public domain. In line with a consciousness of socioeconomic and political transformation, he narrates the story of the Catholic Church's campaign against social injustice in Kenya and argues that "the church, which is the "body of Christ" as hierarchy (leadership) and faithful, has a responsibility to participate in all aspects of a nation's life, be it social, economic, political or otherwise. This is a divine responsibility."[8]

Both Mary Slessor, a young female missionary from Dundee who worked in the hinterlands of Nigeria, and Akanu Ibiam from Unwana – a village in southeastern Nigeria – are outstanding examples of development-oriented

---

6. Jacobson, *Doing Justice*, 15–16.
7. Jacobson.
8. Ruwa, *Principles of Good Governance*, 5.

church leaders. Although she retained some vestiges of colonialism, Miss Slessor demonstrated, deep in the remote areas of Nigeria, an example of the overwhelming benefits provided by a church leader in the public domain. J. H. Proctor relates the story concisely: By discouraging certain traditional practices (such as killing twins at birth, administering the "poison-ordeal" to determine the guilt or innocence of persons suspected of causing another's death, and offering human sacrifices at the funerals of notables) and by settling disputes between individuals and between groups, she contributed significantly to the reduction of disorder and violence. Barely two years after she had set up her station in the area occupied by the reportedly fierce Okoyong people where no government agents had yet established themselves, she claimed that "the influence of our presence has been very marked in the saving of life, and in the laying aside of arms."[9]

Narrating the story of the virtuous Akanu Ibiam – church/community leader, missionary doctor and reputable politician – Anya states that "the late Dr. Akanu Ibiam was the most outstanding and best known of this class of selfless Christian patriots of Nigeria."[10] As a church leader Ibiam made immense contributions to Nigerian society through education, medical practice, community leadership and politics while bringing his Christian virtues to bear as he served in the public domain.

4.3 Social Analysis of Church Leadership Discourse
4.3.1 Setting the Stage

The social discourse of Nigerian church leaders may be said to have been initiated by the missionaries from the inception of Christianity in Nigeria. However, these efforts, which were carried out mainly within the ambit of charity and other projects, did not achieve any notable progress beyond these confines. It may be recalled that, in pursuit of the social vision, those missionaries, who were the church leaders, "established institutions such as schools, hospitals, courts and a printing press as well as initiating social activities such as sport (football, cricket) in Nigerian society."[11] Many of these

---

9. Proctor, "Serving God and the Empire," 48.
10. Anya, "Foreword," ii.
11. Aye, "Foundations of Presbyterianism," 168, 170.

missionaries worked closely with the colonial administration and, in some instances, played dual roles as both missionaries and administrators. Much of these activities within the missionary era were both denominationally and missionary driven within the societies in which such missionary activities were carried out. A typical example is that of Mary Slessor of the Church of Scotland Mission (Presbyterian) who worked in various capacities with several colonial officers, including Sir Claude Macdonald, the high commissioner and consul general of the Niger Coast Protectorate.[12]

These activities brought some benefits to Nigerian society in that they produced both the elite who played a significant role in the struggle for independence and also certain outstanding leaders who played a role in the various sectors of national life. In addition, these activities also led to the sustenance of "community healthcare, destigmatization (lepers who had been healed), the eradication of certain inhumane practices such as the killing of twin babies, trials by ordeal and a measure of economic empowerment."[13]

However, despite these benefits, the pattern of Christianity that had taken root in Nigeria was dualistic; it separated the sacred and the secular, and the Christian view of political, economic and social issues was jaundiced, with grave consequences.[14] Okonkwo has also decried the "passivity of Christians in Nigeria to the affairs of their Nation and, indeed, their political environment,"[15] a passivity which he attributes to the "long processed indoctrination that has placed Christians as mere heads yet with the tail focus." It follows thus, that the engagement of both the church and church leaders in social issues was characterized by a conversionist approach.[16] The generation of church leaders who came after the missionary era did not have a development orientation beyond the propagation of the gospel and the provision of education, medical services and empowerment projects within their immediate communities, with very few exceptions. As such, unlike those church leaders (missionaries) who worked in close collaboration with the government in political, judicial and public policy issues, emergent indigenous church leaders were not able

---

12. Proctor, "Serving God and the Empire."
13. Ogarekpe, "Liberty to the Captives," 223.
14. Musa, *Christians in Politics*.
15. Okonkwo, *Expectation 2003*, 1.
16. Agha, "Unto These Little Ones," 250.

to follow suit for reasons such as the missionaries' disinclination to engage the locals in secular issues and also poor training.[17] Several social issues, including politics, were termed worldly and unspiritual.[18] This attitude on the part of the majority of the church leaders inadvertently shaped the attitude of many church members who, although they constituted the bulk of the elite of the society, were not able effectively to synchronize their sociopolitical and economic responsibilities with their spirituality as a calling from God. Accordingly, the activities of the church and its leaders were confined mainly to the church compound and to the immediate communities where the hospitals and schools were often located with church denominations, such as the Roman Catholic, Anglican, Presbyterian and Methodist churches, playing key roles in this regard in different parts of the country. However, despite the fact that the social engagement of the church and its leaders in this period contributed significantly to Nigerian society, it also identified the approach of church leaders to the socioeconomic and political challenges facing the people with regard to the church's traditional and historical categories of social engagement as in other places, namely, charity/relief and projects. The international bodies sending out the missionaries tended mainly to sponsor charitable activities and projects. However, this approach was paternalistic and created a significant degree of dependency on these foreign bodies and, thereby, produced a church leadership that was not able to respond adequately to the political, socioeconomic and theological challenges facing Nigerians.

The trend in the approach adopted by church leaders to the political and socioeconomic challenges in Nigeria, which had, until then, been restricted to the pulpit, church environment and immediate community and had taken the form of charity and projects, took on a new dimension when General Olusegun Obasanjo became the head of state. As the military head of state, Obasanjo invited some church leaders to Dodan Barracks, Lagos, for a parley, on 27 August 1976. These church leaders who had been invited to meet with the head of state were of diverse denominations. However, the government's sole aim in that meeting was to discuss both the introduction of the national pledge and the salutation of the national flag in the nation's primary and secondary schools. The church leaders agreed to the head of state's request

---

17. Aye, "Foundations of Presbyterianism."
18. Musa, *Christians in Politics*.

provided that the staff and the students of each school would be able to sing praises and offer prayers to God during the morning devotions before the national pledge and the salutation of the flag took place.[19] The government's collaboration with church leaders in this regard is understandable as many of the schools in the country had been established by the mission churches and, thus, government perceived the churches and their leaders as partners of government in the educational system. Had the church leadership made similar inroads in the political and economic spheres, then the influence of the church and its leadership in these areas would, naturally, have earned the church a place within the state and other arms of government. Thus, soon after the meeting with Obasanjo, the church leaders decided unanimously to hold another meeting at the Catholic Secretariat, not far from Dodan Barracks. It was at this meeting that the church leaders agreed to "form an organization which would provide a forum where they could regularly meet together and take joint actions on vital matters, especially on issues which affect the Christian Faith and the welfare of the generality of Nigerians."[20] This was the origin and the beginning of the Christian Association of Nigeria.

The emergence of the Christian Association of Nigeria (CAN), the largest ecumenical body in both Nigeria and Africa, also marked the emergence of what has now become the "most powerful Christian voice in Nigeria."[21] Despite the fact that the various church denominations in Nigeria, through their leaders and structures, engage in social issues in a variety of ways, CAN and its constituent blocs have become the most viable fronts through which church leaders address social issues in Nigeria. The constituents of CAN reflect a conglomeration of groups that include all the various denominational churches in Nigeria, from the national to the local government areas. These groups of churches which constitute CAN are also called blocs of CAN. They include the Catholic Secretariat of Nigeria (CSN), Christian Council of Nigeria (CCN), Christian Pentecostal Fellowship of Nigeria and Pentecostal Fellowship of Nigeria (CPFN/PFN), Organization of African Instituted Churches (OAIC), and Tarrarya Ekkelisiyar Kristi, a Nigeria

---

19. CAN, *Brief Story*, 1.
20. CAN, 1.
21. Mbachirin, "Review of JC Nwafor," 655.

and Evangelical Church of West Africa (TEKAN/ECWA).[22] Accordingly, in collaboration with CAN, Nigerian church leaders are now engaging in the Nigerian social discourse through organizations such as the African Forum on Religion and Government (AFREG), Forum for Righteousness in Governance (FRIG), Congress on Christian Ethics in Nigeria (COCEN) and Save Nigeria Group (SNG).

An assessment of the engagement of church leaders in the Nigerian social debate may, arguably, include such engagements under the following themes: charity and social services, dialogue, advocacy and collaboration.

4.3.2 Charity and Social Services

The most significant contribution of both the church and its leaders to Nigerian society, from the time of the missionaries to modern times, may be said to be in the area of charity and social services with the churches and church leaders having been consistent in this social approach through their denominations and ecumenical bodies. Charity and social services encompass "a substantial range of categories: education, health services, social welfare and some sort of economic development."[23] These charitable and social service activities were aimed at conversion, literacy, poverty alleviation and the improvement of the well-being of Nigerians. During and after the Nigerian civil war, church leaders and churches, with the support of the World Council of Churches (WCC) and overseas partner churches, were deeply involved in relief and reconstruction activities. These activities contributed immensely towards ameliorating the sufferings of both Christians and non-Christians throughout the country. At the beginning of 1969, relief distribution by the World Council of Churches was done in collaboration with the ecumenical church in Nigeria. Several thousand staff attempted to feed over five hundred thousand refugees and local residents. This was a formidable task as despite parallel efforts of Caritas (a Roman Catholic Church relief outfit) and the I.C.R.C., thousands died painfully from starvation or malnutrition. Through the auspices of Christian Council of Nigeria (CCN), now an ecumenical bloc of CAN, there was a stockpile of nearly 15,000 tons of food and 400 vehicles for the movement of relief supplies and personnel, and there were more

---

22. CAN, *Brief Story*.
23. Swart, *Churches and Development Debate*, 18.

than 1,000 relief workers already active. For more than eighteen months, the CCN supplied between 25 and 35 percent of all medical and relief personnel involved in the Red Cross relief program. This commitment of the church through its leaders and institutions during the civil war was very consistent with the response of the church to issues pertaining to health crisis whether it related to the missionaries or the indigenous people.[24]

In line with CAN's objectives, as enunciated in its official documents through the medium of its leaders and as an expression of its social concerns, CAN believes that its role as a watchdog of the spiritual and moral welfare of the nation must, of necessity, include every effort to ensure that all Nigerian citizens, especially the masses, enjoy reasonable and inexpensive healthcare. In this regard, CAN sponsored the founding of Christian Health Association of Nigeria (CHAN) whose membership, at the national level, comprises Catholic Bishops Conference of Nigeria, Christian Council of Nigeria and Northern Christian Advisory Council. CHAN is, thus, more or less derived from CAN and its "main purpose and objective is to encourage and develop the highest level of healthcare for the people of Nigeria within the framework of National Health policies."[25]

The pronouncements and actions of Nigerian church leaders on health issues for the benefit of Nigerians was further supported by the involvement of representatives of CAN in all the committees set up by the federal government to tackle the HIV and AIDS pandemic. It is, however, doubtful whether the "development of the highest level of health care for the people of Nigeria within the framework of National Health policies" is attainable in terms of both CHAN and CAN's memoranda to the federal government of Nigeria. In as much as the efforts of CAN are commendable, a stronger level of engagement with the government may be necessary if CAN truly wishes to deliver affordable and quality healthcare to the millions of Nigerians who are in a deplorable state of health with a few only managing to visit the ill- equipped and poorly maintained hospitals, should they even exist.

With the numerous and recurrent religious, ethnic and political crises and natural disasters that have afflicted Nigeria, the church leaders, through CAN, have also succeeded in playing key roles in the area of relief and social

---

24. Johnston, *Of God and Maxim*.
25. CAN, *Brief Story*, 11.

services. These services have usually been initiated by church leaders and have provided much needed succour in critical times when the Nigerian government has often been found wanting. Church leaders at the local levels usually provide food, shelter, clothing and medical care immediately while reaching out to the various levels of the ecumenical church organization for more support. It is often through such measures that Christians have contributed towards the rehabilitation of ordinary Nigerians who have suffered huge losses because of these crises.

From the inception of CAN in 1976, church leaders have used this channel to call upon the federal government of Nigeria to rise to the challenge of the falling standards in the Nigerian educational system, which is in a state of moral, spiritual and infrastructural decay. Such calls made to the federal government have also included pressure on the government to return to the church the church schools and hospitals that the government removed from the control of the church. Such efforts have "yielded some results as some state governments have returned such institutions back to the churches."[26] However, lofty though such moves may be, the monumental challenges facing the educational system in Nigeria today will need a multifaceted approach. This approach could include the return of schools to churches and the emergence of a political leadership with the foresight and the will to formulate and implement policies that may revamp the educational sector. In addition, a church leadership that is well informed about social change and the way in which such a change may come about would be invaluable to both the Christian community and to Nigerian society.

The initiatives of church leaders over time have led to laudable ventures such as the establishment of educational and medical/paramedical institutions, relief initiatives, vocational centres and other social services. These initiatives have, in turn, led to some measure of empowerment of the many poor and suffering Nigerians. However, one wonders if such measures are addressing the root causes of the challenges facing Nigerians, for example, poverty, underdevelopment, violence, corruption and poor leadership. Are church leaders and, to some extent, the churches not merely engaging in *ad hoc* measures that amount to a "merry go round" which will, eventually, lead to nowhere? Do church leaders and their members lack the resources

---

26. CAN, 12.

to deliver to Nigerians the much-needed social transformation beyond the scope of their current charity and social service initiatives? It is the author's view that church leaders do have the capacity to go beyond their current level of engagement and it would appear that Nigerian church leaders are making meaningful strides towards the transformation of Nigerian society through dialogue.

4.3.3 The Use of Dialogue as a Tool for National Cohesion

The WCC *Guidelines on Dialogue with People of Living Faiths and Ideologies* argues that "dialogue means witnessing to our deepest convictions, whilst listening to those of our neighbors."[27] C. A. Omonokhua argues that dialogue is "a conversation between two or more persons, especially of a formal or imaginary nature; an exchange of views in the hope of ultimately reaching agreement."[28] Lending his voice to the explanation of the concept of dialogue and its implications, John Onaiyekan, President of CAN, Catholic Archbishop of Abuja and co-chairman of the Nigerian Inter-religious Council (NIREC), asserts that "inter-religious dialogue is perhaps the best way to describe what we understand by management of our religious diversities."[29] The concept of dialogue is based on the assumption that the various religious practitioners can actually talk to one another and understand one another; that they can devise a common language to communicate with each other. It is also based on the conviction that religious practitioners have common grounds, despite the differences in the way they practise their religions and, sometimes, also the way the tenets of their faiths are formulated and proclaimed.

Thus, in their postulations and leanings on the concept of dialogue, the WCC, Onaiyekan and Omonokhua may be said to have covered all the religious and sociopolitical dimensions of the basic elements of dialogue.

The perennial challenge of Islamic fundamentalism in Nigeria, which has brought about colossal destruction of human lives and property worth billions of nairas across the country, has given impetus to the need for various forms of dialogue. It is to the credit of Nigerian church leaders, under the auspices of CAN, that the initiative to engage in dialogue with Islamic

---

27. World Council of Churches (WCC), *Guidelines on Dialogue*, 16.
28. Omonokhua, "Dialogue," 1.
29. Onaiyekan, "Dividends of Religion," 7.

leaders constitutes such a giant step towards the sociopolitical and economic development of Nigerian society. The fact that sociopolitical and economic life in Nigeria is significantly informed by religion and that, without the peaceful co-existence of the adherents of Christianity and Islam, there may be no meaningful development in Nigeria, underscores this point. However, it may be argued that, besides the challenge of Islam, the collaboration of churches of diverse doctrinal persuasions under the ecumenical auspices of CAN, inevitably, depends on the instrumentality of dialogue to maintain the bond of unity. In that sense, without dialogue, there could not have been the emergence of CAN. Dialogue is, therefore, one of the key factors that will ensure both the existence and the functionality of both CAN and of other collaborative measures within the Christian community and beyond. Dialogue may take various forms, including dialogue on life, "dialogue on social engagements, dialogue on theological engagement and inter-religious dialogue,"[30] with each of these forms of dialogue impinging on the social contributions of church leaders to Nigerian society. Each of these forms of dialogue will now be discussed.

4.3.3.1 Interreligious Dialogue

In pursuit of one of the objectives of CAN, namely, "to promote understanding, peace and unity among the various people and strata of society,"[31] church leaders in Nigeria, conscious of the presence of other religions in Nigeria such as Islam, have championed the establishment of NIREC and various other activities aimed at the enhancement of interreligious dialogue. It is in this light that one of the objectives of NIREC is "to create a permanent and sustainable channel of communication and interaction, thereby promoting dialogue between Christians and Muslims in Nigeria so that the members of both faiths may have mutual understanding of each other's religious position, co-existence among all the people of Nigeria, irrespective of their religious or ethnic affiliations."[32] In order to actualize dialogue in practical terms, opportunities for dialogue are being created through channels such as discussions, workshops, seminars, conferences and pamphleteering. Affirming the

---

30. Omonokhua, "Dialogue," 1.
31. CAN, *Constitution*, 2.
32. CAN, *Brief Story*, 15.

importance of dialogue and the vital contributions of church leaders under CAN towards interreligious dialogue, Alhaji Muhammad Sa'ad Abubakar[33] maintains that "undoubtedly, relations between neighbours represent the vital nexus in the web of relations that shape the character of the communities we live in. Most importantly, they play a vital role in building peace and promoting social harmony and mutual co-existence in the wider society."[34] Just as CAN has become the main Christian platform on which interreligious dialogue is carried out between representatives of the Christian faith and Islam and other faiths from the level of local government to that of the federal government, it is also essential that the Supreme Islamic Council and other religious bodies institute such structures in order both to broaden and to deepen dialogue. However, it may be possible that the current dialogue between the major religions in Nigeria is confined to some religious leaders only. Hence, if meaningful engagement and result oriented dialogue is to take place, the followers and leaders of the different religions will need to acknowledge, respect and celebrate the diversities of the various religions, both formally and informally. It is then, in the daily interactions of Nigerians in the marketplace, offices of government, Armed Forces and political parties and in the various circles of family, community, local government, state and the nation, that interreligious dialogue may become a normal way of life for Nigerians. The formal structures of dialogue, such as CAN and SCIA, provide a good starting place but the dialogue should move beyond to the grassroots as it is then that the social, political, ethnic and religious upheavals which the issue of religion is being used to fuel with its concomitant high toll on the economic and sociopolitical life of the country may be addressed. In this connection, church leaders have insisted on dialogue with other religious, traditional and political leaders as a way of overcoming the perennial challenge of violence in various parts of the country, including the Plateau State. In one such instance, Archbishop Ignatius Kaigama of Jos and Bishop Ayo-Maria Atoyebi of Illorin pleaded with political, traditional and religious leaders to "dialogue so that peace and unity can reign"[35] in the affected areas. In addition

---

33. Alhaji Muhammad Sa'ad Abubakar is the Sultan of Sokoto, leader of the Supreme Council for Islamic Affairs (SCIA) and co-chair of NIREC.

34. Abubakar, "You and Your Muslim Neighbour," 1.

35. "Nigerian Bishops Plead," 6.

to their plea for dialogue, these leaders had been able to pinpoint ethnicity as the cause of some of the violent eruptions in the nation. For example, the May 2004 outbreak of violence in the town of Yelwa in the Plateau State had been caused by ethnic sentiments which were, in turn, politically motivated. Unfortunately, the crisis ended up taking on religious dimensions.

In addition to the goal of national peace, which is vital for development in Nigeria, interreligious dialogue, through the collaboration of CAN and SCIA under the auspices of NIREC, is bringing benefits to the nation in the fight against both malaria and HIV and AIDS. Such joint actions are a strong indication of the significant contributions that religion could make to the well-being of all Nigerians and of the extensive common interest and constructive engagement that may be explored instead of riots, which lead to wanton destruction of lives and property. The unique concept of the NIREC and its sustained momentum would not have been possible without the ingenuity of, inter alia, Prelate Sunday Mbang, President Olusegun Obasanjo, Prof. Yusuf Obaje, Alhaji Ibrahim Maccido, Archbishop John Onaiyekan, other CAN, SCIA and federal government leaders.

In order to bolster the efforts of government and the CAN, SCIA and NIREC, and as a word of caution for Christians and the followers of other faiths who are opposed to interreligious dialogue, the warning of Bevans and Schroeder should not go unheard. According to them, dialogue with those of other religious ways (and, for that matter, with those who are not members of any religious group or who do not subscribe to any religious doctrine) is not a tactic that the church has been forced to take in order to "get along" in the aftermath of Western colonialism, the worldwide renaissance of the world's religions, or the spread of postmodern secularism. Nor is dialogue to be interpreted from these words to be a subtle tactic or strategy to proclaim the name and message of Jesus Christ to non-believers. "Dialogue is, of course, the only option in today's globalized and polycentric world; it does and must include a moment of proclamation – of each partner to the other."[36]

Bevan and Schroeder's position on interreligious dialogue was inspired by the encouraging and challenging words contained in the 1984 Roman Catholic document on dialogue and mission. The challenge and inspiration contained in their words should also challenge and inspire all persons of

---

36. Bevans and Schroeder, *Constants in Context*, 378.

good will to take on a new mindset that may provide impetus to sustainable dialogue aimed at the advancement of social transformation in all societies. Interreligious dialogue within the various religious persuasions, in particular, and the use of dialogue beyond these religious circles are vital to the general well-being of Nigerian society. One of such patterns of dialogue may be termed dialogue on social engagements.

4.3.3.2 Dialogue on Social Engagements

The critical need for dialogue on social engagement, with particular reference to the issues of ethnicity and culture, is closely linked to interreligious dialogue. This link between ethnicity, culture and religion is so close in Nigerian society that it is often difficult to separate these issues. The ethnic question has constituted a problem in Nigeria with Emezi arguing that "ethnicity is a powerful variable and issue in the Nigerian society."[37] Not only has ethnicity been used as a tool for injustice, oppression and corruption, but it has also been used to reinforce the ineptitude and mediocrity which characterises Nigerian society. Institutions such as the Federal Character Commission, political parties and the church's zoning systems reinforce the issue of ethnicity with Nigerians having experienced the scourge of ethnicity in the civil war. It is also common knowledge that ethnic forces are igniting the current crisis in both Plateau State and in other parts of the country. In all of these instances, the consequences have been both unbelievable and disheartening. The churches and their leaders are a vanguard for the eradication of ethnicity even though they are, in some instances, also guilty of playing the ethnic card. No matter how well intended, all manifestations that promote ethnicity spell doom for all Nigerians, including the secular benefactors of the country.

Nevertheless, it may be possible for both ethnicity and culture to serve as a resource for national development through the dialogue of social engagements with Ekpenyong, arguing that the more than 200 ethnic groups in Nigeria and the cultures they nurture "can constitute the stepping stones for human progress."[38] The opportunity for interaction between the various ethnic groups and cultures included in the regular members of the Christian community affords Nigerians a wonderful opportunity to learn about all the

---

37. Emezi, "Ethnic Foundations," 25.
38. Ekpenyong, *Beware of Gods*, 95.

ethnic groups and their cultures. However, it is also possible for dialogue to take place beyond the religious environment, for example, in the context of social and cultural events such as sport, musical events, marriage ceremonies, and economic activities etc.

The positive impacts of globalization and social networking have become a vital source of the dialogue of social engagements. The church and its leaders have served as instruments of social cohesion and should continue on this path. The challenge of meeting the other in the vast diversity of Nigerian society may be better facilitated when, in the course of engagement, "fellow Nigerian strangers" are approached with wonder, hospitality, recognition and reconciliation. "To make room for wonder we need to suspend judgment. Wonder presumes being in uncertainties without being irritated or needing to establish fact and reason."[39] This approach to the other requires that uncertainty and ambiguity be tolerated, while it also holds the potential to tame arrogance. Such an approach would, naturally, pave the way for the acceptance of each other as having equal worth. As regards hospitality, Anderson further suggests that when we offer hospitality to a stranger, we welcome something new, unfamiliar and unknown into our lives that has the potential to expand our world. Regard for strangers in their vulnerability and delight in their novel offerings presupposes that we perceive them as equals, as persons who share our common humanity in its myriad variations. Thus, it may be possible to eradicate from our society the antagonism and violence felt towards fellow Nigerians from different ethnic groups, cultures and religious beliefs by the practice of hospitality – a practice which is inherent in both African culture and in religious practices. The development of sensitivity towards and consciousness of the presence of the stranger and his/her cultural peculiarities are indispensable in the act of recognition. All Nigerians may admit to the fact that the various ethnic groups and religions have wronged each other at different times and that healing is possible only when Nigerians admit their wrongs, show remorse and make a concerted effort in word and deed to accept others and to live in mutual respect. This may be the sure way to true reconciliation. The role of church leaders, such as Matthew Hassan Kukah, in

---

39. Anderson, "Seeing the Other Whole," 10.

this regard has been of immense value in the dialogue of social engagement concerning the famous Oputa Panel.[40]

Interreligious and social engagement dialogues have served, and will continue to serve, the interest of Nigerians in their sociopolitical and economic development. However, there is also a third type of dialogue, which has also made a significant contribution, namely, theological dialogue.

4.3.3.3 Dialogue on Theological Engagement

It may be claimed that the belief systems of all religions and the dispositions of most of their adherents are shaped by the theological underpinnings of these religions which, in turn, inform their sociopolitical, economic, ecological and general human concerns. The crucial and privileged position of religion in African societies and, indeed, in Nigeria underscores the importance of theological dialogue within each religious community and also between the different religions. Omonokhua terms this type of dialogue the dialogue of experts. "This is where specialists come together to discuss theological issues to seek deeper understanding. This form of dialogue deals more with clarification of terms, understanding one another's view and respecting one another's convictions."[41] In such intercourse, terms such as *"peace and love"* as used by the various religions, may be understood and enriched for both a more meaningful co-existence and for service to the society. Such dialogue also holds the promise of lovingly taming fundamentalism and curbing excesses within the groups of a particular religion and beyond. Much of the religious excesses and fundamentalism, which pose such an immense challenge to the peace and development of Nigerian society, are known to emanate from the ignorance of some religious followers and the selfish manipulations on the part of these followers of certain politicians and religious leaders.

Onaiyekan has noted the need both to incorporate "the remnants of our African Traditional Religion (ATR)"[42] into the NIREC where suffi-

---

40. Justice Chukwudifu Oputa was the Chair of the Nigerian commission that was set up by Obasanjo's administration to look into some of the painful experiences of Nigerians for the purpose of calling the perpetrators to justice and bringing relief to the victims. It was hoped it would function as a truth and reconciliation commission. Kukah was the secretary of the commission which was also known as the Oputa Panel.

41. Omonokhua, "Dialogue," 3.

42. Onaiyekan, "Dividends of Religion," 16.

cient grounds for such inclusion have been established and to resuscitate the Nigerian Association for the Study of Religions (NASR) to work with NIREC. Situating this type of dialogue within the academic setting may give rise to creative exchanges while such endeavours may forge those strands of theologies that may be useful to the religious communities in addressing the current challenges of poverty, underdevelopment, corruption, poor leadership and violence among both the religious families and Nigerian society as a whole. It may, therefore, be argued that, in addition to development, understanding, respect, collaboration, peaceful co-existence and learning, dialogue is aimed at restoring and safeguarding the dignity of both human and other forms of life.

4.3.3.4 Dialogue on the Dignity of Creation

"The dignity of the human person is ultimate in every aspect of dialogue"[43] while that same important dignity is inseparable with the dignity of the extra-human life which co-exists with humankind on the same planet. It is a well-known fact that humankind and the rest of creation, without which it is not possible for humans to exist, are all experiencing severe degradation at an alarming rate. The level of violence being perpetrated on both human beings and the natural environment is a clear indication of the degree of value which is being accorded to both human beings and the natural environment. A conscious and inclusive approach to include the various expressions of life in our dialogue as one of the ultimate goals of this dialogue has become inevitable. In addition to the challenge posed by the proliferation of arms, wars, organized crime, HIV and AIDS, poverty, hunger, inflation and environmental degradation, the negative impact of globalization and the world economic order has left the world increasingly divided between the "haves and have-nots." In this respect, N. Mette has observed that the threat of destruction in the ecological field is surely the most obvious and the one which is most prominent in the public mind. Slower but nonetheless with a lasting effect is the process that exhausts the social and cultural base for human communal life which takes place, beginning with the personal and

---

43. Omonokhua, "Dialogue," 6.

ending up in the international dimension. The social contracts that have been valid up until now are, in fact, dodged and cancelled.[44]

It would appear that the deplorable condition of the nonhuman creation spells doom also for the dignity of the human species. It may, therefore, be argued that the disintegration of other species in the postmodern world is also signalling the disintegration of the human species. It may be in this light that Mudge has cautioned that "the solidarity of the global human community today rests on our being able to see ourselves as belonging in a network of mutual moral obligation."[45] There is, therefore, an urgent need for Nigerian church leaders to be both proactive and innovative in their quest for the redemption and preservation of the dignity of all Nigerians before it is too late. It is essential that church leaders stand in solidarity with the numerous Nigerians who are daily experiencing the stark challenges of injustices in the form of unemployment, corruption, violence, hunger and all kinds of social exclusion. In addition, the position of church leaders on environmental pollution, global warming, deforestation and the preservation of endangered species should be unambiguous. All this calls for the adoption of multivariate approaches beyond the confines of dialogue to include other areas such as the promotion of conditions of life that may enhance the dignity of both human and non-human life.

4.3.4 Church Leaders' Advocacy and Social Transformation

"Perhaps the most important political duty which CAN often performs and must never shirk, is its warning and prophetic function."[46] The author is of the belief that it is this "warning and prophetic function" which encompasses the elements of advocacy which are geared towards the social transformation of Nigeria. Church leaders in Nigeria are in the main engaged in advocacy through communiqués, press releases and messages from both the pulpit and the mass media. It has become characteristic of church bodies – denominational and ecumenical – to issue press statements at the conclusion of their major meetings – statements that relate to socioeconomic and political issues. Depending on the interest of the media houses, such publications may

---

44. Mette, "Economic Context of Globalisation."
45. Mudge, "Human Solidarity," 27.
46. CAN, *Brief Story*, 13.

or may not incur financial charges. A typical example of such a statement is the communiqué of the second general assembly of CAN held at Kaduna from 15 to 17 November 1988. Over 500 delegates (church leaders), drawn from all the Nigerian states, including Abuja, and representing all the church groups in Nigeria, which, at that time, comprised "over 60 million Christians"[47] through the constituent groups that constitute CAN, were present at the conference. The theme of this assembly was "Religion in a Secular State." The assembly reports, addresses, discussion themes and communiqués all capture the sociopolitical and economic discourses of the church leaders. In addition, the assembly carried out the functions typical of such gatherings, for example, evaluating national and ecclesial matters, creating awareness among church leaders regarding issues of concern, taking decisions for joint Christian action and declaring the position of Christians on urgent issues affecting the nation. As mentioned earlier, CAN occupies a unique position through which both the churches in Nigeria and their leaders are able to relate to both the government and other religions such as Islam. For the present, it would appear that CAN remains the most powerful voice and the most viable channel through which the church's advocacy project may thrive. It is in this light that Williams states that "CAN has been the rallying point for all Nigerian Christians, who have, thus, been enabled by the Holy Spirit to speak out, boldly and with one voice"[48] on national issues and on issues that affect the church. However, what is informing the activities of CAN in light of advocacy, and how it has fared and the grounds that still need to be explored are crucial issues that should be addressed.

The public statements of church leaders that are intended to call the attention of both the Nigerian government and the public to the commendable strides taken by government as well as to areas which continue to incur the displeasure of the church are often geared towards social transformation with the issues being raised often covering religion, ethics, poverty, politics and socioeconomic matters. The matters on the subject of religion often include the insistence on the secularity of the Nigerian nation, dialogue among the religious faiths, freedom of religion and the fair treatment of all adherents of the various religions in all spheres of the Nigerian society. Historical antecedents

---

47. CAN, "Communiqué," 48.
48. Williams, "General Secretary's Report," 11.

such as the attempt of some adherents of Islam who occupy top positions in government to impose Islam on non-Muslims inform these statements. Other such issues include marginalization based on religion, the refusal of certain individuals in authority to allocate land to churches in some parts of the country and the infamous registration of Nigeria by Babangida's administration into the Organization of Islamic Conference (OIC) as an Islamic state without due consideration of the tenets of the Nigerian constitution and consultations with other religions such as Christianity.[49]

As regards the call on all Nigerians in all occupations to adhere to the moral rectitude which is indispensable for nation building, Nigerian church leaders have also played some role in this direction. For the Christians, in particular, this is a call to live their faith and to stand up for their Christian values despite the strong presence of corruption and other unethical practices. Reporting on commendable steps taken by church leaders to deal with ethical challenges, Minchakpu reports that "for the past two years, Nigeria has ranked as the world's most corrupt place to do business, according to an independent survey of global business executives. But recently, thousands of church leaders gathered to take aim at the country's corruption problems and agreed to stop shifting blame to political leaders for societies' problems."[50] Pointing out the reason why church leaders should refocus on ethics, Minchakpu also reports that the chairperson of the Ethics Covenant, Dr. James Ukaegbu, insisted that "in Christian ethics, it is never wrong to do right and it is never right to do wrong."[51] The convocation of more than two thousand church leaders, whose main aim was to deliberate on ethical issues, signed a new covenant recommitting themselves to biblical truth and ethics. In Garry Maxey's view, as further presented by Minchakpu, the significance of this covenant is the fact that "covenant signers standing together is particularly important in view of the fact that many of the millions of strong moral-minded Christians in Nigeria feel alone when it comes to open resistance to the massive extortions that surround us."[52] The covenant, which was aimed at transforming Nigerian society through Christian ethics, envisioned church leaders as the

---

49. CAN, "Communiqué."
50. Minchakpu, "Church Leaders Refocus," 72.
51. Minchakpu, 72.
52. Minchakpu, 72.

repositories of the ethics through which not only the faithful but also Nigerian society as a whole could be influenced. The discovery of the significance of Nigerian church leaders as indispensable channels for socioeconomic, moral and political transformation is both revealing and informing. It also stands in the spirit of this study. Thus, the Congress on Christian Ethics is deemed to have taken a step in the right direction. It is expected that such convocation of church leaders should be held from time to time to appraise the extent of the nation's moral regeneration and to chart new courses where necessary.

Church leaders have often reminded both the government and Nigerian society of the precarious conditions prevailing in Nigeria and they have also challenged Nigerian leaders to rise to meet the challenges of poverty, unemployment, the brain drain, the political crisis, criminal activities and the general insecurity of the nation. The challenges of poor infrastructure such as hospitals, roads, education, electricity and pipe-born water have featured repeatedly in the public statements of church leaders. For example, CAN issued the following statement:

> We note with concern the precarious situation our country is passing through, politically, economically, socially and religiously, as evidenced by the atmosphere of unease and depression all over the country. We challenge all Christians in public life, the civil service, the Armed Forces, Statutory Corporations, the judiciary, quasi-Government Institutions, Private Companies, Business and the Professions to live their faith and stand up for their values and convictions. We are greatly concerned about the catalogue of injustices and inequities perpetrated by Government against Christians in this country. We want an immediate stop to such discriminatory actions. The Assembly strongly denounces the complete or partial takeover of Christian schools [and] the attendant harmful effect of this action on the moral and spiritual development of our children. All Christian educational institutions and hospitals, hitherto, taken over by the Government should be returned. We note with great concern the rate at which armed robbery, hired assassins etc. have constituted serious threats to the security of life and property of Nigerian citizens. Soaring unemployment, retrenchment make it

impossible for most Nigerians to afford adequate nourishment, let alone a decent living. Having deliberated on these issues, we, in this Assembly, hereby call on the present administration, the Federal, State, and Local Governments, to take action to save our beloved country from ominous, imminent disintegration.[53]

Arguably, this statement of CAN's Second General Assembly, which is partially cited above, could be said to reflect concern, discontent, a call to duty, a declaration of intents and requests. There is no doubt that the statement also expresses some sort of advocacy for both the church and the Nigerian public. Mbachirin reminds us of the advocacy of Nigerian church leaders when he states that "it is important to note that the Nigerian bishops have confronted and advised the state on human rights abuses, educational policies, religious freedom issues, and religious tolerance. The bishops also educate the local populace on their rights and in most cases, they speak for the people."[54]

Although it is difficult to assess the impact of the engagement of church leaders in advocacy, as there has been no scientific study conducted which could have constituted an authoritative source, nevertheless a simple assessment based on the outcomes of such engagements may provide some sort of foundation from which to work. To begin with, the courage and audacity contained in the text of the statement within the context of a military regime is both outstanding and could be said to be prophetic. However, both this courage and audacity are consistent with the genre of CAN's public statements to the church, government and Nigerian society in general. Although the poverty, employment, development and general well-being indices of Nigerian society have not improved, some state governments have returned previously church-owned schools and hospitals to the churches while the systematic Islamization of the Nigerian society by certain institutions of the federal government at the time has also been curtailed. The allocation of a piece of land for the National Ecumenical Centre, which is symbolic of the "Church Unity Centre," in the central area of Abuja, as was done for the Muslims, may have been made possible as a result of the stance of CAN. The attempt of President Olusegun Obasanjo to prolong his tenure in 2007

---

53. CAN, "Communiqué," 48–50.
54. Mbachirin, "Review of JC Nwafor," 654.

attracted the resistance of church leaders and, to a certain extent, this resistance contributed to his failure to remain in office as he had wished to do.[55]

Despite the acknowledged achievements as well as other achievements which may not have been acknowledged for want of information, it should, perhaps, be admitted that church leaders and church members have not done enough to change the lot of the Christians who represent a substantial percentage of the population of Nigeria and of Nigerians themselves. It may even be said that the church leaders have been more concerned about preserving Christianity against the incursion of Islam than with the huge challenges of nation building, poverty, unemployment, corruption, poor leadership, ecological challenges and other forms of injustice. Accordingly, it may, perhaps, be said that the church has been a greater beneficiary of its own advocacy than Nigerian society as a whole. Admittedly, in terms of their professional obligations, church leaders have both a divine and a moral responsibility to protect their faith, which has often been subject to lethal attacks by Islamic leaders who have tried a number of times to use state power to foist their religion on non-Muslims. However, the question arises as to whether or not such endeavours deserve a lesser amount of their energy while more energy and resources should be channelled into more creative ways of solving such problems. It is presupposed that, among all the other options, advocacy for approaches such as human empowerment through qualitative education that is responsive to the practical challenges of society and the political development and socioeconomic transformation of society are more viable and more lasting options. It is essential that church leaders bear in mind that poverty and ignorance may be the surest ways to both religious fundamentalism and to other forms of recruitment into groups that engage in criminal activities.

The present level of advocacy on the part of church leaders appears to be both weak and, inevitably, extremely limited in its impact. Although advocacy is a powerful means through which sociopolitical and economic injustices may be addressed and transformed, it is vital that the approach of church leaders to advocacy extends beyond news releases, communiqués and pulpit rhetoric. An additional dimension of ecclesial leadership engagement could include public lectures, mass rallies/campaigns, sponsorship of candidates to the various arms of governance and the lobbying of policy makers. Again,

---

55. Salifu, "Christian and Nation Building."

the scope of such advocacy should be broadened to include gender injustice, physically and psychologically challenged persons, animals, the environment and all forms of injustices which are being meted to the various expressions of the created order. However, if this is to be successful, church leaders may have to wrestle with the challenge of religious reductionism, compartmentalism, the full import of the theology of the kingdom of God and missional theology. In other words, church leaders may first have to come to terms with such questions as whether the church should collaborate with government and other social institutions. What does the presence of the kingdom of God mean to Nigerians in their respective socioreligious, political, economic and environmental milieus? What constitutes good news to Nigerians in the midst of their present experiences of poverty, unemployment, underdevelopment, violence, ill health and other forms of suffering? For now, this study will attempt to wrestle with the issue of the collaboration of the church and its leaders with other institutions in their quest to contribute to the socioeconomic and political well-being of Nigerians.

4.3.5 Collaboration of Church Leaders and Churches with Other Institutions

According to Anna Nieman, collaboration and partnership are essential elements of social development theory and practice with collaboration representing "the relationships of stakeholders pooling resources in order to meet objectives that neither could meet individually."[56] It is anticipated that the uneven degrees of power represented by the role players, including church leaders, government officials, community leaders and the poor should be evened out through the process of collaboration. However, it is extremely doubtful whether the current level of collaboration between church leaders and the Nigerian government is on the right track. According to the records available, Nigerian church leaders, under the auspices of CAN and their respective denominations, are working in collaboration with the federal government in the two main traditional areas, namely, education and health while it would appear that possible future areas of collaboration are poverty alleviation, the fight against corruption and collaboration with civil society. According to the records of CAN, "right from its inception in 1976,

---

56. Nieman, "Churches and Social Development," 41.

CAN has always felt very strongly that a crucial part of its mission is to be the watch person of the type of education which our children are receiving. For this reason, the very first memorandum which the Association presented to the Federal Government contained a formidable chapter on education."[57] Emphasising its passion for education, CAN affirms its "readiness to enter into partnership with Government in the ownership and administration of public schools."[58] While further expressing the wishes of both church leaders and the churches to collaborate with the government, Onaiyekan makes "a plea for greater cooperation between the state and religious organizations, especially in the social services that the latter run."[59] Drawing from historical evidence to justify the usual areas on which the church tends to focus in social transformation, both inside of Nigeria and beyond, Onaiyekan argues that "there are good examples to follow from our past history and from what many other countries are doing even today. Health and education are the classical areas of activities of religious bodies, especially the Christian churches. Greater encouragement from the state would put them in a better way to render more service."[60]

It is, thus, not surprising that a number of churches own educational institutions ranging from crèches to universities across the country. In view of the fallen standards of education in Nigeria, church-owned educational institutions rank among the best institutions in contemporary Nigeria with the universities including Veritas University, Babcock University, Madonna University, Covenant University and Redeemer University. From the missionary era, church-owned institutions have been the repositories of morality and excellence. Together with some private-owned institutions, church-owned institutions have custody of most of the wards of Nigerians who fall into the category of the Nigerian elite. The attempts of church leaders to improve the standard of education in Nigeria are commendable although these attempts do entail the high cost of acquiring such education and a lack of development in areas such as sports and social activities. Inevitably, certain challenges arise including the fact that even some church members who contributed their

---

57. CAN, *Brief Story*, 11.
58. CAN, "Communiqué," 49.
59. Onaiyekan, "Dividends of Religion," 33.
60. Onaiyekan, 33.

meagre resources to help start up these institutions in the hope of benefiting from them are being sidelined. Also, quality education should include, at the very least, good academic standards, solid character development and the opportunity to socialise, and the neglect of any of these dimensions may spell doom to any endeavour.

The health sector is another area of traditional collaboration between the church and the state and also reminiscent of the missionary era. Besides the establishment of CHAN, which is a health arm of CAN which aims to provide quality healthcare at a subsidized rate, the Christian community is also engaging in rural health projects and the fight against HIV, AIDS and malaria. In some instances, churches own hospitals, maternity homes and community centres where they provide health services. A number of these projects are run through denominational health projects such as Presby-AIDS. Other projects include the provision of eye operations, routine medical checks and medicines during the annual medical week programmes of church denominations such as the Presbyterian Church of Nigeria. The church and government run some of these institutions jointly while some are run by the church alone.

4.3.5.1 *Emerging Areas of Collaboration*

New areas of the church's engagement in social processes, which are outside of the familiar terrain of education, health and, recently, dialogue, include collaboration with government towards poverty alleviation and collaboration with civil society. As regards poverty alleviation, the Obasanjo administration introduced the Promise Keepers Partners (PKP) under NAPEP which could, as community-based organizations, liaise with religious organizations in poverty alleviation. The programme involved a loan scheme which, in turn, entailed the contribution of a certain amount of money by a religious organization and an equal sum by the government. This amount was then made available to the organization as a revolving loan through which such an organization could give soft loans to its members for investment purposes.

The collaboration between church leaders and NGOs such as the African Forum on Religion and Government (AFREG) may be traced to the efforts of some church leaders such as Rev. Dr. William Okoye, Professors Yusuf Turaki and Jerry Gana, Elder Chief Ojo Maduekwe and Dr. Peter Ozodo, in 2004. These leaders, under the auspices of "Integrity Advocates," which is a nongovernmental organization, conceived the notion of convening an "All African Conference on Religion, Leadership and Good Governance."[61] Further support from key church leaders such as the Most Reverends P. J. Akinola and John Onaiyekan, who were the president and vice-president of CAN respectively at the time, gave impetus to those efforts. The contributions of President Olusegun Obasanjo, his chaplain, Prof. Yusuf Obaje, and Dr. Dela Adadevoh aided these efforts and eventually led to the formation of AFREG in July 2006, thus giving AFREG both a national and an international image. AFREG's vision is to "create a platform for African leaders of integrity who are committed to the transformation of the continent to address the issue of institutionalizing the culture of good governance with a view to tackling the problems of corruption, poverty and underdevelopment in Africa."[62]

The fact that CAN has collaborated with AFREG has, to a large extent, shaped and deepened the approach and scope of church leaders in regard to their more relevant engagement in sociopolitical issues, especially within the Nigerian context. This collaboration also led to the formulation of what is now known as the "Nigerian Christian Creed on Governance," an ideological framework for the engagement of both church leaders and the entire Christian community in governance. As a result, church leaders were able, for the first time, to meet with the major presidential aspirants of political parties who were Muslims, to discuss their attitudes towards issues that are important to Christians. A similar effort was replicated through the CCN, a body under the auspices of CAN in Lagos, through the Forum for Righteousness in Governance (FRIG), in the build-up to the 2007 election for governors.[63] In addition, CAN has now created the office of the National Director on National Issues with Rev. Dr. William Okoye at the helm. The purpose of this office is to address socioeconomic and political issues as they affect Christians throughout the country. With this structure, the church has taken a further step to collaborating with the Independent Corrupt Practices and other Related Offences Commission (ICPC), an anti-corruption agency established by the Federal Government to fight corruption.[64] Thus, the collaboration of CAN

---

61. Okoye, "African Forum on Religion," 2.
62. Okoye, 2.
63. FRIG, "Leadership 2007."
64. Okoye, "African Forum on Religion."

with AFREG, an offshoot of Integrity Advocates, and with the government is a welcome development. These efforts are being driven by a conscientized church leadership which is taking advantage of the resources of the church, including the Christian values which are an integral part of the church, to rectify the moral ineptitude which is contributing to the challenges of poverty, underdevelopment, corruption and poor leadership in Nigeria.

In a more recent development, the leadership of the church, through the activities of Pastor Tunde Bakare of the Later Rain Assembly, is engaging in a new dimension under the aegis of the "Save Nigeria Group." This group is a peoples' movement which, during the Yar'adua health crisis and the National Assembly electoral reforms in 2010, contributed significantly to the transformation of Nigerian society. Through organized protests and rallies, Nigeria was delivered from a leadership vacuum and anarchy and credible leadership was restored in the form of the national electoral body and the Federal Executive Council. This approach to social transformation is in alignment with both David Korten's "Fourth Generation Approach" and the ecumenical radical pragmatic view of Charles Elliot.[65] In terms of both views, the church is situated within the context of cultural power as both a community based and a people's institution. With its spirituality, values and ideas as its main resources, the church is perceived to occupy unlimited space in both civil society and people's movements to transform society on the local, national and international levels. This study concurs with the above viewpoints.

It is the view of this study that the church, through its leaders, has, thus far, made some progress beyond its normal comfort zone in the Nigerian social discourse. However, this progress has, so far, not had the desired impact that is capable of transforming the sociopolitical and economic milieus of Nigerian society. In as much as church leaders are able to sustain the charity, social services and dialogue as well as the advocacy and collaborative efforts with the government, they may need to focus more of their energies towards the transformation of those structures that formulate policies/laws, govern and interpret the laws. In addition, church leaders should be discouraged from keeping a distance from people's movements and they should endeavour to utilize the huge resources at their disposal in order to bring about the spiritual and tangible blessings that would relate to the concrete experiences

---

65. Swart, *Churches and Development Debate*.

of all Nigerians. Using public health as an example, Schmid, Cochrane and Olivier have argued that "when religious organizations become engaged in public health, the challenge is to go beyond providing health services, to take on social justice issues that have an impact on health. Especially those that affect the most marginalized groups in society, to advocate on behalf of these groups, and to participate in the formation of policy in dialogue with the public health authorities."[66] Both the church's consciousness and the influence it is able to wield in the transformation of policies and institutions so as to ensure accountability and render it impossible for the wrong persons to ascend to positions of authority instead of merely praying for "Godfearing leaders," is crucial. Accordingly, Kukah has advised that "to lay a foundation for a nation that will respond to all the ideals we aspire, we need to return to the issues of institution building and rely on these institutions to regulate the behavior of public officers rather than to continue to argue that we need God fearing men and so on."[67] However, are there theological perspectives within the church in Nigeria that may inform and justify the social engagements of both church leaders and Christians?

4.4 Theological Analysis of the Church Leadership Discourse

4.4.1 The Quest for a Nigerian Christian Theology

In a way, the assertion of J. S. Mbiti that the "church in Africa is a church without a theology and a church without theological concern,"[68] and his argument that this trend has been changing in recent years, resonates with the Christian theological experience in the Nigerian context. From the theological curricula of theological/Bible schools to the witness of most of the churches in Nigeria, there is a yawning gap between the theological conditioning of church leaders and the faithful and the daily experiences of the faithful as they journey through life. Accordingly, both church leaders and church members are faced with the challenge of holding on to theologies that are foreign and unresponsive to their spiritual, emotional, psychological,

---

66. Schmid, Cochrane, and Olivier, "Understanding Religious Health," 141.
67. Kukah, "Globalisation and the Rest," 73.
68. Mbiti, *African Religion and Philosophy*, 226.

cultural, sociopolitical and economic experiences. Accordingly, Onwurah has observed that "there is real evidence that Christians often limit Christ to prescribed areas of their lives. When it comes to major crises of life, namely, sickness, suffering and death, Christ is pushed aside and real recourse made to traditional and well-proven methods of countering the effects of evil and gaining assurance in the world of uncertainty and danger."[69] It is for this and other reasons that Idowu, a former Patriarch of the Methodist Church Nigeria, argued in his book, *Towards an Indigenous Church*, for the establishment of an indigenous church in Nigeria as both "an immediate and an indispensable task."[70] He maintains that it is only a church whose "indigenousness" is reflected in both its theology and its ritual that would be able to provide the necessary resources and nurture for the Nigerian Christian. Kwame Bediako has observed that Idowu's stance on the indigenization project, especially within the Nigerian context, was aimed at covering the following: the Bible in indigenous Nigerian languages, the language of evangelization, theology, liturgy, and dress and vestments.[71] Mbiti has blamed the church's struggle to exist in Africa without a theology for African Christians that has evolved within Africa on the poor education and lack of theological exposure of the missionaries and their African helpers. However, he also observed that, from the 1960s, there has been a definite development in African theology and this has gained significant momentum in the years following the 1960s.[72] However, apart from a few exceptions, notably in the African Independent Churches and some Pentecostal churches – although, even in these churches, the theology is still confined to certain areas such as prayer and music – the desire for and efforts towards the development of such a theology have not yielded significant results.

In Nigeria today, issues involving the Christian response to organized crime and violence, extortion, partisan politics, beauty pageants, multiple marriage rites, sex, sexual orientation, divorce and remarriage, negotiated contract awards and many other burning issues are still in desperate need of answers. For example, the issue of organized crime and violence

---

69. Onwurah, "Quest, Means and Relevance," 47.
70. Idowu, *Towards an Indigenous Church*, 1, 9.
71. Bediako, *Christianity in Africa*.
72. Mbiti, *African Religion and Philosophy*.

perpetrated by Muslims against Christians in northern Nigeria highlights the urgent need for an immediate theological response that is realistic to the context and which will provide informed guidance to Christians in such situations. Archbishop Ben Kwashi describes the ongoing experiences of Christians when he states that "Muslim attacks on the church seem to be a permanent feature in northern Nigeria. After each attack many Christians are immediately left with the loss of the lives of their relations (sometimes those killed are the bread-winners of the family), and of property."[73] In view of the perennial nature of these acts of organized crime and terror and in the absence of a practicable and hermeneutical theological disposition, Kwashi further argues that as a result of the "frequent and increasing conflict in northern Nigeria many suffering Christians have changed their attitude to violence."[74] All along, Christians in Nigeria have maintained a strong belief in the Scripture that says: "If someone slaps you on one cheek, turn to them the other also."[75] "Today, some Christians no longer hold strongly to this view. Such Christians will question: 'The Muslims have slapped us on one cheek; we have also turned the other cheek, now which other cheek do we have to turn?'"[76] By this, they tend to imply that they need to fight back and resist the Muslims whenever they are attacked.

The reinterpretation of the teachings of Jesus reflects a serious departure from the usual pacifist and nonviolent resistance disposition which has often characterized the theological understanding of Christians of this doctrinal persuasion as it concerns the passage in Luke 6:29. Admittedly, this may be perceived as an extremely radical departure from the teachings of Christ and it may even be considered to be inconsistent with biblical teaching and, therefore, heretical. It is, however, not possible to dismiss the repeated pain and losses that these Christians have been enduring over the years. But, Christians in different contexts of suffering have often developed a theological framework which has guided and sustained them to "weather their storms." Accordingly, these Christians in northern Nigeria have devised a theology which they assume will satisfy their needs and they will adhere to

---

73. Kwashi, "Conflict, Suffering and Peace," 65.
74. Kwashi, 68.
75. Luke 6:29 (NIV).
76. Kwashi, "Conflict, Suffering and Peace," 68.

this theology unless church leaders provide a more relevant theology that meets their existential needs.

The church in Nigeria is, indeed, still in dire need of developing a theological paradigm that may adequately inform the engagement of church leaders and church members in the socioeconomic and political arena in the country. However, there are some glimmers of such a theological paradigm emerging that must be nurtured and sustained. As argued in this study, it is essential that such a theological orientation is characterized by a biblical underpinning and also a development orientation. In other words, such a theological framework should be biblically rooted and contextually relevant to the current challenges facing Nigerians in the light of the poverty, underdevelopment, corruption, violence and poor leadership in Nigeria. It is in this regard that Mduekwe in Obasanjo has argued that "unless a new generation of African Theologians of both the cross and the crescent, in concert with other serious social thinkers, are able to evolve paradigm shifts that would lead to the urgent internalization of the timeless truths of the two major religions of Africa, our politics will remain hopelessly corrupt, our bureaucracy relentlessly kleptocratic, and the task of nation-building a casualty of the deadly duels of primitive accumulation."[77] Although Maduekwe's argument relates to church and to Islamic and social thinkers or leaders it is, nevertheless, of special significance as it relates to a theological analysis of the discussions of church leaders.

In line with Maduekwe's position, Obasanjo has also raised some extremely relevant questions in the following way: How do we reconcile a global reputation for being a very religious continent with a global reputation for being a very corrupt continent, if the Transparency International Perception Index Report is to be believed? Is there a theology of the African State (Nigerian state), strong and adequate enough to situate states in Africa (Nigeria) as deserving of loyalty in the context of a Pauline theology of the ruler and the ruled, very much different from our enthronement of ethnicity as the first principle of statecraft? How do we begin to internalize the truths of our two historical religions in order to walk our talk and ensure the relative peace so conducive to drive development on the continent (nation)? How can the received faiths of the two of the world's historical religions, namely

---

77. Obasanjo, "Africa Arise."

Christianity and Islam really speak more intimately, and more authentically to our cultural experience, and, by so doing, become more relevant to our situation and conditions?[78]

The necessary, timeless truths which should be internalized by the faithful so as to form the basis of their daily living in all spheres, as suggested by Maduekwe, may be detected in Obasanjo's thesis, namely integrity, state, peace, development and inculturation theologies. In dealing with the theologies that relate to the vexed issues on the African continent in general, and the Nigerian context in particular, it may be argued that there are theological frameworks that may be engaged in order to respond to the issues that are at stake in the Nigerian context.

Meanwhile, the focus of this study at this juncture is to discover and analyse some of the theological exchanges that have taken place within the Nigerian context. These theological discussions may be drawn from the documents, statements and publications of church leaders, CAN, other church bodies and the Nigerian public. A categorization of the topical issues into themes such as church leaders and ecumenism, a theology for church and state relations, Nigerian Christianity and moral questions, inculturation and Nigerian Christianity, the concept of good news, the church in missions as an agent of transformation, church leaders and gender issues, and the church and the environment may be helpful.

4.4.2 Church Leaders and Ecumenism

Article two of the Christian Association of Nigeria clearly defines the association's commitment to ecumenism as pivotal to its existence. "The Christian Association of Nigeria is an association of Christian Churches with distinct identities, recognizable Church Structures and a system of worship of one God in the Trinity of the Father, Son and Holy Spirit. This association makes Christ the Centre of all its works and shall promote the glory of God, by encouraging the growth and unity of the churches, and by helping them to lead the nation and its people to partake of Christ's salvation and all its fruits."[79] Thus, CAN is envisioning the existence of the church as an entity and its mission in Nigerian society as dependent on the ability of both church

---

78. Obasanjo.
79. CAN, *Constitution*, 1.

leaders and the faithful to find common grounds for unity, despite doctrinal differences. The establishment of CAN was the first step in this direction and, since then, the churches in Nigeria have kept on forging the path of unity, despite challenges.

As in the case of the WCC, the formation of CAN had a "deeper motivation, a theological one which caused men and women of different confessions and church bodies to throw themselves wholeheartedly"[80] into the quest for the unity of the body of Christ. These pioneers of the largest ecumenical movement in Africa were aware that Christianity could only bear faithful witness to God's will for all peoples of the *oikoumene*[81] if it was united. The assertion that "human beings are gregarious animals tending naturally to form groups with their fellow beings"[82] is worth recalling. According to Ana, in so doing, they reveal not only their capabilities but also their relationships of power and mutual dependence. Human associations such as CAN have exerted undeniable influence on both member churches and on Nigerian society. In order to consolidate the achievements of the past and to find new ways of responding to current challenges, church leaders in Nigeria, and, in particular, under the umbrella of CAN and its constituent bodies, are involved in theological discussions that relate to ecumenism. Such discussions include, inter alia, issues such as their understanding of ecumenism and the grounds for ecumenical collaboration.

In his theological treatise, "Ecumenism: Bringing Together All Who Confess Faith in God," Fagun has argued that "ecumenism is the bringing together of all who confess faith in God, one and triune, in the incarnate Son of God, our Redeemer and Lord. This may be achieved through growth in reconciliation and a true communal relationship which takes into account legitimate differences."[83] He argues further that it involves interior conversion, knowing our separated brethren, prayer for repentance and receiving the mind of Christ who assures us of peace and unity which the world cannot give. The end is common confession of the one faith and true communal relationship, taking account of legitimate differences.

---

80. Ana, "Preserving Charisma," 382.
81. John 17:21.
82. Ana, "Preserving Charisma," 382.
83. Fagun, "Ecumenism," 45.

Drawing extensively from the Second Vatican Council (1962–65), Fagun affirmed his stance regarding the importance of ecumenism in Nigeria and urged other church leaders to continue on the path of the ecumenical movement. He notes that division among Christians and among human beings generally fills humankind with fear and alarm, while divisions among Christians are in open contradiction of the will of Christ and, therefore, sinful. In addition, such divisions scandalize the world and cause damage to the most holy cause which is the preaching of the gospel to every creature.[84] In order to attain the much-desired unity of the church in Nigeria, the use of prayer, which has the potential to purify the motives and intentions of both church leaders and church members, is inevitable. The expected unity of the body of Christ should also be seen as a gift from God which is dependent on God's mercy.

Cardinal Dominic Ekanem had highlighted the progress of ecumenism in Nigeria by emphasizing the continued existence of CAN and its expansion in the previous decade, dialogue among churches and certain areas of co-operation among churches.[85] However, CAN has now been in existence for several decades beyond the time of Ekanem's reference. The areas of achievement, including dialogue among member churches, theological education, training for Christian communicators, sharing in sacred music, the Chan-Pharm Health Project, the Bible Society Project and the building and maintenance of the National Christian (Ecumenical) Centre also constitute common grounds for ecumenical interaction and provide evidence of an ongoing collaboration between the various Christian denominations.

4.4.3 A Theology for Church and State Relations

It had been observed previously that the missionary era had bequeathed a reductionist type of Christianity to the church in Nigeria – reductionist because it distinguished between the sacred and the secular or the spiritual and the carnal. As also noted, this type of Christianity was not only strange to the worldview of Nigerians as typical Africans, but it also distanced Christians from sociopolitical and economic engagement by dubbing such issues worldly and unChristian. It is for these reasons that statements such as "politics is a dirty game" are common among Christians. Also, questions such as "Can a

---

84. CAN, "Communiqué," 45.
85. Ekanem, "Presidential Address."

Christian participate in partisan politics?" are often posed in question-and-answer sessions of churches. Allied to these developments are questions such as, what are the theological views that justify the Christian's participation in the affairs of the world in which he/she lives? How is it possible for such a person to be true to the teaching of being "in the world but not of the world?" and, how is it possible for the Christian to "give to Caesar what belongs to Caeser and to God what belongs to God"? Accordingly, Maduekwe's concern for a Christian theological framework that may bolster a sociopolitical ethic and Obasanjo's rhetorical questions on a Pauline church/state theology all fall within the same category. Obasanjo's questions may, therefore, be reframed to read: How do we reconcile a global reputation for being an extremely religious nation with a poor reputation globally or with notoriety as regards being one of the most corrupt countries, if the Transparency International Perception Index Report is to be believed? Is there a theology of the Nigerian state which is sufficiently strong and adequate to situate the Nigerian state as deserving of loyalty in the context of a Pauline theology of the ruler and the ruled? How do we begin to internalize the truths of the Christian religion in order to "walk the talk" and to ensure relative peace which would be conducive to driving development in the country? How could the Christian faith speak more intimately and more authentically to our cultural experience and, by so doing, become more relevant to our situation and condition? Nevertheless, church leaders in Nigeria have started offering theological responses that may serve as a guide to Christians on some of these vexing issues.

Arguing from theological and anthropological perspectives, Gbonigi has pointed out that both the Old and the New Testaments provide hints about the relationship between the state and religion. In the Old Testament, such hints may be found in the conflicts that arose between kings and priests or prophets with cases such as King Ahab and Prophet Elijah, and King David and Prophet Nathan providing good examples. Although the examples cited reflect conflicts between prophets and kings in the context of theocratic states, it is remarkable that the prophets, whose primary responsibility it was to defend and uphold the moral and religious ideals and standards, did not flinch in the face of such challenges. On the contrary, they were bold and courageous in the interests of God and of his rule. In the New Testament, the conflicts between the state and our Lord Jesus Christ, and the challenges that the early church and the apostles faced as regards the state provide such examples.[86] Positioning Christianity within the anthropological frame of religion for the purpose of pulling the strands of his argument for the church's participation in sociocultural and political milieus, Gbonigi defines religion as "faith in a divinely created order of the universe, agreement with which is the means of salvation for a society and for the individual by virtue of his having a role in the society."[87] Speaking more broadly, Gbonigi argues that religion may also be defined as "a way of life or a system of belief based upon man's ultimate relationship to the universe or to God or gods." There are three strands to this argument that may be helpful to our discussion on the theology of church and state relations. First, the belief in religion that the world in which we live is made by God. Second, the salvation of society and every individual member of society being dependent upon their agreement with the divine ordering of the society. And third, the belief that every member of the world community has a moral duty to play both a moral and a productive role, in conformity with the moral ordering of the world and for its total salvation. The Christian's belief that God created the world implies that the created order has a definite purpose; it is sustained and governed by its creator; and that, despite the fact that God is transcendent in his divine almightiness, glory, majesty, holiness and honour, he is, at the same time, immanent in the world in his condescending love, grace and mercy. Gbonigi argues that this nature of God corresponds with Jesus's teaching that "God does not forget a single one of them. And he knows the number of hairs on your head."[88] It follows, thus, that God is also a spiritual and moral being and, the ordering of creation by God entails spiritual and moral principles. As such, the salvation of any society of which the members' standards of living are contrary to the spiritual and moral ideals of the creator is in jeopardy. The salvation in question is holistic; and, as such, it encompasses the political, economic, social, cultural, moral and religious spheres.

Accordingly, the role of the church in any society, including Nigeria, is a vocation, a calling and a task or responsibility for which the church has been equipped by God to carry out. As such, the church's role in Nigeria

---

86. Gbonigi, "Religion in a Secular State," 23.

87. Gbonigi, 23.

88. Luke 12:6–7 (TLB).

permeates all facets of life, namely, family, professional, economic, political, social, religious and spiritual. According to Gbonigi, it is for this reason that the question as to whether or not a Christian should participate in partisan politics should not arise. In addition, the true God of the Bible is a God of history who is concerned with the events of history and was active in them, as in the case of the Israelites in their deliverance from Egypt and his giving them the Ten Commandments. Gbonigi further postulates that a reading of the Bible will reveal how seriously the religious leaders of the Old Testament took their responsibilities in the sociopolitical realm. In his view, the essence of the life and teaching of the Lord Jesus Christ was a revolutionary acceptance of involvement with the life of this world, in order that, by completely identifying with humankind in their societies, he might redeem both them and their societies from sin. The far-reaching implication of this is the fact that, although Jesus had come to inaugurate a new humanity with a new kind of relationship, he was not indifferent to the world of humankind as he found it. Gbonigi clarifies the role of the church in the Nigerian state as follows: "This responsibility of Christ, and His followers, towards the world of men as they found it, was a two-fold responsibility of judgment and creative participation."[89] Creative participation, because God has chosen the way of incarnation and intended to save the world by being involved in it; judgement, because there had come into the world a new humanity with a new relationship, in the light of which old things were seen to be passing away and all their values to be only relative. The role of the church in the sociopolitical, economic, moral and cultural order in Nigeria should, therefore, be that of creative or transformative participation and judgement.

As regards the Pauline theology of church-state relationship as enunciated in Romans 13:1–7, Gbonigi affirms that Paul recognized the divinely ordained place of government. He argues that the responsible role of the Christian in relation to the government is dutiful and obedient citizenship, not only through fear of punishment, "but also for conscience's sake."[90] Prelate Sunday Mbang of the Methodist Church Nigeria supports this viewpoint.[91] Thus, according to Paul, civil government is part of the natural order of a moral universe and

---

89. Gbonigi, "Religion in a Secular State," 25–26.
90. Gbonigi, 25.
91. Mbang, "Religion in a Secular State."

this, in turn, is in agreement with our definition of religion, as formulated by Gbonigi. In the spirit of this argument, just as nature will usually reward the hard-working farmer while starving the lazy farmer, so civil government, as part of the same natural moral order, exists to reward honesty and to punish wrongdoing. However, both nature and the state are under the control of God who is the God of both nature and grace. It is, therefore, worth noting that the church, which belongs to both realms of nature and grace, as the God it serves owns both, should maintain the creative tension of judgement and transformative participation as it may otherwise have nothing specifically Christian to contribute to the state. This position also relates to the metaphors of "salt" and "light"[92] in the Bible. The question on how the Christian is "in the world but not of the world" is also portrayed by the teaching of being "different but also involved." According to Gbonigi, the axiom of an unknown Christian in the second century AD, which is assumed to have been written to an enquirer named Diognetus, vividly illustrates these teachings. It states: "What the soul is in the body, thus Christians are in the world. The soul is spread through all parts of the body; so are Christians through all the cities of the world. The soul lives in the body, but is not of the body; so Christians live in the world but are not of the world, the soul is shut up in the body, but itself holds the body together; so, too, Christians are held down in the world, yet is they who hold the world together."[93] The debate in respect of the payment of tributes to Caesar has been addressed in the summary of the duties of the church and its members towards the state, as analysed by Gbonigi in his discussion of judgement and creative participation respectively. As it concerns judgement, the church is urged to hold before men in their legislative, administrative and judicial tasks the standards of righteousness and justice which alone exalt a nation; To lend moral support to the state when it upholds those standards, and to criticize it fearlessly when it departs from them; To be an ever-present reminder to the state that it exists only as the servant of God and man, and that its authority is only relative.[94]

In respect of creative participation, the church has a responsibility to carry out the following: To pray for the state, its people and its government;

---

92. Matthew 5:13–14.
93. Gbonigi, "Religion in a Secular State," 26.
94. Gbonigi.

Loyally to obey the state and to pay whatever is due in taxes and service, to disobey, only if obedience would be clearly contrary to God's will; To cooperate wholeheartedly with the state, in promoting the welfare of its citizens and in removing social, economic, and civic wrongs; To permeate the public mind with the spirit of righteousness and brotherhood, and to train up Christian men and women who can bring whole and stable personalities to the service of the community.[95]

In response to the question which was asked by the Second Assembly of CAN, namely, "Is it lawful to give tribute to Caesar or not? Shall we give or shall we not give?"[96] Yusuf argues that "Christians in Nigeria are not giving God his own share. On the contrary, we always give to Caesar what belongs to God. The huge amounts of money we spend on funerals and weddings; and also on parties, personal houses, cars, dresses, gifts to Obas, chiefs and Obis, in order to be made chiefs or waziri, and advertisements for governors and presidents etc. are far more than we ever give to God."[97] Yusuf's position highlights the moral indifference which characterizes the engagement of Christians in the sociopolitical, economic and cultural circles in Nigerian society. He argues that the Christian's theological framework of service to God and society should inform every Christian's engagement, and take precedence over the attitudes of self-seeking and ethnicity in both the private and public domains. His advocacy for the fight against corruption, nepotism and all forms of injustice is premised on the theological underpinning of Jesus's teaching as regards giving to Caesar what belongs to Caesar and to God what belongs to God. For Yusuf, the fact that Jesus died for the rich and for the poor is important in the Christian's fight for social justice and fair play – a fight which should go beyond mere words to peaceful protests or demonstration. It is in such social involvement that the civil authorities or government (state) may be made to understand that many things have gone wrong in the society.

Salifu asserts that, throughout the ages, the church has been a constant agent of reformation and change. It is on this note that he calls for the political education of the church and society which, he insists, is the way out of

---

95. Gbonigi.
96. Mark 12:14–15 (KJV).
97. Yusuf, "Is It Lawful?," 41.

the ignorance and indifference of both the church and Nigerian society as it concerns the participation of Christians and churches in politics. The church needs to create a wing for the political education of believers and society on contemporary political, socioeconomic issues, their civic roles and their right to participate in the good governance of the society. Our God himself has, over the years and ages and generations, ensured that the expected role that the church should play as "salt" and "light" is fulfilled.[98]

In as much as the creation of an arm for the political and civic education of Christians and the Nigerian public may be vital, it may be debated that such a task would be too enormous for such an arm and the results achieved would be extremely limited. The Nigerian church leadership at all levels of the expression of the church (ecumenical, denominational and congregational) and with a concern for the socioeconomic, political and leadership challenges facing Nigerians may be better served by conscientising their respective Christian communities which would, in turn, conscientize their areas of influence in the process of their normal interactions with the broader society. However, the question arises as to whether the Christian community possesses the moral rectitude that may earn this community a respectful hearing within Nigerian society?

4.4.4 Nigerian Christianity and Moral Questions

The notoriety of Nigerians both at home and abroad and the high number of Christians in a Nigerian society which is haracterized by palpable religiosity in terms of, for example, the number of churches, Christian names, and religious activities remain irreconcilable. Kwashi, thus, remarks: "This nation of Nigeria is blessed with every conceivable missionary church and para-church, and the number of prayer ministries is uncountable . . . And what have we achieved?"[99] It is for this reason that the following questions arise: What kind of Christian morality is emerging or evolving in this predominantly Christian nation? What are the evidences for and consequences of this form of Christianity? How does the Nigerian Christian moral experience conform to the requirements of biblical Christian morality? If Christianity is the norm, why, then, the rize in the incidence of vices such as cultism, bribery and

---

98. Salifu, "Christian and Nation Building," 195.
99. Kwashi, "Christian and Corruption," 42.

corruption, armed robbery, looting of public treasuries, electoral malpractices, kidnappings and other forms of criminal activities? What constitutes the actual moral authority of Christians? Is it the media, internet, secular values, reason, tradition or Scripture? Why have Nigerian Christians, both in moments of crisis and when in political or elevated positions, failed to live up to their professions of Christianity? In as much as these are extremely difficult and disturbing questions to which this study may not be able to proffer adequate answers, given the limited space, the Nigerian church and its leaders would do well to acknowledge the significance of such questions which impact directly on the very essence and presence of the church as the bastion of morality in society, particularly in view of the church's claims to be "salt" and "light." However, a Christian is a follower of Christ and, for that reason, she/he ought to mirror the life of Jesus.

Kunhiyop has observed that the challenge of African and, by implication, Nigerian Christianity may be looked at in terms of moral life and practice; while a discussion on morality would automatically touch on theology and vice versa, as theology and ethics are intimately connected in both the African continent and elsewhere. Kunhiyop has, therefore, decried the fact that the message that was passed on during the missionary era was wrapped in a culture that is alien to Nigerians and that both the message and the culture were treated by the messenger as one and the same thing. It is for this reason that the worldview of the messenger was deliberately transmitted to the Nigerian Christian with the resultant effect of supplanting the Nigerian/African worldview with a Western mindset. Such a Western worldview, which is unfamiliar to Nigerians, includes the compartmentalization of life and issues, negative individualism, a shameless morality which asserts individual moral freedom in total disregard of the community, systematization of Scripture, philosophical methods of dealing with problems and the decline in the role of scriptural authority in shaping morality.[100] Kunhiyop maintains that it is this state of affairs that has impacted negatively on Nigerian/African Christians, leaving them with a moral attitude which is neither rooted in traditional African morality nor in Christian morality. His thesis is, therefore, as follows: "In order to recover our [Nigerian] moral sanity, there is the urgent need to retrieve and restore some positive moral foundations and

---

100. Kunhiyop, "Challenge of African Christian."

beliefs which were the moral fibre of the society. These moral foundations and beliefs, transformed through serious interaction with the word of God and inculturated into African [Nigerian] Christianity, will save and strengthen the moral stance of the Church."[101] Thus, the issue at stake is the identification of the true Nigerian elements to enable the Nigerian Christian to live truly. As a panacea to the Nigerian Christian moral crisis, Kunhiyop advocates that Christians should approach life holistically, live with a concern for one another as a community, recapture the key concepts of shame and honour, devise theological and hermeneutical models that are contextually relevant, shape theological/ministerial education to be contextually relevant, practice double listening and return to the Bible.

As is common to all African societies, the Nigerian society views life as one big whole. In terms of this thinking, it is the whole that brings about the unification of the parts. There is no such thing as the compartmentalization or dichotomization of life, for example, matter and spirit, soul and body, religious tension and daily life, physical and spiritual, theory and practice, religion and politics, religion and economics or academic and life situation. "Speculative reflection without practice has never been the trust of Africans. Practice, reflection, and praxis always go together."[102] Nkemkia calls this situation of "interconnectedness, relatedness or cohesion 'vital force' – the parts are really indispensable to the whole, and enable the whole to include in itself all the parts, though different from them."[103] Church leaders should, therefore, make use of all available opportunities to bridge the existing gaps resulting from this acquired Western worldview – a worldview which is inhibiting the true ownership of Christianity by Nigerian Christians – so as to enable them to evolve moral standards that apply to their own concrete realities.

The concept of community in Nigeria, which resonates with many traditional societies and also the Christian Scriptures, is an indispensable feature of Nigerian and other African societies and it is this concept that informs shame, honour and morality. The question usually asked when acts of shame or honour occur is, "whose child are you"? Such questions were vital to ensure good conduct in the community as every act of shame or honour was

---

101. Kunhiyop, 222.
102. Kunhiyop, 226.
103. Nkemkia, *African Theology*, 166.

tantamount to exposing the family, household, clan, community or kinship that would also be forced to participate in the act committed by the individual concerned. It was the duty of all grownups to look after children and praise and punishment were not necessarily meted out by their biological parents. People looked to the well-being of one another and ensured that the moral codes of the community were upheld. Unfortunately, Western individualism has invaded Nigerian communities and the church is succumbing to such influences and, as a result, people are engaging in unacceptable conduct without shame. It is becoming increasingly difficult to call people to order for unacceptable conduct. "Individual rights and freedom are given as legitimate reasons for children to rebel against parents, girls aborting their babies, and men and women cohabiting."[104] Many of these practices emphasize self and personal achievement, without any regard for the community. Christians and, especially, church leaders should be encouraged to jettison such practices and to emphasize community as a way in which to combat moral decay.

The challenge posed by the degeneration in the morality of Nigerian Christians has been given impetus by the relativism which is now being ascribed to the Bible instead of the Bible being upheld as an authoritative source of moral codes. Much of the theological education curricula in Nigerian seminaries and colleges are patterned on Western theologies and philosophical thought.[105] With the exception of the commendable work in respect of inculturation carried out by some Roman Catholic theologians, African independent churches and Pentecostal pastors, there is still much that needs to be done to interpret the Scriptures and formulate theologies in the context of the daily experiences of Nigerians. Church leaders should rise to the challenge of using Nigerian symbols and models to make the Scripture speak to the "Nigerianness" of the Nigerian Christian. It is in terms of such dimensions that Nigerian Christians may be enabled to navigate the moral questions confronting them by finding moral guidance for their daily lives in their unique circumstances. In addition, this may also help them to resist the numerous morally deficient attacks that saturate the social media, media and internet.

---

104. Kunhiyop, "Challenge of African Christian," 230.
105. Ekpenyong, *Beware of Gods*.

Eme has also argued for the upholding of the Christian Scriptures as the norm for the moral conduct of both Christians and, indeed, of all Nigerians in public office and other places of responsibility. In particular, he suggests that the eighth commandment, "You shall not steal,"[106] could motivate and inform Christians, thus preventing their becoming enmeshed in the corruption which is rife in Nigeria. Accordingly, he urges that "the 8th commandment constitutes an imperative to every Christian, both in public and private service, to avoid stealing of any kind. This commandment requires that every Nigerian Christian should, in concrete ways, reject the culture of embezzlement, kickbacks, fraud, exploitation, indiscipline, prostitution, bribery, and deception because this is God's command."[107] Eme's postulation is crucial for at least three reasons: first, it draws from a biblical norm which is in alignment with an African/Nigerian worldview with regard to the notion of shame and honour in respect of stealing. To be a thief in Nigerian traditional communities attracted stigmatization, and as such thieves were not to be given places of honour in the community. Stealing was also held to be hereditary and it was therefore usually regarded as unacceptable to marry into a family which had a thief as one of its members. Second, this postulation resonates with the critical issue of "corruption" which constitutes a major contributory factor to some of the current challenges facing Nigerian society, namely, poverty, underdevelopment and poor leadership. Stealing is a fitting nomenclature which names the evil by the actual name by which it is known in traditional society as compared to new terms[108] such as "sharing in the national cake," "settlement," "chop make I chop," "sharp, sharp" and so on. This practice weakens the import of the act in the public view and helps the perpetrator to evade the requisite stigmatization. Third, Eme's postulation represents a call to return to the Scripture which requires action that corresponds to Christian principles in order to validate one's Christian faith. This, in turn, would be transformative to all Nigerians of all creeds in terms of their ethical conduct as well as the nation's economy and international image. However, if this vision is to be realized, then the Christian teachings as enunciated in

---

106. Exodus 20:15.

107. Eme, *Ethics in Nigerian Social*, 181.

108. Expressions such as "sharing in the national cake," "settlement," "chop make I chop" and "sharp, sharp" are all related to fraudulent or corrupt practices and they are familiar terms among Nigerians.

the Old and New Testaments, and the doctrines of the Christian faith will have to flourish within the Nigerian context.

4.4.5 Inculturation and Nigerian Christianity

The Christian faith is said to not ever exist except when it is "translated" into a culture and this concept has been an integral feature of Christianity from its inception. According to Bosch, the developments that eventually gave rise to the emergence of what has now come to be termed "inculturation" began in Africa after World War II. More precisely, in 1956, a group of African priests from the Francophone countries published a book, *Des pretres noirs s'interrogent*. This work came to have a significant influence among Roman Catholics. Not long thereafter, Tharcisse Tshibangu, who was, at the time, a student at the Catholic Theological Faculty in Kinshasa, began to question his Belgian mentor's notions concerning a universally valid theology. In the process of time and as a result of more developments along these lines, it was finally recognized that "a plurality of cultures presupposes a plurality of theologies, and, therefore, for Third-world churches, a farewell to a Eurocentric approach. The Christian faith must be rethought, reformulated, and lived anew in each human culture. This must be done in a vital way, in-depth and right to the cultures' roots."[109] If this is to be achieved in the Nigerian context, ordinary Nigerian Christians (laity), church leaders and theologians are advised to interpret the teachings of Scripture in a reasonable and meaningful way by examining the cultural symbols and texts of the Nigerian peoples. However, such an endeavour requires Nigerian Christians, in collaboration with their theologians, to bring the "naked" Christian gospel into dialogue with the symbols, narratives, proverbs, riddles, songs, dances, paintings, names and the socioeconomic and political realities of Nigerians."[110]

So far, there have been ongoing attempts to inculturate the Christian faith within Nigerian society but these have been extremely slow and much still needs to be done. It is possible to locate visible signs of inculturation in some enclaves of the Christian fold such as the Roman Catholic Church, African Independent Churches (AIC), the Pentecostals and certain publications of some Nigerian theologians. However, whereas the Roman Catholics have

---

109. Bosch, *Transforming Mission*, 452.
110. Ekpenyong, *Beware of Gods*, 29.

made inputs in such areas as music, cultural interactions and the healing ministries, the AICs and Pentecostals have made an impact on the Nigerian milieu through their prayer methods and teachings that resonate with the daily experiences and challenges of all Nigerians. It may be argued by some social critics that much of the theological underpinnings of the AICs and Pentecostals lack sound theological foundations and that they are, therefore, deceptive, unscriptural and a platform for scandalous activities. This strain of argument and understanding of the Pentecostal movement has become a source of considerable concern within the orthodox or missionary established churches in Nigeria. For instance, Aboyade, states that "credit must be given to the Pentecostals for this type of attention-grabbing sermons . . . people like me find ourselves asking what message we have received from them but with no positive answer. All one hears often is what God can do, but not what we have to do to receive these miracles, that is, how to do God's will on earth."[111] The seemingly "magical" use of, and emphasis on, symbols such as anointing oil, mantles and the blood of Jesus are assumed to contribute to such scepticism. Nevertheless, it is not possible to dismiss Pentecostalism as a phenomenon simply because of some vital fragments of the inculturation which it is bringing to the concrete realities of Nigerians, as is evidenced by the large followership which it commands. In this respect, Ekpenyong's position may be a pointer in the right direction when he counsels that the "seriousness of Pentecostalism in the local pastoral ministry behooves us to accede to the demands of contextualization and inculturation. There is a need to research into a biblical Christology that correlates the ebullience of Pentecostal Christology practiced in Nigeria. What Scriptural perception of Jesus correlates the popular understanding of Jesus among Pentecostals as power?"[112]

Pentecostalism is, thus, offering solutions to the existential problems of Nigerians in such instances as the Night Bus Ministry which ministers to the safety of travellers in a country where roads are in a deplorable condition and insecurity is palpable. In addition, the prosperity gospel and motivational pep talks are giving hope to many Nigerians who are, because of a myriad of economic woes, unable to find hope in the political leadership

---

111. Aboyade, "Exhibitionists," 13.
112. Ekpenyong, *Beware of Gods*, 84–85.

and government policies of their country. However, despite these positive achievements, clandestine and reckless interpretations of Scripture in the name of inculturation may amount to error and cheap gospel, both of which would be catastrophic and inimical to both the Christian faith and the process of inculturation. In his work, *Christianity and African Gods: A Method in Theology*, Turaki proposes a method of approaching the African traditional religions from an integral biblical perspective with an emphasis on the primacy of both the Bible and biblical revelation as the legitimate basis of defining African traditional religions, cultures and worldviews, which have to submit to biblical authority, definition and teachings.[113] However, he cautions that, before the advent of Christianity as a religious system with its set of beliefs, practices and religious life, the traditional African mind had already been preoccupied with African traditional religious thought which has had a profound and dominant influence on the African Christian and must, therefore, be recognized and taken seriously.

Accordingly, "inculturation suggests a double movement: there is at once inculturation of Christianity and Christianization of culture. The gospel must remain Good News while becoming, up to a certain point, a cultural phenomenon, while it takes into account the meaning systems already present in the context."[114] In addition, inculturation should be viewed in the sense of a continuum as culture is dynamic and there is also the possibility of the church being led by the Holy Spirit to discover previously unknown mysteries of the faith. Furthermore, in a very real sense, inculturation involves what Joseph Blomjous terms "interculturation," the practice whereby theologies from different parts of the world, including the West, can interact, influence, challenge, enrich and invigorate each other.[115] The concept of "good news" is a vital concept that needs to incarnate in the Nigerian context and it is a concept which could easily find a comfortable dwelling in the said environment. This concept is also being considered by Nigerian church leaders.

---

113. Turaki, *Christianity and African Gods*.
114. Bosch, *Transforming Mission*, 454.
115. Bosch.

4.4.6 The Concept of Good News

In his discussion on the "Whole Gospel to the Whole Person," Adadevoh has pointed out that the phrase "good news" was used by the prophet Isaiah in the context of the deliverance of the Jews from the oppression of their enemies. As such, it was an anticipation of the coming of a saviour who would restore the times of *shalom* as they had been enjoyed in the time of King Solomon. Thus, the first proclamation of good news was that "in spite of the difficulties and sufferings under the rulers of other nations, the people of Israel need to be aware that their God was still the King over all the nations of the earth. He still reigns. He had not lost control."[116] The words of the prophet were extremely clear on this matter – "How beautiful on the mountains are the feet of those who bring good news, who proclaim peace, who bring good tidings, who proclaim salvation, who say to Zion, "Your God reigns!"[117] Isaiah also used the term "good news" in respect of God's promise to his people to visit them in Zion with deliverance[118] and, in the passage, "The Spirit of the Sovereign LORD is on me because the LORD has anointed me to proclaim good news to the poor."[119] This contains a prophecy about the Son of God who would come to the people of Israel to bring them deliverance and salvation. Adadevoh is of the opinion that Isaiah's prophecy was fulfilled in the New Testament in the person of Jesus Christ, who secured the salvation of both the Jews and the rest of humanity through the laying down of his own life as a ransom. Although this approach differed from the anticipation of the Jews which had been strictly political, the original plan of God still involves salvation that touches "not only the spiritual aspects of human life, but also the political, economic and social."[120]

In the face of the growing irrelevance of the church in current global, national and local challenges, including morality, integrity, poverty, hunger, violence, irresponsible leadership, social peace, injustice and underdevelopment, Adadevoh advocates for a return to the Scripture for the purpose of taking another look at the nature of "good news" and the mission of the

---

116. Adadevoh, "Whole Gospel," 27.
117. Isaiah 52:7 (NIV).
118. Isaiah 40:9.
119. Isaiah 61:1 (NIV).
120. Adadevoh, "Whole Gospel," 27.

church. In his view, the good news or gospel as understood by the Jews, taught and lived by Jesus, is all embracing with regard to the spiritual and material challenges of both humankind and the environment. A return to this biblical meaning of the good news is essential for the Nigerian church and for the contemporary Christian mission in all parts of the world. In a broader sense, therefore, and in line with the implications of the concept of good news, the church in Nigeria should commit to a broader understanding of the blessing intention of God; not only spiritual, but also economic, political, social, scientific and technological. In addition, the church in Nigeria should engage in national transformation and not only individual evangelism and discipleship; commit to both the kingdom now and the kingdom yet to come; posit "spiritual salvation theology" in the broader context of "kingdom theology."[121] The propagation of the good news in all its ramifications is possible only through the engagement of the church, as an agent of transformation, in the Nigerian mission field.

4.4.7 The Church in Mission as an Agent of Transformation

Writing in the Nigerian context, Anthony O. Farinto and others have made some contributions to the subject of the church in missions as an agent of transformation. Farinto affirms that the church and missions are inseparable and, for that reason, the church would cease to be meaningful if it lost its mission focus. According to him, in a generic sense, the word "mission" is used to refer to a specific goal or operation, either on the part of the church or the state. "Mission" is derived from the Latin word *mitto* which means to send and has the same meaning as the Greek word *apostolos* which means someone who is sent to accomplish a goal or task. Thus, mission is a biblical term which may be perceived to have been at work in God's interaction with Abraham in Genesis and which also flows through biblical history, culminating with the church, not as a building but as individuals who have confessed faith in Jesus. Farinto further posits that the term "transformation," although currently popular and often used by politicians or any individual who is trying to gain the emotional acceptance of people, was first encountered in the 1990s in the United States of America. In this American connection, the word was used in reference to the major plan to overhaul the American

---

121. Adadevoh, 27.

education system – "Education transformation." Besides these usages, Farinto argues that the traditional use of the word, which is derived from Romans 12:2, has been expounded upon by Matthew Poole as to be regenerated and changed in your whole person.[122] This understanding and use of the word "transformation" is in line with the Greek word for biblical transformation, *metamorphoo*, from which the English word, metamorphosis, which refers to complete change, is derived. It is in the light of these that Farinto posits that "the church in mission (as) an agent of transformation indicates the supernatural impact of the presence of God on His creation. When a man first experiences the divine transformation of God, it is spiritual and physical, and then the human society; both the sacred and secular, feels its impact.[123] The implication is, thus, that there ought to be increase in the holiness of life, accelerated growth, reconciliation in relationships, the use of spiritual gifts and an increase in relevance in the participation in the broader society. This would include the radical correction of social ills by the church, a commensurate decrease in crime rates and evidence of the application of biblical justice. Unlike the imperial church (the post-Constantinine church), which was preoccupied with arguments instead of engaging in missions in all its implications, Farinto challenges the Nigerian church to be engaged in missions as an agent of transformation in individuals, groups and corporate entities in the sense of seeking positive change in the whole of human life, spiritually, materially, and socially. The quest to recover the true identity of human beings, as created in the image of God, and the discovery of their true vocation as true stewards faithfully caring for God's world and his people should inform the church's mission as an agent of change in Nigerian society. However, the church would do well not to neglect its resources of persistent repentance, humility, prayer and sacrificial servanthood.

For Maccain, because change is both imperative and a process which has been a part of God's activities in the world in successive generations, the church is placed in human society and in Nigeria in particular, as God's missional agent of societal change. Building on the following two principles, namely human beings as God's instruments of change in the world, and God's process of change through the "hard way, the slow way, the difficult

---

122. Farinto, "Church in Mission."
123. Farinto.

way, the progressive way, and the way that is opposite of the way human beings do things," Maccain proceeds with his thesis. The structures that are not able to elude God's change include individuals (Philippian jailor), families (Philippian jailor's family), the church (church at Philippi), the judiciary (Paul's reaction to the injustice meted out to him as a Roman citizen who may not be flogged), the economy (Joseph's ability to transform the economic fortunes of Egypt), governmental (the change of government from a federation to a monarchy by Samuel), infrastructure (Nehemiah rebuilding the broken walls of Jerusalem), and man's attitude towards God (Daniel's ability to turn men to God by his consistency, obedience and trust in God during the reign of Darius and Cyrus).[124] In Maccain's opinion, each of the biblical accounts show us prototypes of how God is able to use Christians (leaders/members) to achieve social change in the Nigerian society. Arguing further for societal transformation, he cites the struggles in the United States which were championed by a church leader, Martin Luther King Jr., and Rosa Parks, an ordinary black lady. Maccain is of the opinion that the civil rights movements were successful because they encompassed good leadership, they embraced and mobilized all segments of society, and the people refused to take no for an answer.[125] Maccain's position could inform this study in the sense that the engagement of the church in social transformation in Nigerian society could yield more lasting results if the church (leaders) were to explore avenues such as collaboration with civil society to transform policies and institutions in order to eradicate poverty, underdevelopment, irresponsible leadership and corruption.

Meanwhile, Okoye has urged that Nigerian church leaders and members should learn from the example of William Wilberfoce who devoted his life to fight for the abolition of the slave trade and the reformation of character in the British society, as it is in this way church leaders and church members may be enabled to lead the church in mission in Nigeria as an agent of transformation. In arguing for the church as a tool in societal transformation, based on historical evidence, Okoye postulates that it would be possible to entrench in Nigerian society the values such as character, morals, justice and business integrity, which became fashionable in Britain as a result of the

---

124. Maccain, "Church in Societal Transformation."
125. Maccain.

work of Wilberforce. The strategy for realizing this goal would be for church leaders "to encourage a balanced and holistic approach to the preaching, teaching and interpretation of the word of God; to encourage all Christian denominations to return to sound biblical disciplining of their members."[126] In so doing, Christians would set the example in terms of what they both preach and teach for the purpose of carrying the crusade to the broader society. Okoye further suggests that, because the nature of "this moral cancer called corruption" is spiritual, it is essential that the moral crusade be backed by intense devotion and prayer.

Yusufu Turaki, eminent Nigerian scholar and theologian, has emphasized the importance of the private lives of church leaders and, to an extent, of Christians who have a missional mandate to lead change within society. For him, their private lives constitute the foundations of human and social transformation.[127] There is no doubt that the church, in its mission as an agent of transformation, should live out the change it seeks to see in society as the lifestyle of the members of the church would, otherwise, stand in contrast to both the message and the values they propagate. This position calls for church leaders and church members to evaluate themselves in the light of the teachings of Scripture and to ensure that their lives are above reproach. Issues that may raise questions regarding the church's public image include issues related to justice, for example, gender stereotypes, other forms of social exclusions including HIV and AIDS stigmatization, and environmental injustice.

4.4.8 Church Leaders and Gender Issues

Onwunta, Amogu and Eme have argued for the need for the church in Nigeria to rise to the challenge of gender injustice both within the church and within Nigerian society. Onwunta, thus, suggests a collaborative stance on the maximum utilization of the huge resources within the women, who constitute the largest group within the church, in terms of the positions of leadership which they are so often denied. In addition, Onwunta insists on a departure from the stereotypes which the church is party to reinforcing.[128] According to Amogu, it is not possible for the church to make sufficient inroads into Nigerian

---

126. Okoye, "Why Are We Here?," 5.
127. Turaki, "Private Life."
128. Onwunta, *Gender Stereotyping*.

society for the purpose of transformation unless the church deals with the issue of gender from within. The church must first embark on self-theologization on the issue of gender – the male and female image of God – to understand that it can make no progress until both male and female gender partake and attain the transformational objective of the gospel. She further asserts that, "in the Magnificat of the blessed Mary,[129] Mary prophesied that Jesus Christ, as Saviour, has set forth for His church an agenda that encompasses a moral revolution, a social revolution and justice, an economic revolution, a religious revolution and peace."[130] It is this transformative agenda for the church that Jesus summarized in Matthew 5:13–16, when he referred to the church or his followers as the "salt of the earth" and the "light of the world." According to Eme, church leaders and members should go beyond the rhetoric for justice and "As God's deputies on earth, Christian movements should give the necessary concrete attention to issues such as the AIDS scourge, gender discrimination, human trafficking, poverty alleviation and corrupt practices."[131] Instead of stigmatizing and discriminating among persons on the basis of gender and state of health, the church should manifest a different attitude from that which is exhibited by the traditional cultures. Following the example of Jesus who identified with and affirmed all persons, forgave sins and healed the afflicted, the church should treat all human beings with love and compassion.

4.4.9 The Church and the Environment

Population growth, poverty and poor governance are reflected in the pressures on natural resources and the decline in environmental indicators in Nigeria. Soil erosion and the concomitant loss in fertility, deforestation, water scarcity, water pollution, biodiversity loss, municipal and hazardous waste, and the impact of oil and gas development as well as other contributory factors are primary areas of concern with regard to the environmental degradation which is increasingly worsening in Nigeria. However, besides the abovementioned developments which may be said to emanate from the situation in Nigeria itself, there are also imperialist activities which may be

---

129. Luke 1:46–55.
130. Amogu, "Recovering True Sense," 2.
131. Eme, *Gender (In)Justice*, 75.

termed criminal and which are posing monumental environmental challenges to the Nigerian environment. For example, in 1988, five shiploads of toxic waste (3888 tons) originating from Italy, were dumped at the small port of Koko in the Delta state, a predominantly Christian community.[132] The fact that the church, through its respective structures, was not able to respond to this challenge may be understandable as it may have needed experts to detect such toxic disposals. However, other activities which are equally damaging to the environment and hazardous to the lives of even church members and which have not been adequately addressed by the church attest to the church's passive stance in the face of the environmental challenges facing Nigeria. As is usual with many other issues, the Christian community has voiced its concern about the environmental perils through communiqués. Nevertheless, although one could argue that it is not possible for the church to tackle every single issue and that issues such as environmental degradation are best left to the experts and the environmental activists, such excuses cannot be sustained in the light of the church's claims to morality, as both an agent of change and a community-based organization. It is on this note that Okopido is calling on the church to bring its resources to bear on the issues affecting the Nigerian environment. He is calling on both individual Christians and on the church as a body to partner with NGOs, CBOs and the Nigerian government. The views expressed in Okopido's argument, as they relate to environmental concerns, and his call on the church and its leaders to partner with other institutions to address environmental challenges is of special interest to this study's focus on transformation and sustainability.

Okopido anchors his theology for the church and the environment and the reason for the ongoing environmental crisis on Genesis chapters 1–3, and asserts that the creation of the cosmos was the manifestation of God's wise design. This design proceeded from his mind and culminated in the creation of man and woman, who were made in the image and likeness of God to "fill the earth" and to "have dominion over it" as stewards of God himself. Okopido postulates that the harmony between God, humankind and the environment (created world) was disrupted by the sin of Adam and Eve and the result of this sin was the curse on both the earth and the human creatures, ushering in hard labour and death. He further contends that the implication of God's

---

132. Okopido, "Church and Environment."

command to Adam and Eve to "till the earth" and to "have dominion over the earth" was not merely a simple conferring of authority, but also a summons to responsibility. Accordingly, the church has a responsibility towards creation and it should consider it its duty to exercise that responsibility in public and in collaboration with others both to protect the earth, water, land, forest and wildlife as gifts of the creator and to save humankind from self-destruction.

Meanwhile, it is commendable that, in 2010, CAN took the initiative for the first time to raise the awareness of church leaders concerning the task of the church in relation to the environment as an agent of transformation. Okopido's attempt to develop a theology for the environment is also commendable. It underscores the point that theology is not the exclusive preserve of the experts, but it is also the endeavour of the faithful as they grapple daily with the issues of life and find light from the word of God to shed light on their paths.

4.5 Conclusion

The social and theological discourse of Nigerian church leaders has made some progress beyond the usual confines of social services – charity, relief, education, health and a measure of empowerment – and the spiritualization of salvation and evangelism with the narrow scope of the personal salvation within the church community. This progress is evidenced in such areas as dialogue, advocacy and collaboration with civil institutions. A number of such new social and theological grounds could be regarded as both emergent and underdeveloped. However, whereas such steps are highly commendable, it is essential that the engagement be deepened and broadened in order to consolidate the present gains and, thus, make room for further strides with more significant results. A more pragmatic approach to theology is gradually coming into play as Nigerian theologians, church leaders and ordinary Christians struggle to make sense of their biblical understandings in the context of their experiences in religious violence, partisan politics, poverty, underdevelopment, poor leadership, sexism, HIV and AIDS, environmental challenges and insecurity. Again, the efforts made are reassuring but much still remains to be done in order to realize the desired impact – an impact which should be pragmatic, holistic and enduring.

So far, this study has been based on the body of literature that pertains to development and leadership within the sociopolitical, economic and ecclesial realm as applied to the Nigerian and global parameters that relate to the study. There is little doubt that, based on the successes and scope of engagement thus far, church leaders in Nigeria have both the resources and the capability at their disposal to act as agents of change in the country. However, despite the fact that their attainments are both commendable and challenging, more meaningful engagement is required to address the widespread issues of poverty, underdevelopment, corruption and poor leadership which are so deeply rooted in Nigerian society. In order to come to an understanding of the way in which church leaders may contribute more meaningfully to the sociopolitical and economic transformation of Nigerian society and the components that should comprise such engagement, this study will also take into account the dissemination and reflections on the empirical study that was carried out among Nigerian church leaders. In addition, the study will also aim to corroborate some of the assertions that have emanated from the study of the relevant literature.

CHAPTER 5

Dissemination and Reflection on Empirical Study

5.1 Introduction

Some vital milestones were attained when the study of relevant literature on development and leadership was undertaken in chapters 2 and 3 respectively. Nigerian development and leadership issues are related to the subject of this study, which is about how church leaders can contribute more meaningfully to the transformation of the Nigerian society in light of poverty, underdevelopment, corruption and poor leadership, and what would be the main components that would inform such social engagement. The historical antecedents of Nigerian society revealed that the sources of poverty, underdevelopment, corruption and poor leadership may be traced, first, to the exploitation of Nigerians by the European traders and colonialists. Second, from the postcolonial era to present day Nigeria, the exploitation of Nigerians and the perpetuation of poverty, underdevelopment, corruption and poor leadership may be attributed to the poor leadership of the military and political elite. These Nigerian elites have been in collaboration with neocolonialists and imperialists. The abuse of ethnicity, religion, certain traditional/religious mores, and globalization also continue to serve the selfish interests of these individuals and institutions.

In chapter 3, discussions on leadership in precolonial, colonial, postcolonial, military and postmilitary (democratic) Nigerian society revealed that the failure of leadership in each of these eras in Nigerian history has contributed to the perpetuation of the challenges of poor leadership, underdevelopment, poverty and corruption in Nigeria. Furthermore, the important role of leadership as the facilitator of development and social transformation in Nigerian society was brought to light. In chapter 4, a journey was undertaken to investigate the social and theological discourses of church leaders in Nigeria so as to be able to assess their concern for social transformation and the contribution of these discourses to Nigerian society. Based on the analysis of relevant literature it was ascertained that the social and theological discourse of Nigerian church leaders has made some progress and that this progress has, in turn, enabled the church to move beyond the usual confines of charity and social services. However, this progress, although commendable, is also emergent and underdeveloped as is evidenced in such areas as dialogue, advocacy and collaboration with civil institutions. The need to deepen and broaden these new grounds so that the present gains may be consolidated in order to make room for greater strides with more significant results was also established.

The aim in this chapter is to present and reflect on the results of the empirical study. The main focus of this exercise is to understand the way in which church leaders may contribute more meaningfully to the social transformation of Nigerian society in the light of the prevailing poverty, underdevelopment, corruption and poor leadership, and also the vital elements of such an engagement. In order to achieve this, the study intends to concentrate on the responses to the open-ended questionnaires as they relate to the research questions so as to uncover themes which will aid the proposal of a sustainable transformational approach to the engagement of church leaders in Nigeria.

5.2 Empirical Study

The empirical research was based on the main aim of this study as it was presented in the research questions – see chapter 1 section 1.5: How may church leaders in Nigeria, in light of the poverty, underdevelopment, corruption and poor leadership in that country, contribute more meaningfully to the sociopolitical and economic transformation of Nigerian society? In what ways could Nigerian church leadership be able to achieve this? When translated into a sustainable transformational development approach (with a view to more meaningful engagement on the part of church leaders in the sociopolitical and economic change within Nigerian society), what would the possible constituent elements of such an approach be?

The following sections will present the research processes, responses to the questions and the findings of the empirical study.

5.2.1 Research Method

The research design and research methodology used in this study was described in chapter 1. The descriptive research method, as applicable to both social and practical theological research, was adopted in this study and qualitative research method was used. The empirical study was conducted from March 2010 to April 2011 in Nigeria. The exercise presented in this chapter is guided by the descriptive-empirical, interpretive, normative and pragmatic tasks of practical theological methodology, as enunciated by Richard Osmer.[1]

5.2.1.1 Sample

The nonprobability purposive sampling method[2] was used for this study and church leaders from throughout Nigeria were chosen for the project. These church leaders were identified by their roles as past and present serving ecumenical, denominational and congregational leaders. The researcher took care to reflect the broad denominational lines and the ecumenical, denominational and congregational expressions of the church.

5.2.1.2 Data Collection Procedure

Open-ended questionnaires (Appendix A) were issued to nine serving and past national leaders of the Christian Association of Nigeria (CAN) and the same questionnaires were issued to three leaders of each of the ecumenical church blocs respectively, namely, the Catholic Secretariat of Nigeria (CSN), Christian Council of Nigeria (CCN), Christian Pentecostal Fellowship of Nigeria and Pentecostal Fellowship of Nigeria (CPFN/PFN), Organization of African Instituted Churches (OAIC); and the Tarrarya Ekkelisiyar Kristi a Nigeria and Evangelical Church of West Africa[3] (TEKAN/ECWA) – a

---

1. Osmer, *Practical Theology*, 4–12. See also 1.8.1.
2. Babbie, 182–83, 11th ed. See also 1.9.3.
3. The Evangelical Church of West Africa is now known as the Evangelical Church Win them All (ECWA).

total of fifteen questionnaires. The same questionnaires were also given to four leaders of the Lagos Presbyterian Church, namely, the minister, and three ruling elders. Unsuccessful attempts were made to reach three church leaders who were involved in social issues but were nonmembers of their church group classification. In all, thirty-one questionnaires were issued but twenty-two only were returned, representing a 70.97 percent response. Two questionnaires were sent by email, two were sent by registered post as the preferred option of the relevant respondents while the remainder were all handed out by the researcher in person. When the questionnaires were issued the time of collection was also agreed upon. This time of collection was at the convenience of the respondents. The issues of voluntary participation and confidentiality were emphasized at all times. Initial contacts were made with the national office of CAN and the Session of the Lagos Presbyterian Church for consent to conduct the research study with their leaders. In both instances consent was given and, at the conclusion of the study, letters of confirmation that the research had, indeed, been carried out, were issued by the respective institutions.

5.2.1.3 *Instruments of Measure*

This study used open-ended questionnaires as a means of gathering the empirical data. In view of the main focus of the study, as reflected in the research question, the researcher deemed the open-ended questionnaire as the most appropriate tool with which to elicit the relevant responses from the participants on the way in which they could contribute more meaningfully, in a sustainable, transformational manner, to the social transformation of Nigerian society. Just as the questions were informed by Osmer's descriptive-empirical, interpretive, normative and pragmatic tasks of practical theological methodology,[4] the responses will be assessed using this yardstick. In addition, the practical theological methodology will be used to aid the presentation of and reflection on the data. The data will, thus, be used mainly as a description of the findings arising from church leaders in Nigeria to enrich the discussion on a sustainable transformational approach to development in Nigeria. This discussion will be presented in chapter 6.

---

4. Osmer, *Practical Theology*. See also 1.8.1.

5.2.1.4 Data Coding and Thematization

Coding was used in order to conceal the identities of the respondents and to manage the data using the computer-Aided Qualitative Data Analysis (CAQDAS) software program (Atlas/ti software). Gibbs has pointed out the importance of thematic coding and categorizing in qualitative research and what the exercise actually entails. "Coding is how you define what the data you are analyzing are about. It involves identifying and recording one or more passages of text or other data items such as the parts of pictures that, in some sense, exemplify the same theoretical or descriptive idea."[5] Such texts are usually identified and linked with a name for the specific concept – the code and it is this sense that codes are helpful in the management and analysis of data. The codes will also be concept and data driven.[6] This implies that some of the codes represented come from the research literature, from topics from the questionnaire schedule and from hunches about what is going on, and also as a result of reading the empirical data and trying to understand what is happening.

5.2.2 Profile of Respondents

The following data was gathered from the questionnaires which were completed by national church leaders of the Christian Association of Nigeria (CAN), bloc leaders of CAN and the congregational leaders of the Lagos Presbyterian Church. A total of twenty-two church leaders were involved as respondents in the research study. The first factor of importance was the status of the respondents in terms of the positions they occupied as church leaders and their involvement in development, followed by their ecumenical and denominational representation. The respondents also represented the voices of the youth, women, senior citizens, clergy and nonclergy. With the exception of the first two questions which indicate the respondents' national, bloc or congregational connections, positions and number of years in leadership, all the other questions were the same in the sense of the information they sought for. The discussion on the profile of the respondents which encompasses the various categories (national, bloc or congregation), positions, years of service and their engagement in development will be based on the responses that

---

5. Gibbs, *Analysing Qualitative Data*, 44–46.
6. Gibbs.

were elicited by questions 1, 2, 10a and 10 b: Question 1. **How long have you been a leader of CAN (national or bloc) or LPC?;** Question 2. **What positions have you held or are you still holding?;** Question 10a. **Have you been involved in sociopolitical and economic transformational activities? and;** 10b. **Please name these activities and state how you became involved**.

While the aim of question 1 was to ascertain whether the respondent had served as a church leader within the time frame of this study (1999–2010), question 2 was aimed at establishing the position which each respondent occupied to assess his/her authority to speak from such a platform. The aim of question 10a was to seek to understand the lived experience of the respondent as regards development while question 10b aimed to understand the particular activity in which the respondent had been involved in development, so as to be able to confirm such claims, or not. The code DEV.+ (development positive) indicated that the respondent had answered in the affirmative that he/she had been involved in developmental activities and had also substantiated such claims by mentioning relevant activities while DEV.- (development negative) indicated that the respondent had indicated that he/she had not been involved in developmental activities and, thus, was not able to mention such activities in which he/she had been involved.

For the purpose of concealing the identities of the respondents in accordance with the ethical compliance of this study, the respondents were represented by the code P (Person) and a number, for example 1, 2, etc. These codes, for example, (P1) indicating person 1 were generated by the atlas.ti software which was used by the researcher in this study for the purposes of data management. The study adopted this approach in order to simplify the representation of the participants of the study so as to facilitate the readers' understanding of the contents of the study, particularly in view of the fact that certain readers may not have been acquainted with either the software or the codes used in the primary documents. The researcher himself undertook a course to enable him to be able to use the atlas.ti software for the purpose of data management before proceeding with the presentation of and reflection on the data.

5.2.2.1 *National CAN Leaders*

The demographic details of the CAN national leader participants are presented in the following table.

Table 5.1: The position, duration of term, ecumenical bloc of origin and development engagement indicator of the nine national CAN respondents

Position	Duration	Bloc	Dev. Engagement
National President	2007–10	CSN	Dev.+
National President	1995–2002	CCN	Dev.+
National President	1986–94	CSN	Dev.+
National Vice President	2006–10	OAIC	Dev.+
National Gen. Secretary	1993–2010	ECWA/TEKAN	Dev.+
National Treasurer	1999–2010	PFN/CPFN	Dev.+
National Women's Leader	2000–2010	CSN	Dev.+
National Youth Leader	2001–10	PFN/CPFN	Dev.+
Centre Manager	2007–10	OAIC	Dev.-
Total	9	5	8 Dev.+ 1 Dev.-

As indicated in table 5.1, out of the nine national CAN respondents, three had served as president, one as vice president, one as general secretary, one as treasurer, one as women leader, one as youth leader and one as centre manager. With the exception of one respondent, whose tenure of service as a CAN national leader had elapsed before 1999, all the other respondents had served within the time frame of the study. However, the respondent whose tenure had elapsed before 1999 was still playing a vital role as a development-oriented church leader in Nigeria. He was, therefore, included in the study both as a past leader of CAN and also based on his crucial role in the development engagement of church leaders in Nigeria. As the table indicates, the national CAN church leaders were drawn from all the ecumenical blocs which comprise a broad range of the majority of the church denominations representing the Christian community in Nigeria. As regards development engagement, eight of national CAN leaders had indicated, and had been able to substantiate, that they had been involved in one form or other of development activities in Nigeria. One leader only had indicated the contrary.

According to the primary documents, the respondents of CAN national leadership are represented as follows:

National President, President (past), I was the President, Vice-President (CAN), Acting President, President (OAIC), General Secretary – National CAN, National Treasurer, National Chairperson of Women's Wing of CAN (WOWICAN), National President of Youth Wing of CAN and CAN National Centre Manager.

It follows, therefore, that the respondents from the national CAN all occupied valid positions, represented a broad spectrum of the national and denominational divisions in the church in Nigeria as well as occupied positions in the Nigerian sociocultural and political milieus and were, thus, qualified to speak with authority.

5.2.2.2 Bloc CAN Leaders

The demographic details of the respondents representing the constituents of CAN, known as blocs, are presented in the table opposite.

As indicated in Table 5.2, nine CAN bloc leaders representing four blocs of CAN responded to the questionnaires. All the blocs had been issued three questionnaires each. With the exception of CCN, which returned all the questionnaires issued; all the other blocs that responded returned two of the three questionnaires which had been issued. However, the researcher is of the opinion that the response rate is satisfactorily substantial and that it constitutes a valid representation of the blocs of CAN. In addition, all the respondents occupied key leadership positions in their respective blocs, had served within the time frame required in this study and were development-oriented. It is also necessary to mention at this point that the OAIC was not able to respond to the questionnaires issued to it at the bloc level. Accordingly, the only voices representing the OAIC were, therefore, from the national leadership of CAN whose representatives responded to the questionnaire as indicated in Table 5.1.

Table 5.2: Bloc, position, duration of term and development engagement of CAN bloc respondents

No.	Bloc	Position	Duration	Bloc Total	Dev. Engagement
1	CSN	Secretary General	2007–10	2	Dev.+
2	CSN	Secretary General	2001–6		
3	CCN	National President	2003–10	3	Dev.+
4	CCN	General Secretary	2007–10		
5	CCN	General Secretary	2000–2004		
6	ECWA/TEKAN	State Secretary	2003–10	2	Dev.+
7	ECWA/TEKAN	General Secretary	2002–10		
8	PFN/CPFN	National President	2005–10	2	Dev.+
9	PFN/CPFN	Chairman FCT	2005–10		
Total				9	9

The respondents' positions and the blocs they represented, as contained in the primary documents, are as follows:

> Secretary General (CSN), Secretary General (Past) (CSN), General Secretary (CCN), General Secretary (CCN), National President (CCN), General Secretary (ECWA/TEKAN), State Secretary (ECWA/TEKAN), National President (PFN/CPFN) and Chairman FCT (PFN/CPFN).

As regards both the national and bloc leadership of CAN, another interesting index which caught the researcher's attention was the broad representation in the pool of the respondents of the sociopolitical landscape of Nigeria, in the sense of the geopolitical zones in the country or the north, south, east and west national demarcations. Unlike the bloc leadership of CAN where there was no female respondent, the national CAN and the Lagos Presbyterian Church leadership both featured female respondents whose voices brought a different flavour to the discussions.

5.2.2.3 Lagos Presbyterian Church Leaders

The demographic details of the respondents from the Lagos Presbyterian Church, representing church leadership from the congregational expression of the church in Nigeria, are presented in the table below.

Table 5.3: LPC leaders' position, years of service and development engagement

No.	Position	Duration	Dev. Engagement
1	Minister in Charge	2007–10	Dev.+
2	Ruling Elder	1995–2010	Dev.+
3	Ruling Elder	2000–2010	Dev.+
4	Ruling Elder	1993–2010	Dev.+
Total			4

Table 5.3 indicates that four respondents participated in the empirical research. While three were ruling elders, one minister in charge also took part in the research study. Whereas this does indicate the typical congregational leadership configuration with one minister and several elders or other leaders, the respondents had all served for a considerable number of years. The said respondents had also been involved in developmental activities within the life of the local church and beyond. Another interesting dimension of the leadership of LPC is made up of elders rather than clergy, and so was usually closer to the church membership or followership. Such voices, it is hoped, will enrich the discussion on the quest for a more meaningful social engagement on the part of church leaders in Nigeria.

A summary of the profile of all the twenty-two respondents who took part in the empirical study is depicted in the following table:

Table 5.4: Total number of research participants and the groups they represent

No.	CH. Group	Position	Duration	Dev. Engage-ment	CH. Group Total
1	CAN NAT.	President	2007–10	Dev.+	
2	CAN NAT.	President	1995–2002	Dev.+	
3	CAN NAT.	President	1986–94	Dev.+	
4	CAN NAT.	Vice President	2006–10	Dev+	
5	CAN NAT.	Secretary	1993–2010	Dev.+	
6	CAN NAT.	Treasurer	1999–2010	Dev.+	
7	CAN NAT.	Women's Leader	2000–2010	Dev.+	
8	CAN NAT.	Youth Leader	2001–10	Dev.+	
9	CAN NAT.	Centre Manager	2007–10	Dev.-	
					9
10	CAN CSN	Secretary	2001–06	Dev.+	
11	CAN CSN	Secretary	2007–10	Dev.+	
12	CAN CCN	President	2003–10	Dev.+	
13	CAN CCN	Secretary	2007–10	Dev.+	
14	CAN CCN	Secretary	2000–2004	Dev.+	
15	CAN ECWA/TEKAN	Secretary	2002–10	Dev+	
16	CAN ECWA/TEKAN	Secretary	2003–10	Dev.+	
17	CAN PFN/CPFN	President	2005–10	Dev.+	
18	CAN PFN/CPFN	Chairman	2005–10	Dev.+	
					9
19	LPC	Minister	2007–10	Dev.+	
20	LPC	Elder	1995–2010	Dev.+	
21	LPC	Elder	2000–2010	Dev.+	
22	LPC	Elder	1993–2010	Dev.+	
					4
Total No. of Participants					22

Having described the twenty-two respondents in the empirical study, the next task is to seek an understanding of the social or development engagement rating of the church and church leaders themselves. A self-score is for the purpose of hearing directly from the church leaders themselves regarding how well or not they considered their social engagements within the Nigerian milieu with regard to the challenges of poverty, corruption, underdevelopment and poor leadership within the said context. In addition, this exercise may underscore, even slightly or otherwise, the views expressed in the literature review concerning the impact of Christian religious leaders and the church in Nigeria in response to the socioeconomic and political challenges in the country.

5.2.3 The Social Engagement Rating of the Church

Based on the views of the church leader respondents and in line with the descriptive-empirical task,[7] question 3 was asked to help the researcher gain a thorough understanding of how much the Nigerian church has impacted Nigerian society:

How would you assess the church in terms of its activities towards the political, economic and social transformation of Nigeria?[8] The aim of this question was to gauge the feeling of church leaders regarding the church's social ministry so as to enable them to suggest more meaningful ways in which the church, through its leaders and members, could become involved in the transformation of Nigerian society. It was hoped that this would also make it easier to suggest the components of such meaningful engagements.

Based on their responses to the question, a number of the respondents generated their own ratings, for example, "average" and "above average." In addition to the scores of "average" and "above average," the researcher supplied "below average" in order to balance the two score lines as is usual wherever such score lines are used. Each of these categories of responses will now be presented and also discussed.

---

7. Osmer, *Practical Theology*. See also 1.8.1.
8. See Appendix A.

5.2.3.1 Above Average

Four of the respondents who participated in the empirical study rated the church's engagement in social transformation above average or else they alluded to the said score as follows:

> Economic and social responsibilities are quite an above average achievement by the congregation and this has impacted positively on the development of Nigerians within the area of influence of the church (congregation).[9]

> The church in Nigeria is doing its best to contribute to the progress of the nation politically, economically and socially. But one must agree that the problem in Nigeria is very complex. Quite engaged positively.[10]

> The church has always been active. Christians have been in politics to play their roles.[11]

> Very good. We could do more.[12]

5.2.3.2 Average

Fifteen of the participants who responded to the question either rated or alluded to the church's social contributions as average. Some of the responses are as follows:

> Average.[13]

> My personal assessment is that the church, in terms of its activities towards the political, economic and social transformation of Nigeria, is average. Needs more effort.[14]

> The church is more socioeconomic in its approach to the transformation of Nigerians but less political.[15]

---

9. P10.
10. P18.
11. P8.
12. P5.
13. P21.
14. P22.
15. P13.

> Some – especially the mainstream churches – are very active in these areas. But there are others which show little or no attention for these concerns.[16]

> Since the inception of the present democratic dispensation, churches have become more involved and committed to political and social education.[17]

> The church has not been too involved in the political transformation of Nigeria. They have always seen politics as a no-go area for Christians but now the story has changed.[18]

> Quite good but slow and insufficient.[19]

> Politically, the church has maintained a lukewarm attitude to the political transformation of Nigeria until recently. Economically, the church is a major contributor to the economic empowerment of the members but not contributing significantly to the economic policies. Socially, this is where the church has played a significant role in establishing schools, hospitals and orphanages in meeting the needs of the citizens.[20]

5.2.3.3 Below Average

Although the score line of "below average" was supplied by the researcher, a number of the responses regarding the rating of the social engagement of church leaders and church members fitted into this category with three of the respondents alluding to this rating as follows:

> I'll put the fellowship's performance at about 50 percent, considering the activities of its thirteen member churches. This means that the performance is still far below our goal of at least 75–80 percent.[21]

---

16. P20.
17. P19.
18. P14.
19. P2.
20. P12.
21. P6.

Not much effect on the political, economic and social transformation of Nigeria. The proliferation of churches and crusades turn church attention to fund raising events.[22]

Politically, I would score the church quite low because, apart from the regime of Rev. Dr. James Ukaegbu in the late 80s/early 90s, the church has been quite politically shy and timid and would not make any pronouncements, whether through prayers or constructive interviews to condemn the obvious political mayhem in Nigeria.[23]

Despite the fact that there is not a significant difference between the statistics for "above" and "below average," the score registered for "average" is fairly significant as compared to the other scores. This, thus, implies that approximately 68.2 percent of the respondents were of the opinion that the contributions of the church in Nigeria to the sociopolitical and economic transformation of Nigerian society are average. However, whereas this score may be perceived as significant, many of the respondents, including those who had rated the church above average, were clearly of the opinion that such contributions were insufficient. However, this attitude on the part of the respondents is understandable as the seeming average score is far removed from the practical experiences of Nigerians in terms of the poverty, underdevelopment, corruption and poor leadership in the country. Throughout the congregational and ecumenical expressions of the church, although the church was venturing into previously unexplored territories, church leaders were in agreement that both the church and its leaders had not done enough to overcome the sociopolitical and economic challenges facing Nigerians. This claim is substantiated by the responses presented above.

A careful examination of the main areas of the church's social contributions reveals that the church's engagement in this respect is still limited to charity, social services and projects. However, much still needs to be done concerning participation and change in the fields of political economy and economic policy in order to guarantee social justice and self-reliance. Accordingly, if they are to influence the sociopolitical and economic transformation of Nigerian

---

22. P17.
23. P10.

society in any way, Nigerian church leaders will need to suggest what still needs to be done if they are to go beyond the point they have so far reached.

5.2.4 More Meaningful Social Engagement on the part of Nigerian Church Leaders

In order to elicit the feelings of the respondents regarding the more meaningful social engagement of church leaders in Nigerian society, question 9a was posed, namely, **how can church leaders in Nigeria contribute more meaningfully to the sociopolitical and economic transformation of the Nigerian society, in the light of poverty, underdevelopment, corruption and poor leadership?**[24] This question aimed to fulfil the normative and pragmatic tasks of practical theology. The normative and pragmatic tasks seek to provide answers to the following questions: What form ought the current religious praxis take in this particular social context? How might this area of praxis be shaped to encompass more fully the normative commitments of a religious tradition in a particular context of experience?[25] Thus, question 9a refers to the main focus of this study and, thus, the views of the respondents will be presented and discussed. Themes such as advocacy, collaboration, conscientization, leadership, leadership training, projects, protest, religious activities, self-conversion, social services and stewardship all featured in the responses of the participants in the empirical study.

5.2.4.1 Advocacy

The respondents argued that church leaders should continue to engage in advocacy.

> Advocative role.[26]

This advocacy needs to draw the attention of Nigerians to the sociopolitical issues and the biblical standards concerning such issues in respect of which there should be no compromise. This view was presented as follows:

---

24. See Appendix A.
25. Osmer, *Practical Theology*.
26. P6.

> Drawing attention to what God says to any given situation without compromising standards.[27]
>
> They are limited but they should continue focusing on their prophetic mission.[28]

The fact that church leaders cannot resort to the use of arms to compel governments, institutions and individuals to fulfil their responsibilities to the citizens has not deterred them from fulfilling their obligations to the society. It is their consistency in pointing to biblical standards without compromise that portrays their prophetic witness.

The role of church leaders in advocacy should be in the sense of their acting as the conscience of Nigerian society.

> Umpire as conscience of the nation.[29]

In addition to being prophetic and acting as the conscience of the nation in the sense of pointing to biblical standards, this role of church leaders in advocacy should include campaigning against unjust sociopolitical and economic policies and practices.

> Campaign against it.[30]

5.2.4.2 Collaboration

The responses of the participants on the issue of the collaboration of church leaders with government, economic institutions, communities and civil society as a path to a more meaningful social transformation process, suggested a broad range of collaborative engagements.

However, it is essential that the collaboration be genuine and deep in all the requisite areas.

> Being practically and openly involved.[31]

---

27. P13.
28. P5.
29. P9.
30. P17.
31. P21.

The respondents pointed out that collaboration should be among the Nigerian church leaders themselves, the structures they lead and with political leadership.

> Come together to form a strong, cohesive and incorruptible umpire as conscience of the nation.[32]

> Through their own structures first and then tangentially with government.[33]

The extent of these collaborative activities of church leaders should be such that are informed by the significance of the church and its leaders as stakeholders in society and, as such, both the church and its leaders would be willing to go the long haul in order to achieve a better society.

> Both in church and society, be conscious that they are concerned and responsible stakeholders. Go beyond anger and complaints to personal involvement and being ready to pay the price for salvific change – after the example of Christ and his redeeming sacrifice.[34]

Such collaboration is biblically rooted in the metaphor of "salt" as a seasoning, purifying and preserving agent. In the opinion of one respondent, there should be no area in which the church should not be involved. In this light, it is argued that

> The salt is the salt of the earth (not of the church). The church should come out of the four walls and be involved in every sphere of life, politics and governance, media, business, education, arts, etc. everywhere.[35]

In addition, church leaders should collaborate with the business community for the purpose of shaping economic policies.

> Church leaders should be involved in shaping economic policies in the country and constantly engage opinion leaders.[36]

---

32. P9.
33. P5.
34. P20.
35. P14.
36. P12.

Collaboration should involve church leaders' participation in partisan politics and governance, and not just encouraging other Christians to become involved in politics.

> Get involved in politics and governance in the larger society.[37]

Collaboration also includes regular and sustained communication with the Christians in politics, other community leaders and technocrats.

> Open and maintain communication lines between church leaders and Christians in politics, community leaders and technocrats.[38]

> Regular and sustained dialogue with opinion leaders and public office holders.[39]

Church leaders would also need to collaborate with local and international civil society.

> Support civil societies.[40]

> Join social groups to reform the nation, establish NGOs they can afford to sponsor.[41]

> There are serious talks about the ills of corruption and bad leadership. More and more civil groups and professional bodies are rising up to address social issues and press for better policies that will bring about a better society.[42]

> If honest Christian leaders would arise and form serious pressure groups within and outside the national boundaries, if the leaders appreciate that they are answerable to God for what happens to the country even after they expire; if we have leaders who love the country above themselves and their immediate

---

37. P14.
38. P19.
39. P12.
40. P18.
41. P8.
42. P18.

family, then the political and economic change so much desired in Nigeria would come.[43]

According to the respondents, the essence of collaboration in the local and international contexts is that a number of the sociopolitical and economic challenges are informed and sustained by powerful imperialist structures outside of the nation.

> These deviant behaviors have their roots and foundations outside Nigeria.[44]

> The exploitative tendencies of the colonial masters should not be allowed to continue.[45]

The arguments of the respondents on the issue of an all-embracing approach to collaboration as a vital component of a more meaningful social engagement strategy, is not only a call to Nigerian church leaders to strengthen their resolve in this emerging area, but it is a demonstration of the bold approach to be adopted by church leaders to infiltrate all areas for the transformation of Nigerian society. It is thus incumbent on church leaders to be focused in their collaborative efforts so as to avoid being absorbed into the powerful institutions, namely, political and economic institutions. The engagement of church leaders in their collaboration with such institutions should be in the sense of critical engagers. Perlas counsels that critical engagers enter the arena of dialogue and/or partnership with open eyes and an open mind, knowing full well that they are entering an arena of opportunities, traps and perils. "They rely on their intimate understanding of institutional dynamics, are appropriately protective and proud of their independence. They have a less vulnerable source of financial support for their activities, and have a broader concept of power, including an understanding of cultural power."[46]

Such engagement should also be informed by both the church leaders' missional calling to Nigerian society and by a reflexive and self-critical approach to social engagement.

---

43. P10.
44. P15.
45. P13.
46. Perlas, *Shaping Globalization*, 103.

5.2.4.3 *Conscientization*

The respondents also suggested that church leaders should be involved in the processes of conscientization.

> Conscientize.[47]

The process of conscientization should involve a deliberate effort on the part of church leaders to educate Nigerians on those issues that relate to the sociopolitical and economic challenges facing them.

> Deliberate educational effort.[48]

Conscientization should also imply church leaders arrange awareness programmes for their members on social issues.

> Let the church arrange awareness programs for members.[49]

As a part of the conscientizing process, church leaders should bring to the attention of both their members and nonmembers the need for good governance and encourage them to participate in partisan politics.

> Conscientizing the people on the need for good governance.[50]
>
> Encouraging members to participate in leadership elections (vote and be voted for).[51]

According to one respondent, conscientization should be a feature of the nature of all education in Nigerian schools.

> Proper education (academic).[52]

The shaping of the mindsets and attitudes of church leaders and church members as well as the public at large regarding the political engagement of church leaders should be a part of the conscientization vision as it is in this way that both church leaders and the people will cease to frown on the participation of church leaders in partisan politics.

---

47. P20.
48. P6.
49. P17.
50. P4.
51. P12.
52. P3.

> Shape and support the election of church leaders to political posts.[53]

In addition, conscientization should also entail the effective political education of Christians at all levels of the church's expression as well as the creation of a level of awareness with the aim of changing the minds and actions of all Nigerians with regard to the implications of bad leadership, poverty and underdevelopment. It should also entail the use of the media, pulpit, church publications and other methods of communication.

> Vigorous political education at both the ecumenical and denominational levels.[54]

> Educating and informing the masses on bad leadership, poverty and underdevelopment.[55]

> Media and educating the church members through the pulpit and various church programs. Use of church publications to members and nonmembers.[56]

5.2.4.4 Leadership

The respondents mentioned leadership as a vital component of the efforts of church leaders in terms of a more meaningful social engagement in Nigeria. They first pointed to the paucity of good leadership as being responsible for the challenges facing Nigerians before pointing to what church leaders needed to do about the challenge of leadership.

> Bad leadership is the key cause of underdevelopment and the high level of poverty in Nigeria.[57]

> We need leaders who are firm and focused, no matter the odds; who understand our strategic priorities and pursue them. Leaders who can generate the excitement we need in our political, economic and social levels of the Nigerian society. Above

---

53. P12.
54. P19.
55. P2.
56. P12.
57. P10.

all, the leader should be God fearing, yet principled and of high integrity.[58]

The participants in the empirical study were aware of the loss of confidence in the political and economic leadership of Nigeria on the part of many Nigerians. As such, they argued that the type of leadership that would generate the followership required to move Nigeria forward in many ways must be such that Nigerians could feel confident and be excited about it. It is for this reason that it is essential that church leaders in particular, and the church in general, assume the leadership role in sociopolitical and economic transformation, beginning with the way in which things are done within the church. These views were expressed as follows:

> The church should lead by example in all spheres of things, that is, leadership changes in the various church organizations, management of church funds, participation in politics (where they are expected to be salt).[59]

> They lead the people to embrace economic activities that bring about individual and, in turn, corporate development. They should lead the development of these initiatives.[60]

Leadership was seen as pivotal to the anticipated sociopolitical and economic transformation of Nigerian society and, thus, it is incumbent on church leaders to develop the type of church leadership which would enable effective leadership in the broader Nigerian society. Such leadership development should include creative, transparent and exemplary leadership.

> Developing the leadership of the church.[61]

> Creatively establish transparent leadership and inculcate the habit of leadership by example.[62]

In order to be able to provide the type of leadership that Nigerians expect from their church leaders, church leaders in Nigeria would need to be willing,

---

58. P11.
59. P16.
60. P11.
61. P3.
62. P10.

knowledgeable, effective and accountable to both God and the Nigerian people in the way in which they discharge their anticipated responsibilities in social change at this crucial point of Nigerian history.

> Knowledge and willingness to be effective and accountable leaders.[63]

The expectations of the respondents with regard to the leadership they expect from church leaders may be extremely demanding although this does not imply that church leaders necessarily have the requisite knowledge and expertise to perform in this regard, despite the expectations of many Nigerians. Ogbu Kalu however has expressed his optimism with regard to the possibility of religious leaders fulfilling the expectations of Nigerians. In his view, "the numerous followers supporting Nigerian church leaders and the emerging political awareness among the Christians behind these leaders may scarcely be rivalled by political and economic leaders."[64] Accordingly, the advantages inherent in such followership should be explored and tailored to suit the sociopolitical and economic transformation of Nigeria. It is such sociopolitical and economic gains that may substantiate in a sustainable way the spiritual depths of Nigerian Christians as compared to the high numbers attending church on Sundays without a commensurate show of responsibility from Monday to Saturday in their homes, streets and places of work.

5.2.4.5 *Leadership Training*

In an effort to address the leadership problem in Nigeria in an appropriate way, the respondents suggested that there be various types of leadership training programmes instituted, for example, mentoring of future leaders:

> Mentors to the emergence of dynamic political leadership.[65]

In addition, it was recommended that leadership training should be carried out at seminars, workshops and retreats and that it forms part of theological education curricula.

---

63. P6.
64. Kalu, "Faith and Politics," 26–27.
65. P9.

> Leadership retreats, seminars and workshop. Curricula of theological education to include content meant to handle such challenges.[66]

Leadership training through youth development programmes was also suggested.

> Concentration on youth development. This will require [that] church leaders must not just be concerned with proselytizing, but sincere about real all-round formation of the youth.[67]

Leadership training and development could also be carried out by church leaders through leadership foundations such as Lux Terra.

> Some church leaders are already doing something to solve our problem which has been leadership. There is a leadership foundation – Lux Terra – being established by Rev. Fr. George Ehusani for the training of future leaders.[68]

5.2.4.6 Projects

In pursuit of the more meaningful social engagement of church leaders in Nigeria, the participants proposed that church leaders incorporate a wide range of projects into the missional engagement of the church with such programmes being geared towards the actual empowerment of both church members and nonmembers. The proposal for such projects was expressed as follows:

> Consciously build in developmental projects as an integral part of mission.[69]

Such empowerment projects should encompass socioeconomic, political and ethical dimensions and also include programmes that may enhance effective self-help.

> Draw up programmes for socioeconomic and political training in Nigeria. Plan and arrange training programmes in

---

66. P6.
67. P18.
68. P4.
69. P10.

self-sustaining activities and lay emphasis on morality in public affairs.[70]

Provide training facilities and programmes for members. Provide employment opportunities for members.[71]

Organize and empower members for effective self-help.[72]

The respondents suggested the setting up of NGOs in specialized areas and also that skills acquisition centres be set up.

Church leaders should encourage members and assist financially in empowering those less financially endowed. Setting up NGOs with specialized areas like attending to the health issues, educational and financial needs. Need to set up a skill centre to train those who could not be otherwise educated.[73]

Promote and finance programmes that will enable church members to access facilities that will improve their lives.[74]

The respondents also suggested microfinance schemes to provide employment, loans and training for small- and medium-size enterprises. In addition to the small-scale businesses, church leaders could facilitate the engagement of the churches in large-scale businesses.

Empowerment of indigent members through microfinance schemes.[75]

Churches pulling resources together to establish small and large-scale businesses.[76]

5.2.4.7 Protests

All the categories of church leaders represented in the empirical study agreed on the need for church leaders to take more radical steps against social

---

70. P17.
71. P15.
72. P20.
73. P12.
74. P12.
75. P4.
76. P19.

injustice such as organizing or taking part in protests. They presented their reasons for such thinking as follows:

Leaders have focused much on advocacy, but there is now a need to move forward to protests with the aim of making a bigger impact on political leaders.

> The church leaders have spoken on corruption but should do more in leading protests where desirable to make deeper impact to [sic] the political leaders.[77]
>
> More aggressively, not just thinking that whatever happens is the will of God.[78]
>
> There should be a total reformation.[79]
>
> If we can begin to see honest martyrs and some Martin Luthers among church leaders who would stand for what is right rather than be lost in the crowd.[80]

These responses of the church leaders referring to protests led by church leaders in order to send a clear message to political leaders are not a common trend in Nigeria and, this approach is, thus, signalling a new dimension in addressing the sociopolitical and economic challenges faced by Nigerians. Such an approach was first championed by Pastor Tunde Bakare in 2010 and has also proved to be effective from the time of Martin Luther in Wittenberg to the time of the black struggles for liberation in both the United States and in South Africa. The use of protests rightly identifies the church with civil society and peoples' movements in general. Although it may be argued that protests may turn violent, even when violence was not initially intended, the fact still remains that protests constitute a nonviolent approach to wresting power and control from unjust persons and institutions. If, as Wink has argued, "the Lord Jesus Christ subscribed to this means to expose the unjust structures in his time,"[81] there is hardly any viable reason why Nigerian church

---

77. P12.
78. P22.
79. P3.
80. P10.
81. Wink, *Engaging the Powers*, 182.

leaders may not use it to liberate both themselves and the Nigerian masses from similar unjust institutions.

5.2.4.8 Religious Activities

The respondents believed that there is a spiritual dimension to the challenges of poverty, underdevelopment, corruption and poor leadership facing Nigeria and, as such, it will require spiritual means to deal with these challenges. Accordingly, the participants suggested the use of religious activities as a part of the solution. The respondents listed the following activities, in this order, namely, prayer, Bible study and preaching/teaching.

On the subject of prayer, the respondents stated the following:

We cannot over emphasize the role of prayer.[82]

Pray against it.[83]

The Niger Delta issue is more of a spiritual issue which requires the church to take up the warfare to deliver that region which the devil (in my opinion) has decided to use to hold this nation to ransom.[84]

Pray for good leaders.[85]

They can pray for the governments (national, state and local government).[86]

As regards Bible study, the respondents had this to say:

Biblical studies.[87]

Effective Bible studies.[88]

Concerning preaching and teaching, the respondents argued as follows:

---

82. P22.
83. P17.
84. P11.
85. P12.
86. P8.
87. P3.
88. P15.

Teach and preach the good news of our Lord with the simplicity and passion of Christ selflessly.[89]

I do not think that they can do more than sermonizing like Bishop Desmond Tutu did.[90]

The use of prayer as a component of a more meaningful approach to social transformation in Nigeria is in the sense of intercession and warfare. Whereas intercessions and supplications for all levels of governance refer to God's guidance in the move towards successful and fruitful governance, warfare is aimed at countering and bringing to subjection those evil powers that are working against the well-being of Nigerians.

Teaching and preaching were perceived as the "good news of our Lord," to be delivered with the "simplicity and passion of Christ," and "selflessly." The respondents may have thought of the flamboyancy and gospel commercialization that now characterize some of the preaching and teaching in some Nigerian churches. Whereas there are, undoubtedly, some benefits to the wave of Pentecostalism sweeping Nigeria, church leaders should also be concerned about the selfish and dubious ways in which some Nigerian preachers abuse their pulpits in church, media and open-air services. The power in the proclamation of the gospel should always be used for the salvation of humankind, edification of the saints, healing/renewal of creation and judgement of all that is opposed to God and, thus, to the glory of God.

5.2.4.9 Self-Conversion

Some of the respondents indicated that they felt that meaningful social engagement on the part of church leaders should include both internal self-appraisal and conversion of the church leaders themselves. The respondents' views on the subject were expressed as follows:

---

89. P19.

90. P1. It may be necessary to clarify that, as regards the statement of respondent P1, Archbishop Desmond Tutu not only sermonized during the years of apartheid in South Africa, but he also advocated and participated in nonviolent protests. It follows, therefore, that church leaders in Nigeria should do more than just sermonizing, not just because Archbishop Tutu did more than merely sermonize, but because it is both reasonable and necessary in present day Nigerian society.

> Undergo internal self-conversion so that the Christian principles will guide our own actions.[91]
>
> The starting point of the church is self-leadership assessment. The leaders themselves should conduct self-appraisal of themselves and improve on areas of bad leadership being practised by them.[92]
>
> First of all, tackle bad leadership within its ranks.[93]
>
> The church leaders must sanitize the body of Christ before they can be bold enough to face the government. Let judgement start from the house of God.[94]

Admittedly, there is good sense in the leadership of the church undergoing self-appraisal which should also, in turn, lead to self-conversion especially in areas in which church leaders are not faring particularly well. Such a stance could provide greater credibility to the image and practices of church leaders as they confront the government, business institutions and individuals on the issue of social ills. It is in this vein that Ngara argues that responsible leadership should begin within the church before spreading into society as a whole as this would mean that the church and its leaders would be in a better position to effect sociopolitical and economic change.[95] However, it is doubtful whether the notion that church leaders should all be either perfect or faultless before venturing into the rectifying of social ills is realistic or herein canvassed. However, the important point is that internal self-conversion should be an ongoing practice of church leaders as a means of self-accountability and appraisal for a more informed social engagement and not a prerequisite for church leaders before embarking on social transformation. In addition, not all church leaders are held in contempt by Nigerians for participating in the social ills besetting Nigerian society, and the great majority of church leaders, who are well respected by the Nigerian masses and institutions, should pursue the social vision for the good of all. Nevertheless, church leaders

---

91. P18.
92. P11.
93. P7.
94. P16.
95. Ngara, *Christian Leadership*.

are human beings and human beings are not always perfect beings even when they are in pursuit of perfection, as many church leaders appear to be. However, church leaders should ensure that, within the church and in Nigerian society as a whole, they are without reproach and their standards of leadership and conduct impeccable.

5.2.4.10 *Education/Social Services*

Although education and social services have always constituted the major activities in the social engagement of church leaders, the respondents in this study believe that church leaders should continue with these activities in the interests of a more meaningful social transformational agenda. Their views were presented as follows:

> Build schools that are affordable to the poor.[96]
>
> Offer education and social services.[97]

In the view of the respondents, the social services of church leaders should be encouraged to continue as a way of offering relief to the Nigerian masses who are experiencing difficult sociopolitical and economic times. Such services, which include schools, hospitals, orphanages and charitable schemes, should be affordable to the poor. Accordingly, schools should not be established primarily for profit and they should be established and run in such a way that the costs incurred are sufficient to sustain their continued existence and are also affordable to the poor whose children should, at least, receive education as one of the basic human needs.

5.2.4.11 *Stewardship*

As regards the way in which church leaders may engage more meaningfully in the social transformational process of Nigeria, several of the respondents referred to the concept of stewardship as indispensable to the management of the enormous resources in Nigeria. According to the respondents, Nigeria has enough resources to cater for all its citizens and, thus, the present state of affairs of abject poverty is unjustifiable. In this light, a respondent stated that

---

96. P19.
97. P5.

we have a rich country that is the poorest in infrastructure, polity, development and social integration.[98]

Other respondents argued that, even in the present political leadership in Nigeria, the culture of corruption, selfishness and waste was still enduring and hampering development.

> The post military era is indeed the optimization of self-interest and backward development compared with available resources.[99]

> Corruption and wastes as the symbol of governance.[100]

Despite the fact that the resources and the potentials (human, natural, financial, etc.) are available to both the church and to Nigerian society as a whole, the respondents were of the opinion that mismanagement, exploitation, disunity and the nonchalance of both church leaders and church members are responsible for the poor sociopolitical and economic performance registered thus far.

> Much nonchalance towards glaring cases of mismanagement of funds, economic exploitation of church members.[101]

> Lack of unity has robbed the church of the cohesion that it requires to adequately and effectively influence positive governance in spite of its huge and majority followership.[102]

> The potentials are there but disunity is the bane. For example, though the population ratio suggests 60 percent Christians out of the total population of Nigerians, yet the church cannot harness the enormous potentials.[103]

According to the respondents, the absence of a culture of stewardship in the Nigerian polity is responsible for the waste in governance with, for example, the states and local governments expecting a share in the oil wealth at Abuja every month so as to be able to afford the salaries and projects

---

98. P10.
99. P10.
100. P9.
101. P6.
102. P9.
103. P9.

pertaining to the various tiers of government. Such an approach to governance has resulted in the inability of the various states and local governments to generate and manage those resources that are available in their local environments as each area has been richly endowed by God. Accordingly, unproductivity abounds to such an extent that those resources that would have enriched the various localities and other parts of the nation and beyond have remained untapped and, in some instances, even wasted. The absence of stewardship is said to be largely responsible for the total dependence of the Nigerian economy on oil. As a result, food insecurity and poverty are common issues in Nigeria. On this note, the respondents argued that

> Nigeria, at the moment, wastes a lot of resources running its unproductive system. The situation where everyone expects something from the centre where not everyone has really contributed is sickening. The way forward for the nation is the strengthening of the states, and consequently, the local governments. In this way each area will move towards self-discovery, build its potentials, and export to the other part of the country and even beyond.[104]

> Monoproduct dependence on oil is destructive, food insecurity abounds, poverty level is among the worst in the world, religious and ethnic wars by fractured people tear us apart.[105]

If the notion of stewardship had been entrenched in the Nigerian system, the hard working and resilient nature of the Nigerians could have been effectively channelled towards the sociopolitical and economic development of the country. According to the respondents, Nigeria and Nigerians do not deserve to be associated with the semblance of a failed state and with poverty.

> They just managed not to allow Nigeria to become a "failed state." But even this is due to the patience, hard work and resilience of Nigerians themselves – who kept forging ahead *despite* their governments.[106]

---

104. P18.
105. P10.
106. P20.

As a way of encouraging stewardship in Nigeria, one respondent argued that the poor should be taught how to utilize the available resources as opposed to being given handouts.

> Teach the poor "how to fish rather than give them fish." Discouraging all forms of laziness.[107]

In addition, effective time management and commitment to responsibility should characterize the Nigerian civil service and the civil servants as part of a stewardship culture.

> Punctuality, faithfulness in public service.[108]

If the notion of stewardship is to become deeply entrenched in both private and public life in Nigeria, Nigerians and, especially, church leaders will need to develop a sensitivity as well as taking responsible action against all forms of environmental, animal, plant, atmospheric, aquatic, sexist and other forms of injustice.

> Be passionately conscious about their environment. Be able to notice where there are injustices and speak up against all forms of injustice.[109]

One respondent also suggested that it will take a leader with a steward's orientation to transform Nigeria both sociopolitically and economically.

> We need a leader who will challenge the way matters are handled presently. Someone who will use all the resources available to develop and bring change.[110]

The concepts that emerged from the responses of the participants in the empirical study and that are vital in the meaningful socioeconomic and political transformation of Nigerian society include conscientization, leadership, collaboration, protests, self-conversion, advocacy and stewardship. In the view of many of the respondents, these are areas that church leaders should include in their existing areas of engagement of religious activities, projects, education and social services.

---

107. P10.
108. P13.
109. P10.
110. P12.

5.2.5 More Meaningful Social Engagement of Nigerian Church Members

Question 9b – **How can church members in Nigeria contribute more meaningfully to the sociopolitical and economic transformation of the Nigerian society, in the light of poverty, underdevelopment, corruption and poor leadership?** – is a follow-up question to question 9a which referred to the more meaningful social engagement of church leaders. Although not as central to the research study as question 9a, the question was posed to test the views of the respondents regarding their expectations of church members in the hope that church leaders will be equipped with the requisite knowledge of the roles they can help their church members play as co-labourers in the quest for social transformation. As in question 9a, question 9b aimed to fulfil the normative and pragmatic tasks of practical theology.[111]

The responses from the participants in the empirical study will be presented in the following categories: advocacy, collaboration, politics, projects, protests, religious activities and values/culture.

5.2.5.1 Advocacy

One respondent suggested that church members should be involved in advocacy in the sense of speaking out against social ills.

> Speaking out.[112]

5.2.5.2 Collaboration

As was the case with the church leaders, church members were expected to be engaged in collaborative activities with one respondent suggesting that:

> Like church leaders, they, too, have their role to play. They can pray for the government (national, state and local government). Join social groups to reform the nation, establish NGOs they can afford to sponsor.[113]

---

111. Osmer, *Practical Theology*. See also 1.8.1.
112. P5.
113. P8.

5.2.5.3 Politics

Church members should be politically engaged so as to enable them to participate in the decision-making process, especially with regard to solutions to the sociopolitical and economic challenges.

> Getting into politics.[114]
>
> Members should ensure that, during elections, they come out en masse to vote and be voted for in the search for credible and transformational leadership.[115]
>
> By having members of the church participating in politics, particularly being members of the House of Representatives and Senate so that they can be part of the decision-making and solutions to these problems.[116]

5.2.5.4 Projects

The respondents were of the opinion that church members should initiate developmental programmes for both communities and individuals as a way of more meaningful social engagement.

> Initiate poverty and developmental programmes for their communities and individuals.[117]
>
> Form cooperatives for agric and income generation efforts and deliberate development efforts.[118]

5.2.5.5 Protest

Some respondents were of the opinion that church members should engage the Nigerian sociopolitical and economic systems through protest.

> Protest against bad leadership.[119]
>
> Engaging the system.[120]

---

114. P5.
115. P11.
116. P11.
117. P7.
118. P6.
119. P7.
120. P5.

They should rise against bad leadership and, by their own example, fight against the vices of the nation.[121]

5.2.5.6 Religious Activities

Religious activities also featured as a strategic area for social transformation.

> Be willing and active participants in the apostolicity of the church.[122]
>
> Praying for those in leadership positions.[123]
>
> They can pray for the governments (national, state and local government).[124]

5.2.5.7 Values

The participants also pointed out that the cultivation and utilization of Christian values are indispensable to a more meaningful social transformation process.

> Cultivating the Christian virtues of helping one another.[125]
>
> Living exemplary lives.[126]
>
> Holding the clergy responsible for the good which they ought to do.[127]

With the exception of politics and values, the other themes discussed in terms of a more meaningful social engagement have already been discussed under the section on the more meaningful engagement of church leaders in the Nigerian social transformation.[128] The repetition of such themes concerning the engagement of church members reflects the importance of these themes. Despite the fact that the requirements of values and political participation

---

121. P2.
122. P6.
123. P4.
124. P8.
125. P4.
126. P5.
127. P9.
128. See section 5.2.8.

were included under self-conversion[129] and collaboration[130] respectively in our discussion on the more meaningful engagement of church leaders, these themes have also surfaced in our discussion on the more meaningful engagement of church members. This, in turn, proves that the usual assumption that church leaders should maintain a "safe distance" from social engagements, for example, political participation, is no longer valid, at least in the view of the respondents who themselves are church leaders. Accordingly, church leaders are expected to engage socially in all spheres of life as a means of leading their followers through the process of sociopolitical and economic transformation in Nigeria.

5.2.6 More Meaningful Social Engagement of the Ecumenical Church

The study sought to understand how the Nigerian ecumenical church could engage in social transformation in Nigeria in a more meaningful way. In order to elicit valid responses in this regard, question 11a[131] was posed – **"What are your suggestions on the ecumenical church's more meaningful engagement in the sociopolitical and economic transformation of the Nigerian society?"** This question stems from the understanding that, for Nigerian church leaders to engage in a more meaningful social transformation exercise in Nigeria, the ecumenical church's platform and the resources within that church may be indispensable. Thus, the question hoped to engage the normative and pragmatic tasks of practical theology[132] to make its findings on the ecumenical church's more meaningful engagement in Nigerian social transformation.

The themes arising from the responses of the respondents in the empirical study will now be presented and discussed below.

5.2.6.1 Ecumenism

The respondents argued that ecumenism is crucial to the church's social ministry in Nigeria, through the medium of its leaders.

---

129. See section 5.2.4.9.
130. See section 5.2.5.2.
131. Appendix A.
132. Osmer, *Practical Theology*. See also section 1.8.1.

> Experience has shown that the neglect of the "ecumenical imperative" in the Christian community in Nigeria is a great handicap for the church to work effectively in these areas.[133]

> Unity of the church should be encouraged.[134]

In an attempt to sustain ecumenical relations among the churches, the respondents proposed the following: A firm resolve among church leaders and churches to discountenance areas of disagreement among the churches while, at the same time, encouraging a team spirit and a focus on serving the interests of the kingdom of God and the well-being of the Nigerian society.

> Resolve to be genuinely united as the body of Christ.[135]

> They should sink their individual differences and work as a team. They should see the transformation of the society as their common task.[136]

> Embrace genuine and selfless unity, no matter the sacrifice and costs it may entail for the love of God's kingdom and the nation.[137]

Church leaders should organise training programmes for the various church groups that could foster ecumenism and the collaboration of the church leaders among themselves and their churches in sociopolitical and economic transformation through ecumenical structures.

> Hold seminars on this with different groups.[138]

5.2.6.2 Policy Change

One of the respondents suggested that the ecumenical church in Nigeria could play an extremely important role in policy change although, at that point, the argument was that the ecumenical church had not achieved much success in that area.

---

133. P20.
134. P8.
135. P13.
136. P2.
137. P9.
138. P7.

> The church has no effect on the polity.[139]

In order to change the sociopolitical and economic policies of the nation, ecumenical church leaders would need to declare publicly their stance against the wrong policies.

> Be more open to contests with government on wrong national issues.[140]

Ecumenical church leaders would not only have to vote in credible candidates into elective positions in government, but they would also have to ensure the election of church leaders who would be able to help change the economic policies of the nation.

> Church leaders should be involved more in the political events in Nigeria. Shape and support the election of church leaders to political posts. Church leaders should be involved in shaping economic policies in the country.[141]

The ecumenical church leaders, especially through CAN, were urged to pay more attention to as well as to contribute to the sociopolitical and economic policies of the nation by various means, including sponsoring motions in the National Assembly.

> At the ecumenical level of the church, the church should be more visible at the political level of the transformation process by articulating its position to influence (positively) the decisions of government for the betterment of society. So, in effect, this level should be involved more in policy matters at the federal government level. Issues that have to do with electoral reforms, inputs in federal budgets and national development plans, e.g. Vision 2020, should be the concern of the ecumenical church, those are national issues.[142]

> The church should, through CAN, sponsor motions on the floor of the National Assembly to make their positions known on

---

139. P17.
140. P17.
141. P12.
142. P11.

these issues. In this regard, the professional Christian associations can be very handy.[143]

5.2.6.3 *Advocacy*

A number of the participants in the empirical study believed that ecumenical church leaders should continue to be engaged in advocacy:

> The church must remain the voice of the voiceless.[144]

It was suggested that this advocacy involves calling on the government to fulfil its responsibilities to the citizens of the country.

> The church should maintain its standard as light in the world and speak out to the government on its duties to the citizens of the country.[145]

Ecumenical church leaders could fulfil their roles in advocacy through dialogue with both government and other institutions/organizations as this could be of help in alleviating the sufferings of Nigerians.

> Advocate visits to government and organizations on these.[146]

A respondent also argued that while, thus far, the advocacy of church leaders had been in the form of verbal and written statements, if they were to have a greater impact on the political leadership, it was essential that the church leaders take advocacy to the level of protests.

> The church leaders have spoken on corruption but should do more in leading protests where desirable to make a deeper impact to [sic] the political leaders.[147]

It was also pointed out that, although church leaders should be careful not to be labelled partisan, they should not fail to call the government to order whenever the need arose.

---

143. P11.
144. P4.
145. P8.
146. P7.
147. P12.

Let us be wary lest we be dubbed partisan but we should not relent from calling the government to order when [the] occasion arises.[148]

5.2.6.4 Efficiency

The respondents observed that a more meaningful engagement on the part of the ecumenical church in social transformation in Nigeria would require a more efficient ecumenical office and a more effective organizational strategy.

> CAN, however, should become better equipped through a more effective national office.[149]

> Have a committee on national issues and make them [sic] function.[150]

5.2.6.5 Focus on Society

The respondents argued that the focus of the ecumenical church should go beyond the church to Nigerian society as a whole and to the challenges confronting Nigerians. This could be effected by encouraging Christians to participate in the sociopolitical and economic life of the nation.

> They should see the transformation of the society as their common task.[151]

> Encourage Christian participation in politics, economy and social life of the nation.[152]

5.2.6.6 Christ-Centred

It was considered essential that ecumenical church leaders and the church in Nigeria be Christ-centred instead of egocentric.

> As we progress in the ecumenical experiment in Nigeria, our ego and self must grow less and less (destruction of egocentricism)

---

148. P1.
149. P5.
150. P17.
151. P2.
152. P6.

and let God and his Christ emerge at the centre stage of the life of the church.[153]

5.2.6.7 Commitment

Both church leaders and members were in need of a deeper level of commitment to both ecumenism and social transformation in Nigeria.

> We should be more committed. Church members need more engagement.[154]

5.2.6.8 Self-Conversion

The respondents suggested that the ecumenical church required self-cleansing to enable it to engage more meaningfully in the Nigerian social context.

> The church must paramountly do a thorough self cleansing.[155]

5.2.6.9 Conscientize

Ecumenical church leaders should ensure a systematic approach to the creation of awareness in Nigerian society about the challenges faced by Nigerians and how to overcome these challenges.

> There needs to be a deliberate and calculated effort to ensure creation of awareness on these issues.[156]

Some of the ways through which the Nigerian society could be conscientized are curricular development and publications.

> CAN to work with its blocs to ensure deliberate curricular development in CAN member churches to meet these needs.[157]

> Write books. Write on these in newspapers and magazines.[158]

The main findings of the empirical study on the more meaningful social engagement on the part of the ecumenical church in Nigeria gave rise to

---

153. P3.
154. P5.
155. P9.
156. P6.
157. P6.
158. P7.

themes which included ecumenism, policy change, advocacy, efficiency, focus on society, Christ-centred, commitment, self-conversion and conscientising. Although a number of the themes had emerged previously in other discussions, ecumenism now emerged as a key component in the more meaningful social engagement of church leaders in Nigeria. As such, it may be that the social engagement of the ecumenical church leaders would enable church leaders in Nigeria to impact more meaningfully on the sociopolitical and economic policies of the country and to change these policies in a more meaningful way than would be possible if they had engaged in this regard as individuals or denominations. The ecumenical church's social engagement has the capacity to utilize the church's resources on a broad high scale and to enable the presentation of a more organized front to the political, economic, social and civil institutions in Nigeria and beyond. This, in turn, may compel these institutions to take notice of the church as an institution worth listening to and to collaborate with the church in transforming society.

5.2.7 More Meaningful Social Engagement on the Denomination/Congregational Levels

Question 11b – **"What are your suggestions on the denominational/congregational church's more meaningful social engagement in the sociopolitical and economic transformation of the Nigerian society?"** (Appendix A) was posed by the researcher in an effort to understand the way in which the denominational and congregational expression of the church in Nigeria could contribute more meaningfully to the transformation of Nigerian society. Apart from the limitations and challenges that exist within the church itself which could impede the effectiveness of the church in Nigerian society as a whole, this question seeks to understand how the current practices of both church denominations and church congregations may become more effective through the medium of church leaders in the Nigerian sociopolitical and economic contexts. This question is also informed by the normative and pragmatic tasks of practical theology.[159]

The responses from the participants in the empirical study will be presented and discussed under the following themes: Projects, membership care, collaboration, denominations and religious activities.

---

159. Osmer, *Practical Theology*. See also 1.8.1.

5.2.7.1 Projects

The respondents were of the view that both denominations and congregations are vital in the socioeconomic transformation of Nigerian society, especially in the area of empowerment projects.

> All denominations to have their own programme and projects.[160]

The intention behind such projects at the denominational and congregational levels is to rescue people from the abject poverty in which they are living. Such projects should, therefore, be both economically empowering and sustainable while developmental projects should reach beyond the church's membership to society at large.

> Deliver the members from abject poverty through economic empowerment programmes and sustainability.[161]

> Each denomination should identify its area of competency in ministry and use it to impact on society. Also, denominations should ensure that they make it as a point of duty to develop and impact their catchment areas. If a church can raise thirty-five billion Naira in five years to build a deliverance stadium, it means that some churches have the capacity to construct road networks of over 500 kilometers. It should engage in projects that impact on the lives of the people, particularly in the region of its catchment areas.[162]

Strategic and sustainable empowerment projects may represent practical ways of generating a culture of innovation, stewardship and productivity that may, in turn, boost the image of the church and also inspire communities. The following arguments on this issue were presented:

> By creating strategic and sustainable wealth resources and use them to show society the way to go. The congregational level should be engaged in more of socioeconomic activities:

---

160. P17.
161. P13.
162. P11.

> vocational centres, youth development centres, microfinance institutions.[163]

> The church could engage in funding industries e.g. tourism, agric, housing estates. An exercise in this direction will lead to applause of the church and lead to enhancement of its stand and its philosophy.[164]

Thus, the denominational and congregational expressions of the church could be vital to church leaders in Nigeria in the sense of their gaining the respect of their communities and combating youth restiveness through their contributions in the welfare and social services.

> Denominations should involve themselves in social and welfare services of the community where they are located.[165]

> We can give the funding of education in all its ramifications. In an educated society we will be comfortable as a civilized setting than an ignorant and illiterate bunch who will be bad eggs causing disturbances here and there.[166]

A number of such empowerment projects under the auspices of the LPC and mentioned by P11 are also being carried out in a number of church denominations and congregations in Nigeria.

> LPC Yaba started a few years ago to put structures that would transform the church and its members and impact on its surroundings. The structures e.g. primary/secondary school, microfinance bank, investment company etc. are still being developed.[167]

5.2.7.2 Membership Care

The care and nurturing of their members by church leaders may enhance the effectiveness of both congregations and denominations in the sociopolitical and economic transformation of Nigeria, first, by enabling them to

---

163. P11.
164. P1.
165. P14.
166. P1.
167. P11.

understand where their members are in terms of their challenges and capabilities and, second, then enabling these members to become what they should be.

> Denominational leaders need to observe the principle of presence in relating to their members so as to further understand them and the state they are in better.[168]

> Continuous education of the membership of their worth as God's people and how they should keep it.[169]

> Church leaders should be conscious of what they can invest in the members.[170]

5.2.7.3 Collaboration

The respondents argued that church denominations and congregations should also be the means of collaboration within both the Christian community and social institutions for the good of society.

> Each denomination should be encouraged to be involved in nation building, especially the Pentecostals.[171]

> If the churches could work together, especially as it concerns their developmental efforts, the country will certainly gain more level of transformation.[172]

5.2.7.4 Denominations

The respondents were of the opinion that denominational interests were responsible for the poor sociopolitical and economic performance of both the church and its leaders in Nigeria.

> Denominational engagements divide the Christendom rather than make them more effective in socioeconomic and political transformation. Each denomination seeks to be more recognized or be seen to do better than the other. They undertake

---

168. P6.
169. P13.
170. P11.
171. P8.
172. P4.

unholy strives [sic] to acquire more membership for the denominational financial benefit at the expense of the whole of society and God's creation.[173]

In an effort to liberate church leaders and their denominations/congregations from such a limiting and selfish approach to both their ministry and to social transformation, the respondents suggested that:

> every denomination must, first and foremost, be kingdom oriented.[174]

> Denominational beliefs and teachings should be fashioned in such a way that they will enhance the transformation of our society.[175]

5.2.7.5 Religious Activities

Denominations and congregations could, through religious activities, equip themselves for a more effective spiritual, sociopolitical and economic transformation.

> The church and the leaders must allow themselves to know Christ and propagate an unmitigated and undiluted gospel of our Lord not our own gospel.[176]

> Preach the whole counsel of the gospel and shun all heresies and the end time bug on the gospel.[177]

> Also, church programmes need to, first and foremost, be God-centred and then people-centred, not leader-centred.[178]

Based on the responses of the participants, the themes that featured prominently in terms of a more meaningful social engagement of both church denominations and congregations in the social transformation of Nigeria included projects, membership care, denominations and religious activities.

---

173. P10.
174. P9.
175. P2.
176. P3.
177. P9.
178. P6.

Despite the fact that some respondents postulated that undue denominational/congregational interests were responsible for the poor social performance of the church in Nigeria, it is very obvious that it is not possible for church leaders to engage meaningfully in social change without the constructive and optimum use of both denominations and congregations. The arguments presented suggested that, if the resources in church denominations and congregations were properly mobilized and utilized by church leaders with social concerns and a kingdom of God orientation, then the social impact of such positive energy, especially within the areas of their operation, would be enormous. As such, denominations/congregations may be the bastions of developmental projects, the discovery of the resources of members and development of the same and the effective utilization of religious activities as vehicles of empowerment, and spiritual and social transformation. It may, thus, be argued that it is especially within the congregational experience of the church that the seeds of both a kingdom and a socially-oriented mindset and engagement may be sown and nurtured. It is within this context that the wonderful fruits we seek to find in the national engagement and transformation should first be seen before the impact will be felt in and beyond the Nigerian context. Accordingly, what transpires in the congregation is, inevitably, transmitted to the entire ecclesial and national life of the society. Thus, in a sense, the hope of a more meaningful social engagement on the part of Nigerian church leaders is within the congregational, ecumenical, sociopolitical and economic horizons of Nigeria as is the effectiveness with which Nigerian church leaders are able to navigate these realms towards the social transformation of Nigerian society.

5.2.8 Leadership Style and Social Transformation in Nigeria

The literature study in chapter 3 revealed that the sociopolitical and economic challenges facing Nigerians may, in the main, be attributed to the failure of leadership in the various strata of Nigerian society since independence to the present day. In an attempt to meet the challenge of the paucity of good leadership in Nigerian society, the study sought to ask the respondents in the empirical study what kind of leadership style could be expected to bring about the expected, positive transformation of Nigerian society. In order to elicit an informed response, question 12 was posited – **What kind of leadership style do you deem most appropriate to flow from the church and its members** to the Nigerian society that can lead to the political, economic and social transformation of the Nigerian society, bearing in mind the perennial challenge of poor leadership in Nigeria? Please explain the reason(s) for your choice of leadership style.[179] The normative and pragmatic tasks[180] also inform this question.

The respondents varied in their proposals for the kind of leadership style that would be necessary to facilitate the sociopolitical and economic transformation of Nigerian society. The views of the respondents will be presented below, coupled with an attempt to make sense of their responses.

5.2.8.1 Sacrificial/Selfless Leadership

Some of the respondents argued that sacrificial leadership represents the style of leadership that could bring about the desired change in Nigeria. In terms of this kind of leadership style,

> the leader acts for the glory of God in the service of the people, ready to "give his life" – that is, sacrifice – for the flock. This is valid for Christian leadership within the church, and also for Christians leading in the world at large; or the political arena.[181]

> Transparent and selfless.[182]

5.2.8.2 Exemplary Leadership

Exemplary leadership was proposed in the following way:

> Leadership by example is the type I consider most appropriate in our context.[183]

> A back to Bible oriented leadership that is full of the fruits of the spirit. The reason being that by that by our fruits, we shall be known.[184]

---

179. Appendix A.
180. Osmer, *Practical Theology*. See also 1.8.1.
181. P20.
182. P19.
183. P4.
184. P9.

Say it and live it out.[185]

Leadership by example/management by objectives. If church leaders would be more objective about the issues of polity and take a solution-oriented approach within their local areas of influence, if they would preach and challenge the people to follow their footsteps.[186]

5.2.8.3 Participatory Leadership

Some respondents were of the opinion that participatory leadership would be helpful to Nigerian society.

> Participatory democracy in which all in the society have roles to play in the leadership, in this way, each person will be part and parcel of the decisions of government.[187]

> The type of leadership should be the participatory type.[188]

> Communion/participatory model.[189]

5.2.8.4 Servant Leadership

Servant leadership style was proposed in the following way:

> Servant leadership style to be sought at all levels.[190]

> Servant leadership.[191]

> Servant leadership should be demonstrated by the church as exemplified by Jesus Christ. Jesus leadership style is still the best till today.[192]

> Corporate leadership, not egocentric leadership. We should be servant leaders, not rulers.[193]

---

185. P16.
186. P10.
187. P2.
188. P22.
189. P18.
190. P17.
191. P13.
192. P8.
193. P3.

> God and people-centred servanthood/accountable leadership.[194]
>
> Visionary servant leadership because a leadership without vision/purpose and not service-oriented leads to disaster.[195]
>
> Jesus style. Jesus exhibited best love, fair play, justice, honesty, integrity, etc.[196]

5.2.8.5 Transformational Leadership

Some of the respondents also proposed the transformational leadership style as the style most suited to the Nigerian context.

> Nigeria needs transformation. Therefore, to do this requires transformational leaders. Transformational leaders have a vision – a goal, an agenda, a results-orientation that grabs people's attention. They communicate their vision and build trust by being consistent, dependable and persistent. They have positive self regard. In general, they transform vision into reality and motivate people to transcend their personal interests for the good of the group. This is the kind of leadership we need in today's Nigeria.[197]
>
> Transformational, servant leadership.[198]
>
> A transformational leader will be ideal.[199]
>
> Accountability, honesty, discipline, hard work, selflessness, vision and commitment.[200]

The various leadership styles suggested by the respondents may not be clear cut and distinct in a number of instances but they reflect the desires of the respondents for visionary, result-oriented, people-centred, ethical and innovative leadership that they viewed as crucial for the transformation of Nigerian society.

---

194. P6.
195. P7.
196. P15.
197. P11.
198. P1.
199. P12.
200. P5.

Whereas it was anticipated that, in view of the fact that all the respondents were church leaders, many of them would subscribe to servant leadership style as the ideal leadership style for the church and society, it is, therefore, surprising that a significant number of the respondents also subscribed to participatory and transformational leadership as ideal leadership styles for the church and society. This surprise arises from the notion among ecclesial circles that the ideal leadership style is the servant leadership which is assumed to be the kind of leadership that Jesus Christ demonstrated.[201]

The fact that a number of respondents provided more details when suggesting a leadership style rather than being specific regarding the style of leadership is also indicative of the fact that the leadership style that may be regarded as ideal in the context of both the church and society in Nigeria should be able to overcome the challenges facing Nigerians rather than a particular style of leadership that is being touted as being more scriptural than any other. As was argued in section 3.3.4, there are numerous similarities between the servant leadership and transformational leadership styles.[202] It is, thus, not surprising that some of the respondents, for example, P1 mentioned the two leadership concepts as though they were the same and, in some instances, as if the transformational style can improve the servant leadership style. In an instance in which servant leadership was proposed, the respondent then qualified servant leadership with a description (visionary) that, in a discourse on the concepts of leadership, would relate to transformational leadership.[203] In this light, it could even be argued that adaptive leadership could as well suffice in the Nigerian context but the respondents may not have mentioned it because they may not be familiar with this concept of leadership.

5.2.9 More Meaningful Social Engagement on the Part of Church Leaders and the Constituents of a Sustainable Transformational Approach to Development in Nigeria

In an attempt to present and reflect on the results of the empirical study, the study presented many of the responses of the participants in the study, including the questions posed and their objectives. It may be necessary to recall

---

201. Gibbs, *Leadership Next*.
202. Stone, Russell, and Paterson, "Transformational versus Servant Leadership."
203. Stone, Russell, and Paterson.

that, whereas some of the questions were intended to confirm, even marginally, the findings that had been made during the literature study discussed in chapters 2, 3 and 4, there were also some questions that were central to both the main research question and the subsidiary research questions – section 1.5. The lens through which the empirical study was viewed was Osmer's descriptive-empirical, interpretive, normative and pragmatic tasks of the practical theological methodology.[204] This same methodology informs the entire study. In order to be able to draw from the findings of the empirical study so as to guide the proposals which will be discussed in chapters 6 and 7, it will be necessary to build on the important themes that emerged from the empirical study in terms of the way in which they relate to how church leaders may contribute more meaningfully to the social transformation of Nigerian society and the components of such an engagement, so as to be able to address the challenges of poverty, underdevelopment, corruption, poor leadership and other forms of social injustice in Nigeria.

The results of the empirical study led to the emergence of themes comprising broad categories such as the church's existence and self-transformation, key structures through which to exert influence, the means through which such influence may be exercized, and the overarching concepts that should inform the engagement of church leaders with other institutions as agents of change and vice versa. These four broad categories and their subcategories comprise more meaningful social engagement on the part of church leaders and the key components of such social engagement in Nigerian society. It is this approach, with its constituents, that may give rise to a sustainable transformational approach to the anticipated social change in postmilitary Nigeria. Each of the categories, subcategories and the way in which they relate to the study will be discussed in the rest of this chapter.

5.2.9.1 The Church's Existence and Self-Transformation

The church in Nigeria is made up of church leaders and church members and the resources they possess. In order to guarantee the continued existence of the church and its socioreligious, political and economic engagement in the Nigerian society and beyond, it is essential that Nigerian church leaders, who are known in Nigeria to be the major architects of the church's vision

---

204. Osmer, *Practical Theology*. See also 1.8.1.

and mission, pay meaningful attention to the church's mission and societal relevance, denominational/congregational membership care, ecumenism, self-renewal/conversion and religious activities. These main components are vital to the identity and existence of both the church and its leaders. However, in order to function within the ecclesial and social contexts in a more meaningful way, each of these components will have to be imbued with the right content and be engaged in the right manner for the right results.

Mission (*missio Dei*) and Society

The mission of the church and its leaders "as a called and sent out community is inseparable from the *missio Dei* (mission of God)."[205] Accordingly, both the church and its leaders are sent by the missional God into society to proclaim the gospel. Such proclamations should be a verbal and lived out witness. A respondent captured the essence of mission of the church in society in their assertion that

> The church is called to proclaim but also to demonstrate the gospel (compassion).[206]

Guder notes that "the compassion of God is the motivating power of God's mission. God is revealed as the one who has compassion on the poor; the oppressed, the weak and the outcast."[207] Both the verbal proclamation and the practical demonstration of the gospel in acts of compassion should be such that they bring witness of the gospel to all of God's creation and, in this way, make the world a better place. P20 managed to express what the gospel is, its import and scope of influence when they asserted that

> the gospel is for all creation – not just for the "little flock" of Christians. The mandate to "preach to all nations" includes making this world a better place for all of God's people.

In the same vein, Guder recalls God's compassionate nature being demonstrated to the nation of Israel, as a called people. "That calling, however, was not for Israel's benefit alone. God's missional intention was that all the

---

205. Guder, *Continuing Conversion of Church*, 20.
206. P4.
207. Guder, *Continuing Conversion of Church*, 32.

world should be blessed."[208] It is, thus, essential that the church and its leaders in Nigeria show a greater sense of commitment to their missional calling as service to Christ, void of selfish acts such as omitting to challenge social issues and engrossment in proselytizing. This is what P4 meant when they stated that

> the church should render more honest and sincere services to Jesus Christ without consideration for personal gain.

The focus of the church and its leaders in mission should, thus, no longer be primarily church growth, but love and care for all of humankind and for the plant, animal, aquatic and environmental life. It is through this depth of ministry that the church's concern for the conversion of souls may be given a stronger witness as a natural result of the Christian mission to society. In this vein, a respondent noted that

> Christians are not expected to compromise the teaching of Christ concerning love and care for others.[209]

If they are to make a more meaningful social contribution to Nigerian society and be a vital constituent of a sustainable transformational approach to social change, church leaders will need to maintain an informed and biblically based balance between the material and spiritual well being of their members. Emphasis on one to the detriment of the other will weaken the mission of the church and its leaders both within and outside of the Christian community. It is this balance that may ensure that the mission of the church in society remains relevant and meaningful as regards the moral questions that arise in the daily realities of life. The respondents argued that such was the prophetic approach of the Old Testament and also the early church's way of dealing with spiritual, material and moral issues:

> Any church or church leader that cannot keep a good balance between the physical and spiritual well-being of the members may have as well missed God's intention for humanity.[210]

---

208. Guder, 33.
209. P16.
210. P10.

> Biblical history shows that prophets and the church had always given godly and moral direction to the people.[211]

As a vital missional approach to society and in line with the *missio Dei*, Nigerian church leaders should constantly bear in mind that they are God's instruments for the transformation of society; always looking for the signs of God's working in society and keeping faith with God in such activities. Some respondents accordingly asserted that:

> Nigeria, even the Nigerian church, are passing through an evolutionary process and divine reformation. I do believe that the church will [work] as an instrument in God's hand for the transformation and salvation of the world.[212]

> They should see the transformation of the society as their common task.[213]

In their missional agenda for Nigerian society, church leaders should seek to liberate the church in Nigeria from theological, intellectual, liturgical and financial colonialism. In addition, the Nigerian church also needs to be liberated from traditional practices that are contrary to biblical witness. This study is not arguing for a total rupture between the Nigerian church and the Christian church in other parts of the world, neither is it arguing that there should be no interaction between Christianity and traditional beliefs and practices. On the contrary, whereas such interaction should be encouraged, church leaders should, nevertheless, ensure that such relationships do not work against an indigenous Nigerian biblical theology, liturgy and financial capability. A respondent called attention to this enduring challenge facing Nigerian Christianity.

> In post independence period we were financially, liturgically and intellectually colonized by the (so called) mother churches in Europe and the Americas and by the traditional worship. We are still under colonial influence until the *"church"* in Nigeria

---

211. P13.
212. P3.
213. P2.

indigenises the gospel presentation and establishes the *"self-hood of the church in evangelism and liturgical expression."*[214]

As against the missionary and colonial understanding of the church relationship with society which was adopted by Nigerian church leaders after the colonial and missionary eras, in hope that this posture will protect the church from the negative influence of the world, a respondent asserted:

> The church blindfolded the members from their civic rights and responsibilities.[215]

Nigerian church leaders should, as part of their missional strategy in Nigerian society,

> encourage Christian participation in politics, economy and social life of the nation.[216]

In addition, a respondent called on Nigerian church leaders to:

> Consciously build in developmental projects as an integral part of mission.[217]

Denominations/Congregations

Guder posits that "a vital instrument for the fulfillment of the missionary vocation of the Church is the local congregation."[218] As part of both the being and the identity of the church, Nigerian church leaders should ensure the continued existence of church denominations and congregations in Nigeria. Each of these levels of the church's existence/expression has a significant role to play in the spiritual and social roles of the missional church in society.

Included in their other roles, the denominational and congregational platforms of the church provide avenues for the instilling of Christian beliefs and teachings. As noted by one of the respondents, such beliefs and teachings should enhance the transformation of society.

---

214. P3.
215. P17.
216. P6.
217. P10.
218. Guder, *Continuing Conversion of Church*, 145.

> Beliefs and teachings should be fashioned in such a way that will enhance the transformation of our society.[219]

Denominations and congregations provide avenues for church leaders to discover the challenges and potentials of their members with regard to the provision of pastoral care, nurturing and positive influences.

> Denominational leaders need to observe the principle of presence in relating to their members so as to further understand them and the state they are in better.[220]

Denominations and congregations also provide opportunities for church leaders to invest in a broad range of options, including finances, time, etc. As such, a respondent suggested that

> church leaders should be conscious of what they can invest in the members.[221]

In addition, church denominations and congregations are indispensable to the church's existence and self-transformation which, in turn, ensure the existence of both the church and its leaders and without which it would not be possible for their social ministry to be released in the sense of providing a means for continual mentoring, conscientization, sustenance and the restoration of their dignity. Alluding to this notion, a respondent affirmed the need for the

> continuous education of the membership of their worth as God's people and how they should keep it.[222]

Ecumenism

Just as the denominational and congregational expressions of the church are indispensable, it is not possible to overemphasize the importance of the ecumenical church to the existence of the church and its missional engagement in Nigeria. In this vein one of the respondents noted that

---

219. P2.
220. P6.
221. P11.
222. P13.

experience has shown that the neglect of the "ecumenical imperative" in the Christian community in Nigeria is a great handicap for the church to work effectively in these areas.[223]

The ecumenical imperative referred to may be found in John 17:21 and it is from this passage that many ecumenical bodies, including CAN, have taken their motto, namely, "That they all may be one." Whereas the church and its leaders have contributed to Nigerian society through denominations and congregations, it is a known fact that the strongest witness of the church in Nigeria has been brought to bear by the ecumenical church namely, the Christian Association of Nigeria (CAN). Despite its challenges and failures, CAN remains the strongest voice for the church in Nigeria and it is through the medium of CAN that the church has been able to hold dialogue with the state and with other religions, including Islam. This study has revealed that a number of respondents are of the opinion that it is through the ecumenical church that it will be possible for church leaders to influence the policies of government and business institutions for the good of Nigerian society. William Temple in "Sermon at the Opening Service: Second World Conference on Faith and Order, Edinburgh, 1937" notes that "a Church divided in its manifestation to the world cannot render its due service to God or to man."[224]

Churches and church leaders should, therefore, ensure the growth and sustenance of the ecumenical church as both a channel and a constituent of a more meaningful social transformational approach. In order to realise this, one respondent opined:

> embrace genuine and selfless unity, no matter the sacrifice and costs it may entail for the love of God's kingdom and the nation.[225]

Placing greater emphasis on the importance of sustaining the ecumenical church for a more fruitful social ministry, another respondent suggested:

---

223. P20.
224. Temple, "Sermon at Opening Service," 18.
225. P9.

They should sink their individual differences and work as a team. They should see the transformation of the society as their common task.[226]

Religious Activities

Religious activities enable Christians (leaders/members), inter alia, to express worship to God, share fellowship with other worshippers, receive nurture, socialise and deal with the challenges of life. Religious activities are, therefore, not only for the benefit of the Christian or the faithful; but they serve the good of broader society in the light of their ethical, spiritual and social components.

Regarding the spiritual and social resource of religious activities such as prayer, a respondent noted:

> We cannot overemphasize the role of prayer.[227]

Accordingly, the respondents suggested that the church and its leaders pray for the emergence and retention of good leaders in all sectors of the Nigerian society.

> Pray for good leaders.[228]
>
> Pray for the governments (national, state and local governments).[229]

Besides the use of prayer for petition and intercession, as may have been implied in the discussion above, prayer may also be directed against the forces of evil that may be responsible for social ills that contribute to the challenges of poverty, underdevelopment, corruption and poor leadership. Regarding this dimension of prayer, a respondent suggested:

> The Niger Delta issue is more of a spiritual issue which requires the church to take up the warfare to deliver that region which the devil (in my opinion) has decided to use to hold this nation to ransom.[230]

---

226. P2.
227. P22.
228. P12.
229. P8.
230. P11.

Kalu stresses the significance of warfare prayers to the spiritual, ecological and political life of Nigeria and other African nations, from a Pentecostal perspective, which he asserts is efficacious and resonates with African maps of the universe. Premising it on the theological paradigm of "theology of land as gift and covenant signifier,"[231] he argues that the loss of Eden and the exile of Abraham's children became paradigms of loss of gift and covenant through neglected stewardship, idolatry and pollution. Recovery is through a deliberate effort to create a new community of resistance that would employ identifiable repentance to deliver or redeem the land from the hostile occupiers or spirits at the gates of communities and that would intentionally speak a renewal covenant into being. Sometimes they call it "building a new altar." An aspect of the task is to use teaching from and reliance on the word, fervent prayers, fastings and certain specific symbolic actions and instruments (such as olive oil and water) to diagnose the nature of the enemy and regain lost victory.

Other religious activities with spiritual and social significance include Bible study, preaching and teaching. Such activities may instil and rejuvenate ethical standards for the purpose of checking corruption and developing good virtues such as honesty, hard work and love. The respondents, therefore, suggested that churches and church leaders should ensure the sustaining and adequate utilization of such activities.

> Teach and preach the good news of our Lord with the simplicity and passion of Christ selflessly.[232]

> Biblical studies.[233]

Self-Conversion

The respondents presented two aspects of the notion of self-conversion which is crucial to the continued existence of both the church and its leaders and as a vital component of social engagement. The first aspect of self-conversion is in the sense of the church and its leaders repenting of their personal failures in their social ministry which has contributed to the challenges of poverty, underdevelopment, corruption and poor leadership so as to enable them

---

231. Kalu, "Pentecostal and Charismatic Reshaping," 127.
232. P19.
233. P3.

to confront both the government and other institutions. In this regard, a respondent noted:

> The church leaders must sanitize the body of Christ before they can be bold enough to face the government. Let judgement start from the house of God.[234]

In accord with this view of P16, the WCC's "Statement on the Missionary Calling of the Church" reads: "The churches must confess that they have often passed by on the other side while the unbeliever, moved by compassion, did what the churches ought to have done. Wherever a church denies its solidarity with the world, or divorces its deeds from its words, it destroys the possibility of communicating the Gospel and presents to the world an offence which is not the genuine offence of the Cross."[235]

Second, self-conversion is used in the sense of a reflexive approach to the existence of the church and its leaders and to social engagement so as to guard against arrogance and error.

> Undergo internal self-conversion so that the Christian principles will guide our own actions.[236]

In a sense, therefore, self-conversion or self-renewal is closely related to the continuing conversion which is indispensable in an authentic Christian witness in order to prevent the church and its leaders from drifting away from the essence of the Gospel imperatives. According to Guder, "Our faithful witness can only happen when we learn to see and repent of our conformities"[237] and gospel reductionism.

This study maintains that the right understanding on the part of church leaders of the missionary purpose of the church in society, as premised on the church's participation in God's mission in the world (*missio Dei*), the proper engagement of the various levels of the church's expression, namely, denominational, congregational and ecumenical with the attendant roles each structure should perform, the appropriate use of religious activities and the practice of self-conversion may enhance the church's existence with

---

234. P16.
235. WCC, *Guidelines on Dialogue*, 341.
236. P18.
237. Guder, *Continuing Conversion of Church*, 72.

its distinctive identity in Nigerian society and enable the church to act as an important agent of change. These factors will ensure the existence, growth, renewal and fruitful engagement of the church and its leaders in the Nigerian context. Admittedly, the church, including its leaders, has not been called to live for itself alone; it is called by the missional God and sent into the world. As such the church's mission is in the world, and not just in the church. In order to be able to influence the world in general, and Nigeria in particular, the Nigerian church and its leaders will need to put in place these influential structures if the church is to address the challenges of poverty, underdevelopment, corruption, poor leadership and other forms of injustice.

5.2.9.2 Key Areas in Which to Exert Influence

Leadership and policy change in political and economic institutions are among the key structures that church leaders need if they are to exert the necessary influence in order to transform Nigerian society by helping overcome the challenges of poverty, underdevelopment, corruption and poor leadership and engage more meaningfully in social change. It is the view of the respondents in the empirical study that meaningful social engagement on the part of church leaders will have to include these areas of leadership and policy change as vital components of their social engagement.

Leadership

Anya, decrying the afflictions of Nigerians arising from the poor performance of leaders from colonial times, argues that even under the administration of Nigerian political leaders, military as well as civil, the pseudo-colonial economic arrangements have subsisted. The recent controversy over the fabulous payments to members of the legislature is but the latest variation on an old theme of hidden gratification of leaders even as up to 80 percent of the national revenue is devoted to the recurrent budget and overheads. He questions that, in a situation in which leaders are living flamboyant lifestyles as compared to the 70 percent of Nigerians living under the poverty line as in 2007 (the situation may even be worse now), from whence can the resources for capital development, especially of needed infrastructure and social expenditure, come? It is on this note that he insists that "Nigeria has never had a leadership devoted to its development and the welfare of the people."²³⁸ Emphasising the importance of leadership and how the absence of good leadership is afflicting Nigerian society, P10 observed that

> bad leadership is the key cause of underdevelopment and the high level of poverty in Nigeria.

It emerged from both the literature review and the empirical study, that Nigerians, including church leaders, agreed that the challenges of poverty, underdevelopment, corruption and poor leadership are attributable mainly to the poor leadership that has kept watch over Nigeria from the colonial period to the present-day democratic society with this failure of leadership impacting negatively on the sociopolitical, economic and religious structures of Nigerian society. It is thus essential that church leaders address the leadership challenge in a number of ways as, without this, other efforts to address the other challenges will be futile. These ways of addressing the issue of leadership include an emphasis on the importance of leadership to sociopolitical and economic transformation, the appropriate leadership style that may be helpful to Nigerians, bearing in mind the challenges they are facing, and the value of mentoring in sustaining the culture of good leadership in Nigeria.

Just as poor leadership has been identified as the main cause of the challenges facing Nigerian society, so good leadership has also been named as the most significant source from which the anticipated change will come. P11 asserted that:

> we need leaders who are firm and focused, no matter the odds; who understand our strategic priorities and pursue them. Leaders who can generate the excitement we need in our political, economic and social levels of the Nigerian society. Above all, the leader should be God fearing, yet principled and of high integrity.

In an effort to demonstrate effectively the importance of leadership in the transformation of the society, church leaders should take the lead in offering good leadership in all spheres (religious, political, economic and social) and they should teach their church members and Nigerian society as a whole by their own example. P19 lent their voice to this argument in the following way:

---

238. Anya, "Science, Human Behaviour," 12.

> Show good example of selfless leadership in the various areas of authority insisting that it is possible to take righteousness into governance. This must be done without fear of being persecuted.

The emphasis on leadership as a strategic area of influence for social change and a vital component of a sustainable transformational approach to development requires an understanding of the leadership style which would be of crucial relevance to the current Nigerian society. Whereas other leadership styles such as servant leadership were mentioned in the empirical study, the argument put forward for transformational leadership as the critical leadership concept for current Nigerian society, bearing in mind challenges facing this society, was outstanding. P11, for example, stated:

> Nigeria needs transformation. Therefore, to do this requires transformational leaders. Transformational leaders have a vision – a goal, an agenda, a result orientation that grabs people's attention. They communicate their vision and build trust by being consistent, dependable and persistent. They have positive self-regard. In general, they transform vision into reality and motivate people to transcend their personal interests for the good of the group. This is the kind of leadership we need in today's Nigeria.

In support for transformational leadership, P12 argued that

> a transformational leader will be ideal. We need a leader who will challenge the way matters are handled presently. Someone who will use all the resources available to develop and bring change.

However, in addition to the importance and style of leadership, leadership development through mentorship was another factor in leadership which was identified in the study. P9 identified the importance of mentorship in this way:

> mentors to the emergence of dynamic political leadership.

Although referring directly to the role of church leaders in raising future leaders for Nigerian society, the concept of mentoring as regards the socio-political, economic and religious life of the Nigerian society is also indispensable. Whereas other forms of leadership training and development should not be neglected, mentoring, which in a way relates to discipling,[239] remains an outstanding process of leadership development.

Institutional Change

Among the other factors contributing to poverty and underdevelopment, the evolution of institutions and organizations has also been noted as contributing substantially to the sociopolitical and economic challenges facing Nigeria.[240] Korten has also argued that "the problem is the system" and as such, "the whole system of institutional power must be transformed."[241] Unfortunately, the impact of the church and church leaders on institutional change, especially as it relates to political and economic institutions, has been negligible with indications of the paucity of such ecclesial influence on these crucial institutions being reflected in both the literature review and the empirical study. P17, for example, stated:

> The church has no effect on the polity.

Kafang intimates to us the reason why the church and its leaders have had so little influence on the Nigerian political, cultural and economic polity when he states that far too many Christians have, for too long, approached politics as if it lies outside their primary responsibility as Christians. "When the distinction is drawn between 'church' and the 'world,' for example, it usually implies that politics, economics, science, technology and mass media are part of the 'world.'"[242] The Christian life is thus confined to personal piety, to church activities, to family prayer and Bible study.

As regards the church's moving beyond the limited space of its influence into more meaningful and crucial areas for more enduring results, P11 urged:

> The church should be more visible at the political level of the transformation process by articulating its position to influence (positively) the decisions of government for the betterment of society. So, in effect, this level should be involved more in policy matters. Issues that have to do with electoral reforms, inputs in federal budgets and national development plans e.g. Vision 2020.

---

239. Belsterling, "Mentoring Approach of Jesus."
240. Anya, "Science, Human Behaviour."
241. Korten, *When Corporations Rule*, 278.
242. Kafang, *Christians' Integrity and Politics*, 20.

P12 stated further:

> Church leaders should be involved in shaping economic policies in Nigeria.

As in the global arena, political and economic institutions play an extremely vital role in Nigeria with much of the social inequalities and injustices, including environmental degradation and pollution, proceeding from these institutions. In view of the fact that they are such powerful institutions because of the political and economic power they wield as well as their global connections, persons living on the periphery of society find it difficult to understand their subtle operations. Church leaders will therefore need to see these institutions as crucial systems that they should seek to influence with the aim of bringing an end to poverty, underdevelopment, corruption and other vices. Kafang also urges that the participation of church leaders and also church members in politics should be "about defining the very nature of government – about the structures, limits, policy, and responsibilities of government."[243]

5.2.9.3 Channels of Influence

The church and its leadership, living in consciousness of their missional responsibility in society, being conscious of their resources and being open to continued renewal, will also need to understand the persons and systems they seek to transform in the interests of a more effective social transformational process. In addition, the Nigerian church and its leaders will need to locate the channels through which these persons and systems may be effectively changed. These channels, through which persons and systems may be changed, were also identified in the empirical study and include conscientization, advocacy, protests, direct participation, projects and social services.

Conscientization

Over time, the mindset of Nigerians has been conditioned negatively by the influence of colonialism, imperialism, ethnicity, militarization, poverty, underdevelopment and corruption. Such a mindset has not only diminished the dignity and productivity of Nigerians, but it has also led to the prevailing

---

243. Kafang, 21.

culture of mediocrity, sectionalism and being unpatriotic. Many Nigerians have lost faith in their leaders and in the Nigerian nation. Accordingly, given the far-reaching implications of this mindset, transformation in Nigeria will remain a dream. However, changing such a mindset requires a deliberate and systematic process that is geared towards creating an awareness among Nigerians of their negative mindset, what has informed such a mindset, its negative impact, how to change it and the potentials and resources that Nigerians have at their disposal to transform their situations and circumstances. Ultimately, all of these processes should lead to a change of heart which in turn should lead to positive action. Based on the responses from the empirical study, it would appear that conscientization is the concept that has the most potential to transform the mindset of Nigerians with P4 asserting:

Conscientizing the people.

P6, alluding to the implications of conscientization, noted:

There needs to be a deliberate and calculated effort to ensure the creation of awareness on these issues.

However, this process of conscientization should go beyond just creating an awareness of the challenges facing Nigerians and how to overcome these challenges, and it should generate a consciousness of outstanding potential within each Nigerian to act for the benefit of all. Thus, conscientization should create in all Nigerians a yearning for and an engagement with that which is noble, honourable, excellent and virtuous. In addition, conscientization should enable Nigerians to rise above religious and ethnic biases and encourage them to admire that which is good and rise up against that which is bad, no matter its source. Thus, conscientization may well be the process through which Nigerians may begin to be guided by ideologies instead of sentiments.

It may be argued, as compared to other institutions, the church and its leaders are more privileged in that they have an enormous followership while the avenues for conscientization, which include, inter alia, fellowships, sermons, counselling sessions, Bible studies and media programmes, are open to them.

Advocacy

Advocacy remains both a vital channel for and a component of social change. Church leaders have, in general, performed creditably in the area of advocacy.

However, church leaders will need to continue in this advocacy and find better ways in which to engage in it. The point that should be borne in mind in the process of advocacy is that church leaders are under an obligation to speak for God and the people as opposed to speaking for themselves. P13 succeeded in capturing the role of church leaders in advocacy as it relates to God by saying:

> Drawing attention to what God says to any given situation without compromising standards.

On the other hand, P4 reminded us of the role of church leaders and churches in advocacy as it relates to the disinherited and those on the fringes or periphery of society.

> The church must remain the voice of the voiceless.

Protests

As has been observed in the study, the most outstanding action of church leaders in the realm of protests was initiated and accomplished by Pastor Tunde Bakare of the Latter Rain Assembly in 2010 under the auspices of the Save Nigeria Group (SNG). This move was lauded by Nigerians not only because it represented a bold step for the clergy, but also because of its impact. The empirical study revealed that protests should be explored by church leaders as a means through which political institutions and other powerful institutions may be pressurized to live up to the expectations of the nation. P12, for example, stated:

> Church leaders have spoken on corruption but should do more in leading protests.

Protests should therefore be seen as representing a deeper level of engaging the systems beyond the scope of advocacy on the part of Nigerian church leaders. This advocacy is characterized mainly by communiqués and visits to political leaders.

Direct Participation

The direct participation of church leaders in all aspects of society is yet another channel by means of which church leaders may exercise influence on the sociopolitical and economic landscape as a way of more meaningful social engagement. "We should be seeking to exercise as much leadership as possible – leadership in both our states and national assemblies, in our senate, in all our tiers of governments, and in international organizations – to propose principled policies and changes in political structures that advance justice domestically and internationally."[244] Stressing the importance of the participation of both church leaders and church members in the sociopolitical and economic processes and beyond, P14 argued that

> the salt is the salt of the earth (not of the church). The church should come out of the four walls and be involved in every sphere of life, politics and governance, media, business, education, arts, etc. everywhere.

The direct participation of church leaders and church members in all spheres of life does not only assist church leaders to remain in touch with the realities of the joys and challenges experienced by other humans, but it is also necessary in helping generate informed theologies that relate to the everyday experiences of life. The image of church leaders working in the real-life situation depicts church leaders as leading the flock within the sanctuary, into the world, and back to the sanctuary. Direct participation is, thus, one of the powerful ways in which church leaders may bridge the church sanctuary, the market place or the place of work and the home or community and also teach the church members to do the same.

Projects and Social Services

Charity, projects and social services have featured prominently in the domain of the church's social engagement for centuries. As such, churches and church leaders in Nigeria have made vital contributions in education, healthcare, relief, skills acquisition and economic empowerment schemes. However, although projects and social services may be a means through which the poor may be kept alive and, thus, empowered in the sense of relief, they may also be a means through which poverty may be perpetuated and the structures that cause poverty justified or given legitimacy. Thus, in this second sense, projects and social services may be disempowering and therefore prejudicial to the poor. According to Jacobson, the works of mercy reveal our own need for mercy, our own limitations, our own poverty of spirit and, as such, they

---

244. Kafang, 22.

may be beneficial in the revelation they bring about. "On the other hand, the works of mercy are considerably limited if they are done without regard to systemic injustice. Society is pleased to have the church exhaust itself in being merciful towards the casualties of unjust systems."[245]

It is thus essential that church leaders maintain a creative tension between relief and empowerment projects and ensure that there is a transition from relief to empowerment. Self-reliance is a crucial aspect of the empowerment of the poor. This is what P13 was referring to when they stated:

> Deliver the members from abject poverty through economic empowerment programmes and sustainability.

P11 subscribed to this view and went on to mention some of such projects that could enhance economic empowerment, self-reliance and sustainability.

> By creating strategic and sustainable wealth resources and use them to show society the way to go, e.g. microfinance institutions.

However, whereas projects and social services may enhance a more meaningful social transformational process and are therefore necessary as a constituent of a sustainable transformational approach to development in Nigeria, this means and channel of engagement should be supported to the extent that it demonstrates the love of God to the poor in practical ways but does not permit the legitimization of unjust institutions.

5.2.9.4 Overarching Concepts That Should Inform the Social Engagement of Church Leaders

Having discussed the existence and self-renewal of the church and also those areas which church leaders should seek to influence and the means through which they can be influenced in order to bring about social transformation in Nigeria, it will now be pertinent to present the overarching concepts that should inform the social ministry of church leaders in Nigeria. The purpose of these overarching concepts is to enrich the social engagement of church leaders as they engage the individuals and systems they seek to change, and to enhance the channels through which the change process flows. In addition, these overarching concepts place the church and its leaders in a better

---

245. Jacobson, *Doing Justice*, 19.

position in which to serve as agents of change in tandem with other vital change agents within Nigeria and beyond. In essence, the existence and self-renewal of the church, the systems/institutions/persons which the church seeks to change, channels through which the expected change may be realized and the overarching concepts that should guide change in the present-day Nigeria all combine to promote both the more meaningful social engagement of Nigerian church leaders and the components of a sustainable transformational approach on the part of church leaders to social change in Nigeria. The task at this juncture is to present the overarching concepts that should inform the social ministry of church leaders in Nigeria, namely, innovation, stewardship, collaboration and values/culture.

Innovation

It is vital that church leaders in Nigeria come to terms with both the socio-political and economic challenges facing the country and the expectations of Nigerians concerning the role of church leaders in bringing about transformation. However, in view of the enormity of both the challenges and what is required to change the status quo, church leaders will have to abandon their usual stance which they inherited from the missionary and the colonial period. In recalling the traditional approach of church leaders to social issues, using the example of politics, P14 noted:

> The church has not been too involved in the political transformation of Nigeria. They have always seen politics as a no-go area for Christians but now the story has changed.

However, the need for innovation on the part of church leaders does not mean that church leaders take the path of least resistance. According to Kafang, innovation involves avoiding "the easy path of simple going along with democratic, economic, and technological changes as they occur,"[246] the aim of innovation should be to develop a coherent Christian political (and economic) perspective that will allow us to make judgements about the justice and injustice of the changes taking place. While it is true that the situation is gradually changing, much still remains to be done to change the

---

246. Kafang, *Christians' Integrity and Politics*, 22.

attitudes of both church leaders and church members to sociopolitical and economic issues.

P21, P13 and P10 gave some idea of what innovativeness requires when they argued that it entails:

> the ability to understand the dynamics of nation building. Understanding the biblical approaches to nation building.
>
> Acknowledge the fact that the situation exists. Discuss genuinely with the view of taking steps on how to address it frontally.
>
> Be able to take constructive steps to bring about a balance between the mission of care and spirituality.

An understanding of both the dynamics of nation building and the biblical approach to nation building are vital components of the innovativeness required of church leaders in Nigeria as regards social change. Such an approach requires a bold acceptance of the realities of the situation and practical steps that should lead to the anticipated change.

Despite the fact that innovation may not guarantee that the engagement of church leaders in social change will be easy, it does, however, indicate a responsible approach to dealing with challenges and such an approach often leads to success. In addition, innovativeness may be said to be a continuum, as it is not static. As new challenges emerge, new solutions are sought and the process continues. P1 illustrated both the process and the gains of innovation when counselled that

> if you fail, look closely, and seek the reason why. You have the power to conquer. If you only try. Let us accept this philosophy in our striving for a just and equitable country and we will not fail.

It is essential that church leaders be proactive in their innovative stance. This, in turn, requires an understanding of local and global contexts and an anticipation of the unexpected, always seeking for better ways in which to confront challenges.

Stewardship

As an overarching concept, stewardship aims to embody a response to the wasteful and corrupt attitude of many Nigerians. In addition, it may also serve to address the inability of Nigerians to utilize effectively the vast deposits of human, natural, economic and spiritual resources with which Nigeria is blessed. Commenting on the rich resources in Nigeria and the absence of stewardship in the utilization of these resources, P10 asserted:

> We have a rich country that is the poorest in infrastructure, polity, development and social integration.

On this note, Idemudia suggests that "the main reason for widespread poverty in Nigeria is lack of transparency and accountability. Therefore, revenue transparency and accountability will contribute to poverty reduction and eventual eradication."[247] However, the concept of stewardship extends beyond the physical, tangible endowment of resources and it also encompasses the effective management of the resources of time and quality of services which often translate into either wealth or poverty, depending on how well, or not, these resources are used. In common with many Africans, Nigerians are known to have a poor attitude towards time management. P13 supported the view that the inefficient use of time and poor quality of services in public institutions are some of the areas that should be included in the social transformation agenda.

> Punctuality, faithfulness to public service.

Above all, the notion of stewardship calls for all Nigerians, at home and abroad, to perceive the transformation of Nigerian society and beyond as an obligation towards which they should channel all possible energies and resources. Such societal transformation includes the preservation of animal, plant, aquatic, atmospheric and environmental life for future generations. However, in light of the fact that the pursuit of stewardship requires a passionate consciousness of the issues enumerated above and that this consciousness should translate into concrete actions, P10 noted the following:

> Be passionately conscious about their environment. Be able to notice where there are injustices and speak up against all forms of injustice.

---

247. Idemudia, "Quest for Effective Use," 1.

Collaboration

The complexities of poverty, underdevelopment, corruption, poor leadership and social change call for collaborative efforts within the local, national and international contexts. No single institution possesses both the competency and the resources to address these challenges successfully, particularly in view of the fact that some of these challenges are informed by local, national and international interests. As such, it is essential that church leaders in Nigeria not merely acknowledge their collaborative partners, but they should also join hands with them ideologically, pragmatically and in other ways if collaboration is to happen.

In other words, church leaders should seek collaboration within the ecclesial community and then reach out to government. P5 underscored this idea as follows:

> Through their own structures first and then tangentially with government.

Economic institutions and economists are also necessary collaborative partners. P12 suggested:

> Church leaders should be involved in shaping economic policies in the country and constantly engage opinion leaders.

Politicians, community leaders/institutions and technocrats may also make for partners in these collaborative efforts. P19 suggested:

> Open and maintain communication lines between church leaders and leaders in politics, community leaders and technocrats.

The power of people's movements, social groups or civil society is increasingly proving to be extremely potent. Churches and church leaders who, according to Korten and Swart, belong in the category of civil society[248] and should, thus, collaborate effectively with them in transforming Nigerian society. It is in this light that P8 and P10 urged and asserted respectively:

> Join social groups to reform the nation.

> If honest Christian leaders would arise and form serious pressure groups within and outside the national boundaries, then

---

248. Korten, "People-centered Development"; Swart, *Churches and Development Debate*.

the political and economic change so much desired in Nigeria would come.

Values/Culture

Values and culture are both features of the Christian community, African/Nigerian societies and human societies in general, with values driving organizations, institutions and nations and having the power either to make or destroy such entities. This is because appropriate and inappropriate behavior is often informed by values and, as Anya reminds us in his narrative on the encounter between the architect of the Singaporean miracle, Lee Kuan Yew, and a Nigerian finance minister, "values matter." Anya attributes the failure of development efforts in Nigeria in the 1970s, 1980s and 1990s to behaviour and values.[249] However, the situation has not changed much in postmilitary or democratic Nigeria. It is thus essential that the quest for the sociopolitical and economic transformation of Nigerian society acknowledge the importance of those values which are expounded by the Christian faith, other religions and traditional society.

Moral values derived from religion and African culture and instilled in individuals and systems may lead to the development of holistic persons who are mature and capable of assuming responsibility. Using the example of the youth, P18 asserted:

> If we can form youths who are able to properly marry the African cultures with Christian values, we may produce a more holistic person who is matured and capable of taking responsibilities.

Both Christian and African values are community-oriented and, as such, they encourage members of the community to act in accordance with the best interests of the entire community. It is on this basis that the extended family system has reached out beyond the compound or village structure to encompass the church in African communities, including in Nigeria. African values are rooted in the concept of "*Ubuntu*." Desmond Tutu argues that "Ubuntu speaks of spiritual attributes such as generosity, hospitality, compassion, caring, sharing."[250] When translated into the context of poverty, underdevelopment, corruption, poor leadership and other forms of social injustice,

---

249. Anya, "Science, Human Behaviour."
250. Tutu, *God Is Not Christian*, 22.

the virtue of helping one another may assist in ameliorating these negative conditions while, if applied to institutions, this virtue may also be of benefit to society. The exploitative and greedy tendencies of institutions and the rich, which result in corruption and unjust practices, will be curtailed when the understanding takes root that all human beings and the environment are related and they should help one another and share the good things of life together. In support of this view, P4 noted:

> Cultivating the Christian virtues of helping one another.

In addition, in both Christian and traditional African societies corruption, which also includes stealing and extortion, is not tolerated and is in fact associated with shame and stigmatization. As P15 argued, upholding both Christian and African values may assist Nigerians to

> say no to corrupt practices.

Although there is some controversy as to what constitutes ethical and unethical standards in both society and in institutions, this does not diminish the importance of values and virtues in Christian and also in African/Nigerian societies. In Nigeria, especially, a country which is greatly influenced by Christian, Islamic and traditional African values, there is usually a high degree of consensus as to what actually constitutes right values and ethical standards. Such consensus may well inform the moral questions in systems and institutions in Nigeria.

It has emerged from the discussion on the overarching concepts that these concepts, namely, innovation, stewardship, collaboration and values/culture, are vital components of a more meaningful social development agenda on the part of church leaders in Nigeria, an agenda which is geared to addressing the challenges of poverty, underdevelopment, corruption and poor leadership. If this development agenda is to attain the desired results, it is essential that all these concepts be engaged as an overarching paradigm to the existence and self-renewal of the church, the persons and institutions which the church and its leaders are seeking to change and the channels through which such change may be achieved.

5.3 Conclusion

The presentation and discussion of the empirical study, which was conducted in Nigeria among church leaders of the Christian Association of Nigeria (CAN) and its constituent blocs and the Lagos Presbyterian Church (LPC) from March 2010 to April 2011, was premised on the research questions which were, in turn, guided by Osmer's four practical theological methodology tasks.[251] Twenty-one church leaders who are also development-oriented participated in the study. Based on their responses to the questions posed in the open-ended questionnaire, various themes emerged. The Nigerian historical timelines assisted in delineating the study and showed that the negative impacts of the colonial, independence and military eras as they relate to poverty, underdevelopment, corruption and poor leadership are still holding sway in the present democratic or postmilitary period. The social engagement of Nigerian church leaders although rated largely as average is still heavily tilted to charity and social services with many respondents showing dissatisfaction in the achievements so far attained. It is such dissatisfaction that has resulted in respondents urging church leaders and the faithful for better ways of social engagement such as protests and direct participation in politics and economic actions towards policy and institutional change despite a number of challenges which include disunity among Christians and selfishness on the part of some Nigerian church leaders.

The study has revealed what is required for a more meaningful social engagement on the part of church leaders in Nigeria in the face of the poverty, underdevelopment, corruption and poor leadership in the country, and the constituents of such engagement. It emerged from the study that a more meaningful social engagement of church leaders and the constituents of such engagement include the church's existence and self-transformation, key structures by means of which to exert influence, the means through which such influence may be exerted, and the overarching concepts that should inform the engagement of church leaders with other institutions as agents of change.

As regards the church's existence and self-renewal, it was argued that, for the church and its leaders to ensure their continued existence and their engagement in their socioreligious, political and economic responsibilities within Nigerian society and beyond, these church leaders, who are known

---

251. Osmer, *Practical Theology*. See also 1.8.1.

to be the major architects of the church's vision and mission, will have to pay close attention to the mission and societal relevance of the church, denominational/congregational existence, membership care, ecumenism, self-renewal/conversion and religious activities. These components are vital to the church's identity and existence, including the identity and existence of church leaders. The key structures through which church leaders should exert influence include leadership and policy change in persons (leaders and followers) and political and economic institutions while the means through which this influence may be exerted include conscientization, advocacy, protests, direct participation, projects and social services. In addition, the overarching concepts that should inform the engagement of church leaders within the ecclesial community and other institutions as agents of change are innovation, stewardship, collaboration and values/culture.

In the view of the researcher, the strategy for a more meaningful social engagement on the part of Nigerian church leaders and the components of such a strategy may be summarized in the form of "a sustainable transformational approach" through which church leaders and the faithful can engage in the sociopolitical and economic transformation of the postmilitary or democratic Nigerian society in the light of the challenges of poverty, underdevelopment, corruption and poor leadership facing the country. Chapter 6 will focus on the sustainable transformational approach to the social engagement of church leaders in terms of development in Nigeria.

CHAPTER 6

A Sustainable Transformational Approach to Development in Postmilitary Nigeria

6.1 Introduction

This chapter will propose a developmental framework which may be helpful to church leaders and the Christian community in Nigeria in utilising their resources as agents of change in Nigeria. The content of this framework will be based on the major themes derived from the empirical study (see chapter 5) and will be informed by the literature review (see chapters 2, 3 and 4). It is hoped that the framework will assist in enabling Nigerian church leaders to contribute more meaningfully to the sociopolitical and economic transformation of Nigerian society. In order to realise the aim of this chapter, Osmer's pragmatic task of practical theological methodology will be engaged. The pragmatic task focuses on the development of rules of art. Rules of art are open-ended guidelines that may assist those who are either leading or participating in a particular form of religious praxis. This task, thus, asks the question: How might this area of praxis be shaped to embody more fully the normative commitments of a religious tradition within a particular context of experience?[1]

---

1. Osmer, *Practical Theology*.

It may be recalled that the essence of this study was to ascertain how church leaders in Nigeria could contribute more meaningfully to the sociopolitical and economic transformation of Nigerian society in the light of the problems of poverty, underdevelopment, corruption and poor leadership facing the country. Also, when translated into a sustainable transformational development approach (with a view to a more meaningful engagement on the part of the church leaders in the sociopolitical and economic change within Nigerian society), what would the possible constituent elements of such an approach be?

In this study's attempt to analyse the socioeconomic and political scenario in Nigeria from the colonial era to present day for the purpose of discovering the development trends which had been implemented and the kind of leadership that has been accorded Nigerians, one major common factor, in the midst of all other factors which may be termed secondary, resurfaced repeatedly, namely, the failure of Nigerian leadership, be it colonial, independent, military, or postmilitary or civil. It would appear that this leadership factor was the cause of the downfall of both the intentions regarding development in the sense of wrong motives and the exploitative, corrupt tendencies which have derailed any developmental approaches at different stages of Nigeria's history. However, yet another cause for concern, besides the critical challenge of irresponsible leadership, is the lack of a specific and workable development paradigm with a definite goal that would be for the good of all Nigerians. The concept of leadership in terms of which the much-needed development may be attained proved to be the transformational leadership style although the adaptive leadership concept could as well suffice. The social and theological discourse of church leaders in Nigeria was analysed for the purpose of understanding the behaviour of these leaders so as to assess their progress thus far and to ascertain what still needs to be done if they are to have an impact on Nigerian society. It was discovered that, despite the fact that much of the sociotheological discourse of the church leaders is still inadequate, there are indications that there has been some progress in a positive direction. It is possible that these gains may be sustained and, indeed, if the church adopted a development paradigm which takes into account the Nigerian society as discussed in this study. In addition, such a framework should also cater for the contextual challenges confronting Nigeria, as well as embody a theological relevance which aligns with the alternative development framework in terms of which church leaders and church members may function as agents of change in collaboration with other agents of change in both the local and the global context.

In order to be able to propose an approach in terms of which church leaders in Nigeria may contribute more meaningfully to social transformation in the country, an empirical study was carried out. The results of the empirical study were presented and discussed in chapter 5. The dissemination and reflection on the study was premised on the research questions which were guided by the four tasks of practical theological methodology as proposed by Osmer.[2] The study has shown that a more meaningful social engagement on the part of the church leaders in Nigeria in the light of the poverty, underdevelopment, corruption and poor leadership in the country and the components of such engagement include the following – the church's existence and self-transformation, key structures through which to exert influence, the means through which such influence may be exerted, and the overarching concepts that should inform the engagement of church leaders with other institutions as agents of change.

As regards the church's existence and self-renewal, the study revealed that, if the church and its leaders were to ensure both their continued existence and their engagement in their socioreligious, political and economic responsibilities in Nigerian society and beyond, Nigerian church leaders would have to pay careful attention to the church's mission and societal relevance, denominational/congregational existence, membership care, ecumenism, self-renewal/conversion and religious activities with these components being seen as vital to the identity and existence of the church and its leaders. The key structures through which church leaders should seek to exert influence include leadership/people and policy change in political and economic institutions. Conscientization, advocacy, protests, direct participation, projects and social services constitute the channels through which church leaders may transform Nigerian society while the overarching concepts that should inform the engagement of church leaders within the ecclesial community, society at large and other institutions of change are innovation, stewardship, collaboration and values/culture. It is the view of the author that the four major components listed above and their subsets make up a strategy for

---

2. Osmer. See also 1.8.1.

the more meaningful social engagement of Nigerian church leaders and the constituents of a social transformation agenda. As such, this sociopolitical and economic transformation agenda may be summarized in the form of "a sustainable transformational approach" for Nigerian church leaders to help bring about the sociopolitical and economic transformation of postmilitary or democratic Nigeria in the light of the poverty, underdevelopment, corruption and poor leadership facing the country.

I will now proceed with the definition of the sustainable transformational development approach and the goals, domains and processes of sustainable transformational development. This endeavour hereafter will be animated by the findings of the empirical research as presented and discussed in chapter 5. Thereafter, development-oriented church leaders as the key drivers of the sustainable transformational development approach in the Nigerian context will be discussed.

6.2 Sustainable Transformational Development
6.2.1 Definition of the Concept

Sustainable transformational development is the term which this study uses as an alternative to the traditional term of development, and the now often used church/NGO based term of transformational development. The term "development," as used by economic growth theorists, has come to have negative connotations. It is essential that transformational development, although still extremely important to Christian development agencies in social engagements, be broadened to embrace both the new developments and the far-reaching dimensions of change that the church must take into consideration as it seeks to transform society in the local, national and global contexts, and especially in the Nigerian milieu. The need for both a broad-based and a church-based development agenda has given rise to the sustainable transformational development approach, particularly within the Nigerian context. This approach is considered to be a developmental framework which could facilitate the more meaningful involvement of church leaders, churches (ecumenical and denominational) and church development agencies in transforming societies in collaboration with other institutions such as government, economic and civil society in both the local to the global context. However, it is envisioned that the framework will, as motivated by the empirical study and the theoretical frameworks that inform this study, have special significance for the church leadership in Nigeria although it may also be relevant outside of the Nigerian environment.

The term "sustainable transformational development" is used to express this study's focus on seeking positive change, from the perspective of the church leadership, as regards the entire spectrum of human, institutional and environmental life in Nigeria and, as such, it encompasses the spiritual, sociopolitical, economic, moral, psychological, ecclesial and environmental spheres. The adjective "sustainable" is used to reflect the notion that the activities of the Triune God, by means of which the church in Nigeria serves as an instrument in collaboration with him, include the dimensions necessary to transform persons, institutions and the environment, from the local to the global contexts. The adjective also implies that the resources required for the Triune God's change agenda are available in Nigeria and should, thus, be sourced by church leaders in collaboration with both the faithful and other institutions within both the local and the global arenas. However, the discovery and utilization of those resources by church leaders should be guided by the following overarching concepts, namely, innovation, collaboration, stewardship and values, while taking into account the local and global challenges in all of life. The notion of resource generation and utilization in the Nigerian environment is in agreement with the notion of self-reliance, as enunciated in the pragmatic ecumenical development debate and by Burkey.[3]

Sustainable transformational development may, therefore, be defined as a deep, positive change in the spiritual, psychological, moral, social, economic, political and environmental life of both individuals and institutions and resulting from the activities of the church in Nigeria (leaders and members) in collaboration with other institutions of change. These activities of the church are based on its participation, with the Triune God, in mission. As a development approach, the sustainable transformational development framework both acknowledges and draws on existing concepts that have motivated the church in its missional engagements in society. Such concepts are, in the main, *missio Dei* or the mission of God. Outside of the ecclesial community, the sustainable transformational development paradigm seeks to create a common ground for collaboration between the ideas and action

---

3. Burkey, *People First*.

from a church-based development ideology and the alternative development approach of people-centred development, as enunciated by David Korten. Korten's fourth generational approach (people-centred development), which is idea and value based, is in the spirit of peoples' movements worldwide which are making global impact as they seek to address the challenges that economic and political powers are creating for both humankind and the environment.[4] In creating such grounds for the integration of ideas and action, the sustainable transformational development approach intends to encourage the church to move beyond the confines of charity and social services to changing both policies and the institutions that mete out injustice to the poor and adversely affect the environment. The Nigerian context, for which this paradigm is being proposed, is, as a result of historical antecedents and the complexity of issues arising from the poverty, underdevelopment, violence, corruption and poor leadership, a complex one and, thus, it is assumed that an innovative and collaborative approach will be of value. The goals of sustainable transformational development are changed people (leadership/followership), changed institutions and the responsible utilization of the resources in creation, especially in Nigeria and beyond, through the medium of stewardship.

6.2.2 The Goals of Sustainable Transformational Development

6.2.2.1 Changed People (Leaders/Followers)

The first goal of sustainable transformational development is to seek change in people (leaders/followers) as, without such change in people, change is unlikely in either systems, institutions or the environment. P10 observed:

> Bad leadership is the key cause of underdevelopment and the high level of poverty in Nigeria.

Thus, it is essential that the leaders in Nigeria undergo change, although this experience of change also needs to be extended to the people or followers who have been affected by the damage inflicted by poor leadership over the years. As Jayakumar Christian argues, this anticipated change encompasses

---

4. Korten, "People-centered Development."

the recovery of the true identity of both the poor and the rich[5] – in the Nigerian context the followers and the leaders – as well as the discovery of the true vocation of the poor and the rich (followers and leaders). The minds of the poor and rich have been corroded by the lies that have shaped their views and, as a result, their true identities have been damaged. While the poor view themselves as being without the dignity, value and ability which would enable them to make positive contributions to society, the rich play God and are enmeshed in the ceaseless pursuit of the wealth which has now become their standard for measuring both their self-worth and the worth of others. However, in addition to the rich having God-complexes and inflated perceptions of themselves, they live with some measure of guilt and insecurity based on the injustices they have perpetrated against the poor. Thus, if development is to be sustainably transformational, the poor and the rich will have to recover both their identities and their vocations. "The poor and non-poor are made in God's image (identity) and are valuable enough to God to warrant the death of the Son in order to restore that relationship (dignity) and to give gifts that contribute to the well-being of themselves and their community (vocation)."[6] P11 asserted:

> We need leaders who are firm and focused, no matter the odds; who understand our strategic priorities and pursue them. Leaders who can generate the excitement we need in our political, economic and social levels of the Nigerian society. Above all, the leader should be God fearing, yet principled and of high integrity.

The quest to change people should begin with spiritual change as the origin of all human and social transformation is spiritual. Without the change in attitudes and behaviour that is implicit in *metanoia* (conversion), it is certain that human beings will remain self-centred creatures. "They are unlikely to transform the external structures and relationships of their society. The power in society of sin, both individual and institutional, is a basic deterrent to positive change."[7] The influence of human greed and corruption may be part of

---

5. Christian, *God of Empty-Handed*.
6. Myers, *Walking with the Poor*, 115.
7. Bragg, "From Development to Transformation," 46–47.

the reason why some development programmes have failed. P19 supported this argument when he asserted:

> Show good example of selfless leadership in the various areas of authority, insisting that it is possible to take righteousness into governance. This must be done without fear of being persecuted.

The vital component of the power of God to bring change to the lives of people, who are both the captives of evil spirits and who are enmeshed in the lies of the devil aimed at keeping them in perpetual poverty, should not be neglected, especially in the Nigerian and the African context. It is also through this transforming work of the Holy Spirit that the non-poor will be enabled to assume their true human identity in place of their God-complexes and to recover their vocation as stewards of the resources in their possession, while their greed will be transformed into contentment. However, such transformation may only be mediated through religious activities such as prayer, preaching and Bible study. In addition, in view of the pervasive nature of imperialism, corruption, ethnicity and violence, all entities in relationship with Nigeria and with Nigerians of all religious persuasions and social status should take stock of their inclinations and actions for the purpose of seeking change, wherever necessary.

Sustainable transformational development also seeks to see changes in people in terms of respect for human dignity, self-worth, freedom, justice, equal opportunities and thriving relationships. The placing of a high premium on human life that leads, in turn, to a rejection of violence, slavery, sexism and all acts that degrade human beings, both directly and indirectly, is a mark of changed people in the context in which violence is a recurrent feature of life. In addition, in contexts in which people have changed, there is equality of all persons before the law. The treatment of the poor as objects of pity is cast aside and the poor take responsibility for their own development by making decisions and engaging their resources, however meagre, in the processes of social change. However, while change is anticipated to begin in people, there are also systems and institutions that have a life of their own and that are capable of meting out injustice both to humankind and to the environment. Accordingly, it is essential that such institutions should also be changed to make way for sustainable transformational development.

6.2.2.2 Changed Systems (Institutions)

At the centre of most of the crises that result in the destruction of human, plant, animal and environmental life, including the threat to annihilate the planet, are institutions or systems that human beings have instituted. However, some of such systems have now assumed a life of their own and it is incumbent on humankind to seek ways of changing these institutions as the world moves towards disaster as a result of poverty, global warming, nuclear armament and violence. P11 urgesd

> The church should be more visible at the political level of the transformation process by articulating its position to influence (positively) the decisions of government for the betterment of society. So, in effect this level should be involved more in policy matters. Issues that have to do with electoral reforms, inputs in federal budgets and national development plans.

The goal of sustainable transformational development is to seek the engagement of churches and church leaders, together with other concerned groups, in the strategies aimed at changing these systems. However, this engagement on the part of churches and church leaders also involves collaboration between the churches and church leaders and the sociopolitical and economic institutions in order to address the challenges facing humankind, other expressions of life and the environment.

Within the Nigerian context, the vestiges of colonialism and imperialism are still evident in political and economic circles in the sense of foreign manipulation and control of the Nigerian political and economic systems. However, in addition to these negative effects of imperialism, ethnic and religious systems as well as corruption, have become an integral part of Nigerian society and, as a result, good governance, national cohesion and development are, increasingly, eluding Nigerians with the concomitant implications of poverty, suffering and underdevelopment. However, these issues affecting Nigeria are also to be found in other parts of Africa and in developing countries on the other continents. "The current misery and underdevelopment in Africa, which is the consequence of centuries of slavery, colonial exploitation, mismanagement and corruption, must be reversed."[8] Some impediments to

---
8. Antonio, "Challenge for Africa," 73.

the development attempts of Nigeria, and indeed most African countries, including the debt burden, the economic policies of the World Bank and the International Monetary Fund and the negative impact of globalization are attributable to systems that are beyond national and regional control. Such institutions, including transnational corporations (TNCs), are assumed to pose the greatest challenges to most of humankind and to the environment. According to P13:

> The exploitative tendencies of the colonial masters should not be allowed to continue.

Debunking their argument that economic globalization would benefit more people, and that it was both inevitable and irreversible, Korten argues that "its claims and promises are grounded in a flawed ideology that contradicts basic ecological and social realities. A global economy is inherently unjust, unstable and unsustainable."[9] Thus, the infamous Bretton Woods meeting of 1944 at which the major ideas of globalization were institutionalized gave rise also to the establishment of the World Bank and the International Monetary Fund (IMF). Other institutions connected to these major institutions have also been established and pursue policies that enable them to implement the interests of these institutions. In Korten's view, "the removal of barriers to the international flow of goods and money was as a result of conscious choices of a self-interested minority who, over the past half-century, have designed, shaped and now control the institutions that dominate global economic activities."[10] Korten submits that, although the Bretton Woods institutions have met their targets, they have failed to bring prosperity to the people of the world and there are more poor people in the world today than ever before. In addition, the gap between the rich and the poor is ever-widening. As a result, there is widespread violence that is tearing apart families and communities, and the planet's ecosystems are deteriorating. Korten insists that there is a growing consensus outside official circles that the planet's ecological limits, and the economic injustice inherent in the

---

9. Korten, "Limits of Earth," 14.
10. Korten, 15.

Bretton Woods system, doom the system to ultimate failure and require a radical change of course.[11]

In his work, *Shaping Globalization: Civil Society, Cultural Power and Threefolding*, Nicanor Perlas expounds on the position of Jessica T. Matthews on the emergence of social movements as a counterbalance to global economic and political institutions.[12] The significance and potency of civil society organizations in the process of changing individuals and systems has been substantiated over time. The wind of change that swept through the Arab world that led to the eventual removal of governments in countries such as Algeria and Egypt in North Africa and the successful electoral processes in Nigeria in the 2011 national elections are all indicative of the effectiveness of cultural power. Thus, the existence and operation of civil societies at the global level at which the world's most powerful financial institutions such as the IMF, TNCs and the World Bank operate through globalization renders these social movements formidable. The fact that they start at the grassroots level and proliferate throughout national, regional and global contexts reflects the resources at their disposal and their "embeddedness" in all societies and social classes as the hope of the socioeconomically marginalized. Thus, Perlas proposes a threefold partnership in terms of which business represents the economic concerns, government will represent the political concerns and civil society will represent the cultural, social, ecological, human and spiritual concerns which are peculiar to these three vital realms of society for the purpose of comprehensive sustainable development. This threefold concept will ensure the distinctive nature of each of the collaborative components and, thus, avoid the co-opting, especially of civil society, as each strand of the partnership represents a particular constituency.[13] Whereas Perlas's argument and threefolding concept is vital to the vision of sustainable transformational development, its respect for the positive contributions of both the economic and political realms of society which should respect the crucial nature of social movements and their constituency as being crucial to their existence is refreshing. However, in addition to the transformation of the policies and systems of the political and economic institutions (local and global), there

---

11. Korten.
12. Perlas, *Shaping Globalization*.
13. Perlas.

is a spiritual aspect to these policies and systems that should be addressed, otherwise the expected change may be impossible.

Wink has argued that the biblical narratives of the fall of man and woman, the angels and the nations as presented in Genesis chapters 3, 6:1–4 and 11 respectively are indications of certain contexts that should be included in the quest for change. First, in the fall of man and woman, Wink suggests that human sin is, ontologically, prior to all social systems and structures. Therefore, changing social systems and structures "cannot be reduced to social determinism, but it is an act of willful rebellion against God."[14] The second fall is that of the angels and this, in turn, reflects a rupture in the very spirituality of the universe. For this reason, it is not possible for human sin to account for all evil. "There is a 'withiness' or spirituality in things that is capable of covetousness and insatiable greed."[15] Third, there is the fall of the nations. This fall concerns the structures and systems that are meant to prevent human life from becoming idolatrous and unjust. However, these systems, which are meant to serve humans, subject human beings to ends that are contrary to the plan of God. Whereas the change that we seek to bring about in humankind relates also to systems and structures, distinguishing the spirituality of such structures and systems and their capacities to function independently of individuals is an attempt to unmask and name the powers inherent in these systems for the purpose of preventing them from subjugating both humankind and the very systems that these powers control. Wink calls these spiritual forces within systems and structures "*the interiority of earthly institutions or structures or systems.*"[16] This notion invigorates the social dimension of the gospel with these powers with which we are forced to contend being the inner and outer manifestations of political, economic, religious and cultural institutions. The point is that "it is not just that people are making choices about how they will behave in the economic system: the system is also making choices about who will remain viable in the system."[17] Accordingly, changing the systems and persons under the influence of these powers requires both a nonviolent resistance approach and fervent prayer. The place of prayer as a liberating

---

14. Wink, *Engaging the Powers*, 77.
15. Wink, 79.
16. Wink, 77.
17. Wink, 79.

resource is extremely important in this process and such prayer is directed at the spiritual powers that hold these institutions or systems captive and which are against humankind and in contravention of the will of God.

In terms of the sustainable transformational approach to development, the churches and church leaders should collaborate between themselves and with government, socioeconomic and civil society institutions in order to effect change in both individuals and systems while the channels through which this may be achieved should include conscientization, advocacy, protests, direct participation, projects and social services. The researcher believes that changing persons, institutions or systems should also affect the entire creation positively. In addition, such positive impacts, which may be regarded as sustainably transformational, should be informed by the concept of stewardship.

6.2.2.3 Stewardship

As an overarching concept in the sustainable transformational approach, stewardship could inform the change we seek to effect in people and institutions or systems, both in Nigeria and beyond. P10 and P13 have noted that church leaders should:

> Be passionately conscious about their environment. Be able to notice where there are injustices and speak up against all forms of injustice.
>
> Punctuality, faithfulness to public service.

According to the change ideology that drives the goal of sustainable transformational development, when peoples' lives are changed, they will be able to discern the powers that influence those institutions which, in turn, subjugate the very human beings they are expected to serve according to the will of God. However, their liberation from such influences and their liberating the systems will lead to humankind and its institutions serving each other and creation in harmony and abundant life. Arising from the mainstream development discourse, the notion of environmental sustainability is said to be "achieved when the productivity of life-supporting natural resources is conserved or enhanced for use by future generations."[18] To an extent, this understanding of environmental sustainability synchronizes with the

---

18. Ndiyo, *Poverty to Sustainable Development*, 9.

stewardship of creation as a religious and enriching approach to environmental sustainability. Manuel Castells has noted that "most of our fundamental problems concerning the environment remain, since their treatment requires a transformation of modes of production and consumption, as well as of our social organization and personal lives."[19] Thus, global warming looms as a lethal threat, the rainforest still burns, toxic chemicals are in the food chain, poverty denies life, and the governments of both the developed and the developing worlds are busy playing games with the poor in Nigeria and other parts of Africa and in the developing world as the worst victims of these crises as they depend more on the environment and also lack the facilities to cope with these challenges. The interdependence of the various parts of the planet and the global scale of these crises call for solutions, and maybe for a reorientation of institutions and policies toward an environmentally responsible socioeconomic system. The position of the religious steward in respect to the utilization and preservation of nature and its resources is deemed to be relevant to the goal of sustainable transformational development. However, Klop argues that the term "religious steward" is not confined to the Christian faith only as it may also refer to the position of Judaism and Islam.[20] In addition, the notion of stewardship has gained wide acceptance beyond religious circles in the sense that it also concerns humankind's relationship with and use of natural resources for future generations.[21]

Stewardship of creation, as a cardinal goal of the sustainable transformational development approach and in line with the Christian theological view of stewardship, argues that "nature has intrinsic value because it is God's creation that is not her own property, nor the property of humankind. For her, God is the stakeholder to whom she is responsible."[22] Thus, instead of an anthropocentric or ecocentric posture, Klop suggests a theocentric view in terms of which all generations of humankind will understand that they are accountable to God for their use of creation as God's gift to humankind. Accordingly, the strategy of stewardship appeals to biblical mandates to care for, watch over, cultivate, govern, and/or improve the earth on behalf of God.

---

19. Castells, *Power of Identity*, 169.
20. Klop, "Equal Respect," 95.
21. Jenkins, *Ecologies of Grace*.
22. Klop, "Equal Respect," 98.

As opposed to the critics who suggest that this may amount to religious license for anthropocentric domination, Jenkins argues that the pair of action verbs, namely, "guarding and tending" – "*abad* and *samar*," as presented in Genesis 2 are privileged over the pair presented in Genesis 1, namely, "exploiting and subduing" – "*radah* and *kabash*."[23] As such, guarding and tending regulates what exploiting and subduing may mean. He further suggests that one way in which to privilege the second pair of action verbs is to situate the mandates in Genesis within the ambit of God's call to conversion, thus emphasizing repentant obedience rather than free license. So, while actively responsible as God's deputy for care of the world, the steward acts as humble servant to a sacred trust. Accordingly, these mandates stand against reckless exploitation in the sense that they set human authority or power as unavoidably accountable to God. In another sense, the stewardship of creation entails humankind's understanding that, besides God, creation is the very essence of their being which they should value in the sense of it being a precious gift which has been given by God and for which we are accountable both to him, future generations and creation itself. Indeed, it is when we are responsibly accountable in all respects that creation will yield more of itself to both us and to future generations, and God is able to nourish humankind as well as offer humankind more sustenance in his creation.

The stewardship motif suggests that both the nonpoor and the poor in Nigeria should come to terms with the fact that the resources in creation are God's gifts and they are meant to serve present and future generations of humankind and all other creatures that inhabit the earth with humankind. The concept of the stewardship of creation as a goal of sustainable transformational development should motivate the leaders in Nigeria to desist from the corrupt practices and the reckless amassing of wealth that are fuelled by both greed and a gross insensitivity to the plight of the poor. Stewardship of creation is an affirmation that, within the Nigerian context, there are abundant resources that may be responsibly tapped without environmental pollution and extensive damage to animal and plant life. God has distributed these resources diversely to the whole nation and all Nigerians, from all parts of the country and in all social categories, have a responsibility to contribute from the wealth of resources at their disposal to the common good. Thus,

---

23. Jenkins, *Ecologies of Grace*, 80.

stewardship of creation is an invitation to all humankind to a collaborative effort to maintain the earth by living in sensitivity and in consideration of the other inhabitants of the planet, both now and in the future. The establishment of systems and technologies that may foster the well-being of the planet should be driven by the notion that humankind and the institutions or systems they establish and all other endowments as well as the way in which they are used are gifts from God in respect of which we stand accountable. This understanding should also lead to the dismantling of institutions, technologies, habits and practices that are inimical to humankind and to the natural environment. So far, "the participation of churches and Christian NGOs in environmental activism is woefully inadequate."[24] Samuel further suggests that this dismal performance is as a result of the absence of effective models for participation. However, the sustainable transformational development approach argues for churches to collaborate with civil societies for the purpose of positive change in vital areas, including the environment.

Nevertheless, if there is to be a successful translation of the goals of sustainable transformational development – changed people; changed systems and the stewardship of creation – into practice in the Nigerian context, there are domains in respect of which these goals should be grounded and transmitted. These domains comprise the vital areas of individual and community life which have been negatively impacted by poverty, underdevelopment, corruption and poor leadership. These areas, namely people, institutions and creation have also become channels through which poverty, underdevelopment, corruption and poor leadership are reinforced. Accordingly, they require transformation so as to become effective launching pads from which sustainable transformational development may infiltrate the individuals, institutions, communities and environment of Nigeria. The domains are spiritual, moral, psychological, sociocultural, economic, political, environmental and ecclesiastical.

6.2.3 Sustainable Transformational Development Domains

6.2.3.1 Spiritual Domain

The traditional and Christian religious worldview of Nigerians understands that the spirit realm controls many of the activities taking place in all aspects

---

24. Samuel, "Globalization, Christian NGOs," 70.

of physical life. Thus, it is essential that the spiritual component be taken into consideration as Nigerian church leaders and members seek change within society. As part of their missional vocation to Nigerian society and beyond, church leaders and churches will need to penetrate and control the spiritual realm through various religious activities so as to liberate the nation/citizens and release them into righteousness and the enjoyment of their prosperity. In line with this view, P22 noted:

> We cannot over emphasize the role of prayer.

P11 further argued that

> The Niger Delta issue is more of a spiritual issue which requires the church to take up the warfare to deliver that region which the devil (in my opinion) has decided to use to hold this nation to ransom.

In this context, there are spiritual forces that are responsible for the problems of poverty, underdevelopment, corruption, violence and poor leadership currently being experienced in Nigeria. These evil spiritual powers are able to manipulate individuals, systems and the environment in a negative way. Although mainstream development scholars and practitioners appear to be silent on the influence of the spirit realm on poverty, some scholars and Christian development practitioners, such as Hughes and Bennett,[25] and Myers[26] subscribe to this view. In addition, the existence of sin in individual and communal life may attract suffering. On this note, P16 argued:

> The church leaders must sanitize the body of Christ before they can be bold enough to face the government. Let judgement start from the house of God.

The notion of the self-conversion of the church and its leaders also has implications for the Nigerian nation as a whole. Thus, unless the matter of sin is addressed by repentance to God, and the evil spirits are controlled, there is no possibility of meaningful transformation ever happening in Nigeria. Therefore, what is required is a desire to see genuine repentance to God and spiritual transformation among all Nigerians of various religious inclinations

---

25. Hudges and Bennett, *God of the Poor*.
26. Myers, *Walking with the Poor*.

as well as a concrete plan of action. In addition, such genuine repentance should also be backed up by the wielding of spiritual authority in prayer and confessions against the powers of evil that are controlling Nigerians, their systems and the environment. A genuine spiritual transformation should translate into the moral rectitude which is vital for the right attitude to both work and the management of resources. It may also be argued that there are universal ethical or moral standards that are common to humankind, despite regional boundaries and religious and nonreligious inclinations that should be upheld as they could contribute to social transformation in Nigeria.

6.2.3.2 *Values (Moral) Domain*

As an overarching concept of the sustainable transformational development paradigm which is aimed at addressing the challenges of poverty, underdevelopment, corruption and poor leadership in Nigeria, the formation and reinforcement of values in the Nigerian sociopolitical and economic contexts and beyond is indispensable. According to Kung, Michael Walzer's works, "Spheres of Justice" and "Thick and Thin," have taken us beyond the difficult terrain of ascertaining universal ethical standards to a common ethical ground where the values of truth and justice may be termed universal moral standards.[27] Walzer's argument demonstrates that there is "a core morality" which he deems to be "a whole set of elementary ethical standards" in which he includes issues such as "the fundamental right to life, to just treatment, to physical and mental integrity." He terms this a "minimal morality" or "a moral minimalism."[28] Kung notes that

> what is meant here are moral concepts which have a minimal significance and are indicated by a "thin" description: in other words, this is a "thin" morality, the content of which, of course, enriched in the various cultures, appears as a "thick" morality in which every possible historical, cultural, religious and political view comes to be involved, depending on place and time.[29]

---

27. Kung, *Global Ethic*, 95. The expression "universal moral standards" is used here in the sense of moral values, norms and attitudes that are generally accepted as the model, norm, measure or criterion by which proper or improper conduct and behavior in the Nigerian and other societies may be adjudged.
28. Kung, 95.
29. Kung, 95.

Thus, the important point is that, despite religious and cultural differences, there are fundamental ethical standards to which the Nigerian pluralistic society subscribes and which, in turn, enable the people to live and act together. In addition to truth and justice, Kung suggests that we include into ethical standards what he terms the "golden rule of humanity." He is implying here that there is scarcely a religion or human society that does not take seriously the respect or value for humanity. It is in this light that there is no more harsh accusation than that a particular system is inhumane and there is no trial that will deliver a more severe sentence than that of crimes against humanity.

Truth, justice and humanity may, thus, be termed the minimum moral values that are generally accepted within the Nigerian and other societies. Eme agrees that moral values and social development are complementary and that it is not possible to achieve the latter in any meaningful way without the former. He notes that, fairly early in the history of Nigeria, statesmen such as Alvan Ikoku and Eni Njoku, on separate occasions, had warned that men and women of high moral rectitude only should be allowed to hold public office, otherwise political independence would be meaningless and, perhaps, disastrous.[30] Shehu Shagari's[31] "ethical revolution" was aimed at addressing the moral laxity which has taken a toll of development in Nigeria, as had been warned by Njoku and Ikoku. Shagari's ethical revolution statement called for "the deliberate and fundamental change of a long-term decisive impact, to move this nation steadily and permanently in a discernible new direction of self-reliance and dedication to excellence in leadership, in discipline, in orderliness, in hard-work, in honesty, in morality, in mutual respect and tolerance along with the submission of our citizenry to God in national affairs and personal pursuits."[32] There is little doubt that Shagari's administration and that of other Nigerian leaders have not been able to combat the scourge of a morally debased Nigerian society. This has not only negatively affected the image of the nation internationally but it has been detected by both Nigerians and non-Nigerians as being a major impediment to the transformation of Nigerian society.

---

30. Eme, *Ethics in Nigerian Social.*

31. Alhaji Shehu Shagari was a democratically elected president of the Federal Republic of Nigeria under the auspices of the defunct National Party of Nigeria (NPN). His administration was terminated by a coup d'état in 1983.

32. Eme, *Ethics in Nigerian Social.*

The need for the moral transformation of all Nigerians so as to enable them to uphold at least the minimum moral standards of speaking the truth, acting in a just way at all levels and respecting the value and life of every human being in Nigeria, irrespective of social class or religion, is a vital domain of sustainable transformational development. As regards the issue of justice which, in turn, is linked to, inter alia, poverty, gender and the environment, Nyomi is not only in agreement with John Calvin's position on social justice, when he asserts that "all those arts whereby, we acquire the possessions and money at the expense of our neighbours are to be considered as theft,"[33] he continues Calvin's quote to make a salient point relevant to the Nigerian context with regard to corruption. "Although those who behave in this way often win their case before the judge, yet God upholds them to be none other than thieves. For He sees the intricate deceptions with which crafty people set out to snare those of simpler mind; He sees the rigour of the exactions which the rich impose on the poor to crush them."[34]

As a church-based development approach, sustainable transformational development views moral values as vital resources which the church, through both its leaders and its members, may restore to Nigerian society. Such values are within the reach of the church and it is possible that its extensive followership is in a position to transmit them to Nigerian society as a whole. However, seeking to inculcate moral values in the citizens of a society that has been negatively affected by slavery, colonialism, poverty, corruption, violence and poor leadership calls for the special psychological reorientation of these citizens. Accordingly, the development-oriented church leader who seeks to be a catalyst of change should also be open to such psychological reorientation.

6.2.3.3 Psychological Domain

The concept of conscientization was discussed in section 5.2.9.3 as a channel through which the sociopolitical and economic transformation of Nigerian society may be realized. The notion of conscientization concerns the psychological domain which should be included as part of a sustainable transformational development strategy. The psychological conditioning of both

---

33. Calvin, *Institutes* II, viii, 45 cited in Nyomi, "Covenanting for justice," 2. In Calvin's Institutes II, viii, 45, Calvin's position on social justice is elaborated.

34. Calvin, *Institutes* II, viii, 45 cited in Nyomi, "Covenanting for Justice," 2.

individuals and communities has much to do with their ability to progress from poverty and underdevelopment to development and general well-being. However, this understanding may be better appreciated when it is placed within the context of concepts such as human development, human capital and the conscientized, responsible self. Burkey has observed that any meaningful sense of development must begin with, and within, the individual. In Burkey's view, "unless motivation comes from within, efforts to promote change will not be sustainable by that individual."[35] The significance of the psychological domain with which sustainable transformational development seeks to connect as one of its major domains is to be found within the field of human psychological empowerment or development. In this connection, an individual must be motivated to develop self-respect, self-confidence and self-reliance. Such an individual will then become aware of his/her potential for positive change, his/her limitations and the need to collaborate with others for the mutual benefit of the community.

As it relates to human resources, some researchers argue that the concept of psychological capacities, "PsyCap," may, if developed and managed, improve the performance of individuals in both institutions and organizations.[36] Extrapolating the concept beyond the context of paid employment to the broader Nigerian context which is characterized by low morale in the civil service, education, police, military and other sectors, the dense Nigerian population may be regarded as an indispensable asset that should be properly managed and trained to become psychologically healthy. It is, thus, possible that the concept of PsyCap, when used in conjunction with the transformational leadership style which this study proposes, could revamp the level of commitment to the work attitude of Nigerians in the various sectors of Nigerian society. Therefore, given the four main components of self-efficacy, optimism, hope and resilience which are the ingredients of positive psychological capacities, the sustainable transformational church leader,

---

35. Burkey, *People First*, 35.

36. Toor and Ofori, "Positive Psychological Capital," 341. Psychological capital (PsyCap) has gained prominence as an important construct in leadership research. Proponents of PsyCap argue that its development at all levels of organizations has much potential as an important human resources management strategy for helping firms to capitalise on their existing and prospective human resources. The notion was originally presented by Fred Luthans and his colleagues.

as a sustainable transformational development component, could reorient Nigerians as agents of change within their own contexts.

As earlier discussed, both the poor and nonpoor in Nigeria are in need of a positive mental or psychological change. This change may be termed "conscientization" and incorporates a self-awareness of the reason why poverty, underdevelopment, corruption, violence, poor leadership and other vices have become perennial in Nigeria. In addition, this psychological or mental awareness should also encompass an awareness of the resources Nigerians possess to change their shameful situation and the personal acceptance of responsibility to change the situation for the better. Baxter suggests that an understanding of individuals and communities regarding where they are today and where they want to be in "a successful sustainable future" is indispensable to sustainable social transformation.[37] Such a mindset may be nonexistent in many Nigerians as a result of the long years of suffering. However, the absence of such a mindset may mean there is too little motivation to embark on such a daunting venture and initiate any action whatsoever. Nevertheless, the development-oriented church leader may be well positioned to bring about the positive mindset required for a better Nigerian society while the Nigerian sociocultural domain may provide useful resources for such a venture, besides being a domain for sustainable transformational development.

6.2.3.4 Sociocultural Domain

Another perspective of values and culture, as an overarching concept of sustainable transformational development as discussed in section 5.2.9.4, relates to the sociocultural values of the Nigerian communities before the infiltration of corruption. Without intending to delve deeply into the anthropological discourses on culture, the focus of this discussion is to emphasize the significance of the sociocultural life of Nigerian society as one of the areas that sustainable transformational development seeks to affirm, transform and utilise in order to bring about change. The understanding is that, as in any other human society, there are both positive and negative components within the Nigerian sociocultural context. Kwast calls culture the "super-glue" which binds people together and gives them a sense of identity and continuity that is

---

37. Baxter, "Stepping Stones," 22.

almost impenetrable.[38] Asserting the importance of African/Nigerian cultural values and Christian values in the formation of persons and the transformation of society, P18 argued:

> If we can form youths who are able to properly marry the African cultures with Christian values, we may produce a more wholistic person who is matured and capable of taking responsibilities.

Following on Kwast's assertion, the identity may be seen most obviously in the way in which things are done, namely, behaviour. At the very heart of any culture is its worldview which informs the beliefs and values of all who share in the culture.[39] Kraft suggests that patterned behavior is to be found at the surface level of culture while the worldview assumptions lie at the deep level of culture.[40] A new or competing system of beliefs may sometimes be introduced, but the worldview will remain unchallenged and unchanged and the values and behavior will reflect the old system. For Burkey, each individual is defined very much by his/her social relationships and cultural traditions. Whereas in both the developed world and the urban centres of developing countries, individuals function as separate members of society with a greater freedom to choose their social relationships, in the rural communities, social relationships are generally rigidly defined and the cultural traditions strong and relatively static.[41] It therefore follows that, in a pluralistic society such as Nigeria with a colouration which reflects both rural and urban dimensions of the sociocultural mix, the sociocultural domain may be seen as a difficult terrain to navigate. However, there are certain behaviours, worldviews, beliefs and values that may be termed Nigerian and, as such, may be discerned within the rural and urban communities. Some of these sociocultural creatives are positive while others are negative. For instance, belief in God, communal life, hospitality, respect for elders, extended family system, community self-help and other values may be termed positive sociocultural practices that should be affirmed, inculcated, nurtured and directed at sociopolitical and economic transformation.

---

38. Kwast, "Understanding Culture," 398.
39. Kwast.
40. Kraft, "Culture, Worldview and Contextualization."
41. Burkey, *People First*.

However, some negative patterns of behaviour and practices also exist in both Nigerian society and beyond and have come to be identified with Nigerians. As such, these now constitute part of the Nigerian sociocultural identity. Such behaviour and practices include corruption, deceit, apathy or indifference to state matters, political patronage, politicization of religion, ethnicity, poor maintenance of infrastructure, dysfunctional institutions and violence. Although many Nigerians abhor these practices, they have become deeply rooted in Nigerian society and have come to constitute the worldview of some Nigerians. They are, thus, difficult to change. However, whereas some of these practices are seen by some Nigerians as coping mechanisms to address the harsh realities of poverty, these practices also reinforce poverty and underdevelopment. It is, thus, essential that these negative sociocultural practices are targeted by the sustainable transformational development efforts in the sociocultural realm. However, challenging and transforming these practices demands a holistic and consistent approach that may transform the worldview that informs them while some of these worldviews are both economically and politically informed.

6.2.3.5 *Economic Domain*

The sustainable transformational development approach recognizes economic activities as indispensable to the general well-being of Nigerians. P12 accordingly noted:

> Church leaders should be involved in shaping economic policies in the country and constantly engage opinion leaders.

However, if economic activities are to meet the goal of sustainable transformational development, it is essential that such activities be carried out on a sustainable basis. This means that the returns of such economic activities must be greater than the costs if such activities are to be deemed profitable. Burkey has, thus, postulated that "any productive economic activity involves the mobilization and management of some combination of all or most of the factors of production. These factors are land and/or raw materials, labour (skilled and unskilled), capital, energy, tools, machinery, plant, management and entrepreneurship."[42] Capital comes from savings, shares,

---

42. Burkey, 36.

credit and taxation, while management requires the skill of organizing and controlling the factors of production. On the other hand, entrepreneurship requires the willingness and initiative to take up opportunities for the purpose of investing, despite the possible risk of failure. Unfortunately, within the Nigerian context, there is some doubt as to whether the resources in Nigeria have been optimally translated into economic gains. Mills laments that the number of Nigerians living under the international poverty line of one dollar per day has risen substantially, despite an estimated $400 billion in oil revenues generated in the forty years from 1965. Nigeria's income inequality is worse than neighbouring Ghana, and it has the third highest number of poor people in the world, behind China and India. Nigeria would have done better – by some estimations the economy would have been 25 percent bigger – if the Niger delta had no oil. One effect of oil has been to squeeze out the private sector, both because there was less incentive and the economic conditions were not right to export.[43]

The understanding of this study is that the aim of the proposal of the sustainable transformational development paradigm within the Nigerian economic domain is to urge the church, through its leaders, to move beyond the welfare context to authentic economic transformation for all Nigerians. Not only should the church insist on the mobilization and management of the factors of production in economic sectors such as agriculture and manufacturing, but the church should also influence the formulation of policies that would move the government and other stakeholders beyond the oil industry. Churches should set up industries in various sectors of the economy to create employment opportunities for Nigerians and to enrich the Nigerian economy. Issues such as the poor performance of microfinance banks, tax evasion by both multinational companies and Nigerians, poor credit facilities, slow legal processes and labour laws should be of great concern to the church and its leaders.

In addition, economic activities and enabling conditions should be encouraged for the peasants, small and medium scale farmers and manufacturers. Authentic economic development, as a vital domain for this study, aligns with a process by which people, through their own individual and/or joint efforts, boost production for direct consumption and to have a surplus to

---

43. Mills, *Why Africa Is Poor*, 171.

sell for cash. Admittedly, this presentation of development may be slanted towards the self-reliant participatory development approach but, nevertheless, it underscores the fact that it is essential that the notion of development gains momentum amongst the poor and their local communities before it will have the desired impact on Nigerian society. In addition, although Nigerian economists and politicians definitely need to be aware of global economic trends, such knowledge should be adjusted and embodied within the local context, including the application of such knowledge in a manner that accommodates the various strata of Nigerian society.

6.2.3.6 *Political Domain*

The transformation of Nigerian society through the political domain calls for church leaders, Christians and well-meaning Nigerians to participate in politics. Accordingly, politics should no longer be seen as a "dirty game" which people with moral rectitude should avoid. P14 argued:

> Get involved in politics and governance in the larger society.

Mills asserts that the main reason why Nigeria and many other African countries are poor is because their leaders have made this choice. He further argues that records show that countries are able to grow their economies and develop faster if their leaders take sound decisions in the national interest.[44] There is little doubt that successive political leaders in Nigeria are to be blamed for the socioeconomic, political and many other challenges that have come to be associated with Nigeria. The present day Nigerian political culture is characterized by corruption, lack of accountability, lack of political competition, political patronage and insensitivity to actions that undermine the economy and other institutions. Unfortunately, Nigerian political leaders are hardly ever punished by the masses for their inefficiencies, unlike in the developed world where they would have been sacked. Understandably, many of these leaders have not assumed political office with the legitimate consent of the people they govern. Elections are usually rigged and political appointments are often given to the cronies of those in power and not on the grounds of competence. It is therefore assumed that, if sustainable transformational development is to be realized in Nigeria, the political structures

---

44. Mills.

should be made to be responsive to the needs and aspirations of all Nigerians. In addition, the rights and property of all Nigerian should be protected by the political structures. It is for this reason that the Nigerian political context represents a crucial domain for sustainable transformational development.

It is with regard to this political domain that the sustainable transformational development approach argues that the development of the Nigerian political structures should be the concern of all Nigerians, irrespective of religion and social class. However, in addition to mobilizing Nigerians to effective political participation, it is also essential that Nigerians in positions of authority as well as those not in such positions be educated. There are many Nigerians who have lost confidence in the political institutions and they should be made to understand the reasons for the development of the political sector. Burkey's counsel on the meaning and implications of political development are relevant to both this study and the Nigerian context. Burkey argues that political development is a process of gradual change over time in which the people increase their awareness of their own capabilities, their rights and their responsibilities, and use this knowledge to organize themselves so as to acquire real political power in order to participate in decision-making at the local level and to choose their own leaders and representatives at higher levels of government who are accountable to the people in terms of planning and sharing power democratically, and creating and allocating communal resources equitably and efficiently among individual groups.[45]

The quest for the transformation of the political domain by the adherents of the sustainable transformational development approach may assist in the amelioration of corruption, political patronage, irresponsible leadership, ethnicity, violence, political instability and the politicization of religion. In addition, in terms of the political domain this approach is capable of restoring the credibility of leadership, patriotism and the ownership of the Nigerian nation by all Nigerians.[46]

---

45. Burkey, *People First*.

46. As a result of the manner in which the colonial masters amalgamated the various nations to form the political entity now known as Nigeria and the favouring of some parts of the Nigerian nation above others, as evidenced by the number of years some ethnic groups have ruled the country, there is a sense of apathy on the part of Nigerians which has, in turn, led to an unpatriotic attitude. Many Nigerians do not seem to own the nation properly. This attitude has resulted in an inclining towards ethnicity to the detriment of national interests, as was seen in the wake of Nigerian independence when political parties were formed along ethnic lines.

6.2.3.7 *The Environment*

The Nigerian ecosystem comprises the biosphere, land and plant, animal and aquatic life. In as much as these may be included in the category of factors of production in the economic domain which was discussed above, the importance of the environment in the face of the severe global environmental crisis necessitates a separate discussion. In addition to the looming environmental crisis, the Nigerian environment constitutes a crucial domain for sustainable transformational development as it is the source of substantial resources which both the current and future generations of Nigerians may utilize to actualize their vision of well-being. Mills has suggested that, despite the fact that Nigeria and its sister African nations are endowed with vast resources, including fertile lands, forests, wildlife, tin, columbite, gold, copper, and crude oil, some of these resources have come to constitute barriers to Nigerian development.[47] Mills's assertion may be justified by issues such as gas flaring and other kinds of environmental pollution as a result of oil exploitation, communal wars, militancy and other challenges. Unfortunately, some of these natural resources are not renewable while some of the environmental crises are irreversible, for example, global warming, while it would be both extremely expensive and also take a very long time to deal with others. On this note, P10 suggested that church leaders should:

> Be passionately conscious about their environment. Be able to notice where there are injustices and speak up against all forms of injustice.

As has been noted before in section 4.4.9, the church and Nigerian society as a whole have done very little either to arrest the threat to the country's natural resources or to utilise these resources effectively in the interests of both the present and upcoming generations of Nigerians. In terms of the Nigerian environment, sustainable transformational development highlights the need to protect, preserve and utilize the environment in a sustainable way for the well-being of all Nigerians, humankind and the environment. As regards this domain, the proposed approach seeks to draw the attention of the church leaders, church members and all Nigerians to the need to participate in the environmental activism against those individuals and institutions

---

47. Mills, *Why Africa Is Poor*.

conspiring against the well-being of the environment. Thus, the spiritual, moral, psychological, sociocultural, economic, political and environmental domains which the sustainable transformational development approach seeks to utilise in order to create positive change within Nigerian society, view the Nigerian church (leaders/members) as the main domain or channel through which all other domains may collaborate with each other to realise the vision of sustainable transformational development.

6.2.3.8 *The Church*

The church's missional calling and identity, as premised on the *missio Dei*, identifies the church in all its expressions with the mission of God to the world. Accordingly, the church and all its resources, including church leaders, are called to fulfil its charter in this regard. Expressing the role of the church and its leaders in society, P20 asserted:

> The Gospel is for all creation – not just for the "little flock" of Christians. The mandate to "preach to all nations" includes making this world a better place for all of God's people.

P14 also argued:

> The salt is the salt of the earth (not of the church). The church should come out of the four walls and be involved in every sphere of life, politics and governance, media, business, education, arts, etc. everywhere.

As discussed in section 1.12.1, the church may be understood as the followers of Jesus in a particular place (venue, city or country); the congregants who gather to worship Jesus and to honour God through Christian witness anywhere. It is an organization or institution among other institutions. Thus, the church in Nigeria may be seen as an organized community with its component membership drawn from congregations and denominations within Nigeria for the purpose of fostering unity among the followers of Jesus and delivering a collective witness to Nigerian society as a whole. The Nigerian society may be termed the church's host community. Within the various forms of the church, including cells, house fellowships, districts, congregations, denominations and ecumenical formations, there are organizational and leadership structures that enable the church to fulfil its roles and objectives. As a result of the dense and diverse membership of the church, Scripture, value ethics, spiritual capacities, financial resources, international influence, local and global networks, community embeddedness, social networks and other resources, the church is in a privileged position to transform society through both its leadership and its membership. However, it is essential that this anticipated transformation within Nigerian society be expressed simultaneously through the various expressions of the church in Nigeria. It is, thus, envisaged that the sustainable transformational development conscious church leader will deploy these structures, and enormous resources that the church in its various forms has at its disposal within the Nigerian context through the medium of the sustainable transformational development approach.

The church, as the bastion of sustainable transformational development, may, through its development-oriented leadership, instil and enforce its resources through channels such as the spiritual, moral, psychological, sociocultural, economic, political and environmental, for the benefit of all Nigerians. The purpose of such an approach is to ensure a holistic response that is consistent with the goals of Nigerian development in response to the challenges of poverty, underdevelopment, corruption and irresponsible leadership. However, the church that is expected to fulfil such an immense task should not only be deemed to possess viable resources, but should be a church that understands both its calling and the resources at its disposal. In addition, the church should also be willing to go with the missional God to the place of mission in total dependence and obedience to this missional God. It is in this way that the church leaders and members will be able to serve both as a springboard and also as the main domain for sustainable transformational development in Nigeria and enable the other domains to find authentic expression. Clearly, the church must not live for itself alone, but it should live for Nigerian society. In other words, the church must not stand aloof in an assumed posture of self-preservation but should be involved in the daily challenges and sufferings of all Nigerians for the purpose of working in collaboration with other institutions for the liberation of the people and the environment, for the benefit of both present and future generations of the created order. Thus, according to Moltmann, the expectation of the promised future of the kingdom of God which is coming to humans and the world to set both humans and the world right and to create life, prepares the church to expend itself unrestrainedly and unreservedly in love and in the work of the reconciliation of the world with God and his future.[48] The social institutions and their roles and functions are the means through which this self-expending may be achieved and they must, therefore, be creatively shaped by love in order that humankind may live in them in a more just, humane and peaceful way and in mutual recognition of their dignity and freedom.

Spong has noted that it is possible to change society only through corporate action. Jesus called people into purposeful community and, thus, the Christian message has to be communal not individual, and public not private.[49] Affirming the position of this study as supported by Spong, Moltmann has argued that the Christian church, which follows the mission of Christ to the world, is also engaged in following Christ's service of the world. "It has its nature as the body of the crucified and risen Christ only where, in specific acts of service, it is obedient to its mission to the world. Its existence is completely bound to the fulfilling of its service."[50] The implication is, thus, that the church is nothing in itself, but all that it is, is in existing for others. The church is, therefore, the church of God and a church for the world. This in turn implies that personal faith, or the fellowship of the congregation, or the church as an institution, loyally fulfil the social roles expected by modern society. The expected transformation of society is such that it is in line with the vision of God's coming kingdom which also entails the coming of righteousness, peace, and freedom and dignity of all humankind and creation. Within Nigerian society, there are processes through which the ideals of sustainable transformational development may find expression.

6.2.4 The Processes of Change through Sustainable Transformational Development

The sustainable transformational development approach is concerned with enabling Nigerian church leaders to contribute more meaningfully to the sociopolitical and economic transformation of Nigerian society in the light of the challenges of poverty, underdevelopment, corruption and poor leadership. Thus, its vision is the transformation of both persons (leaders/followers) and

---

48. Moltmann, *Theology of Hope*.
49. Spong, *New Christianity*, 227.
50. Moltmann, *Theology of Hope*, 327.

institutions or systems while its means and processes of change are people and community through stewardship.

6.2.4.1 Effecting Change through Persons

In terms of persons, sustainable transformational development, through the church and the church leaders, seeks to reorient both the rich and the poor in Nigeria as well as leaders and followers as regards their relationships with God, themselves, their environment and the rest of the planet. As in relation with transformational development, sustainable transformational development's envisaged development of personhood involves both ourselves and ourselves in relationships; the development of the self; and an understanding of the roles with which we have been entrusted.

Personhood is about both the ability to make moral choices and the ability to see the other by accepting differences, but without excluding the other. It is the ability to resist wrongdoing and to be able to forgive and reconcile even when we have been wronged. It also concerns admitting our limitations, our need for self-renewal and our dependence on others. In addition, personhood also has to do with accepting responsibilities, creativity or innovation and stewardship. Our growth in personhood makes it possible for Christ to feel at home in us through his Spirit and, through us, to reach out to others in our various engagements and involvements in society.

This personhood may be developed through a deliberate effort such as activities on the part of church leaders through denominational and ecumenical activities through which church leaders and church members may be equipped (with knowledge, moral and financial capabilities) to enable the leaders and members to effect change in the society. However, personhood may also be developed through family and traditional societal institutions, norms and values. Those church leaders and church members who are so equipped will also deliberately seek such outcomes in the sense of knowledge, moral and financial empowerment in their interactions in Nigerian society.

As regards the poor in Nigeria, whose personhood has been negatively impacted by past and present exploitative regimes, poverty and underdevelopment, the development of personhood should seek to restore his/her dignity and self-worth through what may be termed the conscientized, responsible self so as to be able to transcend such challenges and, thus, make progress. On the other hand, the recovery of the personhood of the rich in Nigeria, in the sense of being freed from the guilt of the irresponsible acquisition of wealth or by acquiring wealth by corrupt means and their failure to make positive change in the country, is also vital.

This study further suggests that personhood, also involves rising up against all forms of injustice, including poverty, underdevelopment, corruption and poor leadership, through legitimate means, including protests, in order to seek the liberation and transformation of human society and, thus, enable meaningful living.

6.2.4.2 *Effecting Change through the Community*

Community in this context includes all human institutions and nonhuman life. The relevance of the notion of community as a process or means through which sustainable transformational development may take place is in the sense of the theological, African and anthropological understanding of community. In addition, the notion of community relates to the notion of collaboration, which is an overarching concept in sustainable transformational development ideology. As Sugden observes, "personhood takes shape in community, between people in a covenant relationship. Such communities are moral communities and are marked by freedom, justice, righteousness, order, law, truthfulness, love and grace."[51] Such covenant communities include churches, families, villages, ethnic groups, states, nations and the world. They are termed covenant communities in the sense that a bonding has been established between those human and nonhuman beings comprising these communities, either by natural or legislative means. The notion of covenant is also in the sense of the shared obligations and responsibilities of the constituents of these communities in respect of others in the community.

Both the Nigerian churches and the traditional communities reflect a mixture of theological, African and anthropological ideologies of community. Such communities, in general, serve as creative communities through which stewardship, truthfulness and hope may be encouraged. In addition, they are nurturing communities and communities with character through which virtues such as mercy, patience, forgiveness, honesty, long-suffering, compassion and concern for justice may be inculcated and developed over time. Such communities provide security and give their members a sense of

---

51. Sugden, "Transformational Development," 72.

belonging. In times of crisis, they provide the necessary succour by helping to bear one another's burdens, for example, in times of bereavement. The church also serves as a community of worship that reflects the kingdom of God. Through such a community, there may be openness to the actions of God's kingdom, and class and ethnic divisions may be overcome; and hope may be continually renewed as our services to God and humankind are carried out in anticipation of the revelation of the fullness of the kingdom of God.

Morever, political and economic systems and the technologies that drive them are part of the community in which we live. Such systems and technologies of the present time as well as those of the future should be regarded in the light of a continuum of community and, as such, should be treated as being of great value for the benefit of all generations.

In addition to the communities as expressed within the Nigerian traditional, religious, socioeconomic and political contexts, the notion of community connects us to God, the ecosystem/planet and global community, all of which, in our present understanding, are inseparable. Thus, despite religious, ethnic, sociopolitical, economic and human/extra-human categories, everything/everyone sharing the Nigerian geopolitical space stands in covenant with everything/everyone else as members of the same geopolitical community known as Nigeria. In the same vein, they also stand in a covenant relationship with all the other human/nonhuman entities that inhabit earth.

Above all, value for community reminds us of the need for collaboration and synergy among all institutions and human endeavours in their joining hands to address the challenges facing both humans and the planet with the required sincerity in order to realise sustainable results that may enhance life in its fullness. It is this sense of community and all that it brings to the fore that should shape personhood and engender collaboration by giving impetus to value for community. To some extent, stewardship of resources relates to the notion of community.

6.2.4.3 Effecting Change through Stewardship

In addition to the notions of personhood and community that are a part of the processes encompassed in the sustainable transformational development approach, the notion of stewardship of resources is also an indispensable element. Both the individual whose personhood is developed in community and the community, which reflects a high degree of resources, constitute valuable resources that may be translated into reality and sustained through stewardship. Sudgen has defined stewardship "as the content of God's image in humanity, requiring access to material resources and, thus, equality of opportunity, and the call to steward resources and the whole of creation."[52] It is in this context that leadership becomes crucial. P11 asserted:

> We need leaders who are firm and focused, no matter the odds; who understand our strategic priorities and pursue them. Leaders who can generate the excitement we need in our political, economic and social levels of the Nigerian society. Above all, the leader should be God fearing, yet principled and of high integrity.

P11 further argued:

> Nigeria needs transformation. Therefore, to do this requires transformational leaders. Transformational leaders have a vision – a goal, an agenda, a result-orientation that grabs people's attention. They communicate their vision and build trust by being consistent, dependable and persistent. They have positive self-regard. In general, they transform vision into reality and motivate people to transcend their personal interests for the good of the group. This is the kind of leadership we need in today's Nigeria.

Lending their voice in support of transformational leadership and its link with stewardship, P12 argued:

> A transformational leader will be ideal. We need a leader who will challenge the way matters are handled presently. Someone who will use all the resources available to develop and bring change.

In other words, stewardship encompasses leadership of the persons through which persons and communities may be harnessed for social transformation as they engage in public action for the good of all. It is through the notion of stewardship that individuals may come to understand that they are accountable to God, to others and to themselves and, as a result,

---

52. Sudgen, 74.

take responsible actions to curtail both their greed and their abuse of the natural environment.

An appropriate understanding of stewardship enables the leaders in the various institutions and at different levels of responsibility to realise that they function in community and that they are fully accountable to the community to which they belong, both now and in the future. Stewardship reminds both individuals and communities that all should take responsible action for the good of all, both in the present and in the future. In addition, stewardship of resources, as in both ideology and in accepted practice, refers to both the idea and the practice that should inform the transformation of institutions, systems and technologies that are no longer serving the good of the environment, individuals and communities. As such, the notion of stewardship has a bearing on the concepts of innovation and values which are both overarching concepts that inform all the components of the sustainable transformational development strategy.

If Christian activities that are directed towards social transformation are to be sustainable, it has been suggested that there will have to be a link between these activities and the church.[53] Such change activities include religious activities (prayer, fasting, Bible study, preaching and teaching), advocacy, protests, direct participation (in economic, political and sociocultural activities) and projects and social services. It is for this reason that sustainable transformational development argues that an appropriate development paradigm for Nigerian society will have to derive from church leaders via the congregational, denominational and ecumenical expressions of the church and in collaboration with the other institutions (government, business and civil society) that are vital in the social transformation in Nigerian society.

The sustainable transformational development approach will be able to address the challenges of poverty, underdevelopment, corruption, environmental degradation and poor leadership in Nigeria through these processes. However, as previously observed, it is essential that the church in Nigeria be informed, mobilized and engaged by its leadership through the ecumenical, denominational and congregational expressions of the church in Nigeria and, without this, sustainable transformational development may remain an illusion in Nigeria. In addition, Nigerian churches and church leaders will have to

---

53. Sugden.

engage Nigerian society through conscientization, advocacy, protests, direct participation, projects and social services. All of such engagement should be guided by church leaders and informed by the four overarching strategies, namely, innovation, stewardship, collaboration and values/culture.

6.3 Development-Oriented Church Leadership as a Vital Component of Sustainable Transformational Development in Nigeria

So far in this study, the challenges facing Nigerian society and the sources of these challenges have been identified. In addition, the components of the sustainable transformational development framework have also been presented. However, what still remains is the way in which the sustainable transformational development approach may be made to work in Nigeria. This study argues that, despite the huge resources at the disposal of the church in Nigeria, it would not be possible for the church to engage meaningfully in the social transformation of Nigerian society without its leaders developing a positive social consciousness and active engagement which, it is hoped, would culminate into a corresponding consciousness and active engagement on the part of the church membership. Accordingly, P12, P16, P11 and P10 respectively argued as follows:

> Church leaders should be involved more in the political events in Nigeria. Shape and support the election of church leaders to political posts. Church leaders should be involved in shaping economic policies in the country.

> The church should lead by example in all spheres of things i.e . . . participation in politics (where they are expected to be salt).

> They lead the people to embrace economic activities that bring about individual and, in turn, corporate development. They should lead the development of these initiatives.

> If honest Christian leaders would arise and form serious pressure groups within and outside the national boundaries, if the leaders appreciate that they are answerable to God for what

happens to the country even after they expire; if we have leaders who love the country above themselves and their immediate family, then the political and economic change so much desired in Nigeria would come.

P14 stated that:

The salt is the salt of the earth (not of the church). The church should come out of the four walls and be involved in every sphere of life, politics and governance, media, business, education, arts etc. everywhere.

Furthermore, the study suggests that such a positive stance on the part of both the church leaders and the church members at all levels of the church's existence should be in liaison with local, national and global institutions if meaningful and sustainable results are to be achieved. However, the initiative for such an ideology of social change and action should be spearheaded by the Nigerian church leaders as a result of their privileged position within both the church and Nigerian society as a whole. It is in this light that the study will now discuss the development-oriented or development-conscious church leader as the facilitator of sustainable transformational development, the conscientizer of the faithful and of Nigerian society, mentor of transformational leaders, and shepherd of the faithful in the public domain as an agent of change and as the harnesser of the resources of the church, Nigeria and the world in the interests of Nigerian development.

6.3.1 The Development-oriented Church Leader as the Facilitator of Sustainable Transformational Development

Sustainable transformational development has to do with socioeconomic, political and ecological transformation for the well-being of humankind, systems/institutions and nonhuman life. Its goals are changed people, changed systems and the stewardship of creation. These goals are directed towards realizing Nigerian development, attaining which is considered to be a possible response to the challenges of poverty, underdevelopment, corruption and poor leadership. The resources at the disposal of the sustainable transformational development approach are expected to flow into Nigerian society through various domains by the instrumentality of the church and through its leadership. Jayme Rolls has remarked that, from the early days of the church, the clergy have played vital roles in society as agents of change, interpreters and translators.[54] However, their expertise and professional skills are now being called upon again in profound and new ways. Although the clergy is faced with unprecedented challenges, it may be argued that it has the potential to deliver despite its destiny of leading a global society in what may be regarded as nothing less than the reinterpretation of societal, institutional and organizational values. Within Abraham Kuyper's Netherlands, Martin Luther King Junior's United States of America, and Desmond Tutu's South Africa, the clergy have registered their footprints on the sands of time in their respective contexts. Increasingly, the sociological context of theology is shaping society while, in Nigeria and other parts of Africa, it is helping a seeking populace to find both wholeness and meaning. Rolls further argues that "clergy construct a sheltering worldview fabric of meaning, and the profession will be the architect of spiritual meaning-making, acting as steward and culture creator and carrier."[55] Within the Nigerian and African context, clergy are being called upon and will continue to be called upon to be the "artisans who weave the fabric of the emergent *nomos*, a new meaningful order."[56] The religious inclination of Nigerians as typical Africans and the rapid growth of the church in the Nigerian and African contexts is providing impetus to the relevance of the clergy and other church leaders in social change.

The clergy and other church leaders are the coaches, facilitators, stewards, relationship builders, mentors, teachers and role models who are able to help each other, the faithful and non-Christians to navigate their own transformation as they live through change. The moral standards of church leaders fall in the category of postconventional morality.[57] In terms of the postcon-

---

54. Rolls, "Transformational Leadership."
55. Rolls, 78.
56. Rolls, 78.
57. Rolls has suggested three stages of development in moral understanding, namely, preconventional, conventional and postconventional morality. In terms of preconventional morality, people perceive their world as a system of rewards and punishment. This is the immature state in which they appear to be acting very ethically but, inside, they are not responding from a sense of the universal good, but rather in order to avoid pain. In terms of conventional morality, people have a strong need for affiliation and they want to belong to and have the acceptance of a group. While people in this phase are no longer motivated by reward and punishment, the group's opinion and decisions on what is crucial for survival are the deciding factor in their behavior. People in this phase allow right and wrong to be determined more by the group than by the merits of a particular course of action and they do not question group judgement. Rolls, 73–74.

ventional morality, an individual does what is right for no other reason than that such an action seems to be both intrinsically and unconditionally good, and stems from universal values. Such a demand for higher values and the responsibility to uphold these values despite the consequences, are synonymous with transformational leadership and the biblical and sociocultural demands placed on church leaders. Thus, in a sense, the church leader may be termed a transformational leader as the leadership responsibilities, patterns and values in both cases agree. It has been argued in this study that, although the servant and transformational leadership styles are closely related,[58] the transformational leadership style is preferred[59] for the purpose of this study as this approach is in alignment with the development approach proposed by the study and, as proposed in the empirical study, it is the leadership style that may both serve the church as well as Nigerian society.

In order to be able to meet the socioeconomic, political and spiritual challenges facing Nigerian society, it is incumbent on the church leader, as an integral part of the church but privileged by his/her call as a shepherd of the faithful to feed, nurture and guide the flock in line with the missional God's vision, and to develop a sensitivity towards the spiritual, sociopolitical, economic and ecological challenges confronting his/her flock and the context in which the members of the flock live. This consciousness/sensitivity is required by virtue of the church's calling, in which the church leader shares, and by virtue of the church leader's call and responsibility as a church leader and a leader of the wider community of which the church is a part. Thus, the development-oriented church leader who is also considered a transformational leader, enjoys a number of privileges or advantages as a result of which he/she is considered to be the most suitable person to initiate sustainable transformational development in Nigeria. Conscientization represents the first step to be taken by the development-oriented church leader in facilitating sustainable transformational development in Nigeria.

---

58. See sections 3.3.1 and 5.2.8.
59. See section 5.2.9.2.

6.3.2 The Development-Oriented Church Leader as the Conscientiser of the Faithful

Elaborating on conscientization, a concept popularly attributed to Paulo Freire, Magaziner notes: "Conscientisation was the process by which men, not as recipients but as knowing subjects, achieve a deepening awareness both of the sociocultural reality which shapes their lives and of their capacity to transform that reality."[60] Conscientization, thus, was the process by which students would educate themselves to become "selves" and then, when they had achieved critical consciousness, work for societal transformation. In addition, Magaziner has noted that Steve Biko and other activists were greatly influenced by this concept during the years of the struggle in South Africa.

The term "conscientization" has come to be associated with Paulo Freire even though he does not accept that he was the originator of it. In any case, since there is doubt as to the actual originator of the term, Freire's continual use of it and its attendant association with his educational pedagogy has meant that he has come to be regarded as the main proponent of the concept.[61] The notion of conscientization, as used in the works of Freire, may be linked to the sustainable transformational development approach as used in this study. It relates to the ecumenical development debate that informs this study and the psychological domains that constitute one of the channels of the sustainable transformational development approach.

Conscientization involves historical commitment, denouncing, announcing and education. The historical commitment in conscientization means a historical awareness in the sense of a critical insertion into history in terms of which people assume roles as subjects making the world, remaking the world. In other words, human beings are asked to fashion their existence out of the material that life offers them. In this sense, conscientization entails both the realization of one's oppression and the capacity of the oppressed to liberate himself/herself and the corresponding concrete engagement to transform the situation of oppression and injustice. The act of denouncing and announcing involves knowing and naming the structures that dehumanize, and denouncing these structures while, at the same time, announcing that which humanizes. The act of denouncing and announcing portrays a conscientized person

---

60. Magaziner, *Law and Prophets*, 129.
61. Freire, "Conscientisation," 23.

as one who is permanently committed to a radical process of transforming the world for the benefit of all. In this light, the conscientized person and one who contributes to the conscientization of others may also be termed prophetic. As opposed to the wrong use of education to reinforce the structures of oppression and injustice, education for freedom, which is conscientization, strives to expose the inversion of accepted practice at the moment at which it occurs so as to ensure that it will not take place.[62] Whereas religion and education have both been used in a negative way in order to justify and maintain oppressive and unjust systems, religion, religious structures and education have also served as liberating and life-giving structures for the liberation of the oppressed.

The church leader who is both aware of the dehumanising consequences of the poverty, underdevelopment, corruption and ecological injustice which have arisen as a result of the Nigerian leadership crisis that has characterized the Nigerian political and economic culture for several decades and is concerned with changing the situation, occupies a crucial position. The church leader's role as a teacher, pastor, counsellor and leader who meets with his/her members frequently may as well serve as their conscientizer by providing prophetic guidance in denouncing and announcing. He/she is able to expose the dehumanising structures or systems, reveal to the church members the resources they possess to change their reality and enable them to become sufficiently self-motivated to engage in the concrete transformation of the poverty, unemployment, corruption, violence, poor leadership and other unacceptable conditions in Nigeria. In addition, the church leader serves in the capacity of a facilitator of the reflection – critical thought and action – which constitute the processes of conscientization.[63] Church leaders in Nigeria are known for their commitment to high standards of education and the establishment of educational institutions. Such institutions could also serve as venues which could enable their students to develop responsible selves for the purpose of transforming the dehumanising institutions and systems in Nigeria. The religious notions that led to the sociopolitical

---

62. Freire.
63. Magaziner, *Law and Prophets*.

paralysis in Nigeria and the uninformed "God-talk"[64] that helps to perpetuate injustice may be debunked by those church leaders who were, themselves, the originators of such ideas or helped to legitimise them. Thus, the processes of conscientization within the various expressions of the church in Nigeria and the educational institution owned by the church would have a significant and rapid positive impact on Nigerian society. Miller reminds that "conscientisation is a long, often torturous process of many beginnings and abrupt stops, a spiral 'dance' if you will, until we ultimately come to the point where we can no longer go back to the old ways of thinking"[65] and doing things. However, in addition to the processes of conscientization, church leaders occupy the privileged positions of being able to mentor transformational leaders after their own pattern across all levels of Nigerian society and it is such leaders who will contribute significantly to the continual renewal of the church and the transformation of Nigerian society.

6.3.3 The Development-Oriented Church Leader as the Mentor of Transformational Leaders

Dorr posits that "leadership is the influencing, motivating, guiding, directing, or coordinating of individuals, groups, communities, or organizations in a way that affects their behavior or actions, especially in relation to bringing about change."[66] Although this definition typifies effective leadership, it is also consistent with the transformational leadership concept which could apply within both the church and other institutions in Nigeria. Judith Corbett Carter's research on "Transformational Leadership and Pastoral Leader Effectiveness" has provided a significant connection between effective pastoral leadership

---

64. Nigerians often justify certain socioeconomic, political and religious issues as the will of God about which they are able to do nothing and they will often call for prayers instead of engaging in transformation. One such example is the leadership vacuum that occurred during the health crisis of the late President Umaru Musa Yar'adua in 2010. Instead of the ailing president resigning or being impeached for his incapacity to function as president of the nation and his failure to inform the National Assembly, Nigerians were asked by the National Assembly and by those dealing with the president's issues to pray for the president. In the heat of the crisis, instead of the nation being informed of the true state of the president's health, religious leaders were invited to the presidential villa (the president's official residence) to pray for the president. This situation was perpetuated by politicians using religion and god-talk to justify unacceptable political practices instead of dealing with the challenges constitutionally.

65. Miller, "Forming Future Feminists," 101.

66. Dorr, *Faith at Work*, 64.

and the transformational leadership style. Reporting on the research findings, Carter notes: "the results indicated that transformational leadership style showed significant correlation with pastoral leader effectiveness."[67] Carter further argues that in today's world, "Christian community pastors (*and other church leaders*) are responsible for spiritual guidance and development, motivation, restoration, care correction, protection, unity, and encouragement of parishioners."[68] In addition, many church leaders are responsible for the organizational development of the church, as they oversee the management of daily operations, develop leaders and establish a vision for the church. Within the Nigerian context, church leaders are also burdened with the responsibilities of leadership outside of the church in society at large with church leaders now running corporate institutions such as universities, banks, political parties and nonprofit organizations. In addition, church leaders have to deal with the requests of political leaders for advice on matters of governance. Within the church itself, captains of industries, politicians and community leaders, who are members of the church, seek leadership guidance from church leaders.[69] Although this wide range of diverse leadership responsibilities expected of church leaders may be onerous, it does place the church leader in a favourable position to groom transformational leaders for both the church and for Nigerian society. To an extent, leadership is not only provided through positions of authority. Leadership may be termed positive influence if it leads to positive change and, in this sense, every Christian is a leader. Besides, effective leadership requires that the leader sees himself/herself as a member of the in-group as he/she motivates other members of the group to achieve the desired goals for the group. With the large population of Christians in Nigeria, church leaders have the opportunity to groom men and women to influence other Nigerians for positive change in the sociopolitical and economic contexts. Such positive influence is capable of reversing the perennial trends of poverty, underdevelopment, corruption and irresponsible leadership. If church leaders are to groom the transformational leaders so desperately needed in Nigeria, then the concept of mentoring becomes an indispensable tool in the realization of such a vision. What, then, is mentoring

---

67. Carter, "Transformational Leadership," 261.
68. Carter, 261.
69. Maisamari, "Christian Youths."

and how may church leaders successfully engage in mentoring effective leaders capable of infiltrating the respective enclaves of Nigerian society and bringing about positive transformation?

Terblanche has noted that there are numerous definitions of mentoring, depending on the profession involved and the workplace practices where the concept is implemented. "Mentoring is a structure and series of processes designed to create effective mentoring relationships, guide the desired behavior change of those involved, and evaluate the results for the protégés, the mentors and the organization with the primary purpose of systematically developing the skills and leadership abilities of the less experienced members of the organization."[70] Blunt and Conolly have argued that mentoring entails psychological guidance and support to influence or inspire and, therefore, it is voluntary.[71] For Cunningham, mentoring is "a relational process between a mentor, who knows or has experienced something and transfers that something (resources of wisdom, information, experience, confidence, insight, relationships, status, etc.) to a mentoree, at an appropriate time and manner, so that it facilitates development or empowerment."[72] Cunningham further argues that mentorship should be characterized by mutual respect and reciprocity between the "mentor" (the more experienced person) and the "mentoree" or "protégé" (the less experienced person). The two primary domains of mentoring attitudes and practices are the areas of career functioning and psychosocial functioning. Career functions include such practices as coaching, sponsoring, providing exposure and visibility, instructing in corporate culture, and offering challenging assignments. The mentor's own psychosocial attitudes and practices position him/her as the one who serves as a role model, offers acceptance and confirmation, instructs in people skills, counsels, and serves as a friend to the protégé. Thus, the psychosocial, professional and voluntary nature of mentorship which should be carried out in an enabling environment to enhance development and empowerment in an atmosphere of mutual respect and reciprocity could be experienced within the context of the church and its institutions. The notion that the acquisition and development of both leadership skills and other skills regarding which

---

70. Terblanche, "Understanding Mentorship," 96.
71. Blunt and Conolly, "Perceptions of Mentoring."
72. Cunningham, "Who's Mentoring the Mentors?," 35.

a role model, friendship and enduring relationship dynamics between the mentor and protégé are required for successful mentoring underscores the importance of the church leader in the mentoring process. Nevertheless, a theological understanding of the concept and of the way in which it may be harmonized for effective results within both the church and Nigerian society may be relevant at this point.

Belsterling has argued that the source of the concept "mentor" may be attributed to Homeric times.[73] However, long before Homeric times, mentoring relationships were evident in biblical times. "Though the term 'mentor' is never used in scripture, the Greek term, *meno* (enduring relationship), does occur in scripture with the term appearing one hundred and eighteen times in the New Testament and thirty-three times in the Gospel of John."[74] Jesus used the term often in his farewell discourse, particularly in John 14 and 15, to describe an abiding relationship, the type of relationship he desired with his twelve disciples. Although Cunningham has shown the similarities between mentoring and discipling, she argues that discipling is the more comprehensive and encapsulates mentoring. Both mentoring and discipling are developmental alliances involving an individual who is functioning at a more experienced level than the protégé and follower while the protégé and follower both desire the knowledge being shared. Such knowledge is usually not shared in the classroom as both mentoring and discipling use life experience as an opportunity for learning and development. In addition, mentoring and discipling are based on intense and focused relationships. As in the example of Jesus, which reflects a perfect analogy of the interplay of the concepts of discipling and mentoring, there was a sharing of life-on-life with fewer people, with this process also including a modelling. Mentoring and discipling are generative relationships in the sense that, in such relationships, the one cared for and nurtured later becomes the primary nurturer of another. Mentoring is a subset of discipleship. Being a disciple can include a mentoring relationship but it is not a necessary requirement and it does not necessarily

---

73. Mentoring, as a recognized concept, has been around since, at least, 800 B.C. It was noted in Homer's Greek mythology, when Odysseus, the Greek poet, took his son, Telemachus, to his friend, Mentor, and requested him to guide, coach and raise him in life skills as he, Odysseus, would be away from home for a long time. The Bible is also full of examples of mentors and protégés. Belsterling, "Mentoring Approach of Jesus."

74. Belsterling, 77.

make one a more devout disciple. While, on one hand, it may be argued that the familiarity of church leaders with the art of discipling is an advantage which should make the art of mentoring a part of their area of specialization, on the other hand, it may be seen as a disadvantage as mentoring may be viewed as a conversionist approach to non-Christian protégés. The latter result in the church leader's role as a prospective mentor to non-Christians will prove abortive. This observation should inform the church leader's approach to mentoring for the purpose of raising transformational leaders for the well-being of Nigerian society which is in such dire need of responsible leaders. Mentoring should, therefore, not be seen primarily as an opportunity to make converts, but rather to raise leaders who, of themselves, should make their own decisions about their religious views. Types of mentoring programmes include one-on-one mentoring, team mentoring, school-based mentoring, workplace mentoring, faith-based mentoring, career exploration mentoring and academic/tutor mentoring.

It is recommended that Nigerian church leaders use the example of Jesus to make their mentoring of transformational leaders both more effective and more enduring. Jesus invested more in the committed few than in the curious many and, in this way, he was able to weed out the sensation seekers and to relate meaningfully with those who had left all to follow him. Thus, he modelled holistically and not selectively. The disciples witnessed Jesus's ministry to all categories of people and his life's experiences in all situations, including the times when he was tired, hungry and angry. He inspired small group interaction with both him and with the other members of the group during which his disciples asked him questions and held discussions among themselves. Jesus also mentored one-on-one in ways specifically tailored to each individual. He explained his public ministry privately through spontaneous questions and answers in private settings. Jesus also gave those he mentored assignments and involved them in his own ministry through which he modelled. He envisioned his numbers growing and urged his disciples to make disciples who would also in turn make disciples. Thus, Jesus envisioned leadership reproducibility and multiplication. He spent much time with those he mentored and could, thus, be termed a very present mentor. In Crow's view, Jesus's methodology in mentoring differed significantly from the conversional approaches used today to develop leaders. "Although He spoke to huge crowds, His primary focus was on mentoring 'the few' who would then multiply themselves among 'the many'. He started small, went deep, and thought big."[75] Besides mentoring, the development-oriented church leader is one who does not merely urge the faithful to go and effect change in the public space or larger society, he shepherds them himself/herself into the public domain as agents of change.

6.3.4 The Development-Oriented Church Leader as the Shepherd of the Faithful into the Public Domain as Agents of Change

During the course of this study, it has been observed that much of the engagement of the church leaders in Nigeria is restricted to charity and social services.[76] However, charity and social services, no matter how well intended, are extremely limiting as they do not address the root causes of social injustice. Other limiting practices of the church in Nigeria include advocacy, church resolutions and church social statements. A number of such activities and also others may be regarded as falling within the church's comfort zone – the sanctuary from which the church distributes the charity doled out by those government, institutions or individuals wishing to alleviate their guilt for the injustices perpetrated against the poor in the society. Thus, in this sense, the church serves as an instrument that eases the guilt of the oppressor and is, therefore, a collaborator instead of the challenger of unjust persons and systems. The church rightly belongs to the oppressed, weak and suffering and it is essential that that belonging is expressed more in action through effective vehicles for seeking justice in the public arena, and not in words in the sanctuary. On this note, Jacobson has observed that "biblically speaking, the preeminent activity of the church is in the public arena, not in the sanctuary. To resist the summons to public life is to resist the Holy Spirit."[77] Jacobson's assertion translates further into a question which he assumes could help implement what he is saying: "Who takes the church into the public arena if not the pastor"? If the pastoral leadership is resistant to the public arena ministry, even the best-intentioned laity will be blocked or deflated in their efforts to engage in public arena issues.

---

75. Crow, "Multiplying Jesus Mentors," 92.
76. See sections 4.3.2 and 5.2.4.10.
77. Jacobson, *Doing Justice*, 14–15.

Engaging in the public arena may yield effective results if such engagement is coordinated by church leaders in the congregational, denominational and ecumenical structures of the church. Such organized networks of the church would do well to collaborate with the churches, religious institutions, civil society and other institutions of change both in Nigeria and beyond. However, it is possible that the synergy of these collaborating institutions may be better coordinated through a church leadership that is development-oriented. In addition, it is recommended that such church leadership appreciate the resources that may be tapped from these collaborative efforts while remaining sensitive to innovation and manifesting a willingness to engage in new challenges and emerging opportunities and to navigate the change processes and utilise new resources in the process. Interestingly, Cohall and Cooper have observed that "Pastors, besides their traditional roles as liturgists, preachers, and leaders in the ordinances of the church, fulfill other major roles in American life."[78] They further note that pastors provide spiritual and social guidance, as well as leadership in the political system. They are representatives of their communities in a variety of socioeconomic causes. These roles of pastors in the American context are not different from the roles being played by some Nigerian pastors and by other forms of church leadership, including elders and deacons/deaconesses, in Nigeria.

Church leaders should be actively involved in political parties, civil society organizations, cultural groups, NGOs, economic organizations, trade unions and other sociopolitical and economic organizations and they should encourage their members to follow suit. The role of Pastor Tunde Bakare in the establishment of the Save Nigeria Group (SNG) which was mentioned above and the engagement of the SNG in mass protests are good examples of such involvement on the part of both church leaders and their followers. In addition, Bakare's partisan political involvement and the efforts of Pastor Chris Okotie and Deaconess Sarah Jubril as presidential aspirants of political parties are all steps in the right direction of the active engagement of church leaders in sociopolitical issues. In their sociopolitical and economic engagements, church leaders should serve as role models and effective change agents as regards addressing the perennial socioeconomic and political challenges confronting Nigerians. Although the active participation of Nigerian pastoral

---

78. Cohall and Cooper, "Educating American Baptist Pastors," 29.

church leaders in the sociopolitical and economic processes may be fairly in the Nigerian landscape, the engagement of leaders such as bishop Matthew Hassan Kukah (Oputa Panel) and Pastor Tunde Bakare (SNG mass protests) were greeted with enthusiasm by Nigerians and such efforts should be lauded as they hold the promise of changing the mindset of Nigerians concerning the roles of church leaders and Christians in active sociopolitical matters. It is, therefore, pertinent that church leaders utilise the resources available in the church, Nigeria and the global community in the interests of sustainable transformational development in Nigeria.

6.3.5 Harnessing the Resources of the Church, Nigeria and the Global Community for Sustainable Transformational Development through Church Leaders

The quest for sustainable transformational development in the Nigerian society is aimed at addressing the challenges of poverty, underdevelopment, corruption and poor leadership which have ravaged the Nigerian society for many years. However, an adequate response to these challenges entails the church leadership employing the resources of the church, Nigeria and the global community in the various domains which have been affected by these challenges and which, therefore, need to be transformed and then used as channels for the realization of the goals of sustainable transformational development. These domains include all the spiritual, psychological, moral, sociocultural, economic, political and ecological aspects of Nigerian society while the goals of sustainable transformational development include changed people, changed systems and the stewardship of creation. These goals also synchronize with the proposed goals of Nigerian development, namely, conscientization, responsible self, value for community and stewardship of resources, and they provide common grounds through which the collaborative efforts of the church community, the broader Nigerian society and the global community may interact to bring about the desired changes within Nigerian society. The well-being of persons, communities/systems and the environment are all concerns that affect the church, Nigerian society and the global community and they may therefore command an enduring and meaningful collaboration. There is, in the twenty-first century, a strong push for collaborative efforts in addressing common challenges as such collaborative efforts will facilitate action, diversity and the adequate harnessing of resources and expertise. There is no doubt that the challenges that are affecting the Nigerians in the church community are the same problems that are affecting Nigerians in the broader Nigerian society and, to an extent, impinging on the global community. In the same vein, within each of these contexts in which these challenges abound, there are also resources that may be pulled together or harnessed for the common good. In this study, the church leader is considered to be in a privileged position to harness the resources available in his/her immediate constituency (church) for use in the wider community to which he/she also belongs.

6.3.5.1 *Harnessing the Resources of the Church*

It has been observed that in South Africa, as in many countries in Africa, including Nigeria, "no social institution can claim to command the same level of public trust as the Christian Churches."[79] Thus, churches and other faith-based organizations may be regarded as strategic in meeting the challenge of moral regeneration and reaching the various levels of the Nigerian society. This, in turn, constitutes a vital social strength that must not be overlooked if a genuine social transformation of the Nigerian society is envisioned, whilst bearing in mind the pervasive impact of corruption and its adverse impact on Nigerian society.

The capacity of the church to reach out to and serve those people who are most in need as well as the value-laden nature of the church's social programmes, as demonstrated through ecumenical, denominational and congregational church bodies, also reflect a measure of the expertise of the church and also the broad social networks established by the church. The church's emphasis on community in both teaching and mode of existence is in alignment with traditional Nigerian society's value for community which has long sustained Nigerian societies. Accordingly, its reenactment is becoming increasingly relevant to the preservation of values and well-being within the national and global community. Speaking on the value for community which could be said to also relate to the church, Swart notes: "Social capital formation is associated directly with the kind of strategic action that will revive the traditional values of 'ubuntu' and 'neighborly love,' that is, value

---

79. Swart, "Churches as Stock," 325.

that, in turn, could be seen as foundational to meeting the social capital goals of social cohesion and inclusion."[80]

Globally, it has been recognized that churches and other faith-based organizations are not only agents of social capital formation,[81] but, in some instances, they may be regarded as the single most important factor in social capital formation and activity in some communities. In addition, the church's established infrastructure, institutions, connections with business/economics, community and government institutions,[82] large financial resource base, global connections with other church bodies and large volunteer base, are additional strengths and resources in this regard. The ability of church members to develop civic skills – leading groups, running meetings, giving speeches, managing disagreements and the usual encouragement to provide help to persons both within and outside of the church,[83] may enhance the capacities of both church members and church leaders in the social context.

In addition to the sociological aspects of the church's resources, the theological resources of the church include the spirituality and reconciliatory roles of the church in the world. The church, as the "body of Christ," is charged with the responsibility of continuing with the reconciliatory message of the Lord Jesus Christ through which the world is invited to be reconciled with God and with each other. This position and calling of the church is especially significant to Nigerians who, over the years, have been polarized by ethnic, social and religious divisions.

Furthermore, the church and its leaders, more than any other institution, are in a better position to address the negative contributions of evil spiritual forces to the challenges facing Nigerians. With the increased involvement of the church in national prayer conferences, ecumenical relationships and interfaith dialogue, its resources and experiences may enrich its sociopolitical

---

80. Swart, 336.

81. Swart opines that social capital formation as a strategic process more than anything else refers to the strengthening and establishment of social networks that will mediate the newly-found access to opportunities, resources and information. It also refers to the strengthening and establishment of relationships, norms and values as the means towards realizing the new state of social inclusion. It further entails the notion of social trust as a fundamental outcome. Social capital formation as a strategic process is finally directly associated with a developmental approach to addressing the needs of people.

82. Burger, Louw, and Watt. "Challenge of Poverty."

83. Carrolls, *God's Potters*.

and economic collaboration with political, economic and community institutions as regards the transformation of Nigerian society and beyond through the instrumentality of its leaders.

6.3.5.2 Harnessing the Resources of the Nigerian Community

The existence of political governance, the economic system, traditional institutions and civil society organizations in Nigeria also bring to the fore other key role players and the wide range of resources at their disposal. In modern day Nigeria, political institutions wield immense influence in issues pertaining to sociopolitical and economic development with the government being the major provider of the infrastructure that may drive sociopolitical and economic development. Since most of such infrastructure, including roads, electricity, urban and town planning, water and healthcare are capital intensive, government budgets are usually expected to fund them. In addition, government and political institutions are also responsible for legislation as well as for the interpretation and enforcement of laws in the country. Thus, property laws, financial regulations and land use decrees are beyond the control of churches and civil society. Nevertheless, enabling legislations and policies could be put in place to facilitate the socioeconomic and political development that may translate into poverty eradication, political stability, job and wealth creation, functional infrastructure, national security and human development. Such institutions and their resources are, therefore, crucial in the collaborative role they play in national development.

Economic and financial systems possess their resources in corporate managerial skills, wealth and global connections with global financial institutions. Their financial policies, employment policies and profit margins may enhance the well-being of Nigerians and the environment. Among its other resources, Nigerian civil society comprises the dense Nigerian population of more than two hundred million Nigerians with their varied specializations and professional expertise that account for the entire Nigerian workforce and with strong local and international networks with global civil society. Such enormous resources within Nigerian society, when combined with those of the church, may lead Nigerians to transcend their present challenges.

6.3.5.3 Harnessing the Resources of the Global Community

In addition to the church in Nigeria and the wider Nigerian society, the global community possesses its major resources in the positive impact and resources of globalization, and the global civil society. Globalization and informationalization, enacted by networks of wealth, technology and power are transforming our world. They are enhancing our productive capacity, cultural creativity and communication potential.[84]

As regards the global social movements or civil society which the church belongs to, their main resources lie in their ability to generate a process of transformation through the power of ideas, values and communication links by mobilizing voluntary action on a national or global scale.[85] Thus, the use of the mass media, newsletters, recorded media, school curricula, media events, various types of social networks, and study groups to mobilize voluntary action through persons both within and outside of their organizations for the purpose of engaging in social transformation is paramount to the global social movements.

These resources, among others, when properly harnessed by church leaders and the broader Nigerian society, have the propensity to translate the unfortunate challenges of poverty and underdevelopment into fulfilling sociopolitical and economic conditions for all Nigerians. There are possible ways in which Nigerian church leaders may harness these resources from the three sections of society – the church, broader Nigerian society and the global community. Some of these ways include learning about and appreciating the resources possessed by the various structures, adopting and implementing applicable strategies, and collaborating with the other structures in the transformation of the Nigerian sociopolitical, economic and ecological spheres. As has been previously mentioned, this study maintains that it is not possible for the church and its leaders to make significant progress in their quest for social transformation in Nigeria without their collaborating with other change agents within the Nigerian and the global community.

---

84. Castells, *Power of Identity*.
85. Swart, *Churches and Development Debate*.

6.4 Conclusion

Sustainable transformational development in Nigeria has been defined as a deep, positive change in the spiritual, psychological, moral, social, economic, political and environmental life of both people and institutional/systems and resulting from the activities of the church and its leaders in collaboration with other institutions of change in Nigeria and beyond.

The domains of sustainable transformational development, namely, spiritual, moral, psychological, sociocultural, political, economic, environmental and ecclesiastical, through which the goals of changed people, changed systems and stewardship of creation may be realized, were also articulated. It has been argued that, whereas the processes through which social change could occur as proposed in this study are vital in addressing the challenges confronting Nigerians, the role of church leaders as the catalysts of sustainable transformational development is crucial. The proposal of the sustainable transformational development paradigm as the recommended approach for church leaders in Nigeria as regards a more meaningful contribution to the transformation of the sociopolitical and economic challenges of Nigerians in the light of poverty, underdevelopment, corruption and poor leadership has, thus far, been informed by the literature study in chapters 2, 3, 4 and the findings of the empirical study in chapter 5. In addition, Osmer's pragmatic task[86] assisted in the formulation of the proposed development paradigm.

---

86. Osmer, *Practical Theology*.

CHAPTER 7

Development-Oriented Church Leadership in Postmilitary Nigeria: Perspectives, Conclusion and Recommendations

7.1 Introduction

The focus of this study, presented at the beginning of the study and expressed in terms of the main research question and its subsets, is: How may church leaders in Nigeria, in light of the poverty, underdevelopment, corruption and poor leadership in that country, contribute more meaningfully to the sociopolitical and economic transformation of Nigerian society? In what ways may Nigerian church leadership achieve this? When translated into a sustainable transformational development approach (with a view to more meaningful engagement on the part of church leaders in sociopolitical and economic change in Nigerian society), what would the possible constituent elements of such an approach be? The background, motivation, problem statement, goals of the study, research paradigm, research methodology and research design guiding the study were also presented in the first chapter. In addition, the significance, delimitations and definitions of the key terms used in the study were explored.

In chapter 2, the meanings and implications of development were presented, together with an evaluation of the Nigerian historical context from precolonial to present times, as it relates to development. In line with Osmer's practical theological methodology,[1] this chapter fulfilled the descriptive-empirical and interpretive tasks by answering the questions: What is going on in the Nigerian social environment as it pertains to development? And why are these things going on? The chapter succeeded in uncovering the root causes of the perennial challenge of underdevelopment and the resultant consequences in Nigeria, and suggested ideas that may be incorporated into a possible development agenda that may be of benefit to the Nigerian society.

Chapter 3 dwelt on the meanings and implications of leadership and surveyed the Nigerian historical context from precolonial times to the present era, as it relates to sociopolitical leadership. Through the engagement of the descriptive-empirical and interpretive lenses of practical theology,[2] the chapter investigated whether there has been a challenge of poor leadership in Nigeria and, if it is true, the way in which poor leadership has been responsible for the challenges of poverty, underdevelopment and corruption facing Nigerians and how effective leadership may transform the Nigerian sociopolitical and economic landscape.

Chapter 4 focused on a social and theological analysis of the discourse of Nigerian church leaders. This endeavour revealed that although Nigerian church leaders still need to do more in sociopolitical, economic and theological engagements, they are, indeed, engaging in sociopolitical, economic and theological issues and, as such, they are revealing their potential as agents of change in Nigeria, particularly in light of the challenges facing the country. The descriptive-empirical and interpretive approaches[3] proved to be useful tools in the analysis.

In chapter 5, the results of the empirical study were presented and reflected upon. The main focus of this exercise was to understand the way in which church leaders may contribute more meaningfully to the social transformation of Nigerian society in light of the challenges of poverty, underdevelopment, corruption and poor leadership and also the vital components of that engagement. The study in this chapter was able to achieve this concern and also uncovered themes that could assist the proposal of a sustainable

---

1. Osmer, *Practical Theology*. See also 1.8.1.
2. Osmer.
3. Osmer.

transformational approach for the more meaningful social engagement of church leaders in Nigeria. The descriptive-empirical, interpretive, normative and pragmatic tasks[4] were the enabling tools for this analysis.

In chapter 6, the sustainable transformational development approach, including its definition, goals, domains and processes and development-oriented church leaders as the key drivers of the sustainable transformational development approach in the Nigerian context were discussed. The chapter also focused on the way in which church leaders could harness the various resources for Nigerian development, consistent with the sustainable transformational development approach.

The purpose of chapter 7 is to highlight some perspectives of the study and to present recommendations that may aid the sociopolitical and economic transformation of Nigerian society in the light of the challenges of poverty, underdevelopment, corruption and poor leadership facing the country. The perspectives to be presented include the interconnectedness of the development-oriented church leader as a change catalyst in Nigerian society, Nigerian leadership/followership, the various expressions of the church in Nigeria's sociopolitical and economic systems, globalization, civil society and the dignity of creation; and also how the development-oriented church leader and the various perspectives that are vital to social change relate to the sustainable transformational development paradigm. The recommendations to be presented will be drawn from the findings of both the empirical study and the literature study and are intended for the attention of Nigerian church leaders, the Nigerian church and Nigerian sociopolitical and economic institutions as they engage in the transformation of Nigerian society. In alignment with the aim of the chapter, as set out above, this chapter will engage the pragmatic approach[5] in presenting its arguments.

7.2 Development-Oriented Church Leadership in Postmilitary Nigeria: Perspectives

The perspectives to be presented in this section include the development-oriented church leader in postmilitary Nigeria and his/her place in the

---

4. Osmer.
5. Osmer.

sustainable transformational development approach as it relates to the concerns of Nigerian development, Nigerian leadership and followership, the various expressions of the church in Nigeria, Nigerian sociopolitical and economic systems, globalization, civil society and the dignity of creation.

7.2.1 Development-Oriented Church Leadership, Nigerian Development and Sustainable Transformational Development

In section 1.12.3, this study argued that both ordained and nonordained persons who are burdened with leadership responsibilities at different levels within the Christian community and who are concerned about and are engaged in social transformation are the very individuals who may be considered as development-oriented church leaders. In sections 2.3, 2.5 and 2.6, Nigerian historical antecedents, current national and global trends, and the consistent failure of development approaches within the Nigerian context were assessed. In addition, the concerns of Nigerian development were viewed as consistent with African, biblical and ongoing global concerns.

The sustainable transformational development approach argues that it is essential that the engagement of the church in social transformation be led by church leaders (section 6.3) and informed by the mission of God to the world (*missio Dei*), in terms of which the church and its leaders are God's instruments and co-labourers. Such an engagement of church leaders should be geared towards changing persons and institutions spiritually, psychologically, economically, socially and politically, and should include ecological justice. This sociopolitical and economic transformation will be realized through conscientized persons, community or collaborative efforts with relevant change agents and the proper mobilization and use of resources in the sense of stewardship. The sustainable transformational approach also argues that the social transformational engagement of church leaders should include charity/welfare, projects and social services but that it should go beyond such measures to include public policy change and through the direct participation of Nigerian church leaders and church members in socioeconomic and political activities.

The sustainable transformational approach may meet the proposed Nigerian developmental concerns by church leaders through creating an awareness of the challenges facing Nigeria, the sources of these challenges and their ability to deal with these challenges through personal interactions with the various sectors of Nigerian society, print and mass media, Bible study, fellowship and the preaching/teaching of both church members and nonchurch members. The creation of such awareness through the concept of conscientization is vital in instilling a new mindset among Nigerians and redeeming their dignity. The notion of conscientization, as consistent with sustainable transformational development, will remind Nigerians of God's presence and his involvement in their affairs, to transform their challenges in light of poverty, underdevelopment, corruption and poor leadership. In addition, it reminds both the rich and the poor, the leaders and the followers of their responsibilities towards each other, the environment and the sociopolitical and economic systems and the reason why all these must function in the interests of the well-being of all. Social transformation should begin in the mind, move to action and be continued in that reflexive approach. The notion of conscientization, within the framework of the sustainable transformational approach, must represent an entrenched consciousness which should inform the thoughts and actions of all Nigerians as they navigate their challenges and thereafter. The sustainable transformational approach argues that conscientization should be carried out in ways required by each Nigerian context (innovation), church leaders should work in tandem with other interested parties in order to achieve conscientization (collaboration), conscientization should be vigorously pursued (stewardship) and the Christian/cultural ideals (values) should inform the concept of conscientization.

As regards the stewardship of resources as a concern of Nigerian development, sustainable transformational development argues for stewardship as one of the overarching concepts that should inform the engagement of both church leaders and other change agents in Nigeria. However, in addition to the engagement of church leaders and the institutions of change, such as churches, civil society and other institutions, the stewardship motif should inform the ordinary Nigerian citizen in his/her daily endeavours. The church's resources and those of the sociopolitical and economic institutions in Nigeria and beyond should be mobilized in the interests of the social transformation of Nigerian society. Sustainable transformational development argues that church leaders are the best positioned to mobilise the enormous resources within and beyond the church for the use of present and future generations of Nigerians. The notion of stewardship, as proposed by sustainable transformational development, implies that, in every individual and environment, God has provided immense resources which should neither be hoarded nor used recklessly. Although such resources may be in the custody of certain persons or institutions, they should be utilized for the benefit of the immediate and larger society. Stewardship suggests that all positions and responsibilities should be utilized for the benefit of all and exercized with the best intentions and to the best of the abilities of those concerned. Stewardship reminds us that we hold all resources in trust for other human and nonhumans in the present and future generations and, therefore, that we are accountable for the resources within our reach. Stewardship encourages us to see both ourselves and other human beings as possessing capabilities that should be made available for the common good.

Whereas the notion of value for community is understood as one of the concerns of Nigerian development, in terms of the sustainable transformational approach to social transformation, the community and its varied expressions are perceived as one of the channels through which the sociopolitical and economic contexts may be transformed. As previously argued, the notion of community and its importance is reflected in the statement: whatever happens to the individual happens to the whole group, and whatever happens to the whole group happens to the individual. In African/Nigerian communities, the notion of community substantiates the importance of the community as regards meaningful existence. There is no doubt that we are made for complementarity. We are created for a delicate network of relationships, of interdependence with our fellow human beings, with the rest of creation. In terms of sustainable transformational development, the community as church, village, clan, compound, country and the global community is viewed as a covenant structure that is extremely crucial in the formation of values and the forging of persons and institutions. The community is also seen as the sum total of all the components of existence, namely, human beings, animals, plants, institutions, technology and all that constitutes the created order. In view of the fact that all of these aspects of the community comprise the whole and, as such, each is dependent on the other, it is essential that life be lived in a way that is informed by this understanding. Each part of the community should, therefore, be cherished and should, thus, play its part and be allowed to flourish for the good of all. The notion of community is therefore interconnected to the values, collaboration, innovation and stewardship that comprise the overarching concepts of every sustainable transformational development engagement within the Nigerian society and beyond.

It follows from the above that the sustainable transformational development approach envisions that the church leaders bear in mind the goals that should be embedded in any developmental approach, if that approach is to have any value for Nigerian society, must include the conscientization of all Nigerians, the strengthening of communal ties as against individualism and the mobilization and adequate utilization of all resources for the well-being of all Nigerians. In addition, such issues as pertaining to conscientization, community and stewardship should be directed by church leaders through persons (leaders/followers), institutions/systems and stewardship, guided by innovation, collaboration, stewardship and values.

7.2.2 Development-Oriented Church Leadership, Nigerian Leadership/Followership and Sustainable Transformational Development

Those church leaders who are engaged in one form or the other of the Nigerian social transformation process understand the importance of religious, sociopolitical and economic leadership in the transformation of Nigeria. As such, the first task of the development-oriented church leader is to appreciate the extent to which good leadership is crucial to all facets of Nigerian society and how the absence of good leadership has denied Nigerians the much needed sociopolitical and economic development.

The colonial, independent, military and postmilitary or political leadership of Nigeria has been largely blamed for the poverty, underdevelopment, corruption and other social vices that have beset Nigerian society for many decades. However, whereas Nigerians have been highly commended for their resilience and endurance in the face of such harsh conditions, it is becoming clearer to observers that the Nigerian populace should also share the blame for the deterioration in the conditions of life and in the infrastructure. This blame stems from the docility of the Nigerians which allowed their leaders to continue plundering the nation's resources while some of the citizens stood aside and watched and others enjoyed the spoils of the plunder. It is being argued that, if ordinary Nigerians had risen to meet the challenge, the situation would have changed long ago. This conclusion or assumption is based on the examples of countries in the Northern hemisphere that have consistently resisted poor socioeconomic and political conditions at different stages of their development history through protests and a demand for accountability from their leaders. Nigerian church leaders and members, who account for a large proportion[6] of the population of Nigeria, may also be considered to have taken too little action to combat the challenge of poor leadership with its effect on the level of poverty, underdevelopment, corruption and other social evils prevalent in Nigerian society.

The sustainable transformational development approach points to the church leader as a development catalyst and it challenges church leaders to meet the challenge of social transformation by taking the lead and teaching their church members, by their example, to engage in social change and to be leaders in such engagements. The sustainable transformational development encourages church leaders to adopt the transformational leadership approach to ecclesial and social leadership and, in this way, to instil in the Nigerian followership such leadership qualities. In addition, in order to perpetuate transformational leadership in Nigerian society, it is recommended that mentoring also be entrenched in the ecclesial, sociopolitical and economic spheres of Nigerian society. Whereas other concepts of leadership such as adaptive and servant leadership are possible options, the transformational leadership concept holds great promise within the Nigerian context. Supporting this view, P11 suggested:

> Nigeria needs transformation. Therefore, to do this requires transformational leaders. Transformational leaders have a vision, a goal, an agenda, a results-orientation that grabs people's attention. They communicate their vision and build trust by being consistent, dependable and persistent. They have positive self-regard. In general, they transform vision into reality and motivate people to transcend their personal interests for the good of the group. This is the kind of leadership we need in today's Nigeria.

In pursuit of the sustainable transformational development agenda, the development-oriented church leader in postmilitary Nigerian must engage in the Nigerian context – from the ecclesial community to all other facets

---

6. Falola, 4.

of the society – through transformational leadership and the mentoring of transformational leaders. Such a development-oriented church leader will embark on that approach to leadership and mentoring with innovation, collaboration, stewardship and the upholding of values.

7.2.3 Development-Oriented Church Leadership, the Various Expressions of the Church and Sustainable Transformational Development

Development-oriented church leaders proceed from the constituency of the church but they are not limited to that domain. They are bonafide members of the broader Nigerian society and, as such, they also experience the various challenges that other Nigerians experience in their day to day lives. However, in view of their privileged positions as leaders of both the ecclesial and broader society, they are called, by the fact of their ecclesial responsibilities, to be agents of God in society. The various levels of the expression of the ecclesial community, such as cells, congregations, denominations and ecumenical bodies, enable the church and its leaders to be in touch with both the perpetrators of social injustices and those who suffer as a result of such injustices.

Accordingly, sustainable transformational development challenges the church and, especially church leaders, to reach out to the poor in society through their religious activities, charity, social services and projects. Such activities are best carried out through congregations and denominations, especially within their areas of operation. However, whereas such activities should be viewed as temporal measures aimed at looking after the bodies and souls of the poor, and as a concrete demonstration of God's love for the poor, they should not be the final products of churches and their leaders. Beyond the confines of charity and social services, church leaders should aim at the actual empowerment of church members and the larger community. This, in turn, calls for collaborative efforts between churches/church leaders and both the community and other institutions that are focused on empowering the poor. Key tools in empowerment should include conscientization, self-reliance, entrepreneurship, microfinance, education and development projects that create viable jobs and employment opportunities which enable those employed to earn remunerations that will allow meaningful living conditions. Within the congregational and denominational levels of the church, church leaders would do well to instil values and to ensure that these values are upheld in all areas of the church members' lives. In addition, church leaders should insist on members fulfilling their sociopolitical and economic obligations as responsible citizens and they should be encouraged to collaborate with other institutions in using all legitimate avenues to challenge all forms of social injustices perpetrated by sociopolitical and economic institutions.

Sustainable transformational development argues for church leaders to use ecumenical platforms such as CAN and its blocs at their local, state and national levels in order to influence sociopolitical and economic policies. This may be achieved by dialogue, advocacy, lobbying, direct participation in sociopolitical and economic activities, protests, court actions and any other lawful means. However, as enunciated in this study, in all of the social engagements of the church and of church leaders at the various levels of the church's existence, it is essential that the concepts of the mission of God (*missio Dei*), collaboration, innovation, stewardship and values inform these church leaders in their social ministry.

7.2.4 Development-Oriented Church Leadership, Sociopolitical and Economic Systems and Sustainable Transformational Development

As discussed in chapters 3 and 4, many Nigerian church leaders were not trained to be knowledgeable about, and be engaged in sociopolitical and economic issues in Nigeria. This was partly as a result of the missionaries' understanding of church and society, poor education and the inability of Nigerian church leaders to wean themselves from the missionary theological reductionism which separated the church/Christians from sociopolitical and economic engagements. Despite the fact that many church leaders are still not involved in sociopolitical and economic issues, nevertheless, a number of church leaders are becoming increasingly conscious of the importance of sociopolitical and economic institutions to both the church and to society at large. Church leaders in the mainstream denominations and in some Pentecostal denominations have shown a commendable response to social issues by making use of advocacy and the quality education of a new generation of Nigerians to infiltrate various sectors of Nigerian society through church-owned educational institutions and NGOs. However, as observed earlier in chapter 4, a number of these commendable measures may be termed emergent and, as such, have not attained the import necessary to alter the ongoing dynamics of poverty, underdevelopment, corruption and poor leadership in any significant way.

The sustainable transformational development approach to social change acknowledges the extent to which sociopolitical and economic institutions are indispensable as the key to shaping either the well-being or otherwise of both the church and of Nigerian society as a whole. As such, the approach seeks to collaborate with and to transform the said institutions through both the persons who run the institutions and through the institutions themselves that have the capability of influencing the persons that run them. Through the instrumentality of Nigerian church leaders and Christians, the concepts of stewardship, innovation, collaboration and values should be brought into each of these institutions by the direct participation of church leaders and members. Spiritual resources such as prayers, religious symbols, prophetic utterances and nonviolent resistance should be utilized in the process of seeking policy change and promoting the functionality of these institutions for the good of society and the environment. The resources of community and its value in ecclesial, anthropological and ecological terms, as advocated in the sustainable transformational development paradigm, also encompasses resources that may inform and transform the sociopolitical and economic systems in Nigeria.

From the perspective of the sustainable transformational development agenda, church leaders and churches who are socially informed, ideologically critical and politically conscious could make meaningful contributions to political democratization, economic democratization, and trade and investment relations on the idea, ethical and value level. In addition, the ethical and value levels of the engagement of churches and church leaders with sociopolitical and economic institutions and the direct participation of church leaders and churches at these levels, as guided by an idea, ethical and value consciousness, may contribute to more meaningful social engagement.

7.2.5 Development-Oriented Church Leadership, Globalization and Sustainable Transformational Development

It is not possible for Nigerian church leaders who are concerned about social transformation to ignore the positive and negative effects of globalization on the Nigerian sociopolitical and economic context. The increasingly interconnected character of political, economic and social life of the peoples on the planet implies that sociopolitical and economic influences from the various parts of the world will also have a direct impact on Nigerians, whether positive or negative. Thus, Anderson notes that globalization is a worldwide social phenomenon in which things are fragmenting or splintering and reluctantly coming together simultaneously. On the one hand, there are new borders emerging daily in nations and multinational corporations because of parochial concerns within, while, on the other hand, universalizing forces from without make borders more porous and particularly more difficult to maintain.[7]

As a response to the inescapable effects of globalization, sustainable transformational development argues for an engagement of church leaders in the social transformational project in Nigeria which involves utilising the resources of both the local and the global communities. The engagement of the church's resources at the congregational, denominational and ecumenical levels in the Nigerian and global contexts may be of immense help to this endeavour. Such collaborative efforts should also be widened to include local, national and global civil society through the effective use of communication technology and social networks. Whereas the church's vast resources, which include, inter alia, human and financial capital and spiritual resources may foster the social ministry of the church and its leaders, the power of civil society, as expressed in people's movements, may hold tremendous sway in the political and economic institutions which, most often, possess international authority. The social engagement of church leaders would do well to make use of the concepts of sustainable transformational development, including innovation, collaboration, stewardship and values in order to engage the gains of globalization in the social transformation of Nigeria. I suggest that such use of the positive effects of globalization may counter the negative aspects of globalization such as the erosion of values, poverty, arms proliferation, global warming and other environmental crisis.

---

7. Anderson, "Seeing the Other Whole."

7.2.6 Development-Oriented Church Leadership, Civil Society and Sustainable Transformational Development

Some Nigerian church leaders and churches have established NGOs to cater for issues such as leadership training, ethics, poverty alleviation and medical services such as HIV and AIDS awareness campaigns. As relevant as these projects may be, this level of engagement in civil society addresses a fragment only of the major issues that may be addressed by civil society. Pastor Tunde Bakare's SNG stands out as the only church motivated civil society organization that has become involved in issues of political governance in collaboration with well-known activists and with outstanding results. Nevertheless, even though the SNG's public influence may have dwindled due to some internal crisis which was generated by Bakare's political engagement as vice presidential aspirant, under the auspices of Congress for Political Change (CPC) – an engagement which SNG was opposed to as it claimed not to have been properly informed by Bakare, SNG still has the capacity to recover from the setback and to forge ahead in its commitment to rise to the challenge of criticising and resisting irresponsible leadership in Nigeria.

As noted in section 2.6.3, civil society refers to the realm of organized social life that is voluntary, self-generating (largely), self-supporting, autonomous from the state, and bound by a legal or set of shared values. The role of civil society includes limiting state power and the promotion of openness in governmental activities, supplementing the role of political parties in stimulating political participation, and the structuring of multiple channels beyond the political party for the purpose of the articulation and representation of the interests of the masses. Civil society organizations serve sociocultural, economic and political functions. As regards their sociocultural function, these organizations promote social cohesion; combat isolation, alienation and anomie; train future leaders; develop organizational skills; and raise the self-confidence and self-esteem of members. They fulfil their economic roles by providing services, mobilising local resources to satisfy local needs, and by increasing self-sufficiency through decreasing dependence. Politically, civil society may act as interest groups to lobby, and mobilise people who, otherwise, do not have access to state power, and to gather these people together in groups so as to enable them to exert some influence and participate in the decision-making processes of the government.

The sustainable transformational development approach to the more meaningful participation of church leaders in social change in Nigeria advocates that the churches and their leaders should collaborate with local, national and global civil society organizations as they seek to influence socioeconomic and political systems and policies for the well-being of both the masses and the environment. Church leaders are thus expected to take the lead in such engagement and they would do well to engage the various levels of the church's expression. Such engagement should also be informed by innovation, collaboration, stewardship and the values that fall within the gamut of the church's participation in the mission of God in the world.

7.2.7 Development-Oriented Church Leadership, the Dignity of Creation and Sustainable Transformational Development

The extremely disturbing impact of soil erosion and soil fertility, deforestation, water scarcity, water pollution, biodiversity loss, municipal and hazardous waste, and the impact of oil and gas development, and other contributory factors to environmental hazards are primary areas of concern in the environmental degradation which is worsening in Nigeria. However, it would appear that church leaders in Nigeria have yet to be seen to show much interest in these issues, despite the fact that these issues are exacerbating the poverty and underdevelopment both in Nigeria and globally.

Sustainable transformational development argues that the whole of creation is God's gift, not only to humankind at the present, but to the entire created order, including future generations. As such each part of creation should be appreciated, valued and allowed to blossom while creation and its component parts must be seen as an integral part of the community without which it would not be possible for other parts of the community to function. Accordingly, sustainable transformational development proposes conscientization, stewardship of resources and value for community as vital components of the goal of development, especially within the Nigerian context. It further suggests that, when people are changed by the occurrence of *metanoia*, such change will have an impact on their greedy tendencies, which lead to the unnecessary quest for greater affluence, and on the development of technology and more subtle methods of acquisition, including unhealthy economic policies, all of which negatively impact other human beings and the environment.

Development-oriented church leaders, as catalysts of the sustainable transformational development paradigm, may contribute substantially to the dignity of creation by utilising the concepts of innovation, collaboration, stewardship and values to ensure the preservation of the dignity of creation which, in turn, relates to the celebration of the life in humankind, plants, animals, environment and all other forms of the expression of life on the planet.

7.3 Conclusion and Recommendations

The perspectives that have been presented above include the proposed concerns of development in Nigeria, Nigerian leadership/followership, the various expressions of the church in Nigeria, sociopolitical and economic systems, globalization, civil society, the dignity of creation and the way in which the development-oriented church leader relates to these crucial aspects that impinge on the social transformational process in Nigeria in the light of the sustainable transformational development approach. As discussed, the development-oriented church leader is seen as a sociopolitical and economic transformation catalyst within Nigerian society. He/she takes into consideration the perspectives discussed above as he/she mobilises the Nigerian church, Nigerian society and beyond to take action in the interests of the advantage and transformation of the Nigerian society, in fulfillment of the church's missional calling.

As previously argued, the transformational development approach, as a development framework of church development agencies, brings to bear, spiritual and practical resources to social transformation and, at the same time, exposes weaknesses of transformational development in such areas as its disconnect with the institutional church, social movements and ecological issues. However, such weaknesses are addressed by the sustainable transformational development approach with its emphasis on the church and its leaders, collaboration with social movements and other institutions, environmental concerns and policy change for the purpose of social justice and self-reliance. In addition to the connection between sustainable transformational development and the existing Christian concepts, the relationship between the ecumenical church and church leaders constitutes additional motivations to the proposed concept of sustainable transformational development which depends on church leaders, the Nigerian church and other sociopolitical and economic institutions for its social transformation agenda. As such, church leaders, as transformational leaders and facilitators of sustainable transformational development, conscientize the faithful, mentor transformational leaders, shepherd the faithful into the public domain as agents of change and harness the resources of the church, broader Nigerian society and the global community for the socioeconomic and political transformation of Nigeria.

The recommendations presented below are based on the findings of both the empirical and the literature study. Although they are intended primarily for the Nigerian church and Nigerian society, they may inform the practices of church leaders, churches, sociopolitical and economic systems in other parts of Africa that may be facing similar challenges as those described in this study. The recommendations will be presented in different categories as they relate to the church and to sociopolitical and economic institutions.

The Church

- Based on the missionary legacy which distanced the church from sociopolitical and economic institutions, and the perpetuation of that mindset after the missionary era, Nigerian church leaders will need to realign the church's theology with the concept of the mission of God (*missio Dei*) to the world – a concept through which the church, in all its expressions, participates as its royal charter. Such theological realignment should be entrenched in theological education curricula and church teachings while such a theological stance should also give rise to the origination of contextual theologies or inculturation within both the church and society in Nigeria so as to enable Christians to respond adequately to their daily challenges.
- Nigerian church leaders at the congregational, denominational and ecumenical levels of the church should accept the responsibility in the holistic empowerment of both Christians and non-Christians in Nigerian society and engage alongside them in the sociopolitical and economic transformation of Nigerian society.
- Nigerian church leaders and churches should take advantage of their privileged position in Nigerian society and enormous resources at their disposal to overcome the sociopolitical and

economic challenges facing the nation, as reflected in the poverty, underdevelopment, corruption, violence and poor leadership. Such transformational engagement should be channelled through religious activities, charity, projects and social services and direct participation in both sociopolitical and economic activities. However, if the engagement of both churches and church leaders in social change is to have a lasting impact then it is recommended that innovation, collaboration, stewardship and values should guide the social ministry of these church leaders as catalysts of change in Nigerian society. The goal of such engagement should always be to change both the people (leadership and followership) and the institutions or systems (sociopolitical, economic, technological and ecological).

The Nigerian Sociopolitical and Economic Institutions

- It is essential that the sociopolitical and economic institutions in Nigeria, including communities, traditional societies, political parties, government, businesses, civil society, NGOs and others, should begin to see the churches and the church leaders as competent and crucial partners in the transformation of Nigerian society, not only in the sense of the significant role which religion plays in the Nigerian context, despite its shortcomings, but in the sense of the enormous resources at the disposal of the church. As such the church and its leaders should be seen as possessing sociopolitical and economic resources to contribute to society as opposed to their traditional use, which is mainly in respect of spiritual matters and in the distribution of charity, relief and social services.
- Sociopolitical and economic institutions in Nigeria should build into their development vision the concepts of conscientization, value for community and stewardship of resources while these crucial development components should be informed by innovation, collaboration, stewardship and values. However, if all these visions are to materialize, Nigerian political leadership should adopt the concept of transformational leadership and

the mentoring of such transformational leaders in all the socioreligious, political and economic institutions in Nigeria.
- All Nigerians should buy into the Nigerian concern for sociopolitical and economic transformation, transcend ethnic and religious sentiments and build synergies across disciplines to find a rhythm that may stimulate the integrity, excellence, innovation, collaboration, stewardship, values and excitement that are geared towards nation building. In addition, all such efforts should be aimed at the recovery of the dignity and sense of pride of the present and also future generations of Nigerians and their environment.

The enormous and perennial challenges of poverty, underdevelopment, corruption and poor leadership facing Nigeria may have been perpetuated by both external and internal forces, especially within the domain of sociopolitical and economic leadership. It will, thus, require the ecclesial, sociopolitical and economic leadership in Nigeria, in collaboration with the requisite global institutions, to rise to the challenge of reversing these trends for a better Nigerian society which would be characterized by improved standards of living and the restoration of the human and ecological dignity of all Nigerians and of the country as a whole. Church leaders are called upon to be at the forefront of this pursuit of social change through the use of the sustainable transformational development paradigm which, in turn, encompasses the overarching concepts of innovation, collaboration, stewardship and values, geared towards human and institutional change and channelled through leadership, advocacy, protests, direct participation, charity and social services. The urgent need to engage in this endeavour arises from the daily plight of approximately 220 million Nigerians as they face poverty, diseases, violence and even death, all of which could be eradicated. The possibility that this goal may be realized is enhanced by the privileged position of church leaders in the sociocultural, political and economic mileaus in Nigeria in addition to the spiritual and material resources available to such leaders. A positive impact on the Nigerian social environment promises to be of benefit to both the African and the global contexts. However, the time to act is now or else the church and its leaders may lose their relevance, both now and in the future.

Appendix

Questionnaire to Leaders of National CAN/ CAN Bloc/LPC

Development-Oriented Church Leadership in Postmilitary Nigeria

Q1. How long have you been a leader of the Christian Association of Nigeria (CAN)/CSN, CCN, ECWA/TEKAN, PFN/CPFN OR OAIC/LPC?

Q2. What position(s) have you held or are still holding in CAN?

Q3. How would you assess the church in terms of its activities towards the political, economic and social transformation of Nigeria?

Q4 In Nigerian history, what do you understand by (i) Colonial period? (ii) Independence period? (iii) Military period? (iv) Postmilitary period ?

How would you evaluate each of these periods as it concerns their impact on the present day (postmilitary or democratic) Nigerian society?

Q5. What are the contributions of Nigerian church leaders to the Nigerian society?

Q6. What in your thinking are the major challenges of church leaders in their developmental efforts in Nigeria?

Q7 Which of the problems are traceable to colonial, independence, military and post military period?

Q8(a). Do you think church leaders are sufficiently aware and creatively responsive to the challenges of poor leadership, underdevelopment and poverty in the Nigerian society? Give some examples.

Q8(b). Do you think church members are sufficiently aware and creatively responsive to the challenges of poor leadership, underdevelopment and poverty in the Nigerian society? Give some examples.

Q9(a). How can church leaders in Nigeria contribute more meaningfully to the sociopolitical and economic transformation of the Nigerian society, in the light of poverty, underdevelopment, corruption and poor leadership?

Q9(b). How can church members in Nigeria contribute more meaningfully to the sociopolitical and economic transformation of the Nigerian society, in the light of poverty, underdevelopment, corruption and poor leadership?

Q10(a). Have you been involved in sociopolitical and economic transformational activities?

Q10(b). Please name the activities and state how you got involved.

Q11(a). What are your suggestions on the ecumenical church's engagement in the sociopolitical and economic transformation of the Nigerian society?

Q11(b). What are your suggestions on the denominational/congregational church's more meaningful engagement in the sociopolitical and economic transformation of the Nigerian society?

Q12. What kind of leadership style do you deem most appropriate to flow from the church and its members to the Nigerian society that can lead to the political, economic and social transformation of the Nigerian society, bearing in mind the perennial challenge of poor leadership in Nigeria? Please explain the reason(s) for your choice of leadership style.

Q13. For some time now, issues like corruption, electoral reforms, Niger Delta militancy, leadership vacuum due to the ailing President (Yar'adua), bank reforms and religious/tribal crisis have been on the front burner of national issues. In your assessment, how has the church (leadership/membership) fared in dealing with the issues in question?

Bibliography

Aboyade, B. "Exhibitionists as Religious Role Models." *Sunday Guardian*, 4 April 2004:13.

Abubakar, M. S. "You and Your Muslim Neighbour." In *Seminar Paper Presented at Christian Association of Nigeria (CAN), National Executive Committee (NEC)*. Abuja: CAN, 2010.

Abubakar, S. "Jonathan's 6-month Scorecard." *Daily Sun (Nigeria)*, 5 December 2010:7.

Achebe, Chinua. *The Trouble with Nigeria*. London: Heinemann Educational Books, 1983.

Adadevoh, D. "The Whole Gospel to the Whole Person." In *Papers Presented at the National Conference for Christian Leaders. Theme: Church in Mission and Transformation (Unedited)*. Abuja: Christian Association of Nigeria, 2010.

Agbedo, O. "Senate Committee Indicts NAPEP Leadership for Fraud." *Guardian Newspapers Limited (Nigeria)*, 18 December 2010:12.

Agbiji, Obaji M. "Religion and Ecological Justice in Africa: Engaging 'Value for Community' as Praxis for Ecological and Socio-economic Justice." *HTS Theological Studies* 71, no. 2 (2015):1–10.

———. "Religious Practitioners and Ecological Justice: Engaging 'Value for Community' as Lens for Ecological and Socio-economic Justice in Africa." In *Climate Crisis, Sustainable Creaturely Care: Integrated Theology, Governance and Justice*, edited by Christina Nellist, 188–207. Newcastle: Cambridge Scholars, 2021.

Agha, A. U. "Unto These Little Ones: Children Education Programme in the PCN." In *A Century and Half of Presbyterian Witness in Nigeria, 1846–1996*, edited by O. U. Kalu, 249–77. Lagos: Ida-Ivory Press, 1996.

Ake, C. "Socio-political Approaches and Policies for Sustainable Development in Africa." Paper Presented at the Annual Meeting's Symposium of the African Development Bank, May 23. Abuja: Unpublished, 1995.

Aluko, M. A. O. "Poverty and Illness in Nigeria: A Parable of Conjoined Twins." In *Traditional and Modern Health Systems in Nigeria*, edited by T. Falola and M. M. Heaton, 231–45. Trenton: Africa World Press, 2006.

Amogu, N. "Recovering the True Sense of the Church and Its Missional Vocation: Gender Perspectives." In *Papers Presented at the National Conference for Christian Leaders, Theme: Church in Mission and Transformation (Unedited)*. Abuja: Christian Association of Nigeria, 2010.

Ana, J. S. "Preserving Charisma in Institutional Reform: A Sociological Approach." *The Ecumenical Review* 50, no. 3 (1998):382–89.

Anderson, H. "Seeing the Other Whole: A Habitus for Globalisation." In *Globalisation and Difference: Practical Theology in a World Context*, edited by P. Ballard and P. Couture, 3–17. Cardiff: Cardiff Academic Press, 1999.

Antonio, D. "The Challenge for Africa: A Culture of Peace, Good Governance and People-centered Development." *Asia-Pacific Review* 8, no. 1 (2001):63–74.

Anya, O. A. "Science, Human Behaviour and Economic Development: An Old Problem with New Dimensions." *A Public Lecture Given at the Cross River State University of Technology (CRUTECH)*. Calabar, Nigeria, 6 October 2011.

———. "Foreword." In *A Century and Half of Presbyterian Witness in Nigeria, 1846–1996*, edited by O. U. Kalu, ii–iv. Lagos: Ida-Ivory Press, 1996.

Aremu, F. A., and J. S. Omotola. "Violence as Threats to Democracy in Nigeria under the Fourth Republic, 1999–2005." *African and Asian Studies* 6 (2007):53–79.

August, K. Th. *Equipping the Saints: God's Measure for Development*. Bellville: The Print Man, 2010.

Aye, E. U. "The Foundations of Presbyterianism among the Calabar Clans: Qua, Efik, Efut." In *A Century and Half of Presbyterian Witness in Nigeria, 1846–1996*, edited by O. U. Kalu, 1–27. Lagos: Ida-Ivory Press, 1996.

Babbie, Earl. *The Practice of Social Research*. 11th ed. Belmont: Thomson Learning, 2007.

———. *The Practice of Social Research*. 10th ed. Belmont: Thomson Learning, 2004.

Barna, G. *Leaders on Leadership: Wisdom, Advice and Encouragement on the Art of Leading God's People*. California: Regal Books, 1997.

Baxter, K. "Stepping Stones: Seven Insights into Community Sustainability." *Alternative Journal* 35 (2009): 22–23.

Bediako, K. *Christianity in Africa: The Renewal of a Non-Western Religion*. Edinburgh: Edinburgh University Press, 1995.

Belsterling, R. "The Mentoring Approach of Jesus as Demonstrated in John 13." *Journal of Youth Ministry* 5, no. 1 (2006):77–92.

Bevans, S. B., and R. P. Schroeder. *Constants in Context: A Theology of Mission for Today*. Maryknoll: Orbis Books, 2004.

Blackaby, H., and R. Blackaby. *Spiritual Leadership*. Nashville: B&H Publishing Group, 2011.

Blunt, R. J. S., and J. Conolly. "Perceptions of Mentoring: Expectations of a Key Resource for Higher Education." *South Africa Journal of Higher Education* 20, no. 2 (2006):195–208.

Bosch, D. J. *Transforming Mission: Paradigm Shifts in Theology of Mission*. Maryknoll: Orbis Books, 1998.

Bragg, W. G. "From Development to Transformation." In *The Church in Response to Human Need*, edited by V. Samuel and C. Sugden, 20–51. Grand Rapids: William B. Eerdmans, 1987.

Burger, R., M. Louw, and C. Watt. "The Challenge of Poverty and Social Exclusion in Post-apartheid South Africa." In *Religion and Social Development in Post-apartheid South Africa: Perspectives for Critical Engagement*, edited by I. Swart, H. Rocher, S. Green, and J. Erasmus, 61–73. Stellenbosch: SUN Press, 2010.

Burkey, S. *People First: A Guide to Self-reliant, Participatory Rural Development*. London: Zed Books, 1993.

CAN. *Brief Story of the Christian Association of Nigeria*. Abuja: Christian Association of Nigeria, 2010.

———. *Constitution of the Christian Association of Nigeria*. Abuja: Christian Association of Nigeria, 2004.

———. "Communiqué of 2nd General Assembly." In *Religion in a Secular State: Proceedings of the Second Assembly of the Christian Association of Nigeria*, edited by A. O. Makozi and G. J. A. Ojo, 48–50. Abuja: Christian Association of Nigeria, 1988.

Carrolls, J. W. *God's Potters: Pastoral Leadership and the Shaping of Congregations*. Grand Rapids: William B. Eerdmans, 2006.

Carter, J. C. "Transformational Leadership and Pastoral Leadership Effectiveness." *Pastoral Psychology* 58 (2009):261–71.

Castells, M. *The Power of Identity: The Information Age – Economy, Society and Culture*. Oxford: Blackwell, 2004.

Chachage, C. S. L. "Discussion on Development among African Philosophers." In *African Perspectives on Development: Controversies, Dilemmas and Openings*, edited by U. Himmelstrand, K. Kinyanjui, and E. Mburugu, 51–60. Kampala: Fountain Publishers, 1994.

Chambers, R. *Whose Reality Counts? Putting the First Last*. London: ITDG Publishing, 1997.

Chinne, Z. "Building a Future on Falsehood." In *Service with Integrity: The Christian in the Nigerian Project*, edited by Z. Chinne, 1–28. Kaduna: The ECWA Goodnews Church, 2008.

Chipenda, J. B. "Culture and the Gospel in Changing Africa." In *The Church and the Future in Africa: Problems and Promises*, edited by J. N. K. Mugambi, 14–40. Nairobi: All Africa Conference of Churches,1997.

Christian, J. *God of the Empty-Handed: Poverty, Power, and the Kingdom of God*. Monrovia: MARC, 1999.

Chuku-Okereke, G. I. "Evolution of Nigeria as a Political Unit: An Historical Analysis." In *Nigerian Politics*, edited by C. A. Ndoh and C. E. Emezi, 1–16. Owerri: CRC Publications, 1997.

Cohall, K. G., and B. S. Cooper. "Educating American Baptist Pastors: A National Survey of Church Leaders." *Journal of Research on Christian Education* 19 (2010):27–55.

Collinson, L. "Management Isn't Mysterious, It's Just Difficult." In *Leading, Managing and Ministering: Challenging Questions for Church and Society*, edited by J. Nelson, 22–35. Norwich: Canterbury Press, 1999.

Crow, D. M. "Multiplying Jesus Mentors: Designing a Reproducible Mentoring System, a Case Study." *Missiology: An International Review* 36, no. 1 (2008):87–109.

Cunningham, S. "Who's Mentoring the Mentors? The Discipling Dimension of Faculty Development in Christian Higher Education." *Theological Education* 34, no. 2 (1998):31–49.

De Gruchy, J. W. "Christian Community." In *Doing Theology in Context: South African Perspectives*. Maryknoll: Orbis Books, 1994.

Deng, L. A. *Rethinking African Development: Towards a Framework for Social Integration and Ecological Harmony*. Eritrea: Africa World Press, 1998.

Denzin, N. K., and Y. S. Lincoln. *Handbook of Qualitative Research*. Thousand Oaks: Sage Publications, 1994.

De Vos, A. S., and H. Strydom. *Research at Grass Roots: A Primer for the Caring Professions*. 1st ed. Pretoria: Van Schaik Publishers, 1998.

Dingemans, G. D. J. "Practical Theology in the Academy: A Contemporary Overview." *The Journal of Religion* 76 (1996):82–96.

Dorr, D. *Faith at Work: A Spirituality of Leadership*. Blackrock: The Columba Press, 2006.

Egeonu, P. "Trans-national Corporations as Agents of Imperialism." In *Nigerian Politics*, edited by C. A. Ndoh and C. E. Emezi, 148–58. Owerri: CRC Publications, 1997.

Ekanem, D. "Presidential Address: 'That All May Be One' John 17:23." In *Religion in a Secular State: Proceedings of the Second Assembly of the Christian Association of Nigeria*, edited by A. O. Makozi and G. J. A. Ojo, 5–9. Abuja: Christian Association of Nigeria, 1988.

Ekanem, S. A. *How the Military Underdeveloped Nigeria*. Calabar: University of Calabar Press, 2010.

Ekpenyong, M. O. *Beware of Gods: Economics, Ethics and Politics for National Development*. Ibadan: Daily Graphics Nigeria, 2005.

Eme, N. N. *Gender (In)Justice and Nigerian Women*. Lagos: Jonai Press Nigeria Enterprises, 2004.

———. *Ethics in Nigerian Social Development*. Lagos: Mbeyi & Associates Nigeria, 2007.

Emezi, C. E. "Ethnic Foundations of the Nigerian Society." In *Nigerian Politics*, edited by C. A. Ndoh and C. E. Emezi, 17–26. Owerri: CRC Publications, 1997.

Fagun, M. O. "Ecumenism: Bringing Together All Who Confess Faith in God." In *Religion in a Secular State: Proceedings of the Second Assembly of the Christian Association of Nigeria*, edited by A. O. Makozi and G. J. A. Ojo, 44–47. Abuja: Christian Association of Nigeria, 1988.

Falola, T. *The History of Nigeria*. Westport: Greenwood Press, 1999.

Fanon, Frantz. *The Wretched of the Earth*. New York: Grove Press, 1963.

Farinto, A. O. "Church in Mission: An Agent for Transformation." In *Papers Presented at the National Conference for Christian Leaders, Theme: Church in Mission and Transformation (Unedited)*. Abuja: Christian Association of Nigeria, 2010.

Fouche, C. B. "Qualitative Research Designs." In *Research at Grass Roots: For the Social Sciences and Human Service Professions*, edited by A. S. De Vos, 109–15. 3rd ed. Pretoria: Van Schaik Publishers, 2005.

Freire, P. "Conscientisation." *Cross Currents* 24, no. 1 (1974):23–31.

FRIG. "Leadership 2007: Who Is Next?" *Report and Recommendations of Forum for Righteousness in Governance Steering Committee to the Church in Lagos and Nigeria for the Purpose of the 2007 General Elections*. Lagos: FRIG, 2007.

Gbonigi, E. B. "Religion in a Secular State." In *Religion in a Secular State: Proceedings of the Second Assembly of the Christian Association of Nigeria*, edited by A. O. Makozi and G. J. A. Ojo, 23–31. Abuja: Christian Association of Nigeria, 1988.

Gibbs, E. *Leadership Next: Changing Leaders in a Changing Culture*. Leicester: Inter-Varsity Press, 2005.

Gibbs, G. *Analyzing Qualitative Data*. London: Sage, 2007.

Greenleaf, Robert K. *The Servant as Leader*. Westfield: Greenleaf Center for Servant Leadership, 1970.

Guder, D. L. *The Continuing Conversion of the Church*. Grand Rapids: William B. Eerdmans Publishing, 2000.

Heifetz, Ronald A. *Leadership without Easy Answers*. Cambridge: The Belknap Press of Harvard University Press, 1994.

Hendriks, Jurgens. "A Change of Heart: Missional Theology and Social Development." In *Religion and Social Development in Post-apartheid South*

Africa: Perspectives for Critical Engagement, edited by I. Swart, H. Rocher, S. Green, and J. Erasmus, 275–88. Stellenbosch: SUN Press, 2010.

Himmelstrand, U. "Perspectives, Controversies & Dilemmas in the Study of African Development." In *African Perspectives on Development: Controversies, Dilemmas and Openings*, edited by U. Himmelstrand, K. Kinyanjui, and E. Mburugu, 16–36. Kampala: Fountain Publishers, 1994.

Hood, Andrew, and Tom Waters. "Living Standards, Poverty and Inequality in the UK: 2016–2017 to 2021–2022." *IFS Report* no. R127 (2017).

Hughes, D., and M. Bennett. *God of the Poor: A Biblical Vision of God's Present Rule*. Cumbria: OM Publishing, 1998.

Hyden, Goran. "Changing Ideological and Theoretical Perspectives on Development." In *African Perspectives on Development: Controversies, Dilemmas and Openings*, edited by U. Himmelstrand, K. Kinyanjui, and E. Mburugu, 308–19. Kampala: Fountain Publishers, 1994.

Idemudia, U. "The Quest for the Effective Use of Natural Resource Revenue in Africa: Beyond Transparency and the Need for Compatible Cultural Democracy in Nigeria." *Africa Today* 56, no. 2 (2009):1–22.

Idowu, B. *Towards an Indigenous Church*. London: SCM, 1973.

Jacobson, D. A. *Doing Justice: Congregations and Community Organizing*. Minneapolis: Fortress Press, 2001.

Jenkins, W. *Ecologies of Grace: Environmental Ethics and Christian Theology*. Oxford: Oxford University Press, 2008.

Johnson, J. C. *Selecting Ethnographic Informants*. Thousand Oaks: Sage, 1990.

Johnston, Geoffrey. *Of God and Maxim Guns: Presbyterianism in Nigeria, 1846–1966*. Canada: Wilfrid Laurier University Press, 1988.

Kafang, Z. B. *Christians' Integrity and Politics in Nigeria*. Kagoro: Zoe Graphics Nigeria, 2011.

Kalu, O. U. "Faith and Politics in Africa: Emergent Political Theology of Engagement in Nigeria." In *Religion in Africa: Conflicts, Politics and Social Ethics (Vol. 3)*, edited by W. J. Kalu, N. Wariboko, and T. Falola, 11–30. Trenton: Africa World Press, 2010a.

———. "Pentecostal and Charismatic Reshaping of the African Religious Landscape in the 1990s." In *African Pentecostalism: Global Discourses, Migrations, Exchanges and Connections (Vol. 1)*, edited by W. J. Kalu, N. Wariboko, and T. Falola, 109–32. Trenton: Africa World Press, 2010b.

Kanduza, A. M. "Socio-cultural Change in Africa." In *Africa since 1990*, edited by Y. N. Seleti, 77–99. South Africa: MSP Print, 2004.

Kankwenda, M. "Forty Years of Development Illusions: Revisiting Development Policies and Practices in Africa." In *African Development and Governance Strategies in the 21st Century*, edited by B. Onimode, 3–19. London: Zed Books, 2004.

Klop, K. J. "Equal Respect and the Holy Spirit: The Liberal Demand for Moral Neutrality in the Political Sphere and Christian Respect for Creation." In *Public Theology for the 21st Century: Essays in Honour of Duncan B. Forrester*, edited by W. F. Storrar and A. R. Morton, 95–106. London: T&T Clark, 2004.

Komakoma, J. *The Social Teaching of the Catholic Bishops and Other Christian Leaders in Zambia: Major Pastoral Letters and Statements (1953–2001)*. Ndola: Mission Press, 2003.

Korten, David C. "Telling a New Story." In *The New Possible: Visions of Our World beyond Crisis*, edited by Philip Clayton, Kelli M. Archie, Jonah Sachs, and Evan Steiner, 259–67. Eugene: Cascade Books, 2021

———. "The Limits of the Earth." *The Nation* 263, no. 3 (1996):14–18.

———. *When Corporations Rule the World*. West Hartford: Kumarian Press, 1995.

———. "People-centered Development: Toward a Framework." In *People-centered Development: Contributions toward Theory and Planning Framework*, edited by D. C. Korten and R. Klauss, 299–309. West Hartford: Kumarian Press, 1984.

Korten, D. C. *The Post Corporate World: Life after Capitalism*. Sterling: Kumarian, 1999.

Kraft, C. H. "Culture, Worldview and Contextualization." In *Perspectives on the World Christian Movement: A Reader*, edited by R. D. Winter and S. C. Hawthorne, 400–406. Pasadena: William Carey Library, 2009.

Kukah, M. H. "Globalisation and the Rest of Us: Hopes and Impediments." In *Service with Integrity: The Christian in the Nigerian Project*, edited by Z. Chinne, 55–76. Kaduna; The ECWA Goodnews Church, 2008.

Kung, H. *A Global Ethic for Global Politics and Economics*. London: SCM Press, 1997.

Kunhiyop, S. W. "The Challenge of African Christian Morality." In *Service with Integrity: The Christian in the Nigerian Project*, edited by Z. Chinne, 211–44. Kaduna: The ECWA Goodnews Church, 2008.

Kurien, C. T. *Poverty and Development*. Mysore: Wesley Press, 1974.

Kwashi, B. "The Christian and Corruption." In *Service with Integrity: The Christian in the Nigerian Project*, edited by Z. Chinne, 29–53. Kaduna: The ECWA Goodnews Church, 2008.

———. "Conflict, Suffering and Peace in Nigeria." *Transformation Journal* 21, no. 1 (2004): 60–69.

Kwast, L. E. "Understanding Culture." In *Perspectives on the World Christian Movement: A Reader*, edited by R. D. Winter and S. C. Hawthorne, 397–99. Pasadena: William Carey Library, 2009.

Land, P. "What Is Development?" In *In Search of a Theology of Development*, edited by G. H. Dunne, 180–203. Geneva: Sodepax, WCC, 1969.

Lanre-Abass, B. "The Crisis of Leadership in Nigeria and the Imperative of a Virtue Ethics." *Philosophia Africana* 11, no. 2 (2008):117–40.

Lines, T. *Making Poverty a History*. London: Zed Books, 2008.

Long, D. S. *The Goodness of God: Theology, the Church and Social Order*. Grand Rapids: Brazos Press, 2001.

Maccain, D. "Church in Societal Transformation." In *Papers Presented at the National Conference for Christian Leaders, Theme: Church in Mission and Transformation (Unedited)*. Abuja: Christian Association of Nigeria, 2010.

Magaziner, D. R. *The Law and the Prophets: Black Consciousness in South Africa, 1968–1977*. Johannesburg: Ohio University Press, 2010.

Maisamari, D. D. "Christian Youths and the Challenge of Future Leadership: Will Your Seed Bear Good Fruit?" In *Service with Integrity: The Christian in the Nigerian Project*, edited by Z. Chinne, 77–108. Kaduna: The ECWA Goodnews Church, 2008.

Masango, M. "Leadership in the African Context." *The Ecumenical Review* 55 (2003): 313–21.

Maxwell, J. C. *Developing the Leaders around You: How to Help Others Reach Their Full Potential*. Port Harcourt: Spiritual Life Outreach, 1995.

Mbachirin, A. "Review of JC Nwafor, Church and State: The Nigerian Experience." *Journal of Church and State*, 654–55. Frankfurt am Main: IKO, 2003.

Mbachu, O. I. "The Anguish of Federalism in Nigeria." In *Nigerian Politics*, edited by C. A. Ndoh and C. E. Emezi, 159–70. Owerri: CRC Publications, 1997.

———. "Leadership and Accountability in Nigeria." In *Nigerian Politics*, edited by C. A. Ndoh and C. E. Emezi, 57–65. Owerri: CRC Publications, 1997.

Mbang, S. "Religion in a Secular State: A Bible Study on God." In *Religion in a Secular State: Proceedings of the Second Assembly of the Christian Association of Nigeria*, edited by A. O. Makozi and G. J. A. Ojo, 13–22. Abuja: Christian Association of Nigeria, 1988.

Mbiti, J. S. *African Religion and Philosophy*. Oxford: Heinemann Educational Publishers, 1999.

Merino, Gustavo Gutierrez. "The Meaning of Development." In *In Search of a Theology of Development*, edited by G. H. Dunne, 116–79. Geneva: Sodepax, WCC, 1969.

Mette, N. "The Economic Context of Globalisation." In *Globalisation and Difference: Practical Theology in a World Context*, edited by P. Ballard and P. Couture, 19–25. Cardiff: Cardiff Academic Press, 1999.

Miller, J. B. "Forming Future Feminists: Elisabeth Schussler Fiorenza, Conscientization, and the College Class Room." *Journal of Feminist Studies in Religion* 25, no. 1 (2009):99–123.

Mills, G. *Why Africa Is Poor and What Africans Can Do about It*. Johannesburg: Penguin Books, 2010.

Minchakpu, O. "Church Leaders Refocus on Ethics." *Christianity Today* 72, 1998.

Mitchell, M. "Living Our Faith: The Lenten Pastoral Letter of the Bishops of Malawi and the Shift to Multiparty Democracy, 1992–1993." *Journal for the Scientific Study of Religion* 41 (2002):5–18.

Moltmann, J. *Theology of Hope: On the Ground and the Implications of a Christian Eschatology*. Minneapolis: Fortress Press, 1993.

Mongula, B. S. "Development Theory and Changing Trends in Sub-Saharan African Economies 1960–89." In *African Perspectives on Development: Controversies, Dilemmas and Openings*, edited by U. Himmelstrand, K. Kinyanjui, and E. Mburugu, 84–95. Kampala: Fountain Publishers, 1994.

Monsma, T. M. *Hope for the Southern World: Impacting Societal Problems in the Non-Western World*. Loveland: CCW Books, 2006.

Moss, T. J. *African Development: Making Sense of the Issues and Actors*. London: Lynne Rienner Publishers, 2007.

Mudge, L. S. "Human Solidarity in a Global Civilisation." In *Globalisation and Difference: Practical Theology in a World Context*, edited by P. Ballard and P. Couture, 27–31. Cardiff: Cardiff Academic Press, 1999.

Munroe, M. *Becoming a Leader: Discover the Leader You Were Meant to Be!* New Kensington: Whitaker House, 2009.

Musa, D. *Christians in Politics: How Can They Be Effective?* Bukuru: Africa Christian TextBooks (ACTS), 2009.

Muyebe, S., and A. Muyebe. *African Bishops on Human Rights*. Nairobi: Paulines Publications Africa, 2001.

Myers, B. L. *Walking with the Poor: Principles and Practices of Transformational Development*. Maryknoll: Orbis Books, 1999.

Ndikumana, L., and S. Verick. "Two-Way Linkages between FDI and Domestic Factor Markets: Evidence from Sub-Saharan Africa." In *Back on Track: Sector-led Growth in Africa and Implications for Development*, edited by D. Seck and S. Boko, 305–27. Trenton: Africa World Press, 2010.

Ndiyo, N. A. *Poverty to Sustainable Development: A Community-Based Approach*. Calabar: University of Calabar Press, 2008.

Ndoh, C. A. "Pre-colonial Political Institutions in Nigeria." In *Nigerian Politics*, edited by C. A. Ndoh and C. E. Emezi, 27–32. Owerri: CRC Publications, 1997.

———. "Colonial System of Administration in Nigeria: The Policy of Indirect Rule Institutions in Nigeria." In *Nigerian Politics*, edited by C. A. Ndoh and C. E. Emezi, 42–50. Owerri: CRC Publications, 1997.

Ndoh, C. A., and A. Njoku. "Nigerian Nationalism in Nigeria." In *Nigerian Politics*, edited by C. A. Ndoh and C. E. Emezi, 51–56. Owerri: CRC Publications, 1997.

Ngara, E. *Christian Leadership: A Challenge to the African Church.* Nairobi: Paulines Publications Africa, 2004.

Nieman, A. "Churches and Social Development in South Africa: An Exploration." In *Religion and Social Development in Post-apartheid South Africa: Perspectives for Critical Engagement,* edited by I. Swart, H. Rocher, S. Green, and J. Erasmus, 37–43. Stellenbosch: SUN Press, 2010.

"Nigerian Bishops Plead for Peace and Dialogue." *America Press,* June 7–14, 2004. Retrieved online on 24 January 2011 from web.ebscohost.com.ez.sun.ac.za.

Nkemkia, M. N. *African Theology: A Step Forward in African Thinking.* Nairobi: Pauline Publications, 1999.

Nkom, S. A. "Culture, Empowerment and Local Government with Reference to North Western Nigeria." In *People-centred Democracy in Nigeria?* edited by A. Adedeji and B. Ayo, 75–81. Lagos: Ingri Press, 2000.

Northouse, Peter G. *Leadership: Theory and Practice.* Thousand Oaks: SAGE Publications, 2019.

Nurnberger, K. *Prosperity, Poverty and Pollution: Managing the Approaching Crisis.* New York: Zed Books, 1999.

Nwokoma, N. I., and N. A. Nwokoma. "Appraising Employment and Export-led Industrialisation in Post-reform Nigeria." In *Back on Track: Sector-led Growth in Africa and Implications for Development,* edited by D. Seck and S. Boko, 99–113. Trenton: Africa World Press, 2010.

Nyomi, S. "Covenanting for Justice: Where Would Calvin Stand?" Paper presented at the 500th Anniversary of John Calvin, in the Faculty of Theology. Stellenbosch: Stellenbosch University, 2010.

Obasanjo, O. "Africa Arise." *Keynote Address at the Inaugural Ceremony of the African Forum on Religion and Government.* Abuja: AFREG 1, 2006.

Obiezu, J., and C. S. Ugenyi. "The Relevance of the Theories of Imperialism to the Nigerian Development." In *Nigerian Politics,* edited by C. A. Ndoh and C. E. Emezi, 219–34.

Odunsi, B. A. "The Impact of Leadership Instability on Democratic Process in Nigeria." *Journal of American Association of Sociology* 31, no. 1–2 (1996):67–81.

Oduyoye, M. A. *Hearing and Knowing: Theological Reflections on Christianity in Africa.* Maryknoll: Orbis Books, 1986.

Ogarekpe, M. O. "Liberty to the Captives: Presbyterian Social Policy and Practice." In *A Century and Half of Presbyterian Witness in Nigeria, 1846–1996,* edited by O. U. Kalu, 220–39. Lagos: Ida-Ivory Press, 1996.

Ohwofasa, A. J. *Democracy and Issues of Governance in African Politics: The Nigerian Perspective.* Nigeria: Bookwright Publisher, 2007.

Okaalet, P. "The Role of Faith-based Organizations in the Fight against HIV and AIDS in Africa." *Transformation* 19, no. 4 (2002):274–78.

Okonkwo, M. *Expectation 2003: Let Kings be Kings*. Lagos: Pentecostal Fellowship of Nigeria, 2003.

Okopido, I. T. "Church and Environment." In *Papers Presented at the National Conference for Christian Leaders, Theme: Church in Mission and Transformation (Unedited)*. Abuja: Christian Association of Nigeria, 2010.

Okonta, I., and O. Douglas. *Where Vultures Feast: Shell, Human Rights, and Oil in the Niger Delta*. San Francisco: Sierra Club Books, 2001.

Okoye, W. "Why Are We Here?" In *Papers Presented at the National Conference for Christian Leaders, Theme: Church in Mission and Transformation (Unedited)*. Abuja: Christian Association of Nigeria, 2010.

———. "African Forum on Religion and Government." *Speech Delivered in (AFREG 2), August 18–21 Limuru, Kenya*. Abuja: AFREG, 2009.

Olukoshi, A. O. *Governing the African Developmental Process: The Challenge of the New Partnership for Africa's Development (NEPAD)*. Occasional Paper. Copenhagen: Centre of African Studies, University of Copenhagen, 2002.

Omonokhua, C. A. "Dialogue: Anthropological and Eschatological Bases." *Seminar Paper Presented at Christian Association of Nigeria (CAN), National Executive Committee (NEC)*. Abuja: CAN, 2010.

Omosegbon, Oladele. "The Role of Institutional Factors in the Modeling of Economic Growth and in Policy Formulation in Africa." In *Back on Track: Sector-led Growth in Africa and Implications for Development*, edited by D. Seck and S. Boko, 37–58. Trenton: Africa World Press, 2010.

Onaiyekan, J. "Dividends of Religion in Nigeria." *Public Lecture at the University of Ilorin*, Ilorin: Unpublished, 2010.

Onubogu, E. "Modernisation, Globalisation and Africa's Political Economy: The Case of Nigeria." In *African Development and Governance Strategies in the 21st century*, edited by B. Onimode, 72–81. London: Zed Books, 2004.

Onwunta, E. *Gender Stereotyping in Church and Community: A Nigerian Woman's Perspective*. PhD Diss., University of Stellenbosch, 2008.

Onwurah, E. "The Quest, Means and Relevance of African Christian Theology." In *Issues in Theology, Mission, Church and Society*, edited by E. M. Ukah, 146–66, s.l. s.a.

Onyekpe, J. G. N. "Globalization and the Less Developed Countries." In *Governance: Nigeria and the World*, edited by S. Odion-Akhaine, 322–44. Nigeria: Centre for Constitutionalism and Demilitarisation (CENCOD), 2004.

———. "Issues in Development: Nigeria." In *Governance: Nigeria and the World*, edited by S. Odion-Akhaine, 133–47. Nigeria: Centre for Constitutionalism and Demilitarisation (CENCOD), 2004.

Onyeani, C. *Capitalist Nigger: The Road to Success: A Spider Web Doctrine*. New York: Timbuktu Publishers, 1999.

Osaghae, E. H. "Ethnicity in Africa or African Ethnicity: The Search for a Contextual Understanding." In *African Perspectives on Development: Controversies, Dilemmas and Openings*, edited by U. Himmelstrand, K. Kinyanjui, and E. Mburugu, 137–51. Kampala: Fountain Publishers, 1994.

Osmer, Richard R. *Practical Theology: An Introduction*. Grand Rapids: William B. Eerdmans, 2008.

Otobo, E. E. "Contemporary External Influences on Corporate Governance: Coping with the Challenges in Africa." In *African Development and Governance Strategies in the 21st Century*, edited by B. Onimode, 101–21. London: Zed Books, 2004.

Perlas, N. *Shaping Globalization: Civil Society, Cultural Power and Threefolding*. Cape Town: The Novalis Press, 2000.

Power, J. "Forward Nigeria." *World Policy Journal* (Summer, 2008).

Proctor, J. H. "Serving God and the Empire: Mary Slessor in South-Eastern Nigeria, 1876–1915." *Journal of Religion in Africa* 30 (2000):45–61.

"Protesters Demand." *Thisday Newspaper*. 10 December 2010.

Rolls, J. "Transformational Leadership." In *Leading, Managing and Ministering: Challenging Questions for Church and Society*, edited by J. Nelson, 65–84. Norwich: The Canterbury Press, 1999.

Ruwa, M. C. *Principles of Good Governance: The Church's Perspective*. Nairobi: Paulines Publications Africa, 2001.

Sachs, J. D. *The End of Poverty: How We Can Make It Happen in Our Time*. London: Penguin Books, 2005.

Salifu, S. L. S. "The Christian and Nation Building." In *Service with Integrity: The Christian in the Nigerian Project*, edited by Z. Chinne, 187–202. Kaduna: The ECWA Goodnews Church, 2008.

Samuel, V. "Globalization, Christian NGOs and the Churches: An Introductory Note." *Transformation* 20, no. 2 (2003): 68–70.

Sandelowski, M. *Handbook for Synthesizing Qualitative Research*. Battlefield: Springer, 2000.

Schmid, B., J. Cochrane, and J. Olivier. "Understanding Religious Health Assets: Health as a Lens on Religion and Development." In *Religion and Social Development in Post-apartheid South Africa: Perspectives for Critical Engagement*, edited by I. Swart, H. Rocher, S. Green, and J. Erasmus, 137–52. Stellenbosch: SUN Press, 2010.

Schoeman, M. *The African Union after the Durban 2002 Summit*. Occasional Paper. Copenhagen: Centre of African Studies, University of Copenhagen, 2003.

Schreiter, R. J. *The New Catholicity: Theology between the Local and the Global*. Maryknoll: Orbis Books, 1997.

Sen, Amartya. *Development as Freedom*. London: Oxford University Press, 1999.

Seteolu, D. "The Challenge of Leadership and Governance in Nigeria." In *Governance: Nigeria and the World*, edited by S. Odion-Akhaine, 70–78. Nigeria: Centre for Constitutionalism and Demilitarisation (CENCOD), 2004.

Sine, T. "Development: Its Secular Past and Its Uncertain Future." In *The Church in Response to Human Need,* edited by V. Samuel and C. Sugden, 1–19. Grand Rapids: William B. Eerdmans, 1987.

Smith, K. G. *Academic Writing and Theological Research: A Guide for Students.* Johannesburg: South African Theological Seminary Press, 2008.

Stein, H. *Economic Development and the Anatomy of Crisis in Africa: From Colonialism through Structural Adjustment.* Cambridge: Centre for Development Studies, 2000.

Stone, G. A., R. F. Russell, and K. Patterson. "Transformational versus Servant Leadership: A Difference in Leader Focus." *Leadership and Organization Development Journal* 25, no. 4 (2004): 349–61.

Spong, J. S. *A New Christianity for a New World.* Morristown: HarperOne, 2001.

Strydom, H., and A. S. De Vos. "Sampling and Sampling Methods, in *Research at Grass Roots: A Primer for the Caring Professions*, edited by A. S. De Vos, 189–201. Pretoria: Van Schaik Publishers, 1998.

Sugden, C. "Transformational Development: Current State of Understanding and Practice." *Transformation* 20, no. 2 (2003):70–76.

Swart, I. "Churches as a Stock of Social Capital for Promoting Social Development in Western Cape Communities." In *Religion and Social Development in Post-Apartheid South Africa: Perspectives for Critical Engagement*, edited by I. Swart, H. Rocher, S. Green, and J. Erasmus, 325–37. Stellenbosch: SUN Press, 2010.

———. *The Churches and the Development Debate: Perspectives on a Fourth-Generation Approach.* Stellenbosch: Sun Press, 2006.

Temple, W. "Sermon at the Opening Service: Second World Conference on Faith and Order, Edinburgh, 1937." In *The Ecumenical Movement: An Anthology of Key Texts and Voices,* edited by M. Kinnamon and B. E. Cope, 17–21. Geneva: WCC Publications, 1997.

Terblanche, S. E. "Understanding Mentorship and the Development of a Structure to Implement and Manage a Mentorship Program to Support Extensionists towards Professionalism." *South African Journal of Agric Extension* vol. 36 (2007):94–108.

Thomson, A. *An Introduction to African Politics.* New York: Routledge, 2004.

Toor, S., and G. Ofori. "Positive Psychological Capital as a Source of Sustainable Competitive Advantage for Organizations." *Journal of Construction Engineering and Management* 136, no. 3 (2010):341–52.

Turaki, Y. "The Private Life of a Leader: Foundations of Human and Social Transformation." In *Papers Presented at the National Conference for Christian*

Leaders, Theme: Church in Mission and Transformation (Unedited). Abuja: Christian Association of Nigeria, 2010.

———. *Christianity and African Gods: A Method in Theology*. Potchefstroom: Potchefstroom University, 1999.

Tutu, D. *God Is Not a Christian: Speaking Truth in Times of Crisis*. London: Rider, 2011.

Ukaegbu, C. C. "Leadership Fatalism and Underdevelopment in Nigeria: Imaginative Policymaking for Human Development." *Philosophia Africana* 10, no. 2 (2007):161–82.

Van Bergen, J. P. *Development and Religion in Tanzania: Sociological Soundings on Christian Participation in Rural Transformation*. Madras: The Diocesan Press, 1981.

World Council of Churches (WCC). *Guidelines on Dialogue with People of Living Faiths and Ideologies*. Geneva: World Council of Churches, 1979.

Weaver, J. H., M. T. Rock, and K. Kusterer. *Achieving Broad-Based Sustainable Development: Governance, Environment, and Growth with Equity*. Connecticut: Kumarian Press, 1997.

Williams, C. O. "General Secretary's Report." In *Religion in a Secular State: Proceedings of the Second Assembly of the Christian Association of Nigeria*, edited by A. O. Makozi and G. J. A. Ojo, 10–12. Abuja: Christian Association of Nigeria, 1988.

Wink, W. *Engaging the Powers: Discernment and Resistance in a World of Domination*. Augsburg: Fortress, 1992.

Yusuf, J. T. "Is It Lawful to Give Tribute to Caesar or Not? Shall We or Shall We Not?" In *Religion in a Secular State: Proceedings of the Second Assembly of the Christian Association of Nigeria*, edited by A. O. Makozi and G. J. A. Ojo, 40–43. Abuja: Christian Association of Nigeria, 1988.

Langham Literature, with its publishing work, is a ministry of Langham Partnership.

Langham Partnership is a global fellowship working in pursuit of the vision God entrusted to its founder John Stott –

> *to facilitate the growth of the church in maturity and Christ-likeness through raising the standards of biblical preaching and teaching.*

Our vision is to see churches in the Majority World equipped for mission and growing to maturity in Christ through the ministry of pastors and leaders who believe, teach and live by the word of God.

Our mission is to strengthen the ministry of the word of God through:
- nurturing national movements for biblical preaching
- fostering the creation and distribution of evangelical literature
- enhancing evangelical theological education

especially in countries where churches are under-resourced.

Our ministry

Langham Preaching partners with national leaders to nurture indigenous biblical preaching movements for pastors and lay preachers all around the world. With the support of a team of trainers from many countries, a multi-level programme of seminars provides practical training, and is followed by a programme for training local facilitators. Local preachers' groups and national and regional networks ensure continuity and ongoing development, seeking to build vigorous movements committed to Bible exposition.

Langham Literature provides Majority World preachers, scholars and seminary libraries with evangelical books and electronic resources through publishing and distribution, grants and discounts. The programme also fosters the creation of indigenous evangelical books in many languages, through writer's grants, strengthening local evangelical publishing houses, and investment in major regional literature projects, such as one volume Bible commentaries like the *Africa Bible Commentary* and the *South Asia Bible Commentary*.

Langham Scholars provides financial support for evangelical doctoral students from the Majority World so that, when they return home, they may train pastors and other Christian leaders with sound, biblical and theological teaching. This programme equips those who equip others. Langham Scholars also works in partnership with Majority World seminaries in strengthening evangelical theological education. A growing number of Langham Scholars study in high quality doctoral programmes in the Majority World itself. As well as teaching the next generation of pastors, graduated Langham Scholars exercise significant influence through their writing and leadership.

To learn more about Langham Partnership and the work we do visit **langham.org**